Women Writers of the Middle Ages

WOMEN WRITERS OF THE MIDDLE AGES

A Critical Study of Texts from Perpetua († 203)
to Marguerite Porete († 1310)

PETER DRONKE

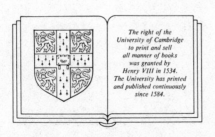

The right of the
University of Cambridge
to print and sell
all manner of books
was granted by
Henry VIII in 1534.
The University has printed
and published continuously
since 1584.

CAMBRIDGE UNIVERSITY PRESS

CAMBRIDGE
LONDON   NEW YORK   NEW ROCHELLE
MELBOURNE   SYDNEY

Published by the Press Syndicate of the University of Cambridge
The Pitt Building, Trumpington Street, Cambridge CB2 1RP
32 East 57th Street, New York, NY 10022, USA
10 Stamford Road, Oakleigh, Melbourne 3166, Australia

First published 1984
Reprinted 1985

Printed in Great Britain by the
University Press, Cambridge

Library of Congress catalogue card number: 83-7456

British Library cataloguing in publication data
Dronke, Peter
Women writers of the Middle Ages
1. Women authors
I. Title
809'.89287   PN471
ISBN 0 521 25580 5 hard covers
ISBN 0 521 27573 3 paperback

UP

Contents

v

Preface

The purpose of this book is to present and interpret a substantial range of texts composed by women from the beginning of the third century to the end of the thirteenth – to explore the ways women helped to shape the earliest Christian writing in a western language, and observe their particular contributions to western literature over a millennium. A comprehensive and authoritative treatment of the subject is not yet possible: the traditional histories of medieval literature, Latin and vernacular, give little help towards it; much certainly remains to be discovered, and much to be charted for the first time.

The value of trying to locate and understand the writings of women from these centuries is more evident today than it was even twenty years ago. Yet while the history of medieval women in its social, legal and economic aspects has made real progress of late, most of their intellectual and imaginative achievements are still neglected, and left difficult of access except to the occasional philologist in one area or another. Whereas the number of books and articles *on* medieval women increases yearly, the greater part of what survives *by* medieval women has remained virtually unknown.

It includes many precious personal testimonies, which historians will doubtless wish to take into consideration in future studies, even while recognizing that such testimonies are inevitably those of literate – and hence privileged, or unusual – women. (From periods before the Renaissance, there are only the fewest authentic records preserved, as if by miracle, of how certain unlettered women thought and felt.[1]) But hitherto the practical and scholarly difficulties of approaching most of the firsthand sources have been enormous. Indeed, with the women who wrote prior to the twelfth century, only a handful of specialists would be able to name them, or would know where their writings are to be found. (Hrotsvitha is the one obvious exception.) And even with two of the most celebrated and most written-about from the twelfth century – Heloise, and Hildegard of Bingen – a large amount of the fundamental work remains to be done. Heloise's *Problemata*, and nine tenths of the writings of Hildegard, do not yet exist in satisfactory modern editions; forty-four of Hildegard's letters, though catalogued in 1916, have never yet been edited at all; on the language, style and sources of these two outstanding women we are in many respects still in the dark.

Nor do I think that most medievalists are aware of how imposing a mass of relevant material does remain, and how great is its range. The thirteenth-century women's writings alone exceed what can be treated adequately even in a sizeable book; but for the preceding centuries too I came to feel it necessary to adopt stringent principles of selection, so as not to let discussion outgrow a coherent structure.

I have focussed on texts that have, in diverse ways, a notable autobiographic or literary or intellectual interest – texts in which women tell how they understand themselves and their world, or construct imaginative worlds of their own. Here I hope to have left no major lacunae, at least as regards western Europe[2] in the period from the first Christian writings till the early twelfth century; after that, even among texts that are truly striking in these ways, it became imperative to choose. Thus Hildegard of Bingen is studied in detail, but not Elisabeth of Schönau; some songs by Provençal *trobairitz* are analysed, but not the works of Marie de France; I have concentrated on Marguerite Porete, but not on Hadewijch or the two Mechthilds or Gertrud of Helfta. At the same time, I have tried to counterbalance this increasing selectiveness by setting out systematically in my Bibliography all the texts written by women that were consulted in the course of preparing this book. There I have also included certain 'borderline' works (such as the *Life* of Christina of Markyate) which, while strictly about women rather than by them, also contain clear elements of autobiographic record.

The theme that runs through the following chapters, then, is that of women's awareness of themselves, their modes of expression and of self-expression. Hence I have looked for the most part at 'free' rather than 'official' writing, though no firm boundary between types can be drawn, and I have trespassed at times, for instance, on the fields of the theologian and the historian of science. I try to suggest what is individual in the various testimonies, bearing in mind that many utterances which in their time were not unparalleled may now, through the loss of recorded analogues, appear as if unique.

The texts before the mid-twelfth century that are here considered were all written in Latin. Often the women who wrote them did not have the opportunity to learn as expert and fluent a Latin as some of their illustrious male contemporaries; at times their expression may remain not only unclassical (which is as it should be, and is – except in cases of pastiche – almost unavoidable), but awkward or unclear; and yet the striving for expression against great odds can also endow texts with unaccustomed, difficult beauties and felicities. Such texts demand unhurried reading: often problems of nuance arise in the many unconventional modes of Latin by which the writers tried to communicate something of their own identity. That is why, in the body of the book, each passage considered is given an English rendering, by which I try to suggest some of the shades of meaning as I see them; the translations are intended as an extension of critical interpretation. Where the original is not easily accessible, or presents special textual interest, it is also cited on the page or in the notes. Some longer texts, in particular those that are unpublished, or have been published imperfectly, are given separately at the back of the book.

The intention throughout is to show a range of testimonies precisely, and to comment on the language, and the articulation of thought and emotion, in a way that may provide a basis for further insights. It will be for scholars in other disciplines, such as social and religious history, to order this evidence within their own framework; for the present it is a matter of enabling certain texts to speak as lucidly and vitally as possible.

This is not, of course, to suggest that one can ever let them 'speak for themselves', as if there were some attainable ideal of clinical neutrality. The selection of what is specially worthy of note is inseparable from questions of assessment and emphasis: it is itself an act of interpretation. It is also an affirmation of the intrinsic value of writings that have been – I believe quite unjustly – undervalued in the past. It is not necessary here to dwell on the history and causes of this, or on the diverse attempts to belittle the rare women whose writing did achieve fame. It will suffice to recall, by way of illustration, that in 1867 Hrotsvitha's works were alleged to be a hoax perpetrated by the humanist Conrad Celtes, who first edited the principal manuscript, and that this 'discovery' gave rise to some coarsely mocking verses; or that till quite recent times, notwithstanding Hildegard of Bingen's meticulous account of her methods of composition, scholars exaggerated the role of her men secretaries to the point of implying that they were the real begetters of her works; again, speculations about male authorship of some of Heloise's letters are still with us, and are still treated much more seriously – there's the rub – than for instance the suggestion that Bacon, or Marlowe, wrote the works of Shakespeare.[3]

The largest chapter (and selection of texts) in the book is devoted to Hildegard. This emphasis needs perhaps less apology today than it did thirteen years ago, when I made a long essay on Hildegard's poetry and drama central to a study of *Poetic Individuality in the Middle Ages*.[4] Since then, an eight-volume selection from Hildegard's writings, in German translation, begun in 1954, has been completed, and a new edition of her works, in the series Corpus Christianorum, is under way.[5] Though much remains to be done in order fully to understand the nature of Hildegard's genius, something of the excitement of that genius has begun to capture the imagination of a wider than specialist audience.

The same is not yet true of the moving and audacious testament of Marguerite Porete, *Le mirouer des simples ames*; though I cannot help feeling that if

Marguerite had been in any way officially approved – if she had been a man, or even better a bishop, or a canonized saint – her work would long since have been studied as intensively, by all who care about French literature, as, for example, the *Roman de la Rose*.

While I was writing this book, a number of friends and colleagues asked me: do you think there is something about these women writers that distinguishes their work from that of men? I would always explain that I was not searching for a Platonic Form, Femininity-in-writing, which would manifest itself similarly in every feminine text. The women writers I was considering showed individuality in all kinds of different ways, and it was this many-sidedness that I wanted to characterize.

At times the femininity is bound up with particular circumstances – for instance, Hugeburc's and Hrotsvitha's self-consciousness that, as women, they are addressing an audience of men, or Dhuoda's awareness that it is as a mother, and a wife abandoned by her husband, that she is depicting ideals of loyalty for her son; or again, Hildegard's special concern to relate women's sexual natures to their temperaments and physiques has no counterpart among the men who wrote medical treatises. We can also, however, hazard a few more general observations on what the authors studied in this book have in common, even if the qualities that might soonest help distinguish them as women writers are the ones hardest to analyse in purely literary terms.

The women's motivation for writing at all, for instance, seems rarely to be predominantly literary: it is often more urgently serious than is common among men writers; it is a response springing from inner needs, more than from an artistic, or didactic, inclination. There is, more often than in men's writing, a lack of apriorism, of predetermined postures: again and again we encounter attempts to cope with human problems in their singularity – not imposing rules or categories from without, but seeking solutions that are apt and truthful existentially. Hence the women whose texts are treated here show excellingly a quality (literary, but also 'metaliterary') of immediacy: they look at themselves more concretely and more searchingly than many of the highly accomplished men writers who were their contemporaries. This immediacy can lend women's writing qualities beside which all technical flawlessness is pallid. So it is Perpetua's thoughts, not those of her eloquent compatriot Cyprian, that are unforgettable; so Dhuoda can reveal herself more profoundly than any of the acknowledged major Carolingians could; so, too, even if none of the Provençal *trobairitz* can match the most spectacular lyrical feats of the finest troubadours, they can still show us movements of thought and feeling of which, if the men's poetry alone had survived, we should never have had a glimmering.

At the beginning and at the end of this survey stand women who were martyred for their beliefs: Perpetua, sentenced to death in the arena at Carthage in 203, and Marguerite Porete, publicly burnt as a heretic in Paris in 1310. The early Christian convert, and the mystic eleven hundred years after her, who was striving with all her being for the perfect Christian life, were equally victims of the official 'State religion' of their time. Though ardent in their beliefs, they were in no way fanatical. But what they had won for themselves was so precious to them that they were ready even to be cruelly put to death, sooner than compromise or reject that inner possession which gave their life meaning. Perpetua's prison diary and Marguerite's *Mirouer* are their attempts to account for themselves: they summon all their resources of mind and imagination in order to confront, not their persecutors, but the world that they leave behind. In different, less tragic ways the other women discussed here seem also to have an inner force that impels and quickens what they write. The same holds, evidently, of some distinguished men who wrote in the Middle Ages. Yet men who wrote, even marvellously well, were also very often 'men of letters' – occasional writers, virtuosi, professional courtiers or teachers. I do not know if before 1300 there were any 'women of letters' in quite this sense: with women, the opportunity and the power to write tended to be too hard-won to make an extrinsic relation to writing possible. This may be part of the secret of the most individual aspects of the texts we shall examine.

I am deeply grateful for the suggestions and comments of Jill Mann and Michael Lapidge, who read this book before publication, and for those of Ursula Dronke, who has accompanied it, sharing my thoughts and writing, through many phases of its composition. The chapter on personal poetry by women began to take shape in some seminars that I held in the Universidad Autónoma de Barcelona in the autumn of 1977, on the invitation of Francisco Rico. Both he and his students gave me the benefit of lively criticism. More recently, Peter Ricketts has kindly and expertly advised me on textual matters in Provençal. The chapter on Hrotsvitha, presented in briefer form as a lecture in the Università di Genova, was read by Ferruccio Bertini, to whom I am indebted for some valuable references. Finally, my warm thanks to the Cambridge University Press, and especially to Michael Black, for the helpfulness and courtesy I have experienced since the manuscript came into their hands.

P.D.

December 1982

From Perpetua to the Eighth Century

In Carthage, early in A.D. 203, Vibia Perpetua, a woman about twenty-two years old, was arrested, tried and imprisoned; on 7 March she was put to death. Her offence was civil disobedience: as a Christian, she refused to perform a compulsory Roman sacrifice in honour of the emperor. At the time of her arrest, she was not yet baptized, only undergoing instruction as a catechumen. She was 'well-born, well-educated and respectably married';[1] her parents were both still alive; she had at least two brothers,[2] one of them a catechumen like herself. At the time of her imprisonment she was breast-feeding her infant son. About her husband we know nothing with certainty.[3]

In her weeks in prison Perpetua made notes, giving 'in narrative sequence an account of her ordeal'.[4] The author of the Passio SS. Perpetuae et Felicitatis,[5] who included what Perpetua had written within his own hagiographic framework, preserved her writing, he assures, 'as she left it, in her own way, and as it was set down by her own hand'.[6] Because of this, we can still today hear Perpetua's voice, and envisage precisely her experience. Her Latin[7] is colloquial and homely, and this too is a special privilege for us: no emotion, no fantasy of Perpetua's appears disguised by stylistic ornaments. Nothing masks her tender – and determined – perceptions or her troubled dreams.

Perpetua's narrative (Passio III–X) includes what might be called an 'outer' depiction of what befell her, and an 'inner' one, of her dream-images and secret thoughts. Among earlier scholars, Erich Auerbach has commented appreciatively on the prose style of an outer passage, E. R. Dodds and Marie-Luise von Franz have illuminated aspects of her dreaming. Specialists in Patristics and hagiology have often looked at the Passio to determine its theological and historical content. What is lacking is a reading of Perpetua's diary interpreting the outer and inner parts in conjunction – for it is this that could lead to a fuller understanding of her self-awareness. (Even Georg Misch, in his great work on autobiography, did not pause long enough at Perpetua's text to attempt this: he mentions her, but passes swiftly by.[8])

To suggest the nature and quality of that self-awareness by way of more detailed indications, it may be best to have a first glance at the notes as a whole, in an English rendering in which I aim, however imperfectly, to remain close to the meaning and style of the original Latin. –

III When we were as yet only under legal surveillance, and my father, out of love for me, kept trying to refute me by argument and to break my resolve, I said: 'Father, do you see that container over there, for instance – a jug or something?' And he said: 'Yes, I do.' And I said to him: 'It can't be called anything other than it is, can it?' And he said: 'No.' 'So too, I can't call myself anything other than I am: a Christian.'

Then my father, angry at this word, bore down on me as if he would pluck out my eyes. But he only fumed, and went away, defeated, along with the devil's sophistries. Then, for the few days that I was without my father, I gave thanks to God – I felt relieved at his not being there. In that short space of time we were baptized. But the Spirit[9] enjoined me not to seek from that water any favour except physical endurance. After a few days we were taken to prison, and I grew frightened, for I had never known such darkness. Oh grim day ! – intense heat, because of the crowds, extortions by soldiers. Above all, I was tormented with anxiety there, on account of my child.

Then Tertius and Pomponius, the consecrated deacons who were looking after us, arranged by a bribe that they let us out into a better, cooler part of the prison for a few hours. Coming out of the dungeon, everyone began to move freely; I breast-fed my child, who was already weak with hunger. Anxiously I spoke to my mother about him, I consoled my brother, I gave them charge of my son. I was worn out, seeing them so worn because of me. Such were my fearful thoughts for many days. Then I managed to have the child allowed to stay with me in prison. And at once I grew well again, relieved of the strain and anguish for him. And suddenly the prison became a palace to me, where I would rather be than anywhere.

IV Then my brother said to me: 'My lady, my sister, you are now greatly blessed: so much so that you can ask for a vision, and you will be shown if it is to be suffering unto death or a passing thing.' And I, who knew I was in dialogue with God, whose great benefits I had experienced, promised him faithfully, saying: 'Tomorrow I'll tell you.' And I asked for a vision, and this was shown to me:

I saw a bronze ladder, marvellously long,[10] reaching as far as heaven, and narrow too: people could climb it only one at a time. And on the sides of the ladder every kind of iron implement was fixed: there were swords, lances, hooks, cutlasses, javelins, so that if anyone went up carelessly or not looking upwards, he would be torn and his flesh caught on the sharp iron. And beneath the ladder lurked a serpent of wondrous size, who laid ambushes for those mounting, making them terrified of the ascent. But Saturus climbed up first (he was the one who at a later stage gave himself up spontaneously on account of us – he had built up our courage and then, when we were arrested, had been away). And he reached the top of the ladder, and turned and said to me: 'Perpetua, I'm waiting for you – but watch out that the serpent doesn't bite you !' And I said: 'He won't hurt me, in Christ's name !' And under that ladder, almost, it seemed, afraid of me, the serpent slowly thrust out its head – and, as if I were treading on the first rung, I trod on it, and I climbed. And I saw an immense space of garden, and in the middle of it a white-haired man sitting in shepherd's garb, vast, milking sheep, with many thousands of people dressed in shining white standing all round. And he raised his head, looked at me, and said: 'You are welcome, child.' And he called me, and gave me, it seemed, a mouthful of the cheese he was milking; and I accepted it in both my hands together, and ate it, and all those standing around said: 'Amen.' And at the sound of that word I awoke, still chewing something indefinable and sweet. And at once I told my brother, and we understood that it would be mortal suffering; and we began to have no more hope in the world.

2

v A few days later the rumour ran that our hearing would take place. My father came over from the city worn out with exhaustion, and he went up to me in order to deflect me, saying: 'My daughter, have pity on my white hairs! Show some compassion to your father, if I deserve to be called father by you. If with these hands I have helped you to the flower of your youth, if I favoured you beyond all your brothers – do not bring me into disgrace in all men's eyes! Look at your brothers, look at your mother and your aunt – look at your son, who won't be able to live if you die. Don't flaunt your insistence, or you'll destroy us all: for if anything happens to you, none of us will ever be able to speak freely and openly[11] again.'

This is what my father said, out of devotion to me, kissing my hands and flinging himself at my feet; and amid his tears he called me not 'daughter' but '*domina*'. And I grieved for my father's condition – for he alone of all my family would not gain joy from my ordeal. And I comforted him, saying: 'At the tribunal things will go as God wills: for you must know we are no longer in our own hands, but in God's.' And he left me, griefstricken.

vi Another day, whilst we were eating our midday meal, we were suddenly taken away to the hearing, and arrived at the forum. At once the rumour swept the neighbourhood, and an immense crowd formed. We mounted the tribunal. The others, when interrogated, confessed.[12] Then my turn came. And my father appeared there with my son, and pulled me off the step, saying: 'Perform the sacrifice! Have pity on your child!' So too the governor, Hilarianus, who had been given judiciary power in place of the late proconsul Minucius Timinianus: 'Spare your father's old age, spare your little boy's infancy! Perform the ritual for the Emperor's welfare.' And I answered: 'I will not perform it.' Hilarianus: 'You are a Christian then?' And I answered: 'I am a Christian.' And as my father still hovered, trying to deflect me, Hilarianus ordered him to be thrown out, and he was struck with a rod. And I grieved for my father's downfall as if I'd been struck myself: that's how I mourned for his pitiful old age.

Then the governor sentenced us all and condemned us to the beasts of the arena. And joyful we went back to prison.

Then, as the baby was used to breast-feeding and staying in the prison with me, I at once sent the deacon Pomponius to my father, imploring to have it back. But my father did not want to let it go. And somehow, through God's will, it no longer needed the breast, nor did my breasts become inflamed – so I was not tormented with worry for the child, or with soreness.

vii A few days later, while we were all praying, suddenly in the middle of my prayer I let slip a word: the name, Dinocrates. And I was amazed, for he had never entered my thoughts except just then. And I grieved, remembering his plight. Then at once I realized that I was entitled to ask for a vision about him, and that I ought to; and I began to pray for him a lot, and plaintively, to God. That very night, this is what I was shown: I saw Dinocrates coming out of a dark place, where there were many people. He was very hot and thirsty, his clothes dirty and his looks pallid – he still had on his face the same wound as when he died. When alive he had been my brother, who at the age of seven died wretchedly, of a cancer of the face, in such a way that everyone saw his death with revulsion. So I prayed for him, and between me and him there was a great gap, such that we could not come near each other. Beside Dinocrates was a pool full of water, with a rim that was higher than he. And Dinocrates stretched up as if to drink. I was full of sorrow that, even though the pool had water, the rim was so high that he could not drink. And I awoke, and realized that my brother was struggling. Yet I was confident that I could help him in his struggle, and I prayed for him every day, till we moved to the military prison – for we were

3

destined to fight in the garrison-games: they were on Emperor Geta's birthday. Day and night I prayed for Dinocrates, groaning and weeping that my prayer be granted.

VIII On a day when we remained in fetters, I was shown this: I saw the place I'd seen before, and there was Dinocrates, clean, well-dressed, refreshed; and where the wound had been I saw a scar; and the pool I'd seen previously had its rim lowered: it was down to the boy's navel. And he was drinking from the pool incessantly. Above the rim was a golden bowl full of water. Dinocrates came near it and began to drink from that, and the bowl never ran dry. And when he had drunk his fill, he began to play with the water, as children do, full of happiness. And I awoke: I realized then that he'd been freed from pain.

IX A few days after that, the adjutant, Pudens, provost of the prison, began to show us honour, perceiving that there was a rare power in us. He allowed us many visitors, so that we could comfort one another. But when the day of the spectacle drew near, my father came in to me, wasted and worn. He began to tear out the hair of his beard and fling it on the ground, he hurled himself headlong and cursed his life, and said such things as would move every living creature. I ached for his unhappy old age.

X The day before our fight, this is what I saw in vision: Pomponius the deacon was coming to the prison gate and knocking urgently. And I went out to him and opened for him. He was wearing a loose, gleaming white tunic, and damasked sandals, and he said: 'Perpetua, we are waiting for you: come!' He took my hand and we began to go over rough, winding ways. We had hardly reached the amphitheatre, breathless, when he took me into the middle of the arena, and said: 'Don't be afraid; here I am, beside you, sharing your toil.' And he vanished. And I saw the immense, astonished crowd. And as I knew I had been condemned to the wild beasts, I was amazed they did not send them out at me. Out against me came an Egyptian, foul of aspect, with his seconds: he was to fight with me. And some handsome young men came up beside me: my own seconds and supporters. And I was stripped naked, and became a man. And my supporters began to rub me with oil, as they do for a wrestling match; and on the other side I saw the Egyptian rolling himself in the dust. And a man of amazing size came out – he towered even over the vault of the amphitheatre. He was wearing the purple, loosely, with two stripes crossing his chest, and patterned sandals made of gold and silver, carrying a baton like a fencing-master and a green bough laden with golden apples. He asked for silence, and said: 'This Egyptian, if he defeats her, will kill her with his sword; she, if she defeats him, will receive this bough.' And he drew back.

And we joined combat, and fists began to fly. He tried to grab my feet, but I struck him in the face with my heels. And I felt airborne, and began to strike him as if I were not touching ground. But when I saw there was a lull, I locked my hands, clenching my fingers together, and so caught hold of his head; and he fell on his face, and I trod upon his head. The populace began to shout, and my supporters to sing jubilantly. And I went to the fencing-master and received the bough. He kissed me and said: 'Daughter, peace be with you!' And triumphantly I began to walk towards the Gate of the Living.[13] And I awoke. And I knew I should have to fight not against wild beasts but against the Fiend; but I knew the victory would be mine.

This is what I have done till the day before the contest; if anyone wants to write of its outcome, let them do so.

Perpetua's father plays the largest role in her narrative. She had always been particularly close to him: as he reminds her, 'I favoured you beyond all your brothers'. So her conflict with him goes beyond ideology: he is claiming her with possessive love, a love that turns to sudden fury as it is rejected.

In her argument, to convince her father of her immutable resolve, Perpetua appeals – as Dhuoda was again to do, six centuries later[14] – to a principle that Jean Jolivet has aptly called 'grammatical platonism' (adding that it can be 'un platonisme quasi sauvage'). It is the notion that names are not arbitrary, that there is a primordial, divinely ordained harmony between names and things.[15] For each thing there is a true name, a name that reflects the nature or essence of the thing. The name may sound variously in various languages – an object may be called *urceolus* in Latin, 'jug' in English – yet this makes no difference to the true, essential aspect of the name. Thus when Adam named the animals, he did not choose words randomly, but found for each creature the true name that had lain waiting for it in the mind of God.[16] To depart from the true name for a thing is to falsify. So Perpetua says, she has chosen the name 'Christian' because that is what she now is – she may even imply that the choice of name makes her what she is.[17] It expresses her essence. To be true to her name means being true to herself. In the *Acta minora* (a shorter, slightly later account of Perpetua, that draws upon her notes), she is twice given a phrase that brings this home by way of a word-play: to the proconsul she says: 'I am a Christian, and I follow the authority of my name, that I may be perpetual (*ut sim perpetua*)'; and to her father: 'Don't be afraid – for if you don't oppose your daughter Perpetua, you'll have a perpetual daughter (*perpetuam filiam possidebis*)'.[18] In her own narrative the argument remains more indirect and subtle, and is not softened by any filial feeling.

Is Perpetua's father roused to sudden anger merely 'hoc verbo' – by her word, 'Christian'? Rather, perhaps, by the way she at once puts his own heartfelt arguments on a purely verbal, academic plane – and outwits him on that plane, with a pert, flippant logic that flouts his paternal authority. The figure of the father returns transformed, I would suggest, in several of Perpetua's dream-images. He who begs 'have pity on my white hairs (*canis meis*, v 2; cf. *canis patris tui*, vi 3)' is echoed in dream in the huge white-haired shepherd (*hominem canum*, iv 8), who nurtures her with his delicious cheese, and again in the fencing-master, also gigantic in size, who rewards her with golden apples and a kiss: 'Daughter, peace be with you (*Filia, pax tecum*, x 13)'. It is a serene father-figure – not tormented and tormenting, but solacing – who appears to Perpetua in her first and last visions.

Yet Perpetua's father is also contrasted with the towering shepherd and fencing-master by being represented so often as grovelling and beaten down. In his last prison-visit he throws himself to the ground (*prosternere se in faciem*, ix 2), and in this he resembles the Egyptian wrestler, who rolls himself in the dust, and later falls on his face (*cecidit in faciem*, x 11). He had flung himself at Perpetua's feet imploringly (*se ad pedes meos iactans*, v 5), whilst the Egyptian, trying to seize her feet (*pedes adprehendere*, x 10), is openly hostile. The father wrestling with Perpetua emotionally is imaged in the Egyptian wrestler, as much as that same father, who brought her to the flower of her youth and favoured her, is imaged in the gently favouring fencing-master. Again, that he tries to prevent Perpetua from mounting the step (*gradus*) of the tribunal where she will be condemned echoes the way the serpent (*draco*) moves out its head in her dream, as if to hinder her from climbing the rungs (also *gradus*) of the visionary ladder. She steps on the serpent's head, confident in Christ – just as she confidently tells her father that 'Christiana' is her proper name. The father who, in his rage, seems about to do her violence, but then holds back, is reflected in the snake which, though threatening, seems to fear her and does not hurt.

From the outset we see that Perpetua records her thoughts in an informal, graphic way, which is moving partly because she is not striving to be literary. There are no rhetorical flourishes, no attempts at didacticism or edification. The dialogue is (I think deliberately) artless in its shaping – 'And he said . . . And I said to him . . . And he said . . .' It retains the imprecisions of living conversation ('a jug or something').[19] Yet Perpetua's command of language is also equal to conveying her psychological insight into her father, and her own complicated mixed feelings about him, including her sense of relief when he doesn't visit her. Her first impressions of prison are set down disjointedly, as if in note form ('. . . tales tenebras. O diem asperum! aestus validus, turbarum beneficio, concussurae militum'), and this allows us to enter the sudden darkness, the heat and overcrowding and harassment, along with the writer: for us as for her it becomes a first experience. Her thoughts about her family – 'tabescebam ideo quod illos tabescere videram mei beneficio' – are a simple but perfect record and analysis of emotion; and the last sentence before the visions begin – when her child, restored to her, makes the prison seem like a palace – is a climax of radiant directness. The heroines in Greek tragedy have moments of comparable intensity, but the intimate and unselfconscious quality of Perpetua's utterance stands alone.

The four visions Perpetua recounts are closely related both to one another and to the outer events interspersed with them. In the interpretation of the dream-images, much must remain conjectural. At the outset I would stress that I believe this is a painstakingly truthful record of authentic dreams, and, because of this, that Perpetua's account must be respected in every detail, not 'smoothed' into more conventional patterns, whether of a Christian or Gnostic or Jungian kind. Thus in the first vision the ladder Perpetua sees must not be equated with Jacob's ladder, nor the shepherd with the Good Shepherd, nor the cheese with the eucharist. The scholars who (following the African Church Fathers that drew on Perpetua's diary for their sermons),[20] have forced interpretations of this type onto her text, have been able to do so only at the cost of ignoring its most individual features. These are precisely what prevents Perpetua's images from being read as parables or turned into Christian commonplaces. Perpetua did not intend to construct spiritual allegories for the benefit of later Christians. Only once, at the close of her fourth vision, does she briefly admit an allegorical meaning, and that for one personage only (the Egyptian), among all her dream-experiences.

The other preliminary point is that the images in Perpetua's dreams clearly have associations that spring not only from what she experienced but from what she had heard and read. And here it is important to remember that, while she was only then being given Christian instruction, she had already, in her early twenties, been 'liberaliter instituta'. That is, she was new to biblical texts, but must have been long familiar with a number of classical ones. This should put us on our guard against investing her imagery with too many Christian, or Christian–Gnostic, meanings: the most important *literary* stimulus to the images in her dreams may well be Vergil rather than the Bible.

Nonetheless, that Perpetua had come to know the biblical image of Jacob's ladder (Genesis 28) seems altogether likely. It too stretched from earth as far as heaven. And yet none of the other connotations of Jacob's ladder has any particular bearing on Perpetua's dream. Jacob himself does not mount his ladder – it is angels who go up and come down on it, revealing a normally invisible communication between heaven and earth. Yahweh leans over the top of that ladder, offering Jacob earthly prosperity. Perpetua's ladder, by contrast, is one that she must climb; it is a means of ascent only, not descent. There are no angels on it, for it is too narrow for more than one being to mount at a time. It is a painful way of climbing, encompassed by terrors: the sharp weapons threaten to rend the climber. Perpetua's ladder is an instance of 'the difficult way up (*Der Schwierige Weg nach oben*)',[21] to cite the title of a wide-ranging study by the folklorist Kretzenbacher, who explores the imagery of some of the ordeals of penance, purgation and judgement that feature a narrow, arduous ladder, or else stairway, mountain-path or bridge. This imagery is popular as well as learned, both in Eastern and Western Europe, and is of great antiquity. Even before there were Christian pilgrims, the difficult climb could express submissive dedication to a god, as when Emperor Claudius, in A.D. 43, climbed the rocky path to the temple of Jupiter Capitolinus on his knees, in thanksgiving for Jupiter's having saved his people in battle.[22] Above all, the ladder had always evoked the challenge of crossing into the beyond. It is, together with the bridge, the commonest image for the shaman's or initiate's means of ascent to heaven.[23]

In Middle Kingdom Egypt, such a ladder was seen as hedged by demonic monsters and snakes; the dead person, about to mount, invoked the heavenly powers for protection.[24] In the myths of many cultures, as Eliade has documented, a bridge linked earth and heaven primordially, but since the time when death entered the world, the passage for any human being has been fraught with danger and suffering.[25] The bridge can be as sharp as a sword, both in the ancient Iranian myth of the Judgement and in the ordeal of the knight Lancelot, who, in Chrétien de Troyes's romance, must traverse the Pont de l'Espee, his hands and feet bleeding.[26] In Japan, women shamans must build themselves a ladder of knives for their celestial ascent.[27] Thus Perpetua, at the close of her ladder dream, sees in it both her *passio* and her otherworldly hopes, won by relinquishing her worldly ones. Symbolically, in the dream, she achieves the initiate's awesome journey.[28]

The moment in which she steps on the serpent's head was doubtless stimulated by God's words to the serpent in Genesis (3: 15): 'she will crush your head, and you will try to bite her heel'. Yet it is also the traditional gesture of the victor in ancient combats: placing one's foot on the head of the opponent betokens having subjugated him.[29] The image recurs in the fourth dream: in her fight against the Egyptian, Perpetua 'struck him in the face with my heels . . . and I trod upon his head' – where the first phrase evokes a moment within the combat and the second the moment of conquering. It is the associations of conquest that are most relevant in the first vision: the serpent is an adversary on Perpetua's way upward, whom her confidence makes tame: like the Egyptian in the fourth vision, and like the false principles and misguided love of her father in waking life, he must be overcome. There may also be a hint of tricking and out-tricking in the encounter: the serpent thrusts forward slowly, 'as if afraid', in order to lull her into security and catch her off guard, while she, pretending she is about to mount the first rung, crushes him by stepping on his head.

Why is the danger of this serpent linked with that of the weapons looming over the narrow ladder of bronze? This cannot be accounted for by Genesis, or by Christian demonology. I would hazard the guess that this configuration of images was inspired at least in part by Perpetua's reading of the *Aeneid*. In *Aen.* II 469ff the enemy of the Trojans, Pyrrhus, breaks into the bronze portals of Priam's palace, tearing them from their hinges (*postisque a cardine vellit/ aeratos*): he is described as

> exulting in *weapons* and sparkling with glint of *bronze*:
> like a *snake* coming into the light, sated with malign herbs . . .
> now, having sloughed its skin, new and gleaming with youth,
> it uncoils its slippery body, thrusting the belly upwards,
> eager for sunlight, with three-forked tongue flashing out.

8

Some reminiscence of Vergil's imagery for Pyrrhus may lie behind the first vision, but also perhaps behind the fourth: the fearsome armed Egyptian, whom Perpetua confronts there, prepares himself for battle with his snakelike wallowing in the dirt.

The shepherd, vast, white-haired, sitting milking sheep in the garden that lies above the ladder, is far from any early Christian iconography of the Good Shepherd. In the Santa Priscilla catacomb-paintings, contemporary with Perpetua, for instance, the Good Shepherd is presented like an Orpheus taming the animals: young and beautiful, standing erect, garlanded. That Perpetua's ancient shepherd is a supernaturally consoling figure (though with more than a casual reminiscence of her father as well) seems clear; so, too, his garden, with its white-robed habitants, is evocative of a paradise. Yet it is important that the consolation the shepherd gives Perpetua is not, as most scholars have suggested, a eucharistic one. He milks cheese (Dodds has perceptively noted the element of time-compression here, so common in dreams),[30] and he gives Perpetua a mouthful, which she takes in her two hands, putting them together. While this might in other contexts be a ritual sacramental gesture,[31] here I think it is primarily a practical one – to prevent the runny curds from spilling. (I imagine a cheese rather like mozzarella, from which some liquid would ooze in the handling.) What Perpetua receives is no Christian sacrament, nor any usual paradisal sustenance – nectar and ambrosia, milk[32] and honey – but the food that, in many times and places, has symbolized the embryo and the process of birth. The 'cheese analogy of conception', expounded by Aristotle and alluded to in Soranus' *Gynaecia*, is also widely and anciently attested in folk belief.[33] Thus Job (10: 10) cries out to his Maker, 'Did you not pour me out like milk and curdle me like cheese?' – and it was this image, enriched by popular medical lore, that was transformed by Hildegard of Bingen into a basis for sketching diverse human destinies before birth, in terms of the coagulation of firm, or insipid, or bitter cheeses.[34] What Perpetua is given with her morsel of cheese is her destiny, her celestial birth – with its inevitable corollary of physical death. We might say that her first vision symbolizes both all she will still have to face on earth, and its serene resolution.

After this vision Perpetua resumes her outer narrative, telling with complete literalness of her father's next visit and of the hearing. She shows her troubled emotional insight into his way of looking. Her father abases himself, pleading with her; at the same time, what he is saying is that she is too proud to give in (*depone animos*), that she is heartless in her lack of consideration for her family. Others – even, presumably, Perpetua's catechumen brother – were getting by, being discreet about their Christian aspirations: why then be as ostentatious as she?

9

On this visit, Perpetua makes clear, her father came together with all her family. Two sentences need special elucidation: his words, 'if anything happens to you, none of us will ever be able to speak freely and openly again'; and her own reflection, that her father, 'alone of all my family, would not gain joy from my ordeal'. This has been taken by many scholars to imply that, except for the father, Perpetua's family were all Christians. And yet, in the light of the *Passio* as a whole, this seems implausible. That the redactor mentions that one of Perpetua's brothers was a catechumen like herself (II 2) is surely meant to demarcate this brother and sister from the rest of the family: if these had all been Christians, it is hard to see how he could have spoken of two being still only catechumens without making this contrast clear. As it stands, the redactor's distinction is evidently between two catechumens and a family of non-Christians.[35]

At the same time, we see from Perpetua's words that all her family, apart from her father, were at least Christian sympathizers. Unlike him, they would admire her decision. This accords well with her father's warning of the danger into which she was plunging her family: what he was saying, I believe, is that if Perpetua faced trial and did not abjure her Christianity, the whole family would fall under suspicion of being Christians secretly, and would then be spied on continually by the authorities.[36]

Perpetua tells of the hearing in a series of short, staccato sentences and rapid exchanges. Her account contrasts strikingly with the speechifying attributed to Christians on trial in the early hagiographic Acts of martyrdom. Perpetua's laconic answers are a world away from the shrill and verbose defiances with which, so we are told, the virgin martyrs answered their judges and persecutors. And when she comes to set down the thoughts about her infant, and breast-feeding, and how a woman's breasts can become inflamed, she articulates movingly and with dignity details such as could scarcely have found a place in ancient literature, except in a key of vulgarity or comedy.[37]

After the death-sentence, a change comes over Perpetua, which is reflected in the texture of the writing. When she first goes to prison and is overwhelmed by the dark horror of it, her account is full of her physical sensations: the exhaustion of her mother and brother adds to her bodily stress, she is still attached to the visible world, and intensely feeling with her family. The prison, when her baby is given her, is transformed into a palace: Perpetua's visionary exuberance, springing from her sense-based emotions, is here prefigured.

With the condemnation, however, she is already altered by the joy of the decision, and feels less anxiety for the child. And the father's cruelty in refusing to return it (did he hope by this still to induce her to yield?) is defeated by the child's change of need. Perpetua's womanly nature no longer feels its condition; her earthly ties are fading.

Then, swift upon this severance of anxiety for the child and its feeding, come the two visions of Perpetua's little dead brother, Dinocrates. Like her baby, he needs to be fed – but his need is for an unearthly drink. When she wakes, Perpetua feels for the suffering not of the living but of the dead. She finds she can make her brother well again by praying. Symbolically, it suggests she can give spiritual help to all her family, and it is this that finally relieves her earthly anxieties over them.

Some details of the pair of visions that now come to her have been finely illuminated by Dölger, in his study 'Ancient parallels to the suffering Dinocrates'.[38] He shows in detail the existence of a substrate of popular conceptions about the otherworld which Perpetua and the pagan writers shared. Yet in one respect I would go further: I would suggest that, particularly in the case of the *Aeneid*, and perhaps of Tibullus too, we must reckon with direct *literary* influences that also helped to shape Perpetua's dreams.

The common popular substrate, moreover, is perhaps most apparent in one detail that Dölger did not consider: Dinocrates' thirst. It was believed throughout the ancient world that the dead, before they reach peace, are thirsty. In Greek tradition, the motif has been traced from an Orphic inscription of the fourth century B.C., where the parched dead person is instructed to beg for water from the Lake of Memory, as far as folksongs collected in modern times, in which οἱ διψασμένοι – the thirsty ones – is a synonym for 'the dead'.[39] Even the custom of placing offerings of wine and water on the tomb for the thirsty soul – which Augustine's mother, Monica, had grown up with in North Africa and was asked to desist from by Ambrose in Milan, 'because those *parentalia* were very like a pagan superstition'[40] – survives in modern Greece.[41] When Propertius curses the bawd who had tried to bewitch him, he cries out: 'may your shade know thirst!'[42]

Yet the special sadness in Hades of those who die young is something Perpetua will have known not only from folk belief but from texts. She would have remembered the wails and weeping of dead infant souls that greeted Aeneas when he had been ferried across the Styx; and she would have retained in her fantasy the dark, muddy place, and the haunting images that follow, of those who, like Dido, perished through their wounds and still bore those wounds in Hades.[43] So too she might have known how Tibullus had pleaded with his beloved, whose little sister had met an untimely death – warning her of the fearfulness of dreams in which the dead child 'will stand, grieving, before your bed, bloodstained as when she fell headlong from an upper window, and came to the lakes below'.[44]

The particular torment that Dinocrates experiences is akin to the one by which the mythic Tantalus was punished – having the longed-for water very near but always unattainable.[45] Yet, unlike Tantalus, he is not being made to suffer by the gods for his crimes, and (here the emphasis is Christian, not pagan) he can be helped towards well-being in the otherworld – not by libations but by prayers.[46] In the dream it is Perpetua's prayers that lower the pool and make it approachable, enabling Dinocrates at last to slake his thirst. I do not think this pool is a dream-counterpart of the baptismal font (thus Dodds), or that Dinocrates' craving for water is a longing for baptism. He wants to drink, not to be immersed. Perpetua describes the drinking lightheartedly, in three stages: first, in his eagerness, Dinocrates drinks straight from the pool,[47] as if he could never have enough. Then he comes to drink more decorously, from the *fiala*, and finds that there too the supply is inexhaustible: this bowl, golden and never-failing, has an immortal aspect. At last, his thirst fully quenched, his exhilaration turns to childish water-play (that seven-year-olds enjoyed this in second-century Carthage, as in present-day Europe, is again a touch, capturing a detail of living experience, such as classical authors seldom record). Dinocrates' wound has healed and become a scar: as Artemidorus notes in his dream-book: 'a scar signifies the ending of every care'.[48]

Perpetua's only hint of interpretation – 'I realized then that he had been freed from pain' – is so brief and simple that it does not warrant any attempt at detailed allegoresis of this pair of visions. If one began by making the pool into a baptismal font, or the water into the 'fountain . . . leaping into eternal life',[49] what meaning could one assign to the 'magical' elements in the episode – the lowering of the pool's rim, the golden bowl – or to the playful ones? Rather, this double vision gives a symbolic insight into the way pain is followed by healing and bliss, frustration by refreshment. And I am inclined to follow von Franz in extending this meaning beyond the overt subject of Perpetua's concern, the dead child-brother, to an inner meaning that concerns herself.[50] For one can plausibly suppose that all her dreams reflect, and stylize, the torments and preoccupations of her waking life. Perpetua dreaming of Dinocrates could indeed be projecting in her dream an aspect of her own being, a childish, 'unredeemed' aspect which she unconsciously senses might still impede her from her heroic goal, and which must first, through prayer, be set at peace.

There is a certain parallelism between this pair of dreams and the initial one. In both something is attained with difficulty: the garden at the top of the ladder, or the pool. And in both the attaining brings with it a nourishment – the cheese, or the water – that proves supernaturally life-giving, and leaves the protagonist with a sense of sweetness or release.[51] I would relate to the close of the Dinocrates visions a sentence about the otherworld attributed to Perpetua outside her own account, by Saturus – a sentence so different from the rest of Saturus' words, so telling and devoid of floweriness, that there is every reason to think of it as authentic Perpetua: 'God be thanked that, as I was full of joy in life, I'm even more joyful here now! (*Deo gratias, ut, quomodo in carne hilaris fui, hilarior sim et hic modo*).'[52] That is how the Perpetua of the diary might have thought about heaven; and it is hard to believe that Saturus, whose heaven is full of roses and angels and 'Holy! holy! holy!', could have made this up.[53]

It is not until the fourth vision that another image of inner conflict emerges. In structure and detail (as has already been hinted) the first and fourth visions are closely related to each other, even though they do not form a true diptych, like the second and third. Before the last vision comes the final scene of conflict in the waking world. Perpetua shows and contrasts two human reactions. Now even an unbeliever, the prison governor, senses her inner strength (of which she herself, through being blessed with visions, had grown increasingly aware). He behaves reverently towards her, and as generously as he can.[54] Only her father embodies till the last a thought in its way as immovable as Perpetua's own: he can see nothing but tragic waste in her dying for her beliefs. Perpetua for the third time describes his sorrow and his entreaties, and still she pities him. Yet, while she depicts him more impassioned and desperate than ever, a tone almost of detachment enters her description, as if her father's behaviour had become more like a histrionic performance, which she was watching sadly but without any impulse to participation. The last phrase – 'I ached for his unhappy old age' – while voicing compassion, comes so abruptly after his extremes of pleading that it has a strangely dry effect. She has made herself deaf to him.

The diary concludes with the most complex and greatest of the four visions. The opening contains a remarkable series of reminiscences, not hitherto noted, from the fifth chapter of the Song of Songs.[55] There (5: 2) the bride lies asleep but with her heart wakeful. Her lover (in the Vetus Latina as in the Greek, literally her brother)[56] knocks at the gate ('pulsat ad ianuam'); she gets up and opens for him ('surrexi et ego aperire . . . aperui ego fratri meo'). The lover's summons, 'veni', that Pomponius uses to Perpetua (x 3), occurs many times in the course of the Canticle, though not in fact in these verses; but his sudden, mysterious departure – 'et abiit' (x 4) – once more echoes this particular passage (5: 5): 'frater meus transivit'. And it is clearly no coincidence that in the Canticle that disappearance is at once followed by the bride's *passio* (5: 7): she is struck and wounded by the city guards, and is stripped of her covering garment ('tulerunt umbraculum meum' – cf. Perpetua's 'et expoliata sum', x 7). We can say that Perpetua's dreaming has here been influenced by a renowned oneiric passage which all early Christians interpreted mystically, as a moment of divine visitation, both summoning and harshly testing the soul that loves God. And the sense, in the Song of Songs chapter, that this dream-visit was both loving and frightening, likewise colours her own vision.

The figure of Pomponius seems to reappear, transformed, in the gigantic fencing-master: both wear an unbelted garment ('discincta...discinctatus') and resplendent sandals, whether damasked or patterned in precious metals ('multiplices galliculas . . . galliculas multiformes'). The first wears white (*candida*), the second purple, and Perpetua adds that his sandals were of gold and silver; here too one cannot but recall phrases used of the Lover in the fifth chapter of the Canticle, who is 'white and red (*candidus et rubeus*)', and whose legs are 'columns set on foundations of gold (*super bases aureas*)'. The fencing-master is also, as we noted with the vast aged shepherd of the first vision, an idealized paternal figure, who at the close, embracing Perpetua, addresses her as 'daughter'. Yet the sense of phantasmagoria obeying their own unreal laws emerges even more from the events narrated. Pomponius says to Perpetua 'Here I am, beside you, sharing your toil' – and at once vanishes and leaves her alone. Perpetua knows she has been condemned to the wild beasts – but the beasts do not come. Nothing is as one might expect in waking life. The details of her combat, too, are surreal throughout. She is stripped of her womanly clothes, and becomes masculine. Here we might see not so much a sexual fantasy as a willed identification, in her dream, with the heroine's end to which she aspires. Like Cleopatra resolving to die with the words 'I am fire, and air; my other elements/ I give to baser life', Perpetua wants to strip herself of all that is weak, or womanish, in her nature. At the same time, the detail of her naked body being rubbed with oil by the handsome young men who are her seconds cannot help carrying erotic suggestion, notwithstanding her disclaimer, that this is customary before an *agôn*.[57]

The Egyptian, her opponent, is seen from the start as an evil figure, 'foul of aspect'. In the Graeco-Roman world, ever since Herodotus and Plato, Egypt had carried the aura of pagan sacred wisdom, the high insight of initiates of the mysteries – precisely what, for a passionately convinced Christian, was bound to appear a forbidden, diabolic knowledge, a threat to the wisdom of the true God. In North Africa, a decade or two before Perpetua's birth, the glitter of the Egyptian initiatory cults had been evoked by Apuleius, in the last book of his *Metamorphoses*, and it may even be his heady account of the mysteries of Isis and Osiris that had shown the adolescent Perpetua how great a force to overcome was that Egypt of the mind.[58]

That something of the world of pagan cults and popular beliefs still lingered in her imagination, and revealed itself in her dream-images, is again clear from many of the details that follow. The fencing-master's robe, as von Franz noted, is that of the African priests of Saturn; his wand suggests the wand of Hermes, guide of souls; the apples of gold, that he promises her as reward if she wins, are the immortal apples of the Hesperides. (In the ninth century the poet Notker, transforming Perpetua's visions in his sequence in praise of holy women, even makes the green branch into Aeneas' golden bough.)[59]

The account of the fight is simultaneously vivid and fantastic. While the wording reflects both the waking-life threats that Perpetua's father had posed to her firmness of purpose and the evocation in Genesis of the hostilities between woman and serpent (see above, pp. 6, 8), the combat becomes truly dream-like when Perpetua floats in the air, able to strike the Egyptian's face from above, as if she were no longer touching ground. Nonetheless I would also stress that in her re-telling Perpetua sees herself as fully lucid throughout the encounter: she is neither in an ecstatic trance nor singing hymns, as von Franz affirmed,[60] confusing Perpetua's dream-account with the purportedly true one of her death by the redactor (XVIII 7, xx 8). The redactor indeed adds many edifying details that are quite alien to the Perpetua of the diary, and are almost certainly fictitious. His picture, for instance, of Perpetua in the arena, covering her legs and tidying her hair after being gored,[61] consorts ill with the dream of the woman who strips naked and is anointed for combat: one who is unafraid to write like that will hardly have gone to her death in a fit of prudery.

In the dream Perpetua wins her combat, wins the apples of immortality. The conclusions of the ladder dream, of the Dinocrates dreams, and of this combat dream, are all serene. In her dreaming, that is, Perpetua always triumphs in the *agôn* she has set herself: to be brave enough to face death, despite all that life holds out – a young son, a family, the joy of earthly existence ('in carne hilaris', XII 7). There is a crescendo in the inner conquests portrayed in these visions, and in the rewards – the cheese, the water that never fails, the golden apples. As von Franz aptly observed, 'The closer destruction comes in the outer sphere, the more do the consoling images in dreams become heightened.'[62] Only thus do we have any awareness – indirectly – of the continuing tensions within Perpetua: overtly, once her dreams have begun, she seems scarcely to give voice to fear.

It is in the light of von Franz's comment that I would see Perpetua's words as she wakes from her last dream: 'And I knew I should have to fight not against wild beasts but against the Fiend;[63] but I knew the victory would be mine.' This brief attempt at allegorical interpretation suggests that here Perpetua has reached a decisive moment of certainty in her waking life – by way of her vision and beyond it. Yet it is one moment of allegory, or rationalization, only. The many vivid details within the last vision – the clothes of Pomponius and the fencing-master, the seconds, her own mode of fighting – cannot be translated into allegoric terms, or could be so only by imposing allegories wilfully. The dream has its own imaginative life, and its own truth as dream. A glance at the banal fabricated visions in such hagiographic works as the *Passio SS. Montani et*

Lucii,[64] or indeed at the vision of Saturus in the later part of the *Passio Perpetuae*, is enough to make this clear. Often details from Perpetua's notes were copied in later Acts of martyrs, and were then deliberately loaded with spiritual meanings. But Perpetua was not writing hagiography – she was recording her own outer and inner world, harrowing and untarnished, with shining immediacy.

The stature of Perpetua's testimony was not fully perceived in the following centuries. Neither the imitation of details from her visions nor the use made of her narrative in sermons reveals more than superficial and conventional understanding. Here the 'reception' of Perpetua by her great North African successor Augustine is especially revealing. While it is Auerbach's lasting merit to have seen in Perpetua's writing the heights of which the 'lowly style (*sermo humilis*)' was capable in the early Christian period, his account of Augustine's attitude to *sermo humilis* was seriously flawed. Augustine did not, as Auerbach claimed, exalt the lowly style over other ways of writing, or 'see the style of Scripture as *humilis* throughout'.[65] On the contrary, in his only detailed stylistic discussion of the Bible (*De doctrina christiana* IV, xx, 39–44), Augustine spends several pages demonstrating with examples that Scripture comprehends the temperate and grand styles as well as the lowly; he sees the value of each style in a relative way – each is suited to certain functions and not others.[66] When Augustine himself turns to the *Passio Perpetuae et Felicitatis*, in three sermons dedicated to these young women saints of his native region, he writes flamboyant, heavily ornamented showpieces, full of rhymes, anaphorai, rhetorical questions and wordplay. (Where the writer of the *Acta minora* had played somewhat crudely upon Perpetua's name, Augustine and his disciple Quodvultdeus take the punning on 'perpetual felicity' to the point of tedium.)[67] Augustine observes no aesthetic distinction between Perpetua's diary and the redactor's hagiographic frame (which is larger than what she herself wrote) – he draws on both parts of the *Passio* indiscriminately. In this he is quite unlike the poet Notker who, five centuries later, went straight to the diary itself, ignoring the frame of the *Passio* entirely, and achieving a concentration and transparency of language worthy of Perpetua's own.

While there is indeed, as Auerbach himself has shown, some compelling prose of a simple realistic kind in the centuries between Perpetua and Notker,[68] I do not believe that this is due to Perpetua's influence, and it is demonstrably not due to Augustine's teaching about *sermo humilis*. Moreover, while there is – as Auerbach (though not Augustine) saw – a profound connection between *sermo humilis* and the new realism found in certain Christian writers, this concept is particularly problematic in the case of Perpetua. Her diary can scarcely be discussed in terms of a 'new realism' – any more than can the diary of Anne Frank, or the Indian memoir of Mary Tyler, or the prison letters of Angela Davis, in

our time. Where writing wells up out of such fearsome events, it seems imperti-
nent, or shallow at best, even to praise the writer's artistry. Nonetheless we can
still marvel at the magnitude of what Perpetua can communicate to us – and
that is, apart from all else, a matter of high art. Perpetua's waking and dreaming
episodes are related to and follow from one another with an inner necessity such
as Aristotle saw to be of the essence of the structure of tragedy. And Perpetua's
language, too, keeps steadily to the essential – no observation seems gratuitous,
no word excessive. While other women must have passed through similar
sufferings, only one young woman gave them such form and meaning.

Perpetua concentrated unswervingly on what was unique in her experience;
she did not try to make her experience exemplary, as the redactor of the *Passio*
and the other African Fathers were tempted to do. In the next testimonies of
women writers that we shall pause at briefly, the sense of by-passing the specific,
individual experience in favour of the paradigmatic, which could be thought to
edify and instruct, is only too apparent.[69]

The collected letters of St Jerome include one (*Ep.* 46) that is by his aristocratic
protégées, Paula and her daughter Eustochium, who from Jerusalem wrote to
their older friend and instructress Marcella, in Rome, to express their joy at
finding for themselves the holy places of the New Testament and the Old, and
their longing that Marcella too would set sail and join them. There are no
reasonable grounds for assuming that the letter was written on their behalf by
Jerome and merely signed by the two women, as some modern scholars have
affirmed, without evidence and without discussion.[70] Jerome's correspondence,
as preserved in the manuscripts, contains many letters by others which have a
connection with his, and in his own epistles to Eustochium and Marcella he
makes explicit reference to the exchange of letters with them, and dwells on
letters of theirs already received.

The letter sent by Paula and Eustochium is stylistically polished and assured,
yet if one hoped to find in it any traces of personal awareness, one would be
deceived. What the two women wish to convey is the bliss and spiritual benefit
that accrues to the visitor of holy places; as regards their own experiences or
reactions, the letters are 'empty'.[71] There is no individual note, and none was
intended. All is exemplary, and hence generalized. We are given not an impression of any particular pilgrims from other lands, but variations on the topos that
people from all lands travel to Jerusalem, centre of the world, centre of Christen-
dom, *visio pacis*:

The Briton, severed from our world, if he has made progress in religion, leaves his western
sun behind to seek the place known to him only by rumour and by scriptural report. Why
should we mention the Armenians, why the Persians, why people of India and Ethiopia,
and of neighbouring Egypt fertile in monks, Pontus and Cappadocia, Celesiria and Meso-
potamia, and all the swarms of the Orient?[72]

Why, indeed, such orotund enumeration? Not just to impress with a rhetorical figure (*occupatio*), but in order to lead effectively into a further topos: this diversity of nations forms a unity, and thereby gives a perfect exemplar of Christian charity:

> . . . they show us a paradigm of the diverse virtues. Their languages are dissonant but in devotion they are one . . . there is no arrogance, no supercilious vaunting of continence: they vie with one another only in humility. Whoever was least among them is here deemed the first. In clothing, no one tries to be different or to attract attention. All walk as they please, without incurring blame or praise.

Clearly such an image of racial harmony and egalitarianism, achieved through love of Christ, would be spoilt irreparably by any 'realistic' touch. Even the addition of specific details would have been precarious. The women do not mention whom they have actually seen, or who precisely has behaved so modestly and charitably towards them. What matters to them is the ideal vision alone, the 'vision of peace' embodied in the name 'Jerusalem'.

They make an impassioned plea to Marcella to come and meet them there:

> Oh, when will that time come, when a panting voyager brings news that our Marcella has been impelled to Palestine's shore? Then all the choirs of monks, all the hosts of virgins, will jubilate! Already we long to run and meet you, hastening on foot, not in a chariot, with ardent body. We shall hold hands, shall see your face – we shall scarcely be separable from your embraces. Will that be the day, then, that we enter the Saviour's grotto, that with you – our sister, our mother – we walk in the Lord's tomb? Shall we then kiss the wood of the Cross, and ascend in prayer and spirit on Mount Olivet with the ascending Christ? Shall we see Lazarus come forth bound in his shroud, and the waters of the Jordan made purer by the Lord's baptism?

Here the women's language takes on a *pathétique* quality which was to become characteristic of Christian expressions of friendship and neighbourly love (*amicitia, dilectio, caritas*) in the following centuries.[73] It becomes the specifically Christian, and especially monastic, modulation of exalted love in the early Middle Ages, and attains its richest gamut, both among men and women writers, in the twelfth century. But again the paradigmatic aspect dominates in what Paula and Eustochium write: they list the principal attractions not as moments they have known (it is not even clear from the wording whether they have visited these holy places already, or are still waiting to do so), but as the epitome of the perfect pilgrim's role, the *imitatio Christi*. As the New Testament events 're-enacted' Old Testament prophecies, fulfilling what had been shown there in *figura*,[74] so the pilgrim can re-enact the New Testament events: these can in their turn become *figurae*, newly fulfilled in individual souls. So, too, the literal voyage the two women beseech Marcella to make has the figural implication of her voyage to the heavenly Jerusalem, to beatitude.

18

Whereas the notion of spiritual ascent is a familiar one, the force of conviction that underlies the pilgrims' ideal emerges remarkably in the phrase, 'shall we see Lazarus come forth bound in his shroud?' Paula and Eustochium do not mean that the impact of seeing Lazarus' tomb will be so moving as to bring on a hallucination, nor that the monks who guard the tomb will arrange for the performance of some sacred mime. Rather that meditation, helped by the numinousness of the place, can recreate the sacred events so intensely that they are lucidly relived in the heart of the believer.

A much longer and more detailed account of a visit to the holy places survives, which may well belong to the same decades as this letter: it is the work known as the 'Itinerary' or 'Peregrination' of Egeria. Since the discovery of the fragmentary and incomplete manuscript in 1884, a vast literature of controversy has dwelt on the identity of the writer (and the correct form of her name), her dates, place of origin, and social rank, the geographic and archaeological details of her account, and above all its language, considered as a treasure-trove of Vulgar Latin. There has been far less literary analysis of Egeria's writing, what she aimed at and achieved, though a brilliant essay by Leo Spitzer (1949) has established a firm base for future critical discussion. Starting with an investigation of some of Egeria's stylistic habits, Spitzer proceeded carefully from these to inductions about her literary intentions and aesthetic decisions; he was able to define perceptively her particular 'epic style'.[75]

The work, insofar as we possess it, has an almost incantatory, litany-like rhythm, both in the procession of brief episodes and in the deployment of language within each larger and smaller syntactic unit. To say that Egeria's account of her travels is monotonous or repetitive would be only a half-truth: she is aiming at a kind of anaphoric writing that had its sacred counterpart in the liturgical ceremonies of her time, and was later, as Spitzer saw, to play a formative role in the verse techniques of *chansons de geste*.[76] –

Meanwhile, walking, we arrived at a certain place where indeed those mountains among which we were passing opened themselves and made an endless valley, huge, all level and extremely beautiful, and across the valley there appeared Sinai, the holy mountain of God. But this place where the mountains opened themselves adjoined that place where the 'Memories of covetousness' lie.[77] In that place, therefore, having arrived . . .

Then, therefore, because I recalled that it was written that St John baptized in Enon beside Salim, I asked of [the priest] how far that selfsame place might be. Then that holy priest said: 'Look, here it is, two hundred steps away. So if you wish, look, I'll at once lead you there on foot. This water, to be sure, which you see in this village, is so copious and pure – it comes from that selfsame spring.' Then, therefore, I began to give him thanks and to ask that he lead us to the place, and so it was done. At once, therefore, we began to go with him on foot through the whole most lovely valley, till we arrived at an orchard garden, an extremely lovely one, where he showed us, in the middle, a spring of water most good and pure, which all at once released an entire stream . . . Then that selfsame holy priest said to us: 'Even unto this day this garden is called in the Greek tongue nothing other than *cepos tu agiu Iohanni*, that is, as you say in Latin, *hortus sancti Iohannis*.' . . .

And so, therefore, giving thanks to God there too, according to our custom, we continued on our route. Again going on that route we saw a valley presenting itself to us on our left, most lovely, and this valley was huge, sending an endless torrent into the Jordan. And there in that selfsame valley we saw the monastery of a certain brother now, that is, of a monk. Then I, as I am most curious, began to ask, what this valley might be . . .

Whatever we may feel at first about the poverty of Egeria's diction and perceptions, it is clear that this web of language has not been woven thoughtlessly. The pattern of iteration can lend its own solemnity, just as such a verse in the *Chanson de Roland* as

> Halt sont li pui e li val tenebros
>
> High are the crags, the valleys tenebrous

acquires new force through its return and variation.

Egeria's echoes are insistent: they insist upon the importance, the holiness of everything in the region, just as the abundance of pseudo-causal connectives conveys a kind of universal connectedness of all the sacred sites with their sacred events and with the pilgrim herself. Not that this pilgrim conveys the quality of any *inner* experience of the sacred – no, she effaces herself in the attitude of the ideal pilgrim, in the posture of limitless travelling, questioning, verifying.

The verifications count for her above all: they epitomize the joy and wonder of seeing for herself all she has learnt about through religious reading. Yet she never tries to communicate joy and wonder direct: she gives only, time and again, the certification that everything was as it ought to be, was as she had been led to expect.

Her *curiositas*, as Spitzer saw, is no individual trait of character but an aspect of this verification-process. Indeed almost nothing about Egeria personally can be safely inferred from her text. That she accepted every explanation she was given without demur does not necessarily mean she was gullible – once more it relates to the quintessential 'pilgrim' frame of mind rather than to her particular temperament. The itinerary she describes sounds arduous: should we infer her keen courage and physical stamina, or that she was immensely wealthy and sheltered from the hardships of the journey by a retinue of regal proportions? This – if the conjecture of some scholars is correct – is the sour interpretation that seems to have occurred to St Jerome;[78] on the other hand, Egeria mentions stretches of riding not only on horseback but on donkey and camel, and scaling inaccessible places on foot. That is, even the princess-like progress – if such it was – had its strenuous moments.

Strangest to me is that the whole of Egeria's surviving account contains no sign of interest in any of her entourage: only casual phrases like 'we all dismounted' make clear that she wasn't travelling alone. But here too it may well be a matter of deliberate exclusion, so as to direct all attention to the places visited and to what the holy men said of them. And the holy men, as Egeria once notes explicitly, talked *only* of holy things; every stranger she meets is presented as an image of the identical plaster saint. There is never a mishap, and gradually one almost begins to long for one. If only Egeria had told of even one monk or bishop who was not gracious but rude, even one who was not a walking textbook of sacred geography but who had told her pious fibs that she saw through, the vivacity of the work would have gained immeasurably. And we can surmise that no voyage so long and tiring could possibly have gone throughout with such preternatural smoothness, with no one ever feeling unwell, or losing the way. But what Egeria wanted to send her 'sisters' – possibly a group of fellow-nuns in Galicia – was not a report truthful in the everyday sense, but a paradigm of perfection.

Thus, while in some respects her techniques can be said to foreshadow vernacular epic style, there is one important difference: in her account, unlike the *chansons de geste*, there is never a *peripeteia*; there is not even narrative development. Egeria does not attempt to unfold a story: she simply itemizes. And every item has been pressed into a similar mould. Because of her overridingly instructive purpose, she shows everything happening in precisely the same exemplary way. It is this that in the last resort imposes limitations on her language; and they are real limitations, as well as symptoms of an unusual artistic-didactic choice.

By contrast, the only other woman's composition known to me from the end of the fourth century is personal and direct: it reveals perceptions so sensitive and lovable that they have something of the same moving beauty as Perpetua's diary. This time the writer is a pagan woman – Paulina, the widow of Vettius Agorius Praetextatus († 384), to whom she had been married for forty years.[79] Praetextatus was illustrious in religion, philosophy and letters, as he was in public life; he was consul-designate at the time of his death. A translator of Greek philosophical texts, a friend of Symmachus and Macrobius, he is portrayed as the host and a leading speaker at the imagined banquet of Macrobius' *Saturnalia*.[80]

The verses that Paulina composed for inscription on his tomb have intimate, touching moments such as epitaphs rarely attain: indeed, only in the last four lines does Paulina speak of her husband's death – the rest is an evocation, in the present tense, of the joys of life with him. Paulina perceives these through a kind of total dedication that in some ways looks ahead to Heloise: she is convinced that, insofar as she has any wisdom, it is because he has taught her; insofar as she has praise and honour in the world, it is because of him. The epitaph – which both in scale and subtlety might more aptly be thought of as a meditation, first rapturous then elegiac – deserves to be translated in full:[81]

> My parents' bright fame gave me nothing greater than this –
> that, at the time we married, I was thought worthy of you.
> Yet my whole light and glory is my husband's name,
> yours, Agorius, who, born of proud ancestry,
> 5   make radiant your land, the senate, and your wife,
> by your mind's integrity, your actions and aspirations –
> you who have reached the highest peak of excellence.
> Whatever has been written in either language,
> by care of the wise, for whom heaven's gate lies open,
> 10   or whatever songs the learned have composed,
> or any works in prose – you pass them on
> even better than you found them in your reading.
> Yet this is little: you, loyal initiate in the holy
> mysteries, bury their insights deep within your mind;
> 15   instructed, you worship a manifold divinity
> and generously make your wife your comrade
> in rites of gods and men: faithful to you, she shares your thought.
> Why should I now mention honours or power
> or any of the joys men seek by praying?
> 20   You, always seeing these as small and fragile,
> set store by the divine tokens of your priesthood.
> Husband, by your good teaching you liberate me,
> innocent and modest, from the bond of death,
> you lead me into temples, dedicate me to gods;
> 25   with you as my witness, I am steeped in all the mysteries,
> and you, blissful companion, admit me – already priestess
> of Cybele and Attis – to the taurine sacrifice;
> you teach me the triple secret of Hecate, whom I serve,
> and make me worthy of Demeter's liturgy.
> 30   Because of you, everyone lauds me as blessed
> and holy: it is you who show me to be good, and so
> I who was unknown am known throughout the world –
> how could I fail to please, since you are my husband?
> Mothers in Rome look to me for example,
> 35   and think their children beautiful if they are like you.
> Now men, now women long for and applaud
> the splendours I have learnt through you, my teacher.
> All this is taken from me now: I waste away, a grieving wife.
> How happy I'd have been had the gods let my husband
> 40   live on – yet in the end I *am* happy:
> I am and have been yours, and soon, after my death, I shall be yours.

Perpetua had taken a lonely road; the sense of controlled excitement in Paulina's words is determined by what she and her husband shared. The opening lines could be simple panegyric, except for the rare sense of blithe self-effacement of the wife before her husband. From line 8 onwards, her account of him and her relation to him becomes specific. From his rôle as teacher she passes on to his greater rôle as spiritual guide. Whilst Augustine could share an experience of mystical illumination at Ostia with his beloved mother, Monica,[82] Paulina's evocation of participating in the highest cognition with her husband is, to my knowledge, unique in the ancient world. The sense of the triviality of worldly honours and power to one whose mind is set on God (18ff) is common enough; but Paulina transforms this into her own crescendo of religious initiations: because Agorius knows that earthly things are unimportant, he has taught her where the true hope of immortality lies. Each of the mysteries into which he had introduced Paulina brings her a step nearer to God and to the immortal world, and (as these lines hint, though it becomes explicit only at the close) to rejoining in that beyond the husband whom she loves.

As she goes on to claim (30ff) that all her worth lies in him, the tone increases in tenderness and exultation. Till line 37, if we did not know these verses were from a tomb, not a word could suggest that what Paulina portrays is anything other than the fullness of harmonious life, informed with love of the divine powers and nearness to them, because informed with conjugal love and nearness. Suddenly, four lines from the close, the bleakness of death intrudes, and at the same time a pang of desperate longing. Then at once serene hope begins to surge again: the oneness in life is a guarantee of oneness in death.

The notion of the human love-union growing into an immortal union in the otherworld is here expressed with an integrity and a conviction that show what heights the pagan mysteries were still capable of inspiring. Paulina conceives herself an initiate as completely as Perpetua had conceived herself a Christian; for both, the way they see themselves is a foundation for luminous confidence, even in the moments of tragic crisis. Jerome, in a letter to Marcella, has a repellent passage in which he mocks Paulina's beliefs and hopes, because they were not Christian ones. He dwells on the outward successes of her husband Praetextatus, 'who ascended the Capitol as if in triumph over enemies laid low, whom the Roman populace welcomed with applause and dancing, at whose death the whole city was moved. Now he is desolate, naked, not in the milky palace of the heavens, as his wretched wife lyingly affirms, but enveloped in foul darkness.'[83] For Jerome the polemicist it was intolerable that there should be any hope of immortality other than the Christian. Yet the Christian women – Jerome's high-born friends, and Egeria – showed no glimmerings of the other-worldly in what they wrote. Theirs was an essentially earthbound spirituality; that of Paulina, like Perpetua's, soars.

Among the vast numbers of funerary inscriptions and verses that survive from the late-antique Roman world, some allow us a glimpse of how women whose utterances would never have been preserved as 'literature' thought and felt. There are touching affirmations of affection, and of keeping memories alive, often in quite artless prose. Thus Placidia Hedone, in Ondara (near Dianium – the modern Denia – on the Gulf of Valencia), at the death of 'her devoted and incomparable husband', builds a monument to be shared by them both, 'so that even in the sepulchre she be not parted from him with whom she lived a joyous life for thirty-five years, in serene harmony'.[84] Seppia Justina, at Beneventum, calls her husband, with whom she had lived for forty-two years, not only 'incomparabilis' but 'amanti mendax' – false to her who loves him, by preceding her in death.[85] Martina, who travels fifty days from Gaul in order to commemorate her husband, buried in Asolo, writes, 'Bene quescas, dulcissime mi marite' – 'Rest well, my sweetest husband.'[86]

Beside these we can place the expression of Cutia Silvana, wife of a freedman at Narbonne, who inscribes on her husband's grave 'I await my man (*virum exspecto meum*)'[87] – whether this intimates a specifically Christian hope of reunion in heaven, as Geist and Pfohl claim, or a more elemental longing; or again, the words of a slave-girl from Aquileia, Anicia Glycera, who had been freed by the man who married her, and who sets down: 'I won favour, I who gave delight to a good man, who led me from the lowest order to the highest honour.'[88] Other slave-girls receive a vengeful warning from the grave, as when a Roman matron, Longinia Procla, builds her vault 'for herself and her freedmen and freedwomen, and their descendants – except for those women who abandoned me whilst I was alive. They shall never have access or admission to this monument.'[89]

Among the *carmina epigraphica* we encounter at times, in simple, not always correctly built verses, a tenderness comparable to Paulina's. Thus for instance an anonymous Christian inscription in third-century Rome:

> Alas, dearest husband, who leave me, wretched, alone!
> Without you, what shall I hold sweet, what shall I believe lovable?
> For whom do I cling on to life and not follow you, villain, into death?
> Let me go with you, hand in hand,
> united to you in the grave that I too much desire!
> Your courtesy, respect and loyalty,
> and being gentle, did not help you – you were doomed to die.
> Only this – if any awareness outlives our bodies –
> I'll let you have my pledge of love forever:
> husband, I'll keep your bed inviolate.[90]

The reproach addressed to him – 'villain (*improbe*)', because he has hastened into death before her – recalls Seppia Justina's 'amanti mendax'; but it foreshadows an even more closely comparable expression in high art, when Juliet, about to die, reproaches Romeo: 'O churl! drunk all, and left no friendly drop / To help me after?' Noteworthy too is the candour with which the ardent hope of some kind of life after death is left inseparable from both the fear that the Christian teaching may not prove true and the idealism of living as if it were true.

A similar emotional beauty can be perceived in some lines from Ecija in southern Spain:

> I, a wife whom her husband held dear, made this vault for my love:
> I had longed to die in his embrace.[91]

At times, as when the inscription is of a dead man speaking *in propria persona*, only an aside may reveal that the epitaph has been composed by his widow; thus for instance with a doctor in second-century Rome, who had died of a knee-infection, and who cries out against the injustice of this to the gods, the verses conclude:

> My wife inscribed this, as best she could, for me, her only one.[92]

Mothers, too, left poignant record of the loss of children. One, in third-century Milan, erects a monument for her soldier son who died in battle, and writes:

> Your comrades could not even bring your body to the grave:
> you have deceived me, left me too-much-orphaned.[93]

Another, by Papiria Tertia of Ferrara, for her own tomb, is filled both with a *planctus* for old age and a defiant bitterness:

> Stranger, you see that, bereft of my own, I raised a monument:
> sad and too old, pitiable, I seek my children.
> Let others learn how my old age was laid waste,
> that barren wives may count themselves truly happy![94]

Perhaps only one late-antique Christian epitaph approaches the imaginative height of the pagan Paulina's: it is the inscription – six elegiac couplets – of Helpis, who dies in Rome perhaps in the sixth century. The older legend, that Helpis had been the wife of Boethius, died hard; and the newer one – still maintained for instance in the *Clavis Patrum* – that she composed two renowned hymns in honour of Peter and Paul, has only recently been scotched by Dag Norberg,[95] who showed that one of these hymns was by Paulinus of Aquileia, the other by a Carolingian imitator of Paulinus. Yet I would also wonder whether the epitaph itself might have been composed not by Helpis but by her husband: as the third couplet indicates, either she wrote it when so near death that she knew her husband would survive her, or else he wrote the verses as if speaking in her name. They begin:

> Helpis was my name; I was nurtured in Sicily;
> a husband's love drove me far from my native land;

without him day was dismal, night anxious, the hour tearful –
not only our flesh but our spirit was one.
My life is not cut off with such a husband surviving,
and I'll live on in the greater half of my soul.[96]

Diehl noted a reminiscence in the fourth verse from St Paul (1 Corinthians 6: 16–17), and in the sixth from Ovid (*Metam.* xv 875–6). Yet Paul's thought is here reversed: where he contrasts the physical oneness of married love ('erunt ... duo in carne una') with the greater, spiritual oneness that man can have with God, Helpis proclaims a human unity of loving spirits as well as bodies. And where Ovid, at the close of his long poem, hopes for *his own* immortality 'in my better part', here the better part is found in the beloved.

The whole piece is a testimony of conjugal love that is not only beautiful but astonishing: as in Paulina's composition for her husband, the hope of reunion in death is expressed in a wholly individual way. Helpis calls the throne of the Christian God, the everlasting Judge, to witness (*iudicis aeterni ... thronum*), in order to introduce a metaphor that, in its fantasy of ultimate one-ness, borders the sublime and the outrageous:

Let no hand violate this tomb, unless perchance my husband
should long to unite these limbs again with his.

From the next period we have little more than a few chance survivals of what women wrote – first, in the later sixth and early seventh centuries, among the highest nobility in Merovingian Gaul, then in the eighth in the Anglo-Saxon world, especially in the monastic circles befriended by St Boniface and disciples of Boniface in Germany.

The Visigothic princess Brunhilda, whose marriage in 566 to Sigebert, King of Austrasia, was celebrated by Venantius Fortunatus in an epithalamium suffused with the florid, essentially pagan, manner of late antiquity, had received an education such that she could appreciate so elaborately learned a piece of courtly flattery. She herself took an active part in the education of her son Childebert, and was praised for the excellence she displayed in this by Pope Gregory the Great.[97] So there is no reason to doubt – as some scholars do – that she was capable of writing the letters that survive under her name. Moreover, while the more formal, official aspects of these letters are of the kind that could in principle stem from a secretary, there are also wholly personal moments, which it would be far-fetched to believe had been penned for her. The most notable occurs in her letter of 585 to Empress Anastasia in Constantinople. Brunhilda's daughter Ingund had married the Visigothic prince Herminigild, whom Bishop Leander of Seville had converted from Arianism to orthodox Christianity. This enraged his father, King Leovigild (569–86) so much that he had the son put to death. The widowed Ingund, attempting to flee back to Gaul with her infant son, fell into the hands of the Greeks.[98] They planned to take her and the child under military escort to Constantinople: the Byzantine emperor, Maurice, was trying to persuade Ingund's brother Childebert to send an army against the Lombards in Italy, and hoped by this means to force Childebert's hand. Ingund, however, died on the way there, in North Africa, and only Athanagild, Brunhilda's grandson, arrived at the Byzantine court. Brunhilda pleads with the empress to have him sent back to Gaul:

Because, most serene majesty, through chance the infancy of my little grandson has learnt to make pilgrimage, and his innocence has begun to be captive in tender years, I ask in the name of the Redeemer of all peoples – as you hope never to see your own most devoted Theodosius taken from you, your sweet son severed from your motherly embrace, as your eyes may always take joy in his presence and your motherly womb delight in its august progeny – that you command arrangements to be made, through Christ's favour, for me to have my little one back again, so that in my inmost being I may be refreshed by his embrace, I who sigh with grievous sorrow at my grandson's absence: let me, who have lost a daughter, at least not lose her sweet child, who remains for me; and, inasmuch as I am tormented by my daughter's death, let me be consoled by you through my captive grandson's swift return – so that, when you look upon my grieving and his innocence, you may, by releasing the captive, receive the reward of glory from God, who is the redemption of all mankind, and thereby too charity may be multiplied and the bonds of peace extended between East and West, with Christ's merciful aid.[99]

This vast sentence, at least as it has been transmitted, is not perfect in grammar[100] or syntax. Brunhilda attempts an excessive, over-ambitious range of hypotactic constructions, which, after the imprecation in the name of Christ and of the empress's own son, continue without entirely clear articulation. The clauses of purpose and result ('ut iubeatis . . .', 'ut . . . relever', 'quatinus . . . multiplicetur') enclose relative and temporal constructions somewhat awkwardly; these clauses look as though they mean to stand in some significant relation to one another, yet the relation is never quite thought through. Brunhilda attempts such a complex, high-flown structure partly so as to convince the empress of the solemn earnestness of what she is saying; at the same time, in the details it is pathos, not ceremoniousness, that prevails. The official style shows us, between the lines, an emotionally tense moment, in which a queen, writing to an empress, appeals to her simply as a mother. You have a young son just like my grandson, she is saying; you don't know what it is to lose a child, as I have done; so that you may never know that sorrow, be merciful now. Even the intimacy that pervades the appeal might be viewable as a rhetorical stratagem, a variation that will enhance the letter's persuasive effect. Yet what is being done here is wholly individual: while palace officials could indeed have drafted an appeal, it would not have sounded like this.

Radegunde, once the queen of Sigebert's father, Chlothar I, had sought shelter from the brutal world of Merovingian power politics in the convent of the Holy Cross at Poitiers. There she exchanged gifts and verses of friendship with the poet Fortunatus, who came to live near her and found delight in her nearness. While he explicitly mentions the verses (*carmina magna*)[101] that Radegunde sent to him, these were unfortunately not preserved alongside his own in the 'collected edition' that was prepared in the convent, doubtless soon after Fortunatus' death. This edition, however, does contain Radegunde's verse epistles to her cousin Amalafred and her nephew Artachis (see below, pp. 85–6), though in these it is hard to rule out some collaboration by Fortunatus in the writing. But the *xenia* that Radegunde and Agnes, her spiritual daughter and successor as abbess, sent to their friend are lost to us: it would seem that the two women were self-deprecating and did not think their own efforts worth preserving. We still have Radegunde's testament (naturally in prose); also a letter to her by Caesaria, abbess of the foundation at Arles, whose rule the Poitiers convent had adopted. Caesaria urges that 'no nun be allowed to enter who does not learn letters'; she warns Radegunde against trying to live too ascetically – 'do everything in a reasonable way' – but also cautions her about the dangers of having the company of men too often.[102] (Fortunatus himself also once hints, in some verses, at the murmurs to which his friendship with Radegunde and Agnes gave rise.)[103]

Apart from Radegunde's two poetic epistles, we have only one other poem by a woman from among Fortunatus' circle of friends. It is by Eucheria, wife of the high-born *litteratus* Dynamius of Marseille. Like her husband and like Fortunatus, Eucheria cultivated preciosity and a delight in mannerism. Her poem (sixteen couplets) is a sparkling variation on the motif of 'the world upside down'. While there are many uses of *adynata* both in learned and unlearned milieux, from antiquity onwards, to express a thought connected with love, to protest fidelity or (more rarely) to reject a lover,[104] Eucheria shows unusual adroitness in working to a witty climax, in staking everything on a provocatively amusing 'curtain line'.[105]

At first she seems to develop her theme of the 'impossible match' in nature systematically, progressing from examples of misalliance in the mineral world to those of plants, and then to fish and animals. But next, as if impelled by the mounting excitement of arguing her case, the instances come pell-mell from every aspect of the world:

> Now let hind couple with donkey, tiger with wild ass,
>> let the swift doe and sluggish ox unite;
> let nectar-like rosy wine be ruined by foul resin
>> and honey be mixed with bitter apple-mash;
> let's wed diamond-like water to a muddy pit,
>> and let the dewy fount proceed from dung;

let the fleet swallow play with the deadly vulture,
   the nightingale harmonize with the dismal owl . . .
Let these monstrosities make fate's course falter –
   then let a peasant slave woo Eucheria!

The whole accumulation exists for the sake of that climax. Was it a pure divertissement, a virtuoso piece for a small refined circle? Sadly, we know too little about Eucheria to gauge the imaginative situation of the piece. We can only guess whether her high-spirited outburst – impish and (at least in jest) destructive – had a real occasion or was entirely fictitious. At all events, what is important here is the way, as pungent as it is elegant, that a woman could show her consciousness of her own worth, and say no to a man whom she thought beneath her ('rusticus et servus'). Whether she really felt the need to say no, faced with a real threat, or devised this purely as a *jeu d'esprit*, the imaginative reality of the situation is one that no social historian should overlook.

Eucheria's poem, like the playful affectionate verses of Fortunatus to Radegunde and Agnes, is a brief respite from the harsher realities of the powerful in the Merovingian world. These obtrude again in the letters of Herchenefreda to her son Desiderius. She had married into a great Gallo-Roman family, the Syagrii, and had helped to give a literary education to her three sons. Desiderius had embarked on a career not as a churchman but as a courtier, and had become treasurer in the palace of King Flothar, and then of his son and successor Dagobert. In 630 one of his brothers, Syagrius, died as governor of Marseille, and the other, Rusticus, who had become bishop of Cahors, was murdered in his cathedral. King Dagobert tried to avenge this murder savagely – 'some men were mutilated, some put to death, some exiled, and some condemned to perpetual servitude'[106] – and then, at the pleas of the people of Cahors, he agreed that Desiderius be appointed bishop to succeed his brother.

Two of Herchenefreda's letters to her son are filled with moral and spiritual advice of the kind that Dhuoda was to give her William – though here the words are brief and colourless compared with Dhuoda's. Once there is a moment of practical solicitude: 'As for the spices which you'll need in the palace, tell me in your next letter, and at once, in God's name, I'll send them.'[107] But the third letter, written after the assassination of Rusticus and before Desiderius' own succession to the see, has a desolate tragic note, which the simple rhetoric, with its word-play in the salutation ('semper desiderabili . . . Desiderio')[108] and its unskilled repetitions and superlatives, does nothing to diminish:

I think you have already been given word how your most gentle brother, the revered bishop Rusticus, was killed by treacherous men who occupied his church. So, most gentle son, since your father too has already passed away, and your brother, Syagrius, has departed, see to it that this cause is pursued manfully,[109] so that a high example come of it.

What shall I, unhappy mother, do, since your brothers are no more? If you should die, I'll be bereft, without any children. But you, most loyal son, my most gentle one, look after yourself always, and whilst you have lost the solace of your brothers, do not lose yourself, do not walk into destruction – far be that from you!

So, too, the eighth-century women who corresponded with St Boniface often display a keenly emotional tone. Yet here it is less because of the violence amid which they lived than because a certain high-pitched effusiveness had become traditional in Christian letters of spiritual friendship, St Jerome's letters serving as the outstanding precedent. This is not to say that these women's letters are affected in their hyperboles and rhetorical imprecations – in the world of the eighth-century missions, where travel was always lengthy and arduous and often dangerous too, and where Boniface himself was finally put to death by the Frisian pagans (754), the relationships bound by mutual prayers and *caritas* must have had a special intensity, partly because of the sombre backcloth against which the travellers' lives were played out.

While five religious women (Aelffled, Egburg, Eangyth, Bugga, and Lioba) wrote letters to Boniface himself which survive preserved with his correspondence, the most passionate and sensitive letters are three near the close of the Boniface collection that have no direct link with the saint. Because of this they have not appeared in modern selections of the Boniface letters, and have been neither translated nor discussed. They are by a nun, Berthgyth, to her brother, Balthard, both children of Cynehild, who was the aunt of Boniface's fellow-worker Lul. Cynehild and her daughter, 'very well-nurtured in liberal learning',[110] had left England and gone, no doubt at Boniface's behest, to teach in Thuringia. There Berthgyth, after her mother's death, remained alone, and became painfully lonely. Three times she writes to Balthard, the only relative she has left, beseeching him for a visit. In her first two letters she employs a poetically heightened prose, full of parallelisms, assonances and rhymes, that go beyond any devices deployed by the women who wrote to Boniface. She uses every stylistic resource at her disposal to persuade Balthard not to neglect her. Her Latin remains essentially simple and limited, capable of relatively few variations on her theme – yet this makes her utterances the more touching. –

Why is it, my brother,
that you have let pass so long a time,
that you have delayed to come?
Why do you not want to remember
that I am alone upon this earth,
and no other brother will visit me,
or any kinsman come to me? . . .
Oh brother, oh my brother,
how can you afflict the mind of me, who am naught,

with constant grief, weeping and sorrow,
day and night, through the absence of your love?
Do you not know for sure
that among all the living there is none
whom I set higher than your love?
Look, I can't suggest all this to you by letter.
Already I feel certain you don't care about me, who am naught.[111]

The language comes close to that of the vernacular women's 'songs for a lover' (*winileodas*), which, according to the famous prohibition of 789, abbesses and the nuns in their charge were forbidden to send from convents.[112] The evocation of solitude and tears and longing has precise parallels in the two extant Anglo-Saxon women's love-laments, known as 'The Wife's Complaint' and 'Wulf and Eadwacer', in the naked emotions expressed, though not of course in the poems' narrative situations. Berthgyth's exclamation that begins 'Oh brother, oh my brother' comes uncannily close to that of Wulf's beloved:

> Wulf, my Wulf, I am sick with longing
> for you, with the rareness of your coming,
> the grief of my heart . . .

And indeed in Berthgyth's second letter she dwells on one of the essential motifs in the *winileodas* – the sea that sunders those who love each other. She enmeshes this vernacular motif in lines whose phrasing is deeply indebted to Old Testament passages.[113] She begins with Job's cry of grief, and then, after pondering her loneliness, sets down David's contrast between human loss and divine solace. This leads her to the thought that true *caritas* does not entail severance in love. Her phrase for the sea, 'congregationes aquarum', echoes the creation of the sea in Genesis; her thought – that spiritual affection is not bound by space – is a reminiscence from a well-loved moment in the letters of Jerome.[114] Yet in the midst of this the sense of the water 'between you and me' is that of 'Wulf is on one island, I on another', or, in 'The Wife's Complaint',

> First my lord went away from here, from his people,
> over the tossing waves. In the dawn I felt sorrow . . .

For her brother's love Berthgyth is unafraid to use the burning expression from the Song of Songs, 'fortis est ut mors dilectio', where even the word *dilectio*, while capable of bearing spiritual meaning, goes beyond the more purely Christian concept, *caritas*. –

My soul is weary of my life,
languishing for our fraternal love.
For I am alone,
abandoned and deprived of the help of kindred;
for my father and mother have left me,

but the Lord has taken me.
There are many congregations of waters between me and you –
still let us be one in love,
for true love is never broken by severance of place.
And yet I tell you
that sorrow has never receded from my soul,
and even in dreams I am restless,
'for love is as strong as death'.

So I ask you now, most beloved brother,
to come to me, or else bid me come,
that I may look on you before I die,
because the love of you has never left my soul.
Brother, your only sister is greeting you in Christ.
I pray for you as for myself, in the days and the nights,
in the hours and the moments,
that you may always have well-being with Christ.

Berthgyth continues with some verses, rhymed octosyllabic couplets such as Aldhelm especially had made popular in the Anglo-Latin world, and Boniface and Lul had written to their friends.[115] Here she is hampered by her form – her phrases scarcely go beyond ones that had become conventional in this type of verse, and her wish – that they may reach heaven together – is a familiar piety. More remarkable is that the ten couplets are followed by a magic spell – 'Elonqueel et Michael, Acaddai, Adonai . . .' It would seem that Berthgyth tried every method known to her in order to obtain the loved brother's assent.

Between the second and third letters, Balthard sends his sister a message and some gifts. She prepares a letter and gift for his messenger to take as he returns. This time the rhythmic patterns and rhymes are much less evident – possibly because the lines had to be written more hastily. Yet there are moments as poignant as in the other letters. Balthard's message must have contained some exhortation to his sister not to cling too deeply to her human attachment, but rather to devote her heart wholly to God. Such advice is essentially of the kind that Abelard was to give at length to Heloise, and in Berthgyth's third letter we can see her struggling with the implications of that advice in a way that is a far-off anticipation of Heloise's sorrows. It will be possible to acquiesce, she thinks – possible not to cling to Balthard too much – if only she can see him once more first. Unlike Heloise, she is ready to admit that God is truly a consolation for human solitude, and that he never abandons her soul. But then the human anguish and longing return, followed again by a great effort to compose herself and summon up inner nobility, to say at last to Balthard: even if you do not come, I shall love you still. –

And now I confess to you that with God's help I long to fulfil all you have commanded me to do,[116] if you will deign to come to me – for [otherwise] I cannot in any way assuage my spring of tears. When I see and hear that other women are about to visit men who are their friends, then I recall that I was bereft of my parents in my youth and have remained here alone. Yet I was not forsaken by the Lord, but I thank God for his immense compassion . . .

And now, my brother, I adjure and beseech you to take away the sorrow from my soul, for it hurts me deeply. For I tell you, even though it were only the space of a single day and you then went home again, the Lord inclining your will, nonetheless the sorrow will then recede from my soul and the pain from my heart. But if it displeased you to fulfil my petition, then I call God to witness, that in me our love would never grow destitute.[117]

It is difficult to assign an exact date to Berthgyth's letters. A letter from Boniface to several of his women friends in England, including Berthgyth's mother Cynehild, is assigned by the editors to the years 742–6.[118] Was Berthgyth not yet born at this time, or perhaps too young to be included in the greeting? At all events, between that letter and those of Berthgyth herself, the mother's and daughter's move to the Continent, and the mother's death, intervene. Moreover, that Berthgyth stresses she was young when her parents died, and closes her third letter saying that, if she came home, it would be in order to die, suggests that the time in Thuringia will have been long. So her letters to her brother may well stem from the same decade, the 770s, as the work of another Anglo-Saxon nun who, shortly after 761, had settled in Germany: Hugeburc, abbess of Heidenheim.

The personal testimony Hugeburc has left us, in the Prologue to her life of the brothers Willibald, bishop of Eichstätt, and Wynnebald, abbot of Heidenheim, reveals a very different temperament and style from those of Berthgyth. Hugeburc is addressing the varied ranks of male clergy, for whom she intends her work. Where Berthgyth uses lucid, uncomplicated vocabulary and syntax, and writes a Latin that seldom strays very far from classical correctness, Hugeburc tries to write exuberantly crammed, complex periods, enhanced by rare words and phrases, new formations and coinages, by alliteration, and by elaborate series of nouns and adjectives dependent (often unsteadily and pleonastically) on one another. Her mastery of 'correct' Latin falls far short of her ambitions, as numerous bizarre cases and case-endings, tenses and verb-forms reveal. Like Berthgyth, Hugeburc echoes or adapts certain phrases with which she is familiar: in the case of her Prologue, as has recently been shown in a fine study of her language,[119] it is especially Sedulius' dedicatory epistle to Macedonius, the prelude to his *Carmen Paschale*, and at the close a riddle of Aldhelm's, that are drawn upon. Nonetheless, Hugeburc's tone and manner are distinctive, even to the ingenious cryptogram by which she conceals – and declares – her name and authorship.[120]

The *Vita* of the two brothers is addressed 'to all priests and deacons and all the princes of ecclesiastical governance'. This is announced in the superscription, and then unfolded far more elaborately in Hugeburc's opening sentence. Next, by way of a modesty-topos, she comes to speak of herself:

To all these abiding here under the guidance of the sacred law, I who am unworthy, of Anglo-Saxon race, I the last of those coming here, not only in years but in behaviour too, I who am as it were a puny creature cómpared with my fellow-Christians, I indeed had decided to expound a little by way of prelude concerning the beginnings of the life of that venerable man Willibald, compressing a few things to allow them to be effectively remembered.

And yet I especially, corruptible through the womanly frail foolishness of my sex, not supported by any prerogative of wisdom or exalted by the energy of great strength, but impelled spontaneously by the ardour of my will, as a little ignorant creature culling a few thoughts from the sagacity of the heart, from the many leafy, fruit-bearing trees laden with a variety of flowers, it pleases me to pluck, assemble and display some few, gathered – with whatever feeble art, at least from the lowest branches – for you to hold in memory.

And now with renewed speech I say, repeating, not relying on the awakening of my own presumption, nor relying insistently on the audacity of my temerity, that I do not – except as it were scarcely – dare to begin.[121]

No matter: Hugeburc feels that she *must* write – for she received from Willibald himself, before his death, an account of all his travels. He dictated this to her, she adds for precision, on Tuesday 23 June. (The year, as scholars have calculated, must have been 778.) And this, Hugeburc stresses, is a true account – far from 'the trifling of apocrypha related in erratic dissertation'.[122] So even if she herself is unlearned (*idiota*), even if 'the Lord our God has deigned to set higher than me prelates who are more outstanding, not only in being of the male sex, but also in their dignity of divine ministry', still she has things of value to relate concerning two blessed men, their lives and deeds and miracles, which it would be wrong to let pass in silence into oblivion. 'Thus it pleases me to set in the reader's hands something to be read that is worthy of remembrance.'

What are we to make of the mixture of confidence and diffidence? The Prologue seems continually to oscillate in tone. Even within a single sentence Hugeburc passes from 'I who am unworthy' to 'I indeed . . . had decided to expound (*ego indigna . . . ego quidem . . . disputare decreveram*)'. From protestations of woman's weak, frail nature she goes on to affirm that her will to write this work was irresistible; then, from 'it pleases me (*libet*)' she retreats again to 'I do not – except as it were scarcely – dare to begin (*incipere nisi ut vix audeo*)'.

Was Hugeburc saying absolutely 'straight' that men are superior by virtue of their sex, and that God has given a sign of this by allowing only men the dignity of priesthood? Or was the elaborate deprecation of herself and her sex a subtle means of self-assertion? St Paul had spoken of himself as 'not worthy to be called an apostle',[123] and yet his rôle in the early Church was unique. Did this not cross Hugeburc's mind as she called herself 'unworthy (*indigna*)'? As Paul sent forth his Epistles, so now all the ranks of clergy were being addressed by one 'unworthy' woman, because she felt she had something unique to impart

34

to them. The to and fro in Hugeburc's Prologue suggests both her determination to write and her playing – half-fearful, half-defiant – upon what the male world will think of a woman trying her hand at things that are normally done by men.

Neither Berthgyth nor Hugeburc was able to forge a wholly unfettered language for herself, a Latin supple enough to convey every nuance of her thoughts and feelings. In the writing of both, many problems of interpretation remain; especially the more ambitious flights of Hugeburc are not always fully clear (quite apart from the many aspects of her syntax, grammar and morphology that a pedagogue using a classical yardstick would castigate). Yet in the writing of both women, so disparate in what they wanted to express, something gleams that is unmistakably their own. In Berthgyth's letters what is memorable is the magnanimous, outgoing tenderness towards her one remaining relative, the one person with whom she longs to maintain a close bond. In this she foreshadows the *Manual* of Dhuoda. Like Dhuoda with her son William, she tries to strengthen the human bond by a Christian bond of prayer, but time and again she is reminded of her loneliness, and thrown back upon the troubling thought: will the person who is to receive her missive understand? Hugeburc, so conscious of writing not just letters but a full-fledged literary work, anticipates Hrotsvitha in the elusive, part-defensive part-ironic way she confronts an audience of men, wavering before them, and verbally assenting to all their preconceptions of male and priestly superiority, but in the last resort determined not to be crushed by them. It is to the two later women, who have left achievements of greater stature – Dhuoda in the ninth century, Hrotsvitha in the tenth – that we must now turn.

2   Dhuoda

It is not till six centuries after Perpetua that we again encounter a woman who, in her writing, reveals a hidden inner world of preoccupations, hopes and sorrows. Where Perpetua has left us only a brief memoir, that had not been finally shaped when she went to her death, Dhuoda conceived and elaborated a work on a large scale. She gave it the form of a manual of advice, moral–religious and practical, for her sixteen-year-old son. Thus ostensibly it belongs to the genre of 'mirrors for princes'.[1] Yet it is the reflection of Dhuoda herself in this mirror which makes her work moving and unique.

The recent edition, by Pierre Riché, contributes much that will make a new and adequate appreciation of Dhuoda's achievement possible. Hitherto, literary judgements have been perfunctory and foolishly condescending: Wilhelm Meyer's claim, that it is 'no joy to read Dhuoda',[2] is still quoted and has never received serious critical challenge. Her Latin is indeed unorthodox and at times incorrect, whether by classical norms or by the standards of Charlemagne's *litterati*; it is also often intrinsically difficult, because of Dhuoda's complex and subtle awareness. Her modes of expression, when they are ungainly, uncertain or unclear, are so chiefly because she was urgently striving to say something in her own way, something that was truly hers. And she does so successfully, I would argue, in that despite – and even because of – the limitations of her Latin, the language she had learnt but never felt fully at ease in, we can still find in her writing a person whom, once we have perceived and understood her, we could never blur with any other, or ever forget.

To arrive at this perception, however, requires patience. Even the parts that are awkwardly and ineptly phrased must be mined for their precious ore. To borrow another metaphor: while Dhuoda seems to record many thoughts and emotions with naïve directness, what she is depicting is much rather 'les choses derrière les choses'.[3] For readers who prefer a more accomplished and melli-fluous, less unconventional Latin, there are other Carolingian authors of con-siderable stature to choose from: Alcuin, Einhard or Theodulf in the first generation, Walahfrid Strabo (almost exactly Dhuoda's contemporary) in the second. Yet none of the major Carolingians, in my view, can match Dhuoda in showing us a mind and presence of such sensitive individuality. The literary

situation seems to me rather like that of Hopkins compared with the major
Victorian poets: that is, while some critics might wish to stress Hopkins' limitations and the more rebarbative aspects of his language, for others (including
myself) the fact of overriding importance is simply that Hopkins saw and com-
municated so much that was beyond the ken of any 'eminent Victorian'.

About Dhuoda we know some things very precisely: she loves recording
dates, often with ceremonious mannerism, just as she loves numerological play,
filling numbers with further meanings.[4] Yet about many other aspects of
Dhuoda's life we know nothing, and are reduced to conjecture. She was born,
it would seem, about 803, into a family of the higher nobility. It is usually
assumed that she grew up in the northern part of the Frankish realm, where the
name 'Dhuoda' is most frequently attested. It is clear – especially from her
verses – that her mother-tongue was Germanic. Yet I do not think one can
exclude the possibility of Dhuoda's having grown up in southern France or in
Catalonia (where the name 'Doda' is also once found in this period).[5] At all
events, it would be easier to understand why her husband, Bernard of Septi-
mania, sent her to live in Uzès if she too had family ties in that region: if her
charge was to safeguard his political interests there, this is something she could
hardly have done as an exile and complete stranger.

Dhuoda married Bernard – she tells us – on 29 June 824, in the imperial
palace at Aachen. Bernard's father, William (later Saint William) of Gellone,
had been a first cousin of Charlemagne, and Bernard became one of the leading
contenders for sovereign power in the intrigue-ridden world of Louis the Pious
(814–40) and his sons. Louis entrusted Bernard with the care of the Spanish
Marches. Dhuoda at first accompanied her husband on his travels and military
adventures. On 29 November 826, she gave birth to her son William. We do
not know how soon Bernard sent her to reside in Uzès, or what his chief
motive was in dispatching her there: her political usefulness to him in that
region, or her personal safety, or even that he had wearied of her and had
become the lover of Empress Judith, Louis's second wife. A number of nobles
hostile to Bernard claimed this, as several contemporary historians record;
though when Bernard challenged his enemies to uphold the accusation against
him in single combat, none dared to do so.

Almost immediately after Louis's death (June 840), Bernard visited Dhuoda in
Uzès, and made her pregnant once again. Her second son was born on 22 March
841. Three months later, Bernard took part in the carnage at Fontenoy, where
the sons of Louis and of Charlemagne made their bid to gain the Empire for
themselves. Bernard fought on the losing, Aquitanian side. To make peace with
the new monarch, Charles the Bald, he sent William, now fourteen, to Charles
as a pledge of good faith. Before his second son was half a year old, before he

had even been christened, Bernard summoned him and had him brought to Aquitaine. Aware of the perilous situation into which he had placed his older son, Bernard was clearly determined to have total charge and control of the younger.

Dhuoda, separated from her husband and both her children, knowing not even the name of her newborn child, began to write. What she wrote could be regarded in outline as a guide to the Christian secular life, and a *speculum principis*. Yet the reasons for her writing lie far deeper. Dhuoda was writing to console herself in her banishment, and to attempt some kind of living contact with the son whom she loved and who, she surmised, might understand her. In the *exemplum* of Griselda, as Boccaccio, Petrarch and Chaucer were to tell it, the inhuman Marquis tests the heroine by depriving her of her children almost at once after she has given birth.[6] Dhuoda (except for her noble origins) comes close to being a Griselda in real life. And like her legendary counterpart, she almost accepts the brutish behaviour of her husband without question and without bitterness. Indeed what she commends to her far-off son is largely what Riché calls 'une religion de la paternité'[7] – a world-picture in which the bonds of loyalty to the human father, to the emperor, and to a Father God are seen concentrically. Yet it is the concealed anguish that we sense as she expounds this which makes her testimony unparalleled.

Many times we realize how deeply conscious Dhuoda is that the loyalties of the world of fathers are precarious – and events bore out her half-voiced terrors. Her book, begun almost at once after her second child was snatched from her (30 November 841), was completed on 2 February 843; the very next year her husband was executed for treason by Charles the Bald, and William, for whom in her book she set up such high ideals of concurrent fidelity to sovereign and father and God, joined the Aquitanian rebels – he was captured and executed four years later. We do not know whether Dhuoda outlived her husband or her son (in the book she often speaks of being near death); nor can we be sure of the fate of the infant, whom Bernard had christened with his own name: much has been written to try and identify this younger Bernard among the high nobility of the next generation, but no certainty has been reached.

In short, we cannot reduce Dhuoda's testament to any of the norms of style or genre current in her time, and many expectations arising from such norms will be dashed (or, I should prefer to say, surpassed). If we approach the work, for instance, through its Christian elements and its piety – while these are warmly and beautifully present throughout, and it would be wrong to belittle them – it is equally important to perceive precisely how unusual many of Dhuoda's expressions of Christian emotion are. To a conventional Christian of her day, the orientation of much that she says might have seemed disturbing, if not subversive – which may well be why her work did not become widely adopted and diffused in learned circles. For hers is a devoutness that, because of her situation and her son's, keeps the 'cares of the world (*mundane cure*)' constantly in view: Dhuoda tries to work out a way of earthly serenity and ultimate salvation *through* these cares, not by rejecting or minimizing them. Again, while much of her practical advice belongs to the tradition of the 'mirrors', it is not here directed to the duties of a prince as such. It becomes intensely personal – it is adapted at every turn to the problems and predicaments of one person, William (though Dhuoda also shows herself aware that he may pass the book on to others, and that it may be copied more than once). It is far more introspective and meditative than one would expect of any advice didactically given. The conventional elements of *sentence*, Christian and political, on which Dhuoda draws, become transfigured. The whole discussion is pervaded by a quest for personal knowledge; there is an almost Socratic aspiration to 'knowing for oneself' rather than abstractly. Each problem is pondered in the light of the questions: who and what am I, as mother, as wife? Who and what is my son? What does it mean that Bernard is the *dominus* and *senior* of us both?

I should like to examine more closely the nature of some of Dhuoda's perceptions. I shall choose moments of three kinds: some of her reflections on herself, others on her husband and son, others again on divine and human values. Often these kinds become strands intertwined in a single thread of thought, so that it would be wilful to separate them completely.

The opening of the *Manual* is remarkable for the number and intricacy of its preliminaries. Dhuoda begins by suggesting a three-branched articulation of her work, and by explaining the meanings of her chosen title, *Manualis*. This first section, *Incipit textus*, is followed by another, *Incipit liber* – which comprises a prose dedication to William and a long verse epigraph for him, which includes another dedication in its acrostic (*Dhuoda dilecto filio Wilhelmo salutem. Lege*), formed by the opening letters of the couplets. She then calls upon Christ for help to begin her book, and for a third time we have an incipit: *Incipit prologus*. This prose Prologue is in turn followed by a Preface (*Praefatio*), and this by a long analytic table of contents, chapter by chapter[8] (though Dhuoda's first proposed division of the work, into three 'branches', seems now to have been forgotten). After this, with the first chapter, on the love of God, the discursive part of the book at last begins.

It is as though a series of barriers had had to be surmounted before Dhuoda felt the confidence to set out a discussion freely and directly. The prolegomena are, as it were, so many hesitations about embarking upon the rôle of instructress; at the same time they constitute the writer's way of gaining assurance towards that rôle, of getting her bearings in it. We shall see something of similar complication in the way that Hrotsvitha prefaces, plans and schematizes her works in sections and sequences. And in our own day a striking instance of such labyrinthine prefacing, introducing and articulating can be found in Anna Akhmatova's masterpiece, *Poem without a Hero*, where numerous epigraphs, a piece 'in the guise of preface' (with its own postscript), three dedications and an introduction precede Part I, chapter 1 (where the verse once more has a prose prelude and, soon after, includes an acrostic). Akhmatova's strategy is like that of Dhuoda, eleven centuries earlier: 'by indirection, find direction out'. For both authors, perhaps, the subjective sense of the stature of their task was inseparable from hardly daring to claim that stature outright and objectively.

The tragic aspect of Dhuoda's loneliness becomes evident from the first moment she calls upon William by name:

Knowing that most women in the world have the joy of living with their children, and seeing that I, Dhuoda, am withheld from you, my son William, and am far away – as one anxious because of this, and full of longing to be useful, I am sending you this little work of mine, copied for you to read, a work that's formative in a mirror-like way. I'd be happy if, since I am not physically present, the presence of this little book call to your mind, as you read it, what you should do for my sake.[9]

What is extraordinary is both the self-awareness and the circumspection – the refinement of sensibility and discretion with which Dhuoda intimates the pain she feels. The contrast she makes could be compared with that so frequent in medieval love-poetry: others have the joy of being together, only I am far from the one I love. So too, the theme of letters rendering the absent person present belongs to the ancient and medieval *koinê* of friendship. Yet here the emotion is at once diverted to something practical and serene: the anxiety and yearning become a 'longing to be useful (*utilitatis desiderium*)'.

The image of the mirror, only glanced at here, is subtly developed in the *prologus*:[10]

To many people many things are clear, yet to me they are obscure; as for those like me, with dimmed perception – they lack understanding: if I say 'lack' [of them], it is still more true of me. He is ever-present who opens the eyes of the dumb and makes the tongues of the inarticulate eloquent.

I, Dhuoda, though frail in sex,[11] living unworthily among worthy women, am nonetheless your mother, my son William: to you the words of my handbook are directed now. For, just as playing at dice seems for a time most comely and apt to the young, amid other worldly accomplishments, or again, as some women are wont to gaze in mirrors, to remove their blemishes and reveal their glowing skin, concerned to please their husbands here and now – in the same way I want you, when you're weighed down by hosts of worldly and temporal activities, to read this little book I have sent you, often, in memory of me: don't neglect it – use it as if it were a matter of mirrors or of games at dice.

Even if, more and more, you acquire books, many volumes, may it still please you to read frequently this little work of mine – may you have the strength to grasp it profitably, with the help of almighty God. You will find in it, in epitome, whatever you choose to get to know; you will also find there a mirror in which, beyond a doubt, you can examine the condition of your soul, so that you can not only please the world, but please him in every way who fashioned you out of clay. So it is altogether necessary for you, my son William, to show yourself, in both ventures, as one who can be of service to the world and at the same time can always, through every action, give delight to God.

The opening phrases are no 'topos of affected modesty', nor are they filled with irony such as William of Conches was to use in the Prologue to his *Dragmaticon*, asking why the things he has taught for twenty years and more, yet still feels he has not understood fully and perfectly, seem so easy to his colleagues, who claim there's nothing they cannot understand instantly: 'is it because I was born in the thick air of Normandy, the land of sheep?'[12] Dhuoda, by contrast, is passionately serious about the threefold conviction she expresses here: her understanding is imperfect; yet God can remedy her imperfection by grace; and she *must* write, whatever her intellectual and personal defects, because her relation to William is unique – 'tamen genitrix tua, fili Wilhelme'. The sense that, because of this, she can communicate something uniquely appropriate to William, something irreplaceable by any other books, no matter how learned, becomes one of the leitmotifs in her work. The mirror she can hold up to him is the one most genuinely his.

How is she to entice him to the ideals finest for him? After all, he is neither monk nor clerk, but of necessity, by his situation in life, overwhelmed (*oppressus*) by thronging temporal concerns. Dhuoda's solution to this problem is very much her own. First, it is a matter of showing William love, and – she hopes – inspiring it. He'll do what is best, not because he has been preached at by clergy, but for my sake – 'ob memoriam mei'. She will bring this about by creating for him a little oasis of reflective calm, where he can gather renewed inner strength – above all, by making that oasis attractive. Not sermonizing as from above, not denouncing, but guiding by way of analogies filled with delight, ones at home in the world that William already knows.

The ethic that Dhuoda unfolds for William in the course of her *Manual* differs from anything the clerical or monastic world of the time could have told him, in one essential respect: Dhuoda's fundamental premise is the validity of a two-fold undertaking (*utrumque negotium*): it is oriented towards the world as well as towards God. Both world and God demand an ideal of gentle service, and in that twofold service there is joy. There is no question of trying to impose renuncia-tion, of overcoming earthly aspirations in favour of an entirely otherworldly goal: on the contrary, this would be a betrayal of the rôle into which William was born, that of a *princeps* in the Carolingian world. At first, Dhuoda's ideal for William is, we might say, simultaneously courtly and Christian, and she sees courtliness as, at its finest, a valid expression of Christian values. Yet as her book progresses, she moves towards a position that in some ways anticipates the radical close of Dante's *Monarchia*: divine providence has proposed *two* goals (*duos fines*) for mankind: one (figured by the earthly paradise), in the felicity of this life, the other (figured by the celestial paradise), in the felicity of eternal life. The first consists in the apt functioning of one's own *virtus*; the second needs a special divine help.[13]

In the verse epigraph, just before the *prologus*, the emphasis is not yet of this kind. Dhuoda still thinks in terms of a single, transcendent goal, even though she sees that goal as extending to courtly virtues and directing these virtues heaven-wards: she invokes God[14] –

> You centre that enclose[15] the whirling firmament,
> folding ocean and fields within your hand,
>
> To you I commend William, my son – at your command
> may well-being be lavished on him in all ways.
>
> In all his course, all his moments and hours,
> may he love you, his maker, most of all.[16]
>
> May he deserve to climb the highest peak,
> swift-footed, happy, with those who are yours.
>
> May his perceptions always be alert,[17]
> open, to you; may he live blissfully for ever;[18]
>
> When he's hurt, let him never burst into anger
> or wander away, severed from your friends;
>
> May he jubilate joyously, through a glad course of life,
> radiant in virtue, may he reach the heights . . .
>
> May your generous grace penetrate him,
> with peace and security of body and mind,
>
> In which he may flourish in the world, and have children,
> holding what's here so as not to lose what's there . . .
>
> Let him be generous and prudent, loyal and brave,
> let him never abandon moderation.
>
> He will never have one like me to tell him this,
> I who, though unworthy,[19] am also his mother,
>
> I who always, at all moments and all hours,
> am asking you with all my strength: have mercy on him.

Here, we might say, Dhuoda projects an otherworldly fulfilment for William by way of his rôle as a perfect nobleman, father of a family, filled with the virtues and graces of his aristocratic way of life. These must be open to the life beyond (just as Dante at the close of the *Monarchia* was to add that the mortal felicity is 'in a certain sense ordered towards' the immortal). Dhuoda in this poem alludes to the four cardinal virtues (p. 76, 58ff); yet she allies these with other notions – the discretion that enables one to control wrath, the joy that is a steady, lifelong state, and itself a virtue, the generosity inseparable from the nobleman's good life: all these coincide with the expressed ideals of Provençal society (*mezura, jois, largeza . . .*) three centuries later.[20]

The verses, here and elsewhere in the *Manual*, are likewise notable for their experiments with form: Dhuoda is one of a group of ninth- and tenth-century poets who (to adapt the expression of Wilhelm Meyer, the great pioneer in this question) introduce 'ancient Germanic rhythms into Latin verse'.[21] Various Latin rhythmic patterns became influenced and modified by Germanic poetic practice; in particular, the Latin rhythmic adonic line ($\acute{\smile} \sim \sim \acute{\smile} \sim$)[22] fused with the Germanic alliterative half-line, which bears two principal stresses and has a variable number of weaker syllables. Dhuoda's verses, with their strongly marked caesura, consisting of half-lines of five to seven syllables (occasionally four or eight), do not reflect precisely all the types and possibilities of the native half-line: the influence of Latin rhythmic adonics is too strong for that. Again, her acrostics are a Christian Latin, rather than vernacular, convention. Yet the sense that the movement of the verse is, as in the vernacular, governed by the two dominant stresses in each half-line is unmistakable.

To trace further some of Dhuoda's thoughts about the 'two goals' she envisages for William's life: at the close of her discussion of the nature of God, she writes:

I urge you, William, my handsome, lovable son, amid the worldly preoccupations of your life, not to be slow in acquiring many books where, through most holy teachers, you should discover and learn something about God the creator – more things and greater than are written here. Implore him, cherish and love him. If you do that, he'll be your guardian, captain, comrade and home, way, truth and life, granting you well-being most generously in the world, and he'll turn all your enemies towards peace. But you must, as is written in Job, gird your loins like a man, be humble of heart and chaste of body; raised to the heights, be greatly glorious and dress splendidly.[23]

The God who is to shelter William's life is, first of all, one who guides him in his earthly concerns. He will not make worldly existence a vale of tears for William, so as to turn the young man's eyes heavenward: no, he will show the same largesse in worldly matters – granting well-being to his liegeman – as the ideal nobleman shows to his vassal on earth. It is even possible that the words *dux* and *comes*, here applied to God, have some of the connotations of 'duke' and 'count' as well as the wider ones of 'captain' and 'comrade'. Then, as

Dhuoda cites the Book of Job (40: 2ff), she transforms the context of her citation daringly: the things that God challenges Job to do 'if you have an arm as mighty as God's and can thunder with a voice like his' – that is, things God puts forward grimly taunting Job, knowing that for one who is not divine they are impossible – here become the ideals William *can* fulfil: he can raise himself up brave, sublime, greatly glorious (Dhuoda adds the intensifying *valde* to *gloriosus* of her own accord), and the splendid clothing is for him no foolish attempt to rival God, as it would have been for Job, but a valid expression of his exalted manhood.

Dhuoda's lines continue, stressing the incomparable way she can perceive what is truly William's finest destiny, in a way that no *doctor*, however learned, could do, because of the world of values, the *speculum*, that she shares with him:[24]

What more shall I say? Your Dhuoda is always there to encourage you, my son, and when I am gone, which will come to pass, you'll have the little book of moral teaching here as a memorial: you will be able to look at me[25] still, as into a mirror, reading me with your mind and your body and praying to God; you will find there too, in full, what tasks you owe me. My son, you will have teachers who will give you more lessons, and more valuable ones – yet not in the same way, with the heart burning within, as I with mine, my first-born one . . .

May the Almighty, whom I, though unworthy, mention so often, make both you and your father Bernard – your lord and mine – happy, and thus jocund in the present world, achieving success in everything, and after this life's course is done, may he let you enter jubilant with the saints.

For her husband and son Dhuoda prays for the two goals simultaneously: the joy of the world – if they are happy (*felices*) in it, they can be jocund (*iocundi*), that is, absorb that joy into their character as a steady outlook and disposition – and the joy of the saints (*laetantes*) in heaven.

Later, similarly, Dhuoda speaks of the biblical Joseph as a model for William, and the way she conceives of Joseph is again significant: he is a perfect embodiment of the 'two goals': 'Beautiful in his looks, more beautiful in his mind . . . very handsome and an enjoyer of the world, he was always acceptable to God and man in everything.'[26]

What is the right way to be acceptable to one's fellow-men? Dhuoda's thoughts on this are too many-sided to be capable of systematization, or even to be seen as fully consistent. On the one hand, she develops the unusual notion that a great court can as such be a school of Christian and chivalric virtue. When he is in the presence of the great, William should

. . . observe their noble example deferentially, and keep to it most steadfastly. For in a great house, such as [the palace of Charles] is, was, and – if the Holy One grant – shall continue to be, many conversations are held. There one person can, if he so wish, learn from another humility, charity, chastity, patience, gentleness, modesty, sobriety, astuteness, and the other virtues, together with the eagerness to do good.

Among these virtues only *astutia* perhaps stands out as a specifically courtly, rather than Christian, attribute.

Dhuoda's next thoughts are headed: 'That you should show deference (*flectas* – literally "bend") to great and small'. While she assumes that the distinctions between classes – *maiores* and *minores* – are part of God's disposition of the world, she also suggests to William that lower people can be a model (*forma*) of life for the higher. For God himself took 'a servant's form (*formam servilem* – cf. Philippians 2: 7)'; he can cast down the mighty and raise the lowly (cf. Luke 1: 52), 'so that they can aspire to a greater height'. She cites the Acts of the Apostles (10: 34), 'God is no respecter of persons', and the words of Paul, urging the strong to remedy the neediness of the weak (II Corinthians 8: 14). William, she says, should regard not only the great as being above him, but his equals too. Yet here nothing is said as to how he should view men of lesser rank than his own. Soon afterwards, however, Dhuoda goes further: William is to show

... service and honour, as much as you are or ever shall be able, to persons who are great and to the least, to equals and to the lowly (*magnis et minimis aequalibusque atque exiguis personis*), not only in words but in deeds, and this with gentleness of address[27] ...

Love all and you'll be loved by all, cherish that you may be cherished. If you love all, all will love you. If you love them in the singular, they will love you in the plural. It is written in the Art [of Grammar] of the poet Donatus: 'I love you and am loved by you, I kiss you and am kissed by you (*osculor te et osculor a te*), I cherish you and am cherished by you, I know you and am known by you.'

Lightheartedly Dhuoda brings together a Christian ideal of *caritas* and a courtly skill in dealing with people, an effective *astutia*. The high goal of loving one's neighbour, serving and honouring him whatever his birth, will also be of practical advantage to the young prince: he should learn to handle human relations as effortlessly as the grammarian handles active and passive in his *Ars*. Now and then (as with *osculor*) the active and passive forms indeed coincide – just as they can in reality in a fully reciprocal love. Perhaps Dhuoda's reference to Donatus as a poet indicates (as Riché suggested) that she had in mind a versification of the *Ars*, one that contained all four of her examples, not only that of *osculor*, which is found in Donatus' own text.[28] Perhaps, again, she herself is elaborating and adding examples, to make a playfully improvised 'poetry' of her own. Underlying the ludic grammar is that 'grammatical Platonism' alluded to above (p. 5): the belief that the relationships expressed in grammar mirror those that subsist in truth, that the reciprocities in language depend upon, and are valid because of, their counterparts in reality.

In a passage that has not hitherto been understood, we see that Dhuoda can even jocularly adapt a line from Ovid's *Amores* to express her conception of the

WOMEN WRITERS OF THE MIDDLE AGES

two human goals. She indicates that she is well aware that, in its original context, the phrase she has chosen had an erotic meaning. She alludes to this only to discard it blithely: the expression can be made to serve her purpose in a different way:

According to the sayings of the sages, two births[29] can be perceived in the one human being: one physical, the other spiritual. But the spiritual is nobler than the physical. In the human race, the one cannot subsist profitably without the other. And, in order that the physical and the spiritual should accord more fittingly, someone says: [they are those] 'with which and without which we cannot live'.[30] And though the meaning in this passage is oriented differently, and there are certain reasons for this divergence, I want you to accept it in the way I have just told.

Where Ovid limned the inner conflict:

> Love and hate, here in my heart, at tug of war –
> and love I suppose will find a way to win.
>
> I'd sooner hate. If I can't I'll be the reluctant lover –
> the dumb ox bearing the yoke he loathes.
>
> Your behaviour drives me away, your beauty draws me back.
> I adore your face and abhor your failings.
>
> *With or without you life's impossible . . .*[31]

and St Paul dwelt on the tussle between flesh and spirit (see especially, for instance, Galatians 5: 16ff) – Dhuoda, aware of both ranges of association, projects a harmony in man's double aspect. To do so, she adapts Ovid's words to Paul's problem, and pulls them in the direction of optimism: flesh and spirit are necessary to each other, as much as their full reconciliation is impossible. The passage casts new light on Dhuoda's intellectual adroitness and on her (generally underestimated) reading: the particular use she makes of Ovid here shows that she knew the context in the *Amores*; she had not merely come across this paradox in some proverbial form.

Towards the close of the *Manual*, Dhuoda attempts a final epitome of the Christian–aristocratic goal she holds out to William, in a set of pseudo-Sapphic strophes composed for him, once again marked by an acrostic that includes his name. While both quantitative and rhythmic Sapphics had enjoyed great popularity among the men of letters around Charlemagne, Dhuoda's is almost certainly the first attempt to fuse the form with the Germanic stress-pattern. For the concluding line of each strophe she keeps to a rhythmic adonic verse (in only two of her eighteen strophes is it hypermetrical):[32]

> Go often to the help of widows and orphans,
> give food and drink to strangers lavishly,
> give hospitality, offer the naked clothing
> with your own hands.

In disputes, be a just, efficient judge,
never accept a bribe from any hand,
never oppress anyone – the bountiful Giver
    will reward you for that.

Generous in giving, ever-watchful and prudent,
at one with everyone, striving to be lovable,
full of joy within – this indeed will be
    your constant face.

Here we have a memorable early formulation of the rôle of the *miles chris-tianus*, whose specific chivalric duty is the assistance and protection of the helpless and weak. From this, and the corollary of being an incorruptible judge and no oppressor, Dhuoda passes to the essentially courtly perfections: the verbal link between the divine *Largitor* and the human quality of the generous giver ('largus in donis') brings out that the nobleman is, in an earthly mode, imitating God. Yet it is the combination of an outer amiability towards all human beings with an inner state of joy from which this gracious behaviour springs that takes us most decisively into that world of courtly values which scholars hitherto have tended to associate with a far later period, in particular with the twelfth century.

Near the end of the verses, we hear the inner cries that often recur in the book: Dhuoda in her loneliness longs to see her son again, but does not dare to hope for a meeting – she has done too little for God to grant her such a joy:

It all seems much too far away from me,
I who long to see again how you look –
if only the strength were given! and yet
    I do not reach that mark.

The moments when Dhuoda speaks of her own state of mind and feelings, or gives voice to her thoughts about her husband and son, are the most precious in the book. A few examples will suffice to show the range and depth of her sensibility.

The transition from Prologue to Preface brings an unexpected change from a touching intimate note to a high-sounding, seemingly impersonal exercise in chronology. The Prologue concludes:

. . . amid my cares, my ardent and watchful spirit frets to let you have, with God's help, what I have written longingly into this manuscript about your birth. In what follows, it may be best to commence with that.[33]

Then the Preface begins grandiosely:

In the eleventh year, by Christ's favour, of the radiant reign of Louis, our late lord, the year of five concurrents,[34] on the third of the Kalends of July, in the palace[35] of Aachen, I acceded to lawful matrimony with Bernard, my lord and your father.

William's birth is recorded with similar pomp, and the death of Louis is given five lines ('With the wretchedness of this age whirling and increasing in calamity . . .') that in their attempted grandiloquence bring us uncomfortably close to the exordium parodied by Hamlet's Player King:

> Full thirty times hath Phoebus' cart gone round
> Neptune's salt wash and Tellus' orbèd ground,
> And thirty dozen moons with borrow'd sheen
> About the world have times twelve thirties been,
> Since love our hearts and Hymen did our hands
> Unite commutual in most sacred bands.

The complex reasons for Dhuoda's mode of opening, however, gradually become apparent as she continues:[36]

After his death, the following year, came the birth of your brother, on the eleventh of the Kalends of April: from my womb a second child came forth, through God's mercy, in the city of Uzès. And indeed Bernard, the lord and father of you both, commanded that this little one, before he had received the grace of baptism, be brought into his presence in the region of Aquitaine – the infant was summoned, along with Bishop Elefantus of Uzès and other men loyal to your father.

But when I had resided a long time in that city, lacking your presence, at my lord's command, happy at his exploits and missing you both, I, well aware of my lowliness, arranged for the copying of this little manuscript and for its dispatch to you.

Moreover, though I am besieged by many anxieties, the only one in the foreground, if God wills and judges it right, is that I may be able at some time to see you face to face.[37] I would have wanted this, indeed, if the power to fulfil it had been given me by God; but, since fulfilment is far from me, sinful as I am, I want it still, and in this willing my spirit utterly fails.[38]

For I have heard that your father, Bernard, has entrusted you to the hands of King Charles. I urge you to carry out the dignity of this charge with complete good will.

Thus with Dhuoda we move from intimate thoughts and concerns to lofty, detached ones, back to intimate ones – or rather, we see how, despite a brave attempt to banish these with dignity, they harass her once again. At first her object is to remind William solemnly: you and I belong with the greatest in the Empire. This she wants to record so as to give him the full sense of his worth, and to retain her own self-respect. Then, as she turns to what has just happened to her second child, she half conceals, half reveals, her own Griselda-like hopelessness. The paragraphs that follow have none of Alcuin's or Einhard's polished lucidity: the phrases, tossing to and fro, convey the turmoil of Dhuoda's emotions directly and unforgettably.

Despite Bernard's harsh command, she still feels with him in his political struggles, or political adventuring, and misses him, as she misses William. All this is interspersed with reminding William of her exile, and indicating, simply

48

and without reproach, that her writing is the one refuge left to her: 'Sed cum diu, ob absenciam presencie vestre, sub iussione senioris mei, in predicta (cum agone illius iam gaudens) residerem urbe, ex desiderio utrique vestrum hunc codicellum . . . dirigere curavi.'[39]

Though she misses both her husband and her son, it is the concern to see William again that causes her most anguish. Is it God's displeasure at her own human weakness that is preventing it? – Such is the rending, helpless thought that crosses her mind. Even if it is against God's will, she says, she cannot help longing for it nonetheless: not bravely, not as one knowing God's plan, but in all her human weakness. With the words 'my spirit fails' she recalls Job in his despondency, Job lamenting his own former height. Her expressions might seem excessive, were it not for the simple, seemingly neutral words that follow, urging William towards perfect good will in his service of Charles the Bald. In the causal link – 'enim' – that bridges 'my spirit fails' and 'I have heard that your father, Bernard, has entrusted you to the hands of King Charles', lurks a secret apprehension. Dhuoda knew that William was, to all intents and purposes, the king's hostage: she knew (as all the imperial allusions to her marriage underline) that Bernard would never submit completely to his great rival in power: could she persuade at least her son to magnanimous loyalty towards Charles, or would he too intrigue and thus risk or forfeit his life? It is what she surmises and foresees that makes every reference of Dhuoda's to the prospect of seeing her son once more an expression fraught with pain.

Many of Dhuoda's allusions to herself in the *Manual* dwell on her *fragilitas* and sinful inadequacy, and one might think it simple to take these as essentially formulaic expressions of Christian humility and piety. Yet this would be to ignore the more individual aspects of such moments, and even more to ignore certain fundamental tensions in what Dhuoda says: to give one striking example, that she feels both an ardent craving to pray to God and misery that she can take no joy in praying.

Certainly I also, though an unworthy woman and frail as a shadow, seek him as best I can, and incessantly implore his help, as far as I know how. For indeed that's absolutely necessary to me. Sometimes it happens that a persistent puppy, under her master's table, can snatch the crumbs and eat them even among the taller male whelps. For he who made the mouth of the dumb creature speak has the might to open my understanding, in keeping with his clemency of old; and he who prepared a banquet for his faithful in the desert . . . can also fulfil his wish in me, his handmaiden, because of my longing for you . . .[40]

Here the expressions of humility lead into a surge of confidence, even if there is also a touch of irony about it. The little *catula*, though weaker in sex, may by sheer tenacity steal a march on the young hounds. There follows a light self-mockery, comparable to that of Gregory of Tours in his Preface to the *Life of*

St Martin. Dhuoda may indeed have had Gregory's passage in mind.[41] Like him, she draws to herself the double comparison of God's intervention with Balaam, and with the exiled Israelites: if he could make an ass speak, he can make me speak too; if he could feed his chosen ones in the desert, he can also choose me, in my desertedness.

And yet Dhuoda, who claims that praying is absolutely necessary to her, likewise admits that she finds praying a difficult, unhappy chore:

But I, Dhuoda, lukewarm and sluggish and frail and always drooping to the depths, take no delight in long prayers – no, not even in short ones. Nonetheless I hope in him who gave his faithful leave to ask. As for you, William my son, be watchful, ask things of him, and pray in brief, concentrated, pure words.[42]

It is when she writes of prayer that Dhuoda tends to reveal her most secret thoughts, as it were slipping them in hesitantly between more conventional utterances:

. . . pray for your father often and assiduously, and make all the ranks of churchmen pray for him, so that, as long as he lives, God may give him peace and concord with all men, if that is possible: may God let his spirit triumph bravely in all things with the strength of one who is patient . . .

One should pray for everybody, especially for those who have received Christ's faith; and not only for strangers, but also for those at home, that is, for those who are near and nearest among our kindred – we should pray for them oftenest. I am saying this so as to come to what I long to tell you. Though I shall die soon, I urge you to pray for all the dead, but most of all for those to whom you owe your birth in the world . . .

For I think that, if you strive towards the blessed one in a fitting and lowly way, he will give you an increase in his frail dignities. If, through the clemency of almighty God, your father commands some of these to be bestowed on you, then as far as you can, thereafter, pray that the reward for this may increase in the souls of those who once possessed it all. Because of his many preoccupations, your father has at present no time for that; but you, since you can do it and have the leisure to, must pray constantly for their souls.[43]

Dhuoda shows her awareness of her husband's psychological difficulties – if anyone can help him towards harmonious relations with his fellow-men, it must be God. For Bernard the greatest victory and feat of courage (*fortiter . . . superare*) would be to learn the strength of the patient (*pacientis vigorem*). As Dhuoda's thoughts turn to praying for others, there is a moving modesty and indirectness about her approach. The train of thought is: pray for all – even pagans and strangers – but more for those near you, and still more for those nearest of all. To come to what I really want to say, pray for your parents. Alluding to the wealth and estates William may later inherit, she stresses that these are God-given, and hence a spur to praying for one's ancestors, through whom God has bestowed them. And in a rueful, almost humorous aside she adds, in effect:

Father is too busy to pray for his parents' souls, he has too much else on his mind
– so you must do it for him.

Much earlier in the *Manual* Dhuoda had appealed to the eloquent passage in
Ecclesiasticus about children's duties towards their parents – though there, in
her spirit of abnegation, she had recalled only the lines relating to a father,
by-passing all the words about what is a mother's due. Again her development
of the scriptural thoughts is intense and wholly individual:

Support your father's old age, if with God's help you arrive at that time; *do not sadden him
during his lifetime or spurn him in your strength*. Far be that from you! Sooner let the earth
cover my body over than that this should happen to him – not that I believe it ever will . . .

Though in the eyes of men the royal and imperial nature or power surpasses all else in the
world . . . nonetheless my own will, my son, is this: that . . . first and foremost, as long
as you live, you never neglect giving a unique, loyal and steadfast homage to him whose
child you are.[44]

Into the biblical admonition Dhuoda inserts the words 'si ad hoc deo per-
veneris auxiliante': would William live long enough to support his father's old
age? His position as hostage at the court of Charles will have been cause enough
for Dhuoda's moment of hesitation – 'if you don't die young'. The biblical
words are followed by one of the most fervent exclamations in the whole work,
which in turn becomes an affirmation, almost hoping against hope, that there
will never be discord between William and his father (the unspoken thought
being, however difficult and tyrannical that father may be). Soon afterwards,
Dhuoda ventures an opinion in her own right, though aware that in doing so
she is setting herself against an established opinion: in the event of a conflict of
loyalties between one's own father and one's sovereign, the dominant loyalty
should still be to the first. We can only speculate whether Dhuoda lived to see
William join the Aquitanian forces against Charles, after his father's execution;
yet if she did, this passage suggests she would at least in some measure have
understood and approved William's rash attempt to vindicate his father, however much a purely personal ambition may have been interfused with his sense
of family honour.

Dhuoda has difficulties and hesitations about ending her book similar to those
she had about beginning. Straight after the pseudo-Sapphic strophes already
cited (which conclude with a strophe, 'Finiunt versiculi . . .'), she says: 'Finita
sunt huius verba libelli.'[45] Then, three pages later, she comes to what might
appear to be a more decisive leave-taking: 'Finit hic liber Manualis. Amen. Deo
gratias.' Yet then Dhuoda remembers that she has left out a number of names
of the dead among those whom William should pray for; she goes on to ask him
to see to it, at her death, that the verse epitaph, which she now composes for

herself, be inscribed upon her tomb. For a moment she looks beyond William alone to 'whoever may read this *Manual*', and to every possible reader (*lector*) of her epitaph. And still Dhuoda proceeds to add a whole further section (xi) by way of postscript, before her ultimate 'Finit hic.' It is as if she were reluctant to let go of the manuscript which is her one-and-only lifeline to her son.

In the pages just before the epitaph, Dhuoda wonders, will she still see the day when William has set his own house in order and has accomplished steady good in public life:[46]

And shall I be able to live till then, that I may behold it? I'm filled with uncertainties – uncertain of my merits, uncertain of my strength, I am buffeted on the waves in my frail effort. Though this is how it is with me,[47] nonetheless all things remain possible for the almighty one.

This leads to the most intimate meditative moments in the whole work. The passage is headed by a verse –

> Ad me recurrens, lugeo
>
> Reverting to myself, I mourn

– where sadness, isolation and inner awareness join. If the verse had survived as a fragment without context, it might well have been thought to belong with the world of *winileodas*, the early medieval women's songs of unhappy love:[48]

> Cum mihi sola sedeo
> et, hec revolvens, palleo,
> si forte capud sublevo
> nec audio nec video.

> As I sit all alone,
> racked with thought and wan,
> if I should lift my head, then I
> do not hear, I do not see.

Here, however, the overmastering love is that of a mother, and of a wife so loyal that she has exposed herself to every danger, has risked everything, both personally and financially, for her husband's sake. And the turning inward is not only something forced on her by solitude, but something in which she finds comfort, as well as renewed pangs of conscience:[49]

neglecting myself, as if forgetting myself, in the sweetness of my excessive love for you and in the longing for your beautiful presence, I long to enter inwardly again, with the doors closed. But, though I am not worthy to be reckoned in the prescribed number, I still ask that, among countless others, you do not cease to pray, with an affection that counts, for the healing of my soul.

It is not hidden from you how much – because of my continual infirmities and certain circumstances (to adapt another's words, 'perils from my kindred, perils from heathen folk . . .') – I have had to bear in my frail body, clogged by my own inadequacies – all these perils, and others like them. Indeed with God's help and thanks to your father, Bernard, I have steadily escaped out of all such dangers – but now my mind reflects on the moments of deliverance. In times past[50] I often remained negligent in praising God, and what I should have done in the seven hours,[51] I always did with a seven times sevenfold[52] sluggishness.

Dhuoda makes the biblical allusions fecund with personal meaning. The words 'with the doors closed' recall the moment when Christ, appearing to the disciples, at last resolves Thomas's doubts (John 20: 26). As Thomas could not believe in Christ's presence in the room, so Dhuoda feels unsure of his presence in her soul: both the human weakness of the doubting, and the sense that the doubt *can* be resolved, weigh in her self-analysis. Touchingly she says: I am not as important to pray for as your father and your paternal ancestors, yet if only you would pray for me, all the same. In the dangers she has passed for Bernard's sake, she compares herself to St Paul in the dangers he endured for Christ;[53] at the same time she dwells on her physical frailty and her spiritual remissness. This leads to a last appeal to William:[54]

And, to enable me one day to attain the final reintegration,[55] I am leaving behind no one like you, none who can champion my cause as you can, and many through you,[56] my noble child.

Here the words 'no one like you (*nullum similem tui*)' echo those in the opening verse epigraph: 'he will never have anyone like me (*Mis michi similem non habebit unquam*).'[57] The two phrases, near the beginning and the end of the *Manual*, complement each other and together circumscribe the unique bond between mother and son as Dhuoda longs to see it. He will be her chevalier, her *nobilis puer*, in the spiritual realm, even after her death.

Yet once more the sense of an earthly goal as well as a heavenly one returns, as Dhuoda goes on to more overtly autobiographic reflections:

To help my lord and master, Bernard – so that my service in his cause, in the Marches and in many places, should not be flawed, and that he should not sever himself from you or from me, as some men are wont to do – I realize I have burdened myself with great debts. To meet his needs, I have often had to borrow large sums, not only from Christians but also from Jews. I have repaid them as far as I could, and always shall in future, as far as I can. So if after my death something remains to be paid, I ask and beseech that you make every effort to find out who my debtors are. When they have been found, see to it that in every case everything is paid back, not only from my estate – if anything is left – but from whatever you have and whatever, with God's help, you still justly acquire.

William, then, must also perform a deed of chivalric honour for Dhuoda in the earthly sphere: the just settling of all her debts. There is an extraordinary beauty in the way she motivates how she plunged herself into debt – in order to keep Bernard's love, or at least not to be abandoned by him, as many husbands leave their wives and families. (The thought that must have occurred to William, as it will to any perceptive reader – 'as Bernard has in effect deserted us' – is left unexpressed). Dhuoda concludes with a notion of human integrity – in the repaying of loans – that embraces Christians and Jews alike. After these lines, with the thought 'Do what you can for your little brother', she looks serenely towards her own death and towards heaven. Her earthly and her spiritual anxieties seem almost overcome, in that she has woven an immense web of prayer which will cover and join all those she loves; it will create and strengthen bonds between the living and the dead, kindred and strangers, and hence also between the lonely woman, 'frail as a shadow', and the joyful family of the saints.

In these last autobiographic passages, most of all, Dhuoda's thoughts can still move us to compassionate fondness. Yet this is perhaps less because of what befell her, in the way of outer events, than because of her sensitivity in confronting those events, and the profoundly original, generous ways of thinking and feeling that can be glimpsed in her reflections.

Hrotsvitha wrote more prolifically than Dhuoda, and planned her major work on a larger scale. Like Dhuoda, she clung to prefaces and preliminaries, dedications and elaborate articulations; but, having far greater literary ambitions than her predecessor, she carried out such manoeuvres with the utmost self-consciousness and craft.

There exists much scholarly writing on Hrotsvitha,[1] yet in it her life and work tend to be misrepresented. Discussion of Hrotsvitha has seldom wholly escaped the assumptions that her existence was 'cloistered' and that her talent was naïve. The stereotype still most widely encountered is that of a woman (usually thought of as a nun) immured in her convent, who unaccountably took it into her head to read the plays of Terence and to 'imitate' them by writing edifying Christian counterparts. It is considered scholarly to add that Hrotsvitha could not have intended her own plays for performance – at most, for reading aloud at mealtimes in the convent refectory.[2]

Specialists, admittedly, have meanwhile recognized how different Gandersheim was from a convent in the usual sense. Founded in 852 by Duke Liudolf, the great-grandfather of Emperor Otto I, Gandersheim was from its beginnings a high aristocratic, then royal and imperial, foundation. Its abbesses were members of the reigning family. When Otto I, in 947, invested the abbess of Gandersheim with supreme authority, she became the ruler of a small autonomous princedom. The situation is well sketched in Ferruccio Bertini's recent study:

Thus the convent had its own courts, an army of its own, was empowered to mint its own coinage, had its own representative at the imperial Assembly, and enjoyed the direct protection of the Papal See without any interference from bishops.[3]

At least in Hrotsvitha's lifetime, that is, Gandersheim was a small, proudly independent principality ruled by women. Such independence will also have suited the Ottonian dynasty politically, since it gave the unmarried women of royal blood a certain power and intellectual scope, and lessened the danger of their marrying princes outside the family, who might loom as rivals for the throne. All who belonged to Gandersheim (except for the servants) were of noble birth, some taking vows as nuns, others remaining canonesses. It is almost certain that Hrotsvitha, born *ca.* 935, was one of the canonesses. It seems likely, too, that she was related to the earlier abbess of Gandersheim, Hrotsvitha I (919–26), and hence was at least a distant relative of the royal house.[4]

The nuns and canonesses at Gandersheim shared certain intellectual aspirations, which were essentially those that had been realized by Radegunde, Agnes and their circle at Poitiers. The intellectual ideal, which implied cultivation of the mind, the study of major authors both pagan and Christian, and literary exchanges with learned men, was combined with a social ideal, a gracefulness of behaviour towards others, in which an aristocratic habit of *gentilezza* blended with Christian love of one's neighbour. These intellectual and social impulses culminated in the spiritual – the attempt to lead a life serenely dedicated to Christ. While the nuns at Gandersheim, however, accepted strict monastic vows, the canonesses kept a number of significant personal freedoms: they could retain their private fortune, have their own servants and buy their own books, they could entertain guests, and come and go without special difficulty. If they chose to leave Gandersheim permanently, in order to marry, no stigma was attached.

Hrotsvitha's abbess, and (we can safely say, despite her many formulaic self-deprecations) close friend, Gerberga II, was the emperor's niece. Born *ca.* 940, and schooled at St Emmeram in Regensburg, she was still young when she came to rule Gandersheim in 959. As abbess she maintained close relations with the imperial court, and especially with the emperor's younger brother, Bruno, the court's chancellor and chaplain, whom Bezzola has called 'the soul of the Ottonian intellectual Renaissance'.[5]

We do not know how old Hrotsvitha was when she entered Gandersheim. It is possible that she spent some of her youth at the Ottonian court rather than in a convent. One detail here seems to me particularly suggestive. In 952, Otto I had invited Rather, the most widely-read scholar and most brilliant prose-writer of the age, to his court: Rather, exiled from his see at Verona because of quarrels and intrigues, arrived virtually as a refugee. Ostensibly he came to give Bruno some advanced literary teaching; but the fact that Rather cultivated a distinctive style of rhymed prose, which has notable parallels in Hrotsvitha,[6] makes it tempting to suppose that, in Rather's years with Otto, Hrotsvitha too received instruction from him, and then tried to model some of her mannerisms on his. Especially her longest and most complicated sentences, often filled with coinages and new formations as well as rhymes, have to me a markedly Ratherian ring.

There are other good reasons for supposing that Hrotsvitha was at the court at an early age. In the passage of transition that links her series of poetic legends to her series of plays, she distinguishes between the various written sources that she used and the one piece for which she was able to rely on an eye-witness account:

the order of events leading to Pelagius' martyrdom was told me by a certain man, a native
of the city [Cordova] where Pelagius suffered, who assured me that he had seen that fairest
of men and had true knowledge of the outcome of the matter.[7]

This native of Cordova can only have been a member of one of Abd ar-
Rāhman III's two embassies to Otto the Great (950 and 955/6). While it cannot
be ruled out that one of the ambassadorial party spent some time at Gandersheim,
it is far more probable that Hrotsvitha met her witness at the court itself.[8] She
must indeed have spoken with him sufficiently long and often to receive not
only the account of Pelagius but some detailed related information about the
life of Christians in Cordova under Moslem rule.[9]

At all events from the 960s onwards, especially through Gerberga, Hrotsvitha's
links with the Ottonian court were far-reaching. And here I believe one should
formulate and advance a hypothesis which, strangely, scholars have not hitherto
entertained. Ruotger's biography of the emperor's brother, Bruno, mentions
not only Bruno's relations with Gandersheim, the foundation ruled by his niece,
but also, among Bruno's wide reading, singles out his enthusiasm for 'the
unseemly jests and mimetic matter (*scurrilia et mimica*) that, in comedies and
tragedies, are presented by various personages: while some people react to these
noisily, shaking with endless laughter, he always used to read them frequently
and seriously; he set least store by the content, and most by what was exemplary
in the style'.[10] The reference (as a passage in Thietmar of Merseburg's *Chronicon*,
II 16, confirms) is clearly to Roman comedies and tragedies, and the *scurrilia*
alluded to must be first and foremost those of Terence. That these were performed 'a personis variis' is presumably not a mere antiquarian aside. The
biographer's contrast between using this material for an occasion of riotous
merriment and using it for earnest stylistic study (as he claims of Bruno, and
Hrotsvitha affirms of herself), suggests that both possibilities were familiar in his
world, and that Bruno's interest – amazing if not scandalous in a holy man – was
too well known for even the author of a *Vita* to ignore. The hypothesis I would
propose, then, is that when Hrotsvitha prefaces her plays with an 'Epistola ad
quosdam sapientes huius libri fautores', Bruno must have been a leading figure
among those 'wise ... favourers'. Hrotsvitha is overjoyed, that is, to have
found favour, not in some monastery or other (as has generally been alleged),
but at the court itself.

If this is correct, then it does not seem too bold to suggest that at the Ottonian
court, with the encouragement of Bruno and others – including quite possibly
Rather of Verona, and another spirited writer, Liutprand, likewise a keen
Terentian, who often visited the court and served Otto as ambassador and
chronicler – the plays of Terence were read aloud with distribution of parts; and

that then, after Hrotsvitha had sent Bruno and his circle five of her own plays (the two on *Gallicanus*; *Agape, Chionia and Hirena*; *Drusiana and Calimachus*; and *Mary the Niece of Abraham*), they showed their appreciation by having these too read publicly in a similar fashion. Hrotsvitha's *Epistola* would represent her delighted reaction at this: it made her feel unafraid to complete her dramatic series, with her two longer, more 'philosophical' plays, *The Conversion of Thais* and *The Passion of the Holy Maidens*.[11]

The question, what precise form a tenth-century reading might have taken, is difficult for want of documentation, and has in the past caused the most heated division of scholars into romantics and sceptics. There is indeed no direct evidence that such a reading, even with the apportioning of rôles to different readers, would have been at all like a fully-fledged performance, with the element of impersonation dominating. The chief relevant indirect evidence is the fragmentary poetic altercation between Terence and his critic,[12] copied probably at Reims in Hrotsvitha's lifetime, but itself somewhat older (perhaps early ninth century). There the indications of movement ('Now Terence comes out, hearing this, and says . . .'),[13] of impersonation ('persona delusoris'), and even of asides ('persona secum'), make clear that the *Altercation* was to be performed, and almost certainly performed as prelude to a play by Terence. For how could the *persona* Terence have answered the mocking challenge of the *persona delusoris*, that his compositions were worthless and outworn, save by having a piece of his own presented for the audience to judge? Yet even here (as with the twelfth-century reference to an 'acted reading (scenica lectio)' of Terence)[14] this does not, I think, warrant an inference to a fully *staged* performance.

On the other hand, the difference between a lifelessly academic reading of a work and one clarified and pointed by looks, gestures and movements, depends chiefly on the inclinations and skills of those taking part. These must have varied in the Middle Ages, whenever a group of people tried out a new piece, whether spoken or sung, with the text in front of them – just as at the concert performance of an opera, or the first public reading of a play today, there will always be some who cling stiffly to their script or score, and others who are able from the outset to enter into the spirit of the work. And there is no reason to suppose that the Ottonian court had only untalented, statuesque readers.

As regards movement, at least a few reasonable conjectures may also be made from internal evidence in Hrotsvitha's texts. When for instance (*Drusiana and Calimachus* VIII) St John goes to Drusiana's tomb with Andronicus, the heroine's husband, God appears to them in the semblance of a most fair young man:

Andronicus: I am trembling![15]

John: Lord Jesus, why have you deigned to appear to your servants in such a place as this?

The Lord: I have appeared so as to waken Drusiana and him who lies beside her tomb, for
in them my name shall be glorified.
Andronicus: How suddenly he was taken back to heaven!

Even in the most unadorned public reading, these last words of Andronicus
would be hard to fathom unless the fair young man were *seen* to vanish before
the eyes of the audience. One need not suppose anything elaborate: he could
quietly ascend steps to an upper gallery, or even make a simple exit behind the
readers. But for Andronicus to speak his sentence while the reader of the Lord's
part was still glued to the spot would have been fatuous then, just as it would be
now.

More problematic is the 'mime-like' element in such a famous scene as the
delusion of Dulcitius, when he embraces the sooty pots and pans in the prison
kitchen, convinced that he is enjoying the bodies of the three Christian maidens.
The idea of having the girls peeping through the cracks in the wall, filled with
mirth at the villain's bewitchment, is Hrotsvitha's own. There is no hint of this
in her hagiographic source, nor is it a kind of humour she could have learnt from
Terence's text. It is the broader, visual humour of *scurrilia*, performed in such a
way as to make people 'shake with endless laughter', in Ruotger's words, that
Hrotsvitha must have witnessed at least now and then. This does not necessarily
imply that, when her own scene was read aloud, it too was fully mimed; but we
can be sure that she would not have shaped her scene in this particular way if she
had never herself watched a mime.

At the Ottonian court, too, she will have witnessed many ceremonies that
involved elaborate rôle-playing. This, it is well known, was taken to extravagant
lengths by Otto III in his years in Rome (996–1002), the young dreamer who
played out the life of a Roman emperor in all its grandeur, conjuring up endless
imperial offices, rituals and charades.[16] But already with Otto the Great and his
son Otto II one has the sense that for them the *imperium* they strove to realize
implied replaying a Roman emperor and court, though in a Christian mode.
Something of this emerges in the resplendent Ottonian miniatures that survive:
men and women are portrayed with grave refinement; the high and low – kings
and shepherds – are subtly differentiated in their looks; gestures are stylized and
hieratic; costumes and settings often deliberately classicizing. Each episode in the
illustrations is solemnly set in its own space, which tends to be demarcated by
pillars or curtains. It is a consciously exquisite, even precious, world – like that
of Hrotsvitha's plays and poems, with which the work of the Ottonian painters
has close affinity. In her dramas especially, Hrotsvitha, like the Ottonian family,
wanted to replay the Roman world in a Christian mode. She was not cut off
from the imperial *renovatio* by belonging to Gandersheim: on the contrary, this
put her in a position to play a key part among the élite who shaped that *renovatio*.

Two of her poems, on the exploits of Otto and on the origins of Gandersheim, are indeed overtly celebrations of the dynasty. But in her poetic legends and plays, too, Hrotsvitha was aware of helping to refashion, for the Ottonians, a culture worthy of the rôle they had chosen – worthy of Charlemagne, of Constantine, and of the myth of Rome.

The double cycle, of poetic legends and plays, gradually became in Hrotsvitha's conception a single *magnum opus*, with vast and elaborate internal symmetries. This was shown in a superb essay by Hugo Kühn.[17] Readers familiar with Kuhn's argument will see at once how much the following suggestions about Hrotsvitha's larger design owe to him, though I also propose certain qualifications and developments of Kuhn's ideas, and do not re-examine every parallel that he indicated.

Let us consider the two cycles side by side:

LEGENDS	PLAYS
Maria/Ascension	*Gallicanus I–II*
Gongolf	*Agape, Chionia and Hirena*
Pelagius	*Drusiana and Calimachus*
Theophilus	*Mary the Niece of Abraham*
Basilius	*The Conversion of Thais*
Dionysius	*The Passion of the Holy Maidens*
Agnes	*Apocalypse*

If we look at them from the vantage of works completed rather than of works in the making, certain parallelisms are at once evident, others become apparent only gradually.

The fifth composition in each cycle is a thematic *reprise* of the fourth: the story of Thais is a variation on that of Abraham's niece Mary,[18] just as the story of Basil (or better, of Proterius' slave) is a variation on that of Theophilus. Central to the series of plays as to that of legends is the treatment of two women and two men, each of whom sinks to the depths by renouncing God, and rises again at last, through repentance, to win heavenly bliss. This theme, with its deep optimism, meant so much to Hrotsvitha that she illustrated it, with the help of deliberate echoes and analogies, in four different ways.

The next parallels that emerge distinctly are those at the beginning of each cycle. It is not hard to see that the first two legends (the life of the Virgin and the ascension of Christ) form a diptych, as do the two *Gallicanus* plays. In each case a long composition is followed by a briefer coda. Like Gallicanus in the sequel to his play, Mary continues as an important figure in the tale of Christ's ascent – indeed his speech of farewell to her, promising her own assumption into heaven, is central to the second piece. There is also a clear thematic parallel between

Maria and *Gallicanus I* – each concerns the conflict between virginity and marriage, and shows the conflict resolved – though I find it harder to see one between the sequels.

Gongolf and *Agape, Chionia and Hirena* stand out in each series by their remarkable conjunction of tragic and burlesque elements. Each unfolds a story that ends in the hero's or heroine's death by martyrdom, yet the most memorable moments in each, poetically and dramatically, are filled with comedy and farce. Hrotsvitha's full title for the legend tells us that Gongolf's story is the *Passio Sancti Gongolfi Martiris*; but he is the martyr of marriage – he dies not at the hands of a pagan executioner, but through a plot hatched by his own wanton wife. At the close of this *Passio* the high-spirited tone of many of the earlier episodes becomes outright fabliau, though Hrotsvitha, while heightening the ribaldry in her source, conveys it by means of elaborate, mock-decorous circumlocutions. Gongolf's wife scoffs at the idea that her late husband has become a saint:[19]

> 'Miracles occur at Gongolf's tomb? –
> only the way that signs and miracles
> occur out of the back of my behind!'
> Thus spoke she,[20] and a wondrous sign followed her words,
> one congruent with that corporeal part:
> thence she brought forth a sound of sordid music
> such as my little tongue is ashamed to tell.
> And after this, whenever she formed a word,
> as often did she sound that graceless note.

In the play of the martyrdom of Agape and her sisters, the villains at each turn are made to look absurd. Always they lose their dignity, routed by the beneficent 'sorcery (*maleficia*)' of the Christian God. It is this that makes Dulcitius deflower pots and pans instead of maidens, that makes the clothes stick to the girls' bodies as they are about to be stripped naked, or that sends the youngest, Hirena, to a mountain-top, made magically inaccessible, instead of to the brothel planned for her. The illusions that seem 'malefic' to the pagans are in fact innocent, and always in a comic mode. I shall return to this point later.

The story of Pelagius and the drama of Drusiana and Calimachus again show a link in theme: both treat of an illicit love. The Caliph's attempt to seduce the beautiful Christian boy (*Pel.* 227–70) is portrayed with insight and daring realism; his words to the reluctant Pelagius – 'o lascive puer, iactas te posse licenter / spernere . . .'[21] – are worthy of the epigrams in the Greek Anthology. So too, Hrotsvitha's presentation of Calimachus, about to violate the dead Drusiana in her tomb – 'I had been happy had I never learnt that her body was still perfect' – shows an imaginative penetration that has no counterpart in her source.

After the 'double bill' in each cycle – the tales of rejecting God and re-discovering him – come two treatments of martyrdom in a serious mode: the legend of Dionysius and the play of Sapientia's three daughters. These too show parallels of theme: the martyred ones are sages – Dionysius, the great philosopher and mystagogue, and Sapientia, the mother who even by her name embodies wisdom, who taunts her judge, the Emperor Hadrian, with the enigmas of Boethian mathematics.

The concluding parallel that Kuhn suggested is in my view correct, though still deeply problematic. The legends conclude with the story of Agnes, the virgin martyr who died refusing marriage, and whose steadfastness led to the conversion of her wooer and his father. Thus this tale both closes the first cycle – reverting to the theme of virginity and marriage in the life of Mary – and foreshadows the first play, where the chaste Constantia's refusal to consummate her marriage brings about Gallicanus' conversion. But what of the counter-piece – if such it is – at the end of the plays, thirty-five hexameters depicting scenes from the Apocalypse? Kuhn noted perceptively how the first line – 'The virgin John saw heaven laid open (*Iohannes caelum virgo vidit patefactum*)' – brought back once more the virginity-motif that is sounded at the opening and close of both series (from Mary to Agnes, from Gallicanus to John), making each series truly cyclic. He added that, while the first and last protagonist in the legends is a woman, and in the plays a man, all the intervening legends have heroes, but all the other plays have heroines.[22] He also suggested that the scenes from the end of time so swiftly evoked here are a meaningful conclusion to the twofold cycle, which had begun with the nativities of Mary and Christ, and with Christ's promise, at the ascension, that he would protect his own till the end of time. Christ coming again, to bind the dragon and open the book of life, is the fulfilment of the cycle of events that began with Mary's birth; and Hrotsvitha, in her own invocation to Mary before she begins to tell of that birth, looks forward to the apocalyptic moment, when she, 'joining the hosts of virgins, may achieve the praise of the crimson-clad Lamb perpetually' (*Maria* 43–4).

What remains unexplained is the use to which this brief hexameter composition was put. Those, like Homeyer, who have reflected on it, can think of these verses only as a group of *tituli* – inscriptions to be placed under book-illuminations or frescoes in a church.[23] Indeed the wording resembles that of *tituli*: 'Here the angel, seeking someone worthy, finds nobody . . . Behold, the secrets of the book lie open . . . Behold, heaven's habitants are silent as at noon. Here he stood with a censer before the holy altar . . .'

Yet the paradox is that these thirty-five lines, which in a sense fit so well thematically as a conclusion to the double cycle of legends and of dramas, could not serve as their conclusion if they were planned for an illustrated sacred text or for a church wall, and not as directly related to the plays. In that case their position after the plays in the manuscript would be fortuitous, and, if we nonetheless accept the idea that Hrotsvitha planned a double cycle, with many precise symmetries between the legends and dramas and between the structures of each cycle, we should also have to say that the second cycle is incomplete – that a final play on the theme of virginity and marriage, or perhaps on the end of time, is lost, or else was planned but never written.

Or is it possible that the apocalyptic verses *were* performed? In principle there is nothing implausible about this. From the decade 965–75 – a time when Hrotsvitha was at the height of her powers – we have the first surviving detailed instructions, set down at Winchester, about how the resurrection-ceremony, *Quem quaeritis*, should be mimed.[24] We also know that the Sibyl's evocation of the fifteen Signs of Judgment – a piece that in length and form (twenty-seven hexameters) as well as content is very close to Hrotsvitha's apocalyptic poem – was performed, both at the climax of the *Ordo prophetarum* and independently, at least from the tenth century onwards.[25] Yet the wording of Hrotsvitha's composition suggests something for which I know no precise parallel in tenth- or eleventh-century sacred performances: a reader who, with expressions such as 'here' and 'behold' (*hic, ecce*), is pointing to and explaining events which, if they were enacted, must have been so silently. If that was the conclusion of Hrotsvitha's dramatic cycle – and it is a big 'if' – does it imply that in the plays themselves there was, after all, more movement than the minimal amount which I believe is all that our other evidence would lead us to suppose? Hrotsvitha's *Apocalypse* raises problems which, in our present state of knowledge, remain unanswerable.

How did Hrotsvitha arrive at her notion of structural and thematic parallels? It is tempting to think of possible iconographic inspiration. The great bronze door of Bernward of Hildesheim, with its subtle parallelisms, was not completed till 1015, a date at which almost certainly Hrotsvitha was no longer alive.[26] Perhaps the likeliest place at which she could have seen paintings or sculptures ordered in series was if she was ever with the court during one of its sojourns in the palace at Ingelheim. This palace had a cycle of reliefs of heroes that began with Cyrus, Romulus and Remus, Hannibal, and Alexander, and went on to Constantine, Theodoric, Charles Martel, Pippin, and Charlemagne. To what extent the cycle showed parallelism is not clear from the description in Ermoldus Nigellus' poem,[27] though the juxtaposition of ancient pagan hero-rulers with the Christian ones, who founded the empire that the Ottonians inherited, must have struck the eye. The church next to the imperial palace had two series of frescoes, twelve Old Testament scenes (from the creation of Adam to Solomon) on the left wall, twelve New Testament ones (from Annunciation to Ascension) on the right. But while there was symmetry, there seems to have been no interrelation, such as could have been achieved by use of *figura*.

In short, Hrotsvitha's scheme for her legends and plays almost certainly went well beyond any visual patternings that she might have beheld. In the harmonies of theme and structure that she succeeded in establishing, she achieved the boldest and most elaborate compositional design in Carolingian or Ottonian literature and art, at least as far as the surviving monuments can show.

It is important to add that the unity Hrotsvitha envisioned comprises the legends and plays, culminating (as on balance I incline to believe) in the apocalyptic verses – but not her other works. Between the legends and plays comes her brief transitional note, headed 'Explicit liber primus, incipit secundus'. The editors, from Winterfeld onwards, have given the erroneous impression that the *Gesta Ottonis* constituted Book III of Hrotsvitha's work, and scholars have often referred to this poem as 'the third book'. But neither is it called 'liber tertius' in the manuscript nor has it thematically any link with the double cycle: its links are, if anything, with the poem on Gandersheim, which likewise sets narrative in the service of dynastic commemoration.

At what stage in her writing Hrotsvitha began to think out a sweeping overall design for her legends and plays, and when she committed herself to that design decisively, can no longer be fully ascertained. From the close of *Theophilus*, and the new dedication to Gerberga preceding *Basilius*, it is evident that Hrotsvitha had first submitted to Gerberga the group of poems from *Maria* to *Theophilus*, and added the rest later. So when writing *Theophilus*, it seems, she had not yet thought of returning to the motif of renouncing God with a second tale. From the epistle to her favourers it looks as if there may have been a comparable break (what Kuhn called a 'Schaffenspause') in her playwriting, after the drama of Abraham's niece, when once more she felt uncertain whether or not to go on. Yet the notion of a larger design must have been in Hrotsvitha's mind before she determined on her second *reprise*, with *The Conversion of Thais*. Beyond this we are reduced to conjecture.

What we can still trace with some precision, however, especially in Hrotsvitha's Prefaces, is her growing – and changing – awareness of herself as artist. These Prefaces are written in the most artificial prose of which Hrotsvitha felt capable – yet paradoxically they are also full of self-revelations, at least between the lines. If we can look beyond Hrotsvitha's overwrought façades, beyond her topoi of humility that become almost presumptuous through sheer over-insistence, we can discover what was really on her mind.

In the discussion that follows, I shall quote from the Prefaces and the Epistle substantially, in translation. With the first Preface, it seemed relatively easy to give at least some impression of Hrotsvitha's mode of rhyming as well as an accurate picture of what she says; with the others, conveying her convolutions and nuances of expression was so demanding that rhyme-effects would only have diminished precision, and hence were not attempted.

The Preface to the series of legends begins:[28]

This small book, adorned with little grace of beauty but elaborated with no little loving care, I offer to the benevolent gaze   of all who are wise   for correction, or at least to those   who take no delight in belittling one who errs,   but rather in the correcting of the errors.

I confess, indeed, to more than average erring –   not only in discerning   the length of syllables, but also in the forging   of poetic style – and many things in this series of poems should go in hiding,   as deserving blame; yet forgiveness is easily given to one who admits her errors, and faults merit the correction that's their due.

But if it is objected that certain things in this work are drawn from writings that some hold apocryphal, there's no blame here for sinister presumption,   only an ignorant assumption: for, when I began to weave the thread of this chain, I did not know that things I resolved to work on were held up to doubt. And when I came to know it, I refused to undo the work – since what seems falsity may perhaps prove truth.

This being so, I am the more in need of many champions for my finished work, inasmuch as, at its inception, I could rely on too little strength of my own: I was not yet mature enough in years, or advanced enough in knowledge. But I did not dare   to lay bare   my impulse and intention to any of the wise   by asking for advice,   lest I be forbidden to write because of my clownishness. So in complete secrecy,   as it were furtively,   now toiling at my compositions alone,   now destroying work that was badly done,   I tried as best I might to produce   a text of even the slightest use,   based on passages in writings I had gathered to store   on the threshing-floor   of our Gandersheim foundation.

There follows a tribute to the guidance of Rikkardis, and of Gerberga, who, 'though younger than I, was more advanced in learning, as behoved an emperor's niece'. Hrotsvitha continues:

Though metrical composition seems difficult and arduous for women, frail as we are, I,   relying only on the help of the ever-merciful grace on high,   never on my own strength, decided to harmonize the songs in this trifling work in dactylic measures. The talent of a little imagination, entrusted to me, was not to lie sluggish in the heart's dark cavern and be destroyed by the rust of negligence,   but rather, struck by the hammer of unfailing diligence,   was to echo some small ringing note of divine praise, whereby, if no chance came to win more, by commerce with it,   it could still be transformed into an instrument of some – however paltry – profit.

The Preface concludes by asking the indulgence of the reader, who should ascribe to God whatever in the work might perchance prove well-composed.

It was one of the much-worn topoi of prefaces and dedications, from the first century onwards, to offer one's work to a reader, or readers, for improvement, asking that they correct the imperfections which remained.[29] Hrotsvitha, playing upon such a device, makes many asseverations of her inadequacy – yet each is immediately in some way qualified, the rhymes pointing her dialectic of balance and antithesis.

If there are errors of prosody and style, there should also be easy pardon for them, as she admits them freely; if she has erred in her choice of subject-matter, drawing on apocryphal texts, is not the concept 'apocryphal' itself something relative? Or perhaps Hrotsvitha is saying: Can legends not be true in their own way, in that they ring true imaginatively? (As we shall see, she reverted to this troubling question several times.) There is a particular double edge to Hrotsvitha's next 'modest proposal'. She was only a beginner when she started her poems, too timid to ask advice from experts at the time; yet the reason she was too timid, it at once emerges, was because she feared experts might hinder her from composing – and she was determined, come what might, to compose. Her writing secretly was grounded as much in inner resolution as in fear.

Whenever Hrotsvitha alludes (as she often does) to womanly weakness, she is saying something rich in ambiguities. Here the suggestion that writing in classical metres is especially hard for women, because they are frail, is deliberately preposterous, and is said tongue in cheek. At the same time, there is a sly recognition that the 'dactylic measure', the hexameter, was generally deemed the heroic metre *par excellence*, and that the heroic was a masculine prerogative. (This also suggests at least one reason why Hrotsvitha later dwelt so often on the heroism of women.)

Once more the feigned doubt has its answer ready: writing hexameters seems hard for fragile women – yet (relying on God's help) I chose to write them nonetheless. The reason that Hrotsvitha alleges again plays upon a topos: one writes so as not to be accused of idleness. She gives the thought a subtle, individual modulation by her use of the image of the talent. Here she does not quite claim *ingenium* – an imaginative gift, or imaginative genius – as she was to do in her later Prefaces: only *ingeniolum*, a 'little genius'. Yet this too is a 'talent' in the biblical sense, a coin that must not be buried but be used with profit. She sustains the metaphor: the coin–talent can be hammered and sound forth in praise of God. Even if it acquires no worldly surplus-value, it is not valueless: it can be made into an instrument, on which divine jubilations can be played.

Thus in this Preface each admission of weakness is inseparable from an impulse of self-assurance, or self-reassurance. Partly Hrotsvitha *is* diffident about her venture, partly she pretends to be. It is the wavering between real and pretended diffidence that reveals to us the Hrotsvitha beyond the topoi, the woman who says, in effect: 'Some of my legends are apocryphal? But there's no absolute certainty in such matters ... I didn't ask the advice of sages? No, I was too shy – and I was so determined to write anyway, that I did so secretly. Hexameters are too hard for weak women to compose? Perhaps, but, weak as I was, I still decided to.'

This preface is followed by a verse dedication to Gerberga, more conventional in tone: the abbess of royal race is to correct and polish Hrotsvitha's graceless compositions. That this here is formula rather than reality is indicated, I think, by the next lines:

> When you are weary, after your varied labours,
>   deign to read these songs by way of play.[30]

If reading Hrotsvitha's verses is to be relaxing (*ludens*) for Gerberga, the task of refining them (*purgare*) cannot be meant too strenuously.

Certain moments in the course of the legends should perhaps also be noted for the self-awareness they display. The heading of the first, *Maria*, contains a strong hint of self-justification: it is 'the story . . . of the immaculate mother of God, which I found in written form under the name of St James (*quam scriptam repperi sub nomine Sancti Iacobi*), the brother of the Lord'. After completing the poem, Hrotsvitha had been told that this text was not by St James at all. Yet her rejoinder in the Preface implies that, even if the ascription to James seems to be *falsitas*, it may nonetheless emerge (through the rediscovery of other early documents?) that this text contained truth. Possibly Hrotsvitha's wording here in the heading even suggests an implicit challenge: how do such ascriptions, if they are incorrect, arise?

A further, almost defiant, allusion to the question of apocrypha comes within the poem – in a passage that Hrotsvitha left unchanged, or perhaps even deliberately added, when she felt it necessary to defend her choice of subject-matter. She does not need, she says, to dwell on Joseph's suspicion of Mary, or on his dream, for these things are known to all from the Gospels, and they surpass her own frail powers to tell: 'I shall base my composition only on those things which are held to be too rarely told in church' (*Maria* 541–2). Hrotsvitha uses the generalized passive construction (*Rarius in templo quae creduntur fore dicta*) – but who else thought the apocrypha were too much neglected in church? Does not the impersonal *creduntur* conceal a very personal *credo*?

The Marian diptych closes (*Ascensio* 147ff) with Hrotsvitha expressing her conviction that poetry is for her a means of winning bliss in heaven. Whoever reads these verses should call down God's mercy on her, so that she may continue celestially, in divine songs, the songs she has composed about God's awesome deeds ('tua facta stupenda'). A similar phrase ('facta dei') occurs in the renewed dedication to Gerberga before *Basilius*, and here it is a sign of greater confidence than before. Offering Gerberga her 'new little verses', Hrotsvitha says: Do not despise them, even though they're full of faults,
>   but, with your gentle heart, praise the deeds of God.[31]

Does the last line imply that it is one of God's deeds to have made Hrotsvitha a poet, or that her poems themselves are 'facta dei', in that they are designed as a means of giving glory to God? On either interpretation, Hrotsvitha's growing sense of a divine calling to compose poetry is unmistakable.

It emerges, too, in the Prelude of *Basilius* itself: now Hrotsvitha insists that the matter of her story, the illustration of forgiveness and of the generosity of divine compassion, is so important that she summons her reader to 'peruse these little verses with submissive heart' –

> And let him not scorn the frail sex of the woman of no importance
>   who played these melodies on a frail reed pipe,
> but rather let him praise Christ's heavenly mercy:
>   he does not want to destroy sinners . . .[32]

The sinner recovering from his or her total rejection of God is, as we have noted, the major theme that Hrotsvitha chose to portray in four different plots in the legends and dramas.

In her brief transitional note between the two series, Hrotsvitha reverts once more to the question of sources and their reliability:

All the subject-matter of this little work [the plays], as of the preceding one, I have taken from ancient books transmitted under the names of certain authors (*sub certis auctorum nominibus conscriptis*), except for the passion of St Pelagius [for which, as she had told, she relied on a firsthand report] . . . So if in either book I have included anything false in my composing, I have not misled of my own account, but only by incautiously imitating misleading sources.[33]

If the texts used by Hrotsvitha reached her as the works 'of certain authors', much depended on whether the ascriptions were correct: if so, then the texts were indeed by witnesses in a position to know. But were the ascriptions 'certain' in the sense of admitting no doubt? Or could some of the texts Hrotsvitha used be imaginative reconstructions, or fabrications, of more recent date and authorship? Abelard, as is well known, set a cat among the pigeons when he questioned the status of the sources concerning Dionysius – the same sources for the most part as Hrotsvitha used.[34] Had she too a suspicion that for instance Hilduin, writing the life of Dionysius only a century before her own birth, was perhaps not the best authority on things said to have occurred at the time of Christ's death? At all events Hrotsvitha's levelheaded and decisive contrast between the eye-witness account from Cordova, of which she had no doubt, and the written sources, where she cannot vouch for greater veracity than that of the materials available to her, is subtle and acute.

Where the use of apocrypha posed problems for the legends, the use of Terence did so for the dramas. This comes out in Hrotsvitha's astonishing tactics in her Preface to the plays, where she says little of what she really means and means almost nothing of what she says. –

Many Catholics can be found who prefer the vanity of pagan books to the utility of holy Scripture, because of the pagans' greater eloquence and grace of style – nor can I clear myself wholly of having such a preference. There are others again who cling to the sacred page and who, though they spurn other works by pagan authors, still rather often tend to read the fictive creations of Terence; and while they take delight in the mellifluence of the style, they become tainted by coming to know an impious subject-matter.

So I, the 'Mighty Voice of Gandersheim', have not demurred at imitating Terence in composing, while others cultivate him in their reading – so that, in the same genre of composition in which the shameless unchaste actions of sensual women were portrayed, the laudable chastity of holy maidens might be celebrated, inasmuch as my little imaginative gift has power to do so.

Not rarely does it cause embarrassment, and suffuse me with a deep blush, that, compelled by the nature of this mode of composing, I have had to ponder while writing and to set down with my pen the loathsome lunacy of the love-struck and their wickedly sweet conversations, which our ears are not allowed even to entertain. Yet had I passed such matters over bashfully, I could never have done justice to my plan: I should not even have set forth the praise of the innocent as fully as I was able; for, the more seductive the caresses with which the love-maddened ones allure, the more sublime the glory of the helper on high, the more glorious the victory of those shown triumphing, especially when womanly frailty emerges victorious and virile force, confounded, is laid low.

I do not doubt that some will raise the objection with me, that the poorness of this composition is far inferior to the writing of him whom I resolved to imitate – more limited, and altogether unlike him. I admit it; yet I would explain to objectors that they cannot rightfully reproach me on the ground that I was trying perversely to compete with those who have far outstripped my want of art in loftier knowledge. I am not of such boastfulness as to presume to compare myself with even the least of their pupils. I aspire only to this, that, though I can by no means do so fittingly, still with submissive devotedness of spirit I might redirect the gift of genius I have received back to the Giver. I am not so filled with self-love, then, that – in order to avoid human reproach – I would cease to proclaim the power of Christ, manifest in the saints, in whatever way he himself empowers me.

If my labour of love gives pleasure to anyone, I'll be glad; but if, because of my worthlessness or the boorishness of my flawed style, it pleases no one, what I have created still gives delight to me – because, while in the other little works that spring from my ignorance, I gathered my poor efforts bound in a chaplet of heroic verse, here I have plaited them in a dramatic chain, avoiding the baleful delights of the pagans by keeping them at arm's length.

It has not I think been pointed out before that none of what Hrotsvitha claims, ostensibly solemnly, at the opening of this Preface can conceivably be literally true. In the fourth century there were, to be sure, some Christian men of letters who preferred reading pagan authors, because of their more elegant style, to reading the Bible – Augustine's and Jerome's admissions of weakness in this matter are especially well known. And it is possible that a handful of the most literate people at Otto's court once again made such a stylistic comparison and came down in favour of pagans – Bruno perhaps, or Rather or Liutprand,[35] and (as she concedes, with feigned reluctance, in a knowing aside) Hrotsvitha herself. But that 'many Catholics (*plures . . . catholici*)' showed this preference in Hrotsvitha's time, or had the knowledge to discriminate among styles in this way, is at least a wild exaggeration, and almost certainly a joke. The joking becomes patent, and more outrageous, in the next sentence: could anyone seriously imagine readers who, out of sheer devoutness, spurn for instance Vergil and Cicero, but still cling to Terence because he is so great a stylist? This may indeed be a teasing allusion to Chancellor Bruno's fondness for Terence, a mischievous hyperbole, pretending that this was his exclusive taste, his addiction. But the sentence can no more be taken straight than if we were to read, in a history of modern literature, that twentieth-century England was full of High Anglicans who rejected all non-sacred writing, yet who could never stop themselves from reading Congreve.

Those who read Terence (naturally only for his style!), Hrotsvitha adds, become corrupted. The question that occurs irresistibly – was she then *not* corrupted by reading Terence? – is the one that, by this mock-serious statement, she wittily passes by.

Or we might say, she redirects the question: *she* reads Terence in order to save those *litterati*, those delicate stylists who are so easily corruptible, from themselves! With her ironically placed Latin equivalent for her name – *Clamor Validus* = Old Saxon *Hrôthsuith*[36] – she even intimates that writing chaste, Christian plays in the Terentian genre, and thereby redeeming the genre, was a kind of prophetic mission she took on. Hers is the 'mighty voice': the expression 'ego Clamor Validus' can hardly help carrying a reminiscence of John the Baptist's 'ego vox clamantis'. At the same time, *clamor* can have an objective as well as subjective force: then her Latinization of the name would suggest something more like 'the big noise of Gandersheim', and be a self-mocking recognition that the spreading rumour of her composing was making her known as a prodigy – or a freak. Once more the diminutive *ingeniolum* comes – her 'little genius' will celebrate chaste maidens, where Terence's great genius had turned to lascivious women. It sounds irreproachable – until we recall that at the centre of her dramatic series are two plays which are not about chaste maidens at all, but which have two zestfully lascivious heroines.

Yet at once Hrotsvitha concedes this: she had to portray sexual love and love-talk, however embarrassing to do so, for the sake of her greater aim – to show the workings of redemption. In order to value chastity, one must first know what love-madness is, and not be so shocked by the very idea that one fails to understand it. Only by showing love, 'wickedly sweet', in all its attractiveness, and lovers in all their lunacy, will the heroic nature of repentance become clear. Hrotsvitha's word-plays here – 'amantium dementiam . . . male

70

dulcia . . . amentium' – are characteristic of a pagan way of talking about love. These are Plautine, Terentian and Ovidian turns of phrase,[37] that were still to have a long fortune after Hrotsvitha, and ones that she uses lightly, hardly with prophetic fervour. Yet here, arguing that sin must be shown in all its seductiveness in order to show the sublimity of recovering from it, she is fashioning her own counterpart to the ancient paradox of human love:[38] to experience love's blissful sweetness, the lover must know its bitter sorrow first. She is also touching seriously on that process of redemption which she depicts in her central pair of legends and of plays: the ultimate victory of virtue is a triumph of God, but Hrotsvitha also sees it 'especially (*praesertim*)' as a feminist triumph. Weak women show their power, strong men go under.

Mary and Thais show their strength by renouncing their lives as courtesans (lives in which, Hrotsvitha makes clear, they both enjoyed themselves immensely). Does Hrotsvitha herself, another weak woman, display a power comparable with theirs by renouncing the philosophy of Terence's plays, replacing it by celebrations of Christian mercy? Or is her power merely an arrogant pretence – like that of Terence's Delusor in the *Altercation* – as if she could vanquish a great ancient author? This is the objection to which she next turns.

Again her extravagant protestations of modesty have a twinkle about them. Of course she does not write as well as Terence, she assures – yet even in saying that her plays are 'altogether unlike' his (*penitusque dissimilis*), is she not also making an implicit claim for their originality? And when she goes on to affirm, I am not competing with those (living scholars) who are far wiser than I, does she not equally mean, I am attempting something they have not attempted? Theirs is the 'loftier knowledge (*scientia sublimior*)' of theology, ethics, sciences – yet they never thought of composing in the Terentian mode.

The pair of justifications that follow ('Nec enim tantae sum iactantiae . . . Ideoque non sum adeo amatrix mei . . .') likewise contain both an affirmative and a negative element. Anticipating criticisms that she is boastful, or full of self-love, she both abases herself and insists that her *ingenium* (now no longer diminutive) must – like the talent in the parable – be moved serviceably towards the God who gave it to her, and, even, that her *ingenium* is itself a proclamation of Christ's power, one that no censure of human beings ought to silence.

With the last sally in the Preface, an impish sense of self-possession gains the ascendant. Hrotsvitha says in effect: you can take my work or leave it – I'm glad if you like it, and if you don't, at least I've given myself some pleasure. Yet the sentence continues craftily, with 'because': 'memet ipsam tamen iuvat quod feci, quia . . .' The reason Hrotsvitha alleges that her work helps, or delights, her (even if it's no good as literature) is because writing it was for her an effective antidote against pagan delights! In this last sentence the wit directed, not against pagan delights but against Christian hypocrisies, is devastating. It is (to resume my analogy) as if the High Anglican who disapproved of secular writing wrote his own plays, ones that kept Congreve constantly in view, and then answered charges of inconsistency by saying: 'But I write them as my protection against Congreve!'

Admittedly, Hrotsvitha claimed she had gone to Terence for style and form, changing the content completely. And yet it is not hard to see that this is disingenuous. Her stylistic debt to Terence is not in fact large. She copies a number of Terentian mannerisms and phrases (exclamations such as 'Pro Juppiter!', 'Ridiculum!', 'Eccam!', 'Atat!' are obvious examples).[39] She likewise imitates certain techniques: the use of rapid exchanges and repartee, or the device of bringing on characters in the first scene of a play to provide needed background information. Yet Hrotsvitha does not imitate Terence metrically, and her diction owes more to Vergil and Prudentius than to him.[40] Where her debt to Terence is far-reaching is not in style but in subject-matter.

For Terence, like Hrotsvitha, had presented with imaginative sympathy a number of young women who were innocent victims.[41] The girls in the *Andria*, *Eunuchus* or *Adelphoi* do not speak, yet in each case they are the focal point of the play's plot. Always the victimized girl triumphs at the close: she wins her freedom, wins her love-match. In the *Andria* and *Eunuchus* the girls, like Hrotsvitha's heroines, are even hedged by 'miracles' – wondrous revelations that lead to the discovery of their true identity and their distinguished birth. In the *Adelphoi* we see a young girl being rescued, like Hrotsvitha's Mary, from a brothel. In the Terentian plays, as in Hrotsvitha's, we often witness trickery, deception and disguise employed in a good cause, in order to confound the men who think themselves mighty – the blustering, boastful or tyrannic ones. As in Hrotsvitha's scenes of confrontation and martyrdom, there are continual threats of whipping and torture, which hardly ever have any effect: in Terence as in Hrotsvitha, there is a hair's breadth between the comic and the horrible. Terence's emotional gamut – the spheres of tenderness, of trickery, and of blustering force nimbly defeated – is (if we leave the specifically Christian motifs out of account) humanly close to Hrotsvitha's.

I am certain that Hrotsvitha was fully aware of this, and that she couched her elusive defence for having turned to Terence in a deliberately misleading way. To carry off the coup she intended, she created her own weapon of literary coquetry. Her shape-shifting, her 'weak little woman' pose, her headily exaggerated modesty-topoi, her diminutives, her graceful to-and-fro of affirmation and negation, can all be seen as in the service of that coquetry: all are witty, skilled means of commanding recognition and respect for her way of looking.

Hrotsvitha was aware of double standards throughout the world of her experience. First and foremost, a different range of expectations for men and women, and for their capacities. Here her coquetry takes the form of comically stressing women's weakness, never minimizing it, yet always pointing it in such a way as to foil expectations and paradoxically show women's strength.

She is equally conscious of other anomalies: between the values of Terence and those of hagiographic writers; between the counsels of perfection of the Christian life and the lapses from it in the world of court and Church; between the demands of entertainment and those of edification. I am not suggesting that her wit resolved these anomalies in complete relativism (such as we might ascribe, far later, to someone like Jean de Meun). Hrotsvitha is indeed committed to the Christian life, the hagiographic goal and the didactic aim; at the same time, she never for one moment ignores their profane and wicked counterparts. Her art is, while pursuing the first, to keep the second constantly in view – to allow for confrontations that can range from violent clashes for the sake of an ideal (the pagan persecutors versus the martyr-heroines) to humorous recognitions of real frailty (as when St Gongolf, with his magic fountain, out-tricks – rather than punishes – his unfaithful wife). And wherever Hrotsvitha dwells most ardently on the 'higher' values, she cannot help hearing echoes of the 'lower': in this sense both Terence and the Christian antidote delight her simultaneously.

Even her frequent condemnations of lasciviousness in the poems and plays are not incompatible with her fascination with it. Hrotsvitha is well aware that the one sheep which is lost and found again is more interesting than the ninety-nine which have no need of penance ('quanto extitit foedior, tanto appareat nitidior'), and that it gives more delight ('magis delectatur').[42] Chastity becomes an absorbing theme for her as much for its penumbra of wantonness as for its own radiance. The many scholars who have seen Hrotsvitha's aim only in terms of a 'straight' didactic and ascetic intention have not read her Prefaces or her writings sensitively.

The Preface to the plays is followed by the letter to her wise *fautores*.[43] In her relief and joyful gratitude that her work has found a welcoming echo among them, Hrotsvitha's euphuism and overacted womanly submissiveness at first seem boundless:

I can scarcely marvel sufficiently at the magnitude of your praiseworthy condescension,[44] nor can I fittingly requite, with recompense of condign thanks, the plenitude of your magnificent benignity and charity towards my inadequacy: for, even though you are nurtured above all in spiritual study and are of surpassing excellence in knowledge, you have thought the paltry work of me, a worthless little woman, worthy of your admiration, and, rejoicing with brotherly affection, have praised in me the Giver of operative grace:

you think to find in me some little knowledge of the arts, the subtlety of which far exceeds my womanly genius.

In a word, hitherto I hardly dared to show the clownishness of my little composition[45] even to a few people, and if at all, then only to intimate friends. So the task of composing something further of this nature almost ceased.

Now, however, Hrotsvitha says she has found the confidence she needed to continue, to complete the greater design she had projected, for (playfully she gives her patrons a biblical *auctoritas*, from Deuteronomy 19: 15) 'what is confirmed by three witnesses is true'. In what follows, Hrotsvitha makes her most serious analysis of her calling as poet: she is convinced there is a divine element in human creativity:

In the midst of this I am torn between diverse impulses – joy and fear: indeed I feel joy deep in my heart that God, through whose grace I am what I am, is praised in me; yet I am afraid to seem greater than I am – I have no doubt that both denying the spontaneously given gift of God and pretending to have received what was not received are equally wrongful.

She is genuinely awestruck by the burden that such a gift imposes; yet she is also unafraid to adapt to herself the words that Paul had used (1 Corinthians 15: 10): 'by the grace of God I am what I am'. Hrotsvitha's *fautores* (unlike her editors) will have recognized her Pauline citation and been aware of its context – a mingled pride and humility close to Hrotsvitha's, as Paul passes from 'I am the least of the apostles, I who am not worthy to be called an apostle' to 'but I laboured more abundantly than all the apostles – not I, however, but the grace of God with me'.

A moment later, with renewed excessive declarations of her own inadequacy, her sense of humour returns irrepressibly:

Hence I do not deny that through the Creator's grace I have knowledge of the arts potentially (*per dynamin*), since I am a living being with the capacity to learn; yet I confess I am utterly ignorant in actuality (*per energian*). I realize that a penetrating imaginative insight was divinely conferred on me, yet when the loving care of my teachers (*magistrorum*)[46] ended, it remained uncultivated.

Hrotsvitha 'demonstrates' her ignorance by using deliberately recherché language – the Greek philosophical expressions *per dynamin . . . per energian* – that she will have drawn from a letter by St Jerome.[47] Here we are not far from the games-playing of Wolfram von Eschenbach two and a half centuries later – Wolfram who, after claiming that he can neither read nor write, proceeds to record the names of the planets in Arabic![48]

Again there is much in the thoughts that follow that is not what it seems:

Therefore, lest God's gift be annulled in me through my own negligence, I have tried to tear some threads, or even shreds, of cloth, snatching them from Philosophia's robe, to interweave them with the present work, so that the wretchedness of my ignorance be illumined by the intermingling of nobler stuff, and that the bestower of genius be praised rightfully, and the more copiously in that women's understanding is held to be more retarded.

Hrotsvitha is indicating that, encouraged by the reception of her earlier plays (presumably those from *Gallicanus* to *Mary the Niece of Abraham*, which survive as a group in the twelfth-century Cologne manuscript), she felt emboldened to try to give her last ones a further, philosophical dimension, with the help especially of Boethian materials. Yet the way she says this is characteristically double-edged. She knew well enough that in Boethius' *Consolation of Philosophy* those who tore shreds from Philosophia's dress were blindly skirmishing sects of pseudo-philosophers, men who thereby degraded Philosophia, grabbing at her dress as if she were a *meretrix*.[49] It is another expression of mock-humility to suggest that she, in her use of Boethius, had done no more than that. But her follow-up – that through the borrowed shreds in the fabric of her work God will be magnified the more, 'in that women's understanding is held to be more retarded' – alludes not only to the common masculine stereotype of women, but indirectly, with telling irony, to Philosophia herself (who in Hrotsvitha's time was mostly identified with Sapientia – divine Wisdom). In the very moment she plays upon the chimera of women's intellectual inferiority, Hrotsvitha reminds her sages that philosophers have always been inspired by Philosophia, she who could be called 'womanly understanding' incarnate.

At the close Hrotsvitha, with the established gesture of submissiveness, asks her patrons to correct and improve her work. Yet even here she slips in a remarkable phrase – 'it behoves you to examine and emend [my little book] with no less affectionate solicitude than if it were a product of your own labour' – that deliberately leaves the reader guessing whether it is meant to be charming or challenging. If Hrotsvitha's *fautores* still had any illusions about women's weakness, reading this letter of hers must have been a chastening experience.

There is one other Preface by Hrotsvitha, accompanying the *Gesta Ottonis*, which Gerberga had charged her to write. The *Gesta*, composed *ca.* 965 and concluded before 968, are generally held to be later than both the legends and the plays. If this is correct, we can say that by the time she was thirty Hrotsvitha had completed her *magnum opus*, her twofold cycle, and that she had won full recognition by her *fautores* at the imperial court. Thus it is not surprising that Hrotsvitha was then asked, as the price of her reputation, to do something expected in many ages of court poets, or poets laureate: to celebrate her sovereign in the epic manner. The commission, her Preface tells, was given her directly by Gerberga, Otto's niece; but in some dedicatory verses to Otto II, still only of schoolboy age when the poem was completed, Hrotsvitha recalls that he too had asked her for it personally: 'if you deign to remember, you yourself, your eyes sparkling, recently bade that the text be presented to you'. In a verse Prologue to his father, Otto I, we see Hrotsvitha's characteristic ambiguity, half-concealing both humility and pride:

Even though many books praising you fittingly may be written after this, books that will deservedly give pleasure, yet let this little book not be the last in rank, for it was clearly written first, without a model.[50]

Hrotsvitha's play on the close of the parable – the last shall be first – here implies a shrewd claim to originality: her work is the lowliest, and yet, in another sense, it takes precedence over all others.

Nonetheless Hrotsvitha was not entirely happy in her commission, or in her rôle as imperial panegyrist. Unlike the Archpoet, who, two centuries later, was asked in vain for an epic on the *gesta* of Frederick Barbarossa, she at least tried to do as she was bidden. Yet she felt – in this instance quite genuinely – unsure of herself. Principally because, for the first time in her composing, she had to work without the help of written sources,[51] or indeed, for many major episodes, without detailed firsthand reports, such as she had had for *Pelagius*. Amid the flourishes that open her Preface for Gerberga, Hrotsvitha is plaintive about the situation in which she had been placed, as well as wonderfully perceptive about the problems involved in composing official *gesta*:[52]

My sovereign lady, you that shed light with the sparkling iridescence[53] of your spiritual wisdom, may it not irk[54] your benignity to look through what, you are not unaware, has been fashioned at your command. Indeed it was you who imposed this burden, that I set forth the deeds of great Caesar in poetic form – deeds that I could not assemble comprehensively enough, even orally. You can imagine how much difficulty I in my ignorance encountered in the toil of this process of composition, for neither did I find these matters previously written down, nor could I elicit an account of them from anyone in a well-ordered and sufficiently full way.

I journeyed like one who, not knowing the route, is about to travel through a vast unknown ravine, where every path lies concealed, covered by thick snow: led on by no guide, only by signals of direction received beforehand, such a one would now stray onto by-paths, now unexpectedly hit the right path again, until at last, having reached the midpoint of the densely crowding trees, he would choose a spot for his longed-for rest, and there, staying his step, would not dare continue, until another came across him and could guide him, or he found a previous traveller's footprints he could follow. No otherwise did I, commanded to penetrate the vast region of glorious events, traverse the manifold paths of the royal deeds faltering and wavering, very ill at ease, and, utterly exhausted by them, sink to rest in silence in a suitable spot; nor do I undertake to climb the pinnacle of imperial excellence without guidance.

Here too Hrotsvitha's diffidence has as its obverse her positive sense of doing something wholly new. Yet the last clause, where she is overtly claiming she is too lowly to celebrate, unaided, Otto's deeds as emperor, after his coronation at

Rome in 962, is in effect more of a *recusatio*, comparable to the Archpoet's when he was asked to magnify his emperor's deeds.[55] She has, she implies, written the 'epic' composition that was demanded (though indeed she kept it relatively brief); and she is not prepared to go on, unless she were provided with a coherent written prose account from which to work. In the poem itself, typically, it is always 'womanly weakness' that is offered as pretext: Hrotsvitha refuses to attempt battle-scenes, because a frail woman cannot hope to do them justice, especially not one who leads as sheltered a life as she (*Gesta* 237ff). And at the close (1487ff) Hrotsvitha revels in a mock-solemn device of *praecisio*: she has sung the deeds of Otto as king, but she is afraid to touch his deeds as emperor, 'for I am forbidden by my womanly nature'. Yet at once Hrotsvitha goes on to tell all the things she is 'forbidden' to write about: how Otto was able to defeat and banish King Berengarius and his odious queen, Willa, to depose one pope and install another in Rome, and to arrange for the imperial coronation of his son. Perhaps this close gives the best pointer to what did not come fully alive in the course of the poem: Hrotsvitha's *ingeniolum* was too mercurial, too much accustomed to mingling the comic and the serious, to adapt well to the kind of panegyric expected from a poet laureate. Like the Archpoet, she could not keep a straight face quite so long.

Finally, I should like to suggest that other aspects of Hrotsvitha's self-awareness become clear if we scan her writings for what I would call indirectly autobiographic moments. This is perhaps a precarious undertaking, yet at times it too can lead to illuminating insights. I shall illustrate by looking closely at three moments: two are chosen from Hrotsvitha's best-known plays, and one from the poem on the origins of Gandersheim, which is virtually unknown save to a few specialists.

Hrotsvitha's play about Agape, Chionia and Hirena (generally, but erroneously, called *Dulcitius*) draws on a strange source, a late Roman *Passion of St Anastasia*, which troubled its twentieth-century editor, the great Bollandist Delehaye, because of the amount of 'fantasy' and 'audacious fiction' that had contaminated what was doubtless a 'good' original.[56] The very features that disquieted Delehaye were those that attracted Hrotsvitha: in fact, she chose to focus on these and ignore all else, discarding even the figure of St Anastasia, the protagonist in the source. Hrotsvitha selected, and brought to life, especially the three sisters (whom her source introduced only as minor characters, protégées of Anastasia) and the villain-buffoons, Dulcitius and Sisinnius, who are mocked and confounded by those girls.

The implicit self-references in the play can, I submit, be perceived by way of a series of verbal echoes that link it with Hrotsvitha's Preface and Epistle at the opening of the dramatic cycle. There Hrotsvitha tried to excuse her concern with the deeds 'of lascivious women (*lascivarum . . . feminarum*)'; she admitted to blushing with shame ('verecundari gravique rubore perfundi . . . erubescendo') when she turned to such matters as lasciviousness, and yet, she stresses, she was trying to show how 'womanly frailty emerges victorious and virile force, confounded, is laid low (*feminea fragilitas vinceret et virilis robur confusioni subiaceret*)'. And in the epistle she speaks of her work as that 'of a worthless little woman (*vilis mulierculae*)'. All these thoughts return, with identical or very similar expressions, in a different modulation in the play of the three maidens. For the Emperor Diocletian, these maidens are 'viles mulierculae' (IX); for the deluded villains, the prison governor Dulcitius and Count Sisinnius, they are 'lascivae puellae' (VII, IX). And at the close it is the men – Sisinnius and his soldiery – whom Hirena provokes to blush ('erubesce . . . erubesce'), as their show of might is set at naught by a *tenella virguncula*.

Hrotsvitha lays special stress on the strength-in-weakness of the youngest of the three girls, Hirena. At the opening, the Emperor expects her to be more amenable than her sisters, because of her youth; instead, punning on her own name ('Peace'), she cries out: 'You'll find the third rebellious and utterly resistant!' She, the littlest, argues the most ferociously and magniloquently ('Conquiniscant idolis, qui velint incurrere iram celsitonantis!'),[57] and at the close she launches her supreme defiance against pagan 'virile force':

Unhappy man, blush – blush, Sisinnius, and groan at being vanquished ignominiously: for you could not defeat a tender little girl's youth without a panoply of arms . . . You shall be damned in Tartarus; but I, about to receive the palm of martyrdom and the crown of virginity, shall enter the ethereal bed-chamber of the eternal King.[58]

Thus Hirena, like Hrotsvitha the author, turns the language of the aggressive male world to her advantage.

The pagan men continually ascribe their powerlessness against the Christian girls to the girls' witchcraft (*maleficia*). Thus the soldiers lament (XIV): 'We are all "illuded" in wondrous ways (*Miris modis omnes illudimur*)'. In that notion of illusion, too, there may be a poetic connotation relevant to Hrotsvitha herself. The worthless little women, whose defeat of male strength the men see as wantonness and evil illusion, are seen by Hrotsvitha as the blessed, innocent ones, whose illuding is divine grace, and whose 'lasciviousness' is satisfied in the bed-chamber of the divine lover. And here the implicit parallel between the innocent virgin–fighter, Peace, and Hrotsvitha the dramatist, emerges in its full complexity: Hrotsvitha designates herself a *vilis muliercula* as regards her writing; she knows she could be censured as *lasciva* for her fascination with Terence and for some of her own choices of subject-matter; yet she also knows that the intention of her *lascivia* is a blessed one, a celebration of the girls' divine love-union, not of earthly delights – a voluptuousness through chastity. But like the girls, she too 'illudes in wondrous ways', by means of her art: in place of *maleficia*, she achieves the innocent magic of dramatic fiction, and her power in this she, like the heroines in the play, attributes to God's grace. Like Hirena, she stresses (in her Preface to the legends) how young she was when, by beginning to write, she in her own way issued a challenge to the masculine world of her time.[59] But it is precisely the young, fragile girl, Hirena–Hrotsvitha, who, with the help of grace, can conquer the frightening world of men, whether that means the real court of Emperor Otto or the imagined one of Emperor Diocletian. There – in the real as in the imagined court – she can win a moral victory over the mighty pagan (Sisinnius or Terence), she can substitute for the pagan's sexual ruses (the humiliation of the girl-victim, her being sent to a brothel) the 'ethereal bed-chamber' of the Song of Songs.

From Hrotsvitha's play *Mary the Niece of Abraham* I would single out a moment that is filled with borrowed language and literary allusion and is at the same time one of the most moving and personal in all her work. Abraham, who came to the brothel disguised as a lover, so as to rescue his fallen niece, Mary, has persuaded her to repent and return to the desert with him. With a phrase that is close to the lyrical *albas*, where lovers part at dawn, he says to her: 'Dawn grows bright; light is coming; let us leave.'[60] (Where secret lovers in the lyrics must sorrowfully go their separate ways, here the pair, bound by a different love, depart serenely together.) Submissively Mary says she will walk behind him; but Abraham rejoins:

Not so: I shall walk, but set you on the horse, lest the roughness of the way should cut your tender feet (*secet teneras plantas*).

She answers:

Oh what name can I give you (*O quem te memorem*)? What reward of thanks can I offer you, you who do not force me by terror, even though I deserve no pity . . .

Into this exchange Hrotsvitha has set a key-phrase from Vergil's *Eclogues* and another from the *Aeneid*.[61] She could be sure that some of her first audience – Gerberga and Bruno among the imperial family, and the finest scholars who had come to the Ottonian court – knew Vergil well enough to recall the original contexts and perceive the full symbolic value of their use here. In the tenth Eclogue, Gallus laments that his beloved Lycoris had (like Mary) become wanton – she had followed the soldiers to the Rhine, far from her home; yet, still in love with Lycoris, he feels nothing but compassion, and imagines how harsh the journey along the Rhine will be for her, 'cutting her tender feet'; for Gallus (like Abraham) is one in whose thoughts 'Love conquers everything.' Hrotsvitha has transformed Gallus' fantasy, his sublimation of sensual obsession, into Abraham's fatherly tenderness. And Mary answers, overcome, in the words Aeneas had used to Venus, as she appeared to him disguised ('O quam te memorem?'). Like Aeneas, Mary has at this moment the sense of a superhuman destiny revealing itself to her in human semblance: the journey back into the wilderness with Abraham ('asperitas itineris') is her life.

As Hrotsvitha tried to 'redeem' Terentian episodes – the girls who are victimized, the brothel-scenes – so here she is 'redeeming' Vergilian language. For her it is no longer Gallus' erotic reverie, or the appearance of a pagan goddess to Aeneas: she has taken the language and transmuted it in her own design. We might say that, in the whole process by which Abraham rescues Mary, Hrotsvitha identified imaginatively with both parts. As Mary left her monastic cell to go and live in Alexandria, Hrotsvitha is in fantasy a Mary, who had deliberately decided to dwell in the *lupanar* of Terence's world. While (as her Preface hints) many churchmen of her time will have found that decision shocking, she was exhilarated and happy in the Terentian world, just as Mary is in her house of sin. She is fond of Terence, as Mary is of the innkeeper for whom she works, the host who, amazed to see her weeping suddenly, says 'Haven't you lived here for two years, and never a moan or a sad word escaped you?' At the same time, Hrotsvitha sees herself in imagination as someone stronger – as an Abraham who temporarily pretends to be of that wanton world, but who has not really succumbed to it. Like Abraham, she enters the world of wantonness in order to challenge it, or at least to redeem from it what she – or Abraham – holds most dear.

The last of Hrotsvitha's extant works, the poem on the origins of Gandersheim, composed in 973 or slightly later, is the only one without a Preface. Perhaps there was a Preface, which has been lost (the poem no longer exists in manuscripts; its text survived only in the *editio princeps*); yet it is also possible that Hrotsvitha had now gained sufficient reassurance and recognition to be able to open with tranquil directness:

> Behold, my spirit, lowly and submissive,
> breaks forth to tell the origins of blissful Gandersheim.

The site for Gandersheim came to be chosen, Hrotsvitha relates, because of an inexplicable repeated apparition of lights in the depths of a forest, an apparition that was held to be a sign from heaven:[62]

> As the report of many well-informed people tells,
> near our foundation there was then a small forest, circled
> by shadowing hills – that circle us even today.
> There in that wood was set a little farm
> where Liudolf's swineherds used to lodge
> in the farmer's fenced enclosure, letting their weary

bodies sink into rest in the hours of the night,
while the swine in their charge were pasturing.
Here, once upon a time, two days before the high
feast of All Saints was to be celebrated,
the swineherds saw many bright lamps in the wood,
blazing in the dark of the night.
Perceiving this, awestruck, they wondered
what the new vision of sparkling light could mean,
that cleft night's blackness with strange radiance.
Trembling, they told the owner of the homestead,
pointing to the place the light had flooded.
He, eager to verify what he had heard,
determined the next night to stay awake,
joining the men in the open, beyond the eaves:
he would not shut his eyes, heavy with sleep's persuasion,
till they had seen the lit lanterns glint again.
They saw them, vanquishing the first in number,
in the same spot as before, though earlier.
Scarcely had Phoebus shed his first beams from heaven
when this sign of happy omen, so serene,
was made known, with jocund Rumour telling all.
Nor could it be kept hidden from great Duke Liudolf –
swiftly it reached his ears.
And he himself, on holy Halloween,
went with a crowd to keep vigil in that forest,
keenly scanning to see if the apparition
would again betoken something heavenly.
At once, as thick night covered the land with mist,
all around, circling the wooded valley
where the surpassing noble temple was to be built,
many lights were beheld, set in harmonious order:
they cleft the tree-shadows, and the dark night too,
with their radiantly penetrating gleam.
All affirmed that this spot should be made holy,
in the service of him who had filled it with such light.

While there are parallels to wondrous visions of light in hagiography,[63] I
think there can be little doubt that the primary inspiration for this episode lies
in the Gospel account of the birth of Christ. Hrotsvitha, telling of the swineherds, assuredly has in mind the shepherds (Luke 2: 8ff) who kept the night vigil
guarding their flocks, when a divine radiance flashed round about them, filling
them with fear. This fear turned to joy when the radiance was revealed as a
divine omen, the shepherds then telling it to the people all around (2: 18). That
the supernatural light is seen first by the lowly and only then by kings (the Magi
of Matthew 2) is not stated in the Gospels, yet this was the clear implication of
the 'synoptic' account, which became the basis for Christmas homilies.

As *in illo tempore*, in the Christmas night, the harbinger of the divine event was beheld first by shepherds, so with the gleams of light in the darkness that betokened the birth of Gandersheim. The foundation that was destined to have such regal splendour is first seen augured by the humblest folk, and it is their telling what they see that makes the fulfilment of the lights possible.

Yet the Gandersheim of 852 is the same place, Hrotsvitha insists, as the Gandersheim of her own day. Still there is a dark forest, and shadowing hills. Can there still be lights in that forest, heralding a special divine grace? The secret answer lies, I believe, in Hrotsvitha's conception of her own rôle. She constantly affirms herself to be the lowliest, 'last of the last (*ultima ultimarum*)'[64] of those who dwell at Gandersheim; yet may it not be because of this that she, like the swineherds, is the first to be blessed by descrying new lights? Gradually the greater world learns of what the lowly one has seen – it reaches the ears of Otto, as the first apparition of lights reached those of his ancestor Liudolf. Then the great themselves begin to watch, and the lights appear 'set in harmonious order': an implicit – even if not fully conscious – equivalent to that *ordo*, that symmetrical twofold cycle, which Hrotsvitha came to present. The lights, that is, were once symbols of Gandersheim the foundation, but they are also – at least potentially – symbols of the chronicler of Gandersheim, Hrotsvitha herself. She is the *vilis muliercula* who, in a special, divinely granted way, receives illumination.

Deep within, Hrotsvitha was certain she had been blessed with this illumination – or better, she became increasingly certain of this as her writing progressed. So in a sense, despite all her protestations, she is not humble – except in the way of the poet who says 'Not I, not I, but the wind that blows through me'.[65] Her insistences on her frailty, lowly submissiveness, and incompetence all contain an element of deliberate over-acting: they can be seen as so many ironic glances at the double standards of the world she knew, and especially of the powerful male-dominated world. So, too, her constant use of diminutives is more than a stylistic mannerism. They reveal an aspect of her thought: they are self-assured, even self-assertive, by being self-deprecating. When she speaks of her *ingeniolum*, or of the *gratiola* she receives, she is saying in effect, these may be of little moment in the world of warriors, sovereigns and popes, yet she is also hinting that she *has* imaginative genius (*ingenium*) and does receive true grace for writing.

The evaluation of that writing poses many problems. It has sparkling moments, and profound ones; it can be cherished for the complex – and I think attractive – personality it reveals. One can admire both Hrotsvitha's many-sided resourcefulness and the high aspirations revealed by the design of her double cycle of legends and plays. Yet technically that design remained imperfect. This is chiefly because Hrotsvitha never came to feel wholly at ease in the classical metres (as the finest Carolingian poets had done); nor, on the other hand, did she take experiment a step further and transform classical verse into a medium wholly her own (as the author of *Ruodlieb* was to do some decades later). The hexameters cited in translation from the *Primordia coenobii Gandesheimensis* are among the freshest, most unforced in her writing; yet even here a slight stiffness of movement and somewhat repetitive wording suggest that in quantitative measures Hrotsvitha never reached the flexibility and vivacity of expression that came to her so readily in her rhymed prose, and especially in dialogues.

Hrotsvitha's finest qualities and her limitations are comparable to those encountered among the painters who were her contemporaries. We might say, especially with her poetry in ancient forms, that she tried to press too much of her own thoughts and feelings into frames as classically elegant, and as confining, as those used by the Ottonian miniaturists, where, for all the finesse, something a little aloof and rigid tends to remain.

She began her twofold cycle with Marian legends and ended it with an apocalyptic tableau. It is worth recalling that in the seventh century an unpredictable artist, whose stylistic sources are still in many aspects enigmatic,[66] had painted at Castelseprio a double series of frescoes – Marian and apocalyptic. It is this artist's immediacy, his fluid and dynamic qualities, that neither Hrotsvitha nor the illuminators of her time recaptured. True, they did not aim to – but that does not prevent one from sometimes longing for it.

Hrotsvitha remained, by and large, without influence in the later Middle Ages. Yet some of her plays were copied several times in the eleventh and twelfth centuries,[67] and once *Gallicanus* was even furnished with stage-directions. Hrotsvitha's distinctive literary coquetry, however, has parallels in the eleventh century, among some of the women poets to whom we shall now turn: Constance's way with Ovid's *Heroides*, for instance,[68] comes very close to Hrotsvitha's with Terence. And one intriguing possibility of Hrotsvitha's direct influence must at least be broached. The unique comprehensive manuscript of her writings, copied in the late tenth or early eleventh century, was preserved at St Emmeram in Regensburg, where Gerberga had been educated. Did the learned young women at Regensburg who, in the later eleventh century, wrote verses of love, flirtation and teasing wit,[69] ever look at Hrotsvitha's writings? Was their particular brand of coquetry learnt as well as cultivated spontaneously? Did they find their oscillations between deference and proud assurance wholly for themselves – or (as I suspect) with a little help from the *ingeniolum* of their supersubtle predecessor?

4   Personal Poetry by Women:
the Eleventh and Twelfth Centuries

While from the later eleventh and twelfth centuries a considerable range of poetry by women survives, much of it belongs to objective genres. To delimit the enquiry, to concentrate on the most direct testimonies of how women thought and felt about themselves, about men, and about the world around them – or better, how they gave their more intimate reflections poetic shape – it is necessary to leave out of account such genres as the narrative and hymnic ones. Little insight into self-awareness can be gleaned, for instance, from the cycle of religious narrative written by Frau Ava in early twelfth-century Austria, or from the hymns and verse inscriptions composed by herself that Herrad of Hohenbourg included, later in the century, in her illustrated encyclopaedia, *Hortus deliciarum*.[1] Ava admittedly has an Epilogue, a strophe of seven lines – telling that it was her two children who had joyfully explained to her the inner meaning of those episodes (from John the Baptist to Antichrist and Judgement) which she recounted in her verse; she tells also that one of the children had meanwhile died.[2] Yet no human detail quickens her laconic close. With a subtler and more versatile poet, Marie de France, one could deduce much, or at least conjecture copiously, about her personal awareness simply by reading 'between the lines' of her *Lais* and *Fables*, quite apart from Marie's direct utterances in the renowned, enigmatic Prologues to these works.[3] Yet this would demand a separate, long and complex, investigation. So, too, the extent to which the lyrical cycle of Hildegard, her 'Symphony of the harmony of heavenly revelations', can be seen, beyond praise and meditation in a liturgical mode, as a testament of unique subjective perceptions, is too precarious a question to be broached here.[4] The poetry that is in primary intention personal is, in effect, confined to two genres – verse epistle and lyric. The texts that remain as witnesses are chiefly in two languages – Latin and Provençal; they stem from milieux privileged in their learning or their aristocratic way of life, or both.

A number of the women's poems in Latin survive anonymously, but I should like to begin with a poetic letter about whose author at least a little is known. Constance, a young nun at the convent of Le Ronceray in Angers, answered an epistle by her admirer Baudri of Bourgueil, who was also her godfather.[5] His missive was in eighty-nine elegiac couplets; her reply of identical length. I say 'her reply' because, even though the suggestion that the answering letter was a fiction perpetrated by Baudri himself has been mooted by two distinguished older scholars,[6] I find this historically implausible. For, in the letter that spurred Constance's reply, Baudri explicitly says it was her poetry (*tua musa*), her letter (*tua littera*) – that is, an earlier one, now lost – which had moved him so.[7] Moreover, not only do we have a second poem of Baudri's to Constance, but also one in which he begs another young woman in the convent, Muriel, to send him verses, since she is equally skilled in reciting and composing them. Because those he has heard 'have already inserted you in the ranks of illustrious poets', Baudri asks Muriel for an exchange of verses (*mutua carmina*) at times when they cannot meet.[8] Muriel was educated at Le Ronceray like Constance, but unlike her had not taken vows and could well leave the convent to marry – though Baudri hopes she will stay on. In short, one could not consistently take Constance's poem away from her without at the same time accusing Baudri of a far more elaborate series of fabrications. That this would be far-fetched is shown by the existence of other such verse exchanges between young women and their *magistri* or clerks in a neighbouring region: those, from the same decades, preserved in a Bavarian manuscript (to which we shall return), with at least thirty pieces composed by various women, would be particularly hard to see as anything but genuine. Besides, Baudri's slightly older contemporary Marbod of Rennes composed a group of love-poems for the young women of Le Ronceray,[9] and whilst only one reply of a *puella* is preserved among them,[10] the fact that three of Marbod's pieces are called *Rescripta* suggests that these too were answering other verses by the girls, which have not survived. Finally, as Manitius rightly saw, there are clear differences of style and tone between Baudri's letter and that of Constance: 'her answer is more intimate than Baudri's piece; in hers genuine human emotion mingles with biblical–Christian elements'.[11]

Here, however, a complementary observation is needed: Constance's letter is mingled even more with Ovidian elements than with biblical–Christian ones. She is consciously writing a modern *Heroides* epistle. And this poses a problem almost as acute as with Hildegard's *Symphonia*: how to distinguish the genuine human emotion – which, like Manitius, I am convinced is there – from the elaborate literary craft.

For it is not only Ovid's *Heroides* themselves that play a part in the design: they are interleaved, we might say, with motifs from a Christianized mode of *Heroides*, most memorably exploited by Venantius Fortunatus five centuries earlier. Fortunatus' mystic love-letter of a holy virgin to Christ, that begins:

> Weeping I lie flung on the ground, I do not see what I long for –
> Sadly I press the rocks to my breast, embracing them . . .

takes the language and imaginative situation of Ovid's Ariadne abandoned by Theseus and transposes it, an extended conceit, *a lo divino*.[12] So too in the epistles attributed in one manuscript to Fortunatus, though the speaker, and at least partial author, is his dearly loved friend, Queen Radegunde.[13] (That she herself composed Latin poetry is certain, the extent of Fortunatus' collaboration, more difficult to gauge.[14]) In one, Radegunde pathetically beseeches her cousin Amalafred, lost in Byzantium, for news: has he forgotten her, who would gladly cross the stormy seas to find him? In another she begs her nephew Artachis to come to her and console her, now that she has learnt of Amalafred's death in battle.[15] Her verses owe conception, form and tone to the letters of Ovid's heroines of love. Radegunde's love for her cousin and her nephew may be wholly unsensual, yet Ovid's influence led her to express it, like Fortunatus' maiden longing for Christ, in the language of high passion.

Baudri, as is well known, loved to compose in the *Heroides* manner: he wrote his own version of Ovid's exchange of letters between Paris and Helen, and out of the elegies of Ovid's exile created a new pair of letters between the ancient poet and his friend Florus.[16] But when Baudri writes to Constance, a new note is heard in the genre. This is a flirtatious letter, crammed with witty artifice. It is a young man's letter: as he says in it, 'iuvenis sum, iunior es tu' (41). Though *iuventus* can, in medieval sources, extend from the age of twenty-eight to forty-nine or fifty,[17] the context does not suggest that Baudri was approaching what was termed 'the graver age' or 'old age' (*gravior aetas, senectus*). While in theory, as Baudri was born in 1046, his poem could be as late as 1096, it seems likelier that it was a good ten years older than that. Constance, younger than Baudri, may well be the 'domna Constantia' who is attested later in the cartulary of Le Ronceray, around 1100 and again in 1129.[18] We should probably not be too wide of the mark if we imagine the two compositions in the period 1080–5, with Baudri still in his thirties and Constance perhaps nearing twenty.

Baudri's letter glitters with paradox, anaphora, and word-play: he wants to take advantage of all the innuendoes of erotic love while claiming incessantly that his love for Constance is pure, free of sensual poison. It is the worldliest, wittiest celebration of the Christian ideal of spiritual friendship, with an impish eye for all that such friendship is not:

> Your naked hand will touch my naked page . . .
> You can safely lay it in your lap.[19]

His declaration of love is filled with playful hyperbole:

> You are more to me, better and greater,
>   than goddess, than maiden, than any love there is;
> You are more to me than Paris was to Helen,
>   Venus to Mars, Juno to Jupiter.

Lest any of these comparisons might carry a hint of unfaithful loving, Baudri, in three refrain-like couplets, addresses her who is Constancy personified: 'I shall never be able to forget you, Constantia.' May their bond be mutual love (*fedus amoris*), never lascivious love (*fedus amor*). The cascade of word-play continues ('Tu virgo, vir ego . . .'), passing into a description of Constance's beauty, in the language and images that had become fixed since late Antiquity; yet here it stops teasingly short of telling the beauty of her body – 'let me embrace this briefly: it is such as befits your face'. Even the rhetorical *brevitas*-formula[20] ('Corporis ut breviter complectar composituram') has a sly suggestiveness.

The hyperboles are accompanied by asides that restore an ironic sense of proportion:

> You could draw mighty Jupiter down from heaven
>   (if the Greek myth of Jupiter were true) . . .

Yet Baudri also warns: there are many young Jupiters around today! The ancient myths can suggest many temptations – yet you and I can fulfil what is good in them:

> If you want to live as mine – and you shall – then live as Diana:
> I'll try to follow Hercules, or Bellerophon.

To live as Diana is, in more serious terms, to live as a virgin, dedicated to the Christian Jove. Towards the close Baudri admits he had been speaking in jest. Momentarily he becomes more earnest: friends are compelling him to complete a poem on Genesis, which he had left half finished. Yet as he entreats Constance to answer his epistle, one line deserves note: 'My verses know no woman other than you.' This declaration of constancy is belied by the poem to Muriel[21] ('No one but you, my girl, has ever received my verses'), as well as by an admission to Godefroy of Reims (†1095) of having written many love-verses, both to boys and girls, but always jocularly (*Musa iocosa*), with no dishonourable counterpart in his life.[22] The lines to Muriel were written to the same address as those to Constance, and were not necessarily far from them in time. It is even possible that Baudri placed his fib deliberately, knowing he would be caught out in it, giving away the game of his 'exclusive' loves, his amatory poses.

How was Constance to answer this mercurial virtuoso display, in which emotions seem to be purposely concealed, rather than revealed? For her, to exploit the emotional range of Ovid's heroines was an ideal solution. The *Heroides* could suggest many ways of handling changes of mood, of expressing warmth and of taunting the man with coldness or neglect, flashes of blithe longing and stretches of being forlorn. At the same time, the differences between physical passion and the more rarefied friendship, blended with coquetry, such

as Constance knew with Baudri, allowed for certain kinds of deliberate incongruity that the *Heroides* had not foreseen. The hyperboles of praise save themselves from being infatuation by always verging on humour, and the reproaches
can – precisely because Constance has not been abandoned in the grievous way
of Dido, Phaedra, Ariadne and the rest – have a shade of comedy likewise.
Fundamentally, what Constance feels for Baudri is, I would suggest, a blend of
hero-worship, tenderness, solicitude and even possessiveness. She wants him to
be in a special way hers. But because she knows he cannot be hers as lover
without causing a scandal that would destroy their delicately built structure of
ardent friendship, she relies on all the expressions of more extravagant fervour
to intimate that an element of wit is, after all, dominant. Paradoxically, it is the
heated language that, by its continual hints of an inherent inappropriateness,
enables her to keep a certain cool composure.

She begins – 'Perlegi' – with a deliberate echo of his opening, and acknowledging that she had perceived his innuendoes: 'With my hand I have touched
your naked songs.' She wants to read his poem even into the night:

> Night hateful to my study, envious of her who reads . . .
> I put the letter under my left breast –
>   they say that's nearest to the heart . . .
> At last, weary, I tried to get to sleep,
>   but love that has been wakened knows no night . . .
> I lay asleep – no, sleepless – because the page you wrote,
>   though lying on my breast, had set my womb on fire.

Like Laodamia or Ariadne in Ovid, Constance pines for her absent loved one
most of all by night.[23] Yet the differences in situation also lend a touch of
incongruity: Baudri has neither died like Protesilaus, nor abandoned her like
Theseus.

At the same time, hers is not the urbane, teasing note with which Baudri had
addressed her. In the movement that begins with her longing to see 'so great a
prophet', to speak with him even a brief while, though 'tantus propheta' is a
conscious hyperbole, the wish to pass from exchange of letters to personal
encounters, which becomes a leitmotif, has no real counterpart in Baudri's poem.
Here it is first followed by flamboyant praises of his mind, and later of his looks.
His poetry and wisdom would have made him a Cicero, a Cato, an Aristotle
many times over, and another Homer – which indeed he is! He has plundered
hidden meanings from the Greek myths like a David slaying Goliath. We might
imagine that Constance was here using a topos of Christian exegesis – the pagan
myths are rendered harmless by such methods as euhemerism. Yet what she does
is double-edged: when she says 'He knows and has expounded the meaning of
Mars, of Juno, and the other gods', is she thinking of his suggestion that the

gods' actions are embodied in human vices, or of his wishful fantasy that went with it – seeing her as Diana, himself as Hercules?

The word *carmen* itself (57) may be ambiguous – suggesting both Baudri's poetry and the spell he casts over her. Though he sent *carmina* only yesterday, it is a whole year since she has seen him. A mock-prudish note enters when Constance says, if they met, at least two or three of her companions would have to attend as chaperones – 'though he'd be pledge enough of his own faith; / yet at least my loyal sister should be with us, / lest any complaint of suspect things arose'. Baudri's *fides* would consist, naturally, in withholding any impulse of a passionate kind. Yet immediately afterwards Constance again expresses herself in the most impassioned terms. She feels like Laodamia and Ariadne – filled with imaginings during the night of their lover's return, yet knowing it is hopeless:

> But what am I doing? What tosses in my mind all night
>   is nothing – nothing, all I plead for with anxious heart.

From here onwards the twists and turns of thought, the fluctuations of impulse, become more and more those of an Ovidian heroine, even though the sense of rôle-playing is never absent. 'Perhaps his letters are a deception? – Alas, what should I *not* dread then? I'll never rest secure . . . I fear he may be entangled, straying in some way: every girl envies my fair fortune!'

Here Constance anticipates, though in a playful modulation, the claim of Heloise: 'What wife, what girl did not long for you from afar or burn in your presence? What queen or great lady did not envy my joys and my bed?'[24] Then, as day breaks, the anguished uncertainties of the night recede and Constance resolves to trust her 'lover', to declare her feelings on her wax tablet – 'for the wax cannot blush'. Her expression here has many ancient echoes (e.g. Phaedra in *Heroides* IV 10, or the princess in the *Historia Apollonii* 20), and returns in a slightly different form in Abelard's *Historia calamitatum* (298).[25]

Theirs is to be a chaste love – 'since you yourself, my beloved, command it' – yet there are difficulties, real and imagined, of varying seriousness:

> Oh if only I could live as bride of God!
> Yet I don't hate your love on that account:
>   the bride must love the servants of her God . . .
> But if you prefer and want another woman –
>   know that this is no jest . . .
> God condemns double-tongues and evildoers,
>   and you are one or other, or even both!
> But may God mend your ways, curb this in you –
>   I can't forget you, troubled as I am.

Constance mischievously extends the divinely enjoined loving of one's neighbour to this sportive semblance of amorousness, into which – perhaps only half counterfeiting – jealousy intrudes. Still, she wants to protect her lover from himself. As Hero warns Leander of the dangers of the Hellespont, or Laodamia pleads with her bridegroom not to step ashore first in Troy, so Constance implores Baudri: don't be tempted by perilous places such as Rome, or Mainz. They are barbarous people there – let another man tame those beasts! The solicitude is essentially jocular (with perhaps a touch of anticlerical or nationalist feeling), yet it conceals possessive affection, too: she would miss him so much if he were away on a long journey. She even throws out a provocative hint that, if he stayed away too long, another man might snatch 'the acres you have only just cultivated'. But at once she changes mood again:

> Then others will laugh, but I, most loyal, shall always
> share your laments and tears with you.

That the tears are those Baudri would shed for losing her through his own neglect gives this too an edge of willed absurdity.

In the concluding distichs a series of passionate calls seems to dominate: do not neglect me, come to see me, or else I'll come; I would have come already if I could – what am I saying, madly? If you don't come you do not love me; yet you must come, you do not know in what sickness I languish. Here even a Song of Songs note enters ('amore langueo');[26] and the concluding distich takes us back by echo – 'Expectate, veni . . . sepe vocate, veni' – to the very opening of the *Heroides*, to Penelope's plaint for the absent Ulysses.[27] Yet even here none of this is separable from witty devices of two kinds. In her pressing invitations, Constance thinks up for Baudri all the pretexts he could offer for making a visit to her: he could allege an imaginary summons from bishop or clergy or abbots or the count, on urgent business. And secondly, the reason he is freer in his movements and can visit her more easily than she him is – she is kept from travelling by her 'savage stepmother (*seva noverca*)'. The phrase is used in the *Heroides* by Hypsipyle, of Medea[28] – but here it must mean the Mother Superior of Le Ronceray. Yet even she, adds Constance, is afraid of you.

The subterfuges of the clerical world, and the appropriate and inappropriate uses of Ovid, come together to create a space in which an iridescent, emotionally fluctuating, range of thoughts and fantasies can find expression. In the last resort, I would suggest, there is deep and sensitive feeling, and great delicacy: the literary knowingness and wit provide a cover for these, a way of shape-shifting, lest certain implicit social pacts should be transgressed, and thereby the more-than-half-feigned agitations of attachment become a real (and inevitably in this milieu destructive) unbalancing. Yet my impression is that it was easier for Baudri than for Constance to maintain the safer, jesting tone – that she had an intuition of the kind of anguish Heloise was to live out some decades later, and was determined – with the *Heroides* and her own adroit wit aiding her – to keep that at bay.

Some of Constance's strategies and concerns can be perceived also in the technically less skilled verses that young women in Regensburg composed in the later eleventh century.[29] What is distinctive in some of theirs is a womanly assertion of dominance in relation to men: it is they who lay claim to elaborating norms of elegant behaviour for the men who frequent their company.

Thirty of the brief verse compositions in the Regensburg collection are addressed by young women – whether lay pupils, novices, or nuns – to their *magister* and his friends. It is not certain how many are engaged in the correspondence – whether we should credit a single girl with Cleopatra's 'infinite variety' of mood, and see her as writing at times on behalf of her companions, or (perhaps more plausibly) suppose several writers are involved, as we pass for instance from doting submissiveness to the *magister* to teasing him with exuberant mockery. Other uncertainties arise from the difficult, often obscure language of the verses. The demands of metre and rhyme on 'amateur' poets, not writing in their native tongue, were considerable. Particular kinds of stylistic awkwardness – trying to express complex emotions in the somewhat intractable form of leonine hexameters – have their precise counterpart in the Latin romance *Ruodlieb*. In each case the leonine verse-form is less supple than the mind and imagination that shine through.

At times the girls at Regensburg speak in the challenging, spirited tone that the Herilis, the châtelaine's daughter, uses at her wedding to Ruodlieb's nephew, to ensure that she will not be deceived and taken advantage of once she is married.[30] In both contexts there is a sparkle – or even crackle – of wit, which is·the woman's device to elicit attention and a certain deference from the menfolk. At other times, as in the fragmentary lines of the girl who writes

> You praised my beauty – as if that deserved it.
> If a creature consumed by a ghastly fever deserves any praise . . .[31]

the stark directness is like that with which the older women in *Ruodlieb* – the châtelaine, and the hero's mother – express themselves in painful moments. Not only in language and versification, but in range and articulation of feeling, the girls who composed at Regensburg are close to the author of *Ruodlieb* – close too, I believe, in time and intellectual milieu. In other ways they are nearer to major women writers of earlier centuries. The unusual shifts between sophistication and seeming ingenuousness that we encounter among them can be paralleled to some extent in Hrotsvitha; the fusion of proverbial expressions with intimate personal ones – or the use of established *sententiae* in order to say intimate and affectionate things – has an older counterpart in Dhuoda.

Whatever the artistic limitations of the women at Regensburg, their conquest of new areas of self-expression is evident. In particular, that of assuredness: in at least two of the poems we see women who no longer feel the need to stress (like Dhuoda or Hrotsvitha) that they are *merely* women – frail, lesser creatures compared with men. Instead, they see themselves as 'makers of manners':

> We love only those men whom prudent Excellence has moulded,
> whom Measure has advised to look on her with deference . . .
> Ovid, that knight of the unchaste *Amours*, has tricked you,
> persuading you to love that poem
> by which unhappy men are seduced, and not made finer . . .
> A lady's grace will grant whatever is honourable –
> this she will give to one who always asks fittingly.[32]

Or again:

> Let men whom lewdness delights depart from our company –
> if you should be of that sort, stay away!
> Even men tested in a thousand ways are only just admitted . . .
> As for those to whom Excellence wants us to give our pledge . . .
> let them be duly refined, with manners of distinction.
> For him who has acquired a name for courtesy like our own,
> our maidenly company desires the grace of joy.[33]

These young women are propounding to the men who frequent their society an ideal of gentle and gracious, cultivated behaviour. Against male notions of sexual adventure and conquest, they set those of refinement and restraint, of the man's taking account of the wishes of her whom he admires. She sees herself as able to increase his delicacy and considerateness; she can test his character, and turn him away if he is too coarse for her. There are clearly parallels to these conceptions in the vernacular poetry composed by men in Provençal and German two or three generations later: Theodor Frings and Elisabeth Lea explored a number of analogues semantically in an essay published in 1968.[34] What still seems to me problematic is their claim that 'the independent, self-assured attitude of the woman arises from an ancient popular stratum'.[35] Was it not perhaps rather the rarity and unusually privileged position of educated young women in the eleventh century that enabled them to speak in this way? And *Ruodlieb*'s Herilis, be it remembered, well-born though she was, had to argue skilfully and to fight against firmly-held prejudices before she won assent to her goal of a marriage on equal terms: 'Cur servare fidem tibi debeo, dic, meliorem, / Quam mihi tu debes?' ('Why should I be more faithful to you, tell me, / Than you to me?')

If one accepts the careful and perceptive arguments of Ewald Könsgen, in his edition of the *Epistolae duorum amantium*, we have a much larger group of compositions by one woman writer from a generation or two after Regensburg. Unfortunately what survives consists chiefly of excerpts rather than complete letters. There are forty-nine from the woman, for the most part in profusely rhymed prose; but many of her epistles also contain verses, and five are entirely in verse. They were set down, together with a slightly larger number of excerpts from her lover's letters, by a Cistercian, Johannes de Vepria, at Clairvaux in the 1470s. Könsgen shows convincingly that what Johannes copied were the remains of a genuine interchange between one man and one woman, each with their own habits of style and expression – he was not excerpting a series of model letters devised by a rhetorician for teaching purposes. Könsgen's assignation of the letters to the earlier twelfth century, and to the region of Troyes, seems to me highly probable, even if not wholly certain. Könsgen was concerned, among other things, to underline those elements in the letters which appear to have close parallels in the relation between Abelard and Heloise: thus, the man in the Troyes collection admires the woman for her unique learnedness as well as her beauty; she praises him as both philosopher and poet, and deplores the envy that French rival teachers show towards him.[36] In many respects one can agree with Könsgen that this loving pair of writers 'was *like* Abelard and Heloise'[37] (he judiciously stops short of outright identification). I propose, however, to make some suggestions here of a converse kind – to indicate some elements in these letters that seem to me distinct from all that medieval sources can tell us about Abelard and Heloise; in particular I wish to observe the woman more closely in the way she writes, especially in her verses.

The relationship between the lovers that emerges in these letters is many-sided: there are numerous expressions of exultant adoration, both from him and from her; at times he addresses her in language of courtly obeisance, at others he is palpably domineering. There are misunderstandings, quarrels, alleged infidelities, reconciliations. Even though Johannes de Vepria tended to copy passages primarily of rhetorical interest, the letters continually give hints of an emotional range so varied and unusual that it can scarcely be paralleled either in a romance or an *ars dictandi*. If anything, it is once more Ovid's *Heroides* that can – considered in their full scope – offer certain analogies.

When the man writes: 'I am your servant, most ready for your commands' (30), or 'To his reverend *domina*, her humble servant sends his devoted service' (36), we may think of the language of twelfth-century vernacular *courtoisie*, or again of comparable expressions in the *Heroides*, as when Ovid's Acontius submits to the sovereignty of Cydippe's love: 'Command me to come, as a *domina* commands / . . . You will say to yourself, when you've seen me endure everything, / "Let him serve me, this man who serves so well!"'[38]

The second of these modes of address in the Troyes collection, however, introduces something very different from either courtly or Ovidian love-service. This letter becomes a complaint:

For I must call you so, and say not 'tu' but 'vous', not 'sweet, dear one' but 'my lady', since I am no longer your familiar as before, and you have become much alienated from me.

At other times the man intimates his sexual longing by provocative word-play and even by irreverent biblical allusion:

To my most longed-for hope and so great good that, possessed, it would leave nothing to be longed for, let me deserve to be incorporated in that good ... With what exultation of spirit I'd run to meet your love for me, I want to show by deed rather than prove by words. (46)

As we do not observe the Lord's command unless we love each other, we must be obedient to divine Scripture. (52)

Then again, there are exchanges filled with recriminations: she writes:

If it was necessary for the bond we had established to be broken, even though that bond comprises much bitterness, it will not be broken a second time! (60)

He counters by writing:

Either I have sinned against you greatly, or you had little love for me before – if you reject it now so easily, with so little concern to find out the truth ... And yet, oh my soul, dry your tears, though I cannot dry my own. (61)

And she, in a loving and forgiving answer, says: 'I don't want the tears to stream from your eyes – it's not seemly for a man to weep.' (62)

Again, while in one letter he praises her intellect and eloquence as 'surpassing both your age and your sex' (50), in another, where he pleads with her to forget what he had written, 'impelled by a sudden insult, in the midst of grieving' (75),[39] the words he adds –

For me you are not old: each day you are renewed in my heart, just as the joyous warmth of the year is always new, though spring is showery ... let us enjoy the time that is given us! –

would seem to imply that the woman is now in reality not so young, and that the two had already loved each other a long time.

At moments the man expresses an ideal of perfect mutual love:

The more I drink my fill of your sweetness, the more I thirst. All my wealth has gathered in you alone, all I have power to do has its source in you. So, that we may devote ourselves to each other, you are I and I am you.[40] (77)

Nonetheless, it emerges from one of her letters that this high bond of love, though full of erotic intensity, had not yet led – or perhaps would never lead –

to physical fulfilment. With a bold sacred parody comparable to his, she adapts language that St Paul had used of heavenly love to speak of their love-affair:

till now you have remained with me, with me you have manfully fought the good fight, but you have not yet received the prize. (84)

There are times when she writes to him with deepest deference (here again playing on a phrase in St Paul):[41]

It pleased your nobility to send letters to my littleness, in which, addressing me and promising me the solace of your love . . . you caught me up into the third heaven. (112)

At other times, full of reproach, she claims to regret loving him:

Your feelings no longer match mine, you have changed your ways; so no fidelity anywhere is safe. I repent no little that I have set you alone, beyond all others, so firmly in my heart. (95)

The woman organizes the expression of all that is positive in her love by way of varied literary devices which, taken together, convey her complex thoughts and imaginings. One letter (45) begins in the realm of Christian litanies and passes over into that of Ovid and Terence:

> To her house of cedar,
> (from) the ivory statue on which the whole house rests:
> from whiteness of snow,
> gleam of the moon,
> radiance of the sun,
> splendour of stars,
> perfume of roses,
> beauty of lilies,
> softness of balm,
> fertility of the earth,
> serenity of the sky,
> and whatever sweetness is embraced in their circumference . . .

For I can no more deny myself to you than Byblis to Caunus, Oenone to Paris, or Briseis to Achilles. What more can I say? I send you as many joys as Antiphila had when she received her Clinia. Do not delay in coming – the more swiftly you come, the more swiftly you'll find a reason for joy.

Both for herself and him she uses expressions ('domus cedrina', 'statua eburnea') close to ones that are traditional in the liturgical praise of Mary. She sees herself as providing rest and support for him ('innititur'), as the caryatid of his being. To him she longs to give all that is radiant, sweet and fecund in the world. Yet the classical allusions near the close of the letter at first sound darker notes. She compares the love she feels to that of Byblis, doomed to an unbearable passion for her brother Caunus, to whom Byblis writes a pathetic love-letter before she dies, deranged and grieving (Ovid, *Metam.* IX 453ff); or to that of

Oenone, abandoned by Paris when he captures Helen, loving Paris still and pleading with him 'Have pity!' (*Her.* v 157); and then to that of Briseis, she who reproaches Achilles that he has not claimed her back from Agamemnon, who longs merely to be Achilles' slave-girl, not even aspiring to become his wife (*Her.* III). Only the last recollection, from a play of Terence (*Haut.* 405ff), implies no sorrow: Antiphila faints with joy as she catches sight of Clinia after their long separation, and she recovers consciousness in his arms. This thought here leads into an ardent – and it seems openly sensual – invitation on the writer's part.

In a brief letter that includes a quatrain in verse, her sensual eagerness gives way to a more courtly reflection on the qualities of love, and then, after the verses, her fearless, wholly uncalculating love is once more plain:

> Lover to lover, the greenness of love.
>> No one shall live
>> or grow in good
> * who cannot love
>> and guide their loving.

What further need of words? Kindled by your love's fire, I want to love you forever. Farewell, my one-and-only salvation and only being in the world that I love. (48)

In the verses she sees human love as a source of increase in goodness; the 'guidance' of loving ('amores regere') may well suggest both the courtly quality of *mezura* – discretion and control – and a more elemental concept of fidelity: the many impulses of love, to be good, must be directed towards one alone.

Most arresting, perhaps, is a longer verse message that she sends, though sadly it was not preserved intact by Johannes the copyist:

> I send you the greeting that I would wish sent to me.
>> I know nothing that could be more reviving than this.
> If I possessed all that Caesar ever owned,
>> such wealth would mean nothing to me.
>
> 5 [. . . . .]
>> I shall never have joys except when you give them,
> and grief and mourning follow us constantly.
>> Unless you give it, nothing will be reviving.
> Among all things that the orb contains,
>
> 10   you will be my only glory, always.
> As stones laid on the earth dissolve in fire,
>> and the pyre set above melts in the flame with them,
> so our body wholly fades away in love[42] . . . (82)

There are innumerable formulaic expressions of affectionate greeting in medieval Latin, but these verses, enigmatic not only through their fragmentariness, shine out among greetings by their intensity. The allusion to Caesar's measureless wealth, whilst it is not made into an outcry like Heloise's ('it would seem to me dearer and worthier to be called your harlot than his empress'[43]), is here used for that gentler hyperbole of love – probably popular in origin – which we know from one of the German *Carmina Burana* ('If all the world were mine . . .') and from a thirteenth-century mystical variation upon it by Mechthild of Magdeburg.[44]

In line 7 above, I would take 'us (*nos*)' not as a simple variant of 'I', nor as a 'plural of majesty', but as a sign that the woman here feels able to speak in the name of her lover as well as herself: they share a special closeness when they are dogged by sorrows. After a couplet that expresses loving adoration (9–10), the three verses that follow are remarkable for all that they leave open. Is 'our body' the bodies of the two lovers joined, or is it the human body in general? Is there a death-wish in these lines, the pyre consuming stones and wood and body alike? Or do they evoke an experience of physical ecstasy? I think rather that they may evoke an ideal image of ecstasy, for one who has not known it physically, but who projects by a simile her sense of what total surrender and oneness must be like. That is, the emphasis in the image may be of 'fading away *in love*' rather than fusing with the body of the lover, and it seems artistically right that the word chosen in the human part of the comparison ('vanescit') should be more abstract, less physical than the words in the inanimate part ('liquescunt', 'liquitur'). The phrase already cited from another letter, with its strange combination of sensual provocation and declared lack of fulfilment – 'with me you have manfully fought the good fight, but you have not yet received the prize' – suggests that such a reading may not be unfounded, and that the wistful, moving quality of these verses of greeting is bound up with – in one sense – inexperience.

When we turn to personal poetry by women in the vernaculars, the *trobairitz* who composed in Provençal occupy a unique position, at least as far as the extant records can show. We still know twenty *trobairitz* by name[45] – though only two have more than a single piece ascribed to them. In the Anglo-Norman world, by contrast, there are the variegated works of one keenly conscious woman artist, Marie de France, and there are some illustrious women patrons of poetry; yet we no longer have any personal poems by women from northern France or England. The same holds of Germany and Flanders, at least before the women mystic poets of the thirteenth century. Among early Italian poets, only she who was known as 'the accomplished girl' (Compiuta Donzella) of Florence surfaces among the Tuscans of the Duecento with two sonnets and part of a *tenzone*, and even her historical existence was called in question by many older scholars.[46] In Spain and Portugal the situation is different again. The surviving songs that are put in the mouths of women, the *cantigas de amigo*, in effect constitute a corpus of art-songs composed by men *trovadores*. That such pieces were often performed by women (*jograresas*) is certain, and it seems wholly unlikely that the *jograresas* did not compose as well: nowhere in Europe do we know of any hard and fast demarcation between composing and performing. And one does not need to be a disciple of Herder and the Romantics to see that behind some of the songs by *trovadores* lie more archaic songs composed by women.[47] Yet songs by *jograresas* are not recorded under their names – just as, in the eleventh century, not even one of the women's lyrics enshrined or adapted in the Mozarabic *kharjas* was attributed as composition to a woman, though here too there were women performers who may well also have improvised or composed. The *jograresas* whom we know by name were remembered for jests about their adventurous or scandalous lives, not for their lyrics. So too, from eleventh-century Andalusia, we still have a complete *diwān* by the Cordovan poet Ibn Zaidūn, but merely a handful of couplets by his beloved Wallāda. These are preserved for the most part among reminiscences about Wallāda's love-life, not because anyone cared to copy her collected poetry. For each language and culture, we are much at the mercy of the selectors – the predominantly male world of chroniclers and copyists.

This makes the existence of personal poetry by women in Provençal doubly precious. The amount surviving is, predictably, very small compared with that of the men. To try to characterize what is distinctive here, I shall focus on four examples. I have not chosen the one extant *canso*, historically of great significance, where a woman, Bieiris de Romans, expresses both physical longing and courtly admiration for another, called Maria. For Bieiris's diction and outlook are hard to distinguish from those of men's love-poetry:

> Grant me, fair lady, if you please,
> what I have set my hopes in to have joy,
> since my heart and my longing are in you . . .[48]

Only the manuscript rubric reveals that this is a woman speaking. So too I leave aside the *tensos* between men and women poets, where again it is hard to identify characteristic women's thoughts and feelings or to distinguish these from the rôle-playing which is inseparable from genres of poetic debate. Women poets step into a world where men have already composed for them; at times, in the debate-poetry, the answers given by women may also be fictional, put in their mouths by feigning troubadours. And when women did answer themselves in a *tenso*, they implicitly accepted the rules laid down by men. Yet there are other poems where women deliberately assumed – or prescribed – their own rules, just as the young Latin-writing ladies at Regensburg had done.

Like them, the *trobairitz* – insofar as their identity is known or can be guessed (and much guesswork has indeed been lavished) – belonged to the nobility. Yet they were not, like the Regensburg poets, *in statu pupillari*, and their closest links were not with the clerical world. Thus their *règle du jeu* was less restricted: not less idealistic, but moving towards a different ideal.

To evoke that ideal, a modern analogy may help. In 1959 Simone de Beauvoir published a study of Brigitte Bardot. Bardot, she claimed, incarnated a new kind of heroine: one who is emancipated but not libertine, attractive and ardent, unafraid to express openly her desire for the man she wants. She chooses her lover rather than waits passively to be chosen by him. She has a disarming confidence, free of any sense of moral lapse or social unseemliness:

Desire and pleasure seem to her more convincing than precepts and conventions . . . She does not ask questions, but she brings answers whose frankness may be contagious . . . (This) is to refuse to transform oneself into a remote idol. It is to assert that one is man's fellow and equal, to recognize that between the woman and him there is mutual desire and pleasure. . . . A free woman is the very contrary of a light woman.[49]

This persona, that Simone de Beauvoir saw as something new in the film *Et Dieu créa la femme*, is remarkably close to the persona evident in a number of poems by the women of Provence in the later twelfth and early thirteenth centuries. While at times they take over the rhetoric of the troubadours who are their contemporaries, the most individual expressions of the *trobairitz* are those of a woman who voices her desires candidly, who chooses her man, who (to cite de Beauvoir once more) 'in the game of love is as much a hunter as she is a prey'. One word of caution, however, lest the analogy be extended misleadingly. Although such women as Simone de Beauvoir describes were, then as now, concerned with emancipation in the personal emotional sphere, it would be wrong to think of them as striking a blow for women's freedom in a wider sense. That would have meant raising questions such as occurred neither to the *trobairitz* nor to the heroine of *Et Dieu créa la femme*.

Probably the earliest of the texts we have is a fragment by Tibors, older sister of the high-born poet Raimbaut d'Aurenga:

> Fair sweet friend, I can indeed tell you truly
> that at no time have I been without desire
> since it pleased you that I hold you as my noble lover;
> nor was there ever a time that I had no wish –
> fair sweet friend – to see you often,
> nor ever a season that I repented it,
> nor ever a time, if you departed angry,
> that I had joy until you had returned;
> nor ever . . .[50]

99

Here there is no question of a woman's outcry, such as we know from Anglo-Saxon and Celtic poetry, or from the *kharjas* in Spain. Nor is the love evoked by Tibors a one-sided, unrequited feeling. Many troubadours explore a realm in which 'the one who loves more makes himself the weaker'. (The words are Thomas Mann's, in his story *Tonio Kröger* – designed to epitomize the vulner-ability of the sheer romantic.) Tibors, by contrast – or better, the persona in her lyric – is self-assured; she expresses her joy in loving frankly, without grief or remorse. The tone is 'realistic' – if he went away angry, she couldn't be happy till he came back – yet the real is not allowed to appear indelicate.

This will have been a long strophe – ten verses perhaps, or even twelve.[51] The form is not highly wrought: a simple rhetoric, with much anaphora, prevails. The row of monosyllables in Tibors' first verse ('Bels dous amics, ben vos puosc en ver dir') would have been – at least in Dante's eyes – an artistic blemish.[52] It is the poet's attitude, open about her erotic wishes, and at the same time so measured and composed, which is unusual, and which has no exact parallel, to my knowledge, in the lyrics of men troubadours.

The next piece comprises question and answer: two strophes by two different women. One of them, Almucs (or Almueis) de Castelnau, appears in documents from *ca.* 1155 onwards, in the region of Vaucluse. –

> Lady Almucs, if you allow,
> I'd like to ask you this at least –
> that you curb your anger
> and ill-will for the sake
> of the man who is sighing and lamenting,
> dying, languishing and complaining,
> and humbly asking pardon;
> or else, prepare him the sacrament,
> if you want to make an end of him –
> that'll teach him to fail you!
>
> Lady Iseut, if I knew
> that he repented of the great
> deceit he showed towards me,
> it would be right for me to have
> pity; but it would not befit me –
> since he doesn't extenuate his wrong
> or repent of his failing –
> to give him fresh opportunity;
> yet, if you lead him to penance,
> you can convert me easily.[53]

This time the theme is that of the lady who has been abandoned by her dis-loyal lover. In tone, however, we are worlds away from the genre of *planctus* –

the laments of women bereft or betrayed. In the first strophe, Iseut intercedes for the inconstant lover, asking that Almucs pardon him. The whole of the wording has a particular – I think ironic – edge, because so many of the expressions also have religious connotations. The Virgin Mary's rôle is to intercede for sinners in the spiritual realm, and it is to that realm that certain key words in the strophe belong: 'prejar', 'merces', 'quier perdon humilmen', 'sagramen'. At the same time, the juxtaposition of such expressions with those that belong to the traditional posture of the noble lover – 'qe sospir e plaing / E muor languen e·s complaing' – show that the two ladies are looking at this faulty lover with a critical, even sardonic, eye. A courtly lover asks for his lady's mercy – this fickle creature will certainly need mercy!

In Almucs' reply, we see the playful use both of legal terms ('dreichz', 'tort') and again of religious ones. The leitmotif here is that of penitence and contrition ('qu'el se pentis...n'agues merces...ni·s pentis...faitz lui pentir'). Especially the concluding word, 'convertir', is evocative: if her lover repents, Almucs will be 'converted' – not to the religious life, but back to the rôle of the gracious *domna*, who shows mercy to the man she cares for.

What is striking here is again the note of confidence. The lady looks at the lover who had been casual towards her with a humorously probing, almost supercilious gaze. It is for her to choose whether or not she will see him again, whether or not she will again grant him favours. Once more – even in the case of one jilted – Simone de Beauvoir's image of the woman who makes the active choice is relevant.

My third illustration is a fascinating and enigmatic lyric, in which three women take part in a discussion of love and marriage. Unfortunately we know nothing of their dates or identities: the song survives, in somewhat garbled condition, in only one manuscript, of Italian provenance. Alais begins:

> Lady Carenza, you whose body is so lovely,
> give some advice to my sister and me,
> and, since you know best how to discern what's better,
> advise me as your experience suggests:
> Shall I, in your opinion, take a husband,
> or shall I stay unmarried? – that would please me,
> for I think to breed has little to commend it –
> yet it's too troubling to be husbandless.

Then Yselda, her sister, says:

> Lady Carenza, I'd enjoy taking a husband,
> and yet I think having children is a penance –
> for after that the breasts will hang right down,
> and the belly be wrinkled and wearisome.

Together they receive Carenza's answer:

> Alais and Yselda: I know you have been
> well-educated, you have merit and beauty,
> youth and fresh colour, you are courtly and prized,
> and more sagacious than all other girls;
> thus I advise you, for the seed to be well sown,
> to take as husband the One crowned with knowledge,
> in whom you will bear fruit of glorious children.
> She who marries him remains a maid.
>
> Alais and Yselda: keep a memory
> of me, and keep the shade of his protection;
> when you are with him, beg the glorious one
> that at my death he set me by your side.[54]

The first half of the song is lighthearted, with a number of satiric touches; the second appears to be entirely serious. The two young women ask advice in a way that seems not so much ingenuous as coquettish. Especially in Yselda's way of thinking: it would be amusing to have a husband – yet what a bore to lose one's figure and attractiveness with childbearing! Her evocation of the woman who grows ugly thereby is both pungent and humorous.

In the light of the serious answer given by Domna Carenza, we may well ask whether this satiric image of giving birth does not have a learned source. Indeed such a technique had been used, especially by Saint Jerome, as a means of persuading young girls to a life of virginity, a life dedicated to God alone. Jerome's caricatures of marriage survived in some measure in the medieval treatises De virginitate. In the early twelfth century, according to Abelard's Historia calamitatum, Heloise, trying to convince Abelard that they should not get married, painted a vivid picture of the miseries of married life with children – children who cry and make messes and noise, and prevent the life of pure contemplation – a picture that, although freshly elaborated, owes something likewise to passages in Jerome.[55]

The two lively, pert sisters, Alais and Yselda, receive an answer to their provocative questions which is solemn but also deliberately obscure. It is a challenge to make them pause to think, to resolve the hidden meanings. The seed well sown by the divine lover has as its fruit virginity, highest fruit on the tree of virtues.[56] Those dedicated to it are so near to the bridegroom, Coronat de Scienza, even in this life, that they can mediate with him for others. The thoughts and images here reveal themselves as traditional; yet the existential difficulty of accepting them for those who are young and beautiful finds its rhetorical counterpart in the difficulty of Carenza's language. A pair of strophes which is colloquial in tone is answered by another pair (a strophe and a four-line tornada) where the tone is grave and withdrawn. Yet the identical rhyme-scheme spanning the strophes of question and those of answer establishes a unity as well as a dialectic play in this unique composition.

My final illustration, from the Comtessa de Dia (probably later twelfth century), belongs with the summits of poetic art in Provence:[57]

> I have to sing of what I would not wish,
> so bitter do I feel about him whose love I am,
> as I love him more than anything there is;
> with him, grace and courtesy are no avail to me,
> nor my beauty, merit or understanding,
> for I am deceived and am betrayed as much
> as I would rightly be had I been unwelcoming.
>
> Friend, comfort me in this – that I never failed you
> through any behaviour of mine;
> rather, I love you more than Seguis loved Valensa,
> and it delights me that I vanquish you in loving,
> my friend, for you are the most excellent.
> To me you show arrogance in words and presence,
> and are well-disposed towards everybody else.
>
> It amazes me that your being turns to proudness
> with me, friend – and for this I am right to grieve:
> it is not fair that another love takes you from me,
> however she may address or welcome you; –
> and remember how it was at the beginning
> of our love . . . God forbid
> that the separation should be fault of mine!
>
> The great merit that shelters in your person,
> and the rich worth you have, disquiet me –
> since there's no woman, far or near,
> who, if she would love, does not submit to you;
> yet you, my friend, have enough discernment
> to know who is the loyalest.
> And remember our understanding.
>
> My worth and my nobility must speak for me,
> and my beauty, and still more my loyal heart,
> and so I send you, where you are staying,
> this song, which shall be my messenger;
> and I want to know, my fair gentle friend,
> why you are so hard and strange with me –
> I don't know if it is pride or evil spite.
>
> But I also want you to tell him, messenger,
> that many suffer great loss through too great pride.

While this song is in *canso* form, it is a love-letter rather than a purely lyrical expression. This means that here the poet is able to examine and analyse her love-relationship in much greater psychological detail than is usual in *cansos*. The song is, above all, a meditation: on her own character and qualities, on the seemingly contradictory qualities of her lover, so admirable in himself and yet having become so arrogantly indifferent towards her. It is a series of questions, to discover what has gone wrong in the affair, an attempt by the woman who speaks to justify herself and remove any possible blame from herself. And finally, as becomes more and more clear, it is an attempt to persuade the lover, so that he will think of her lovingly again.

The persuasion remains inseparable from reproaching him, and even from the hint of warning at the close – his own pride may bring him low. Yet uppermost is her longing to make him remember: if only he will recall how it was, then he will want it to be like that again. Thus in the third strophe – 'e membre vos cals fo·l comensamens / de nostr'amor' – and again in the fourth – 'e membre vos de nostres covinens'. The seemingly inconsequential use of 'e' to introduce these pleas is dramatically masterly: it suggests the impulsiveness of her thinking, as if this memory had only then crossed her mind, yet with such force that she must interrupt her argument to tell him.

There is much in the song that seems, superficially, repetitive – yet the reiterations too have subtle dramatic purpose. For the rhetoric mirrors the obsessive quality of the lady's questioning and rebuking: she turns the same thoughts over and over, reverting to them each time with a new attack. Each time we are brought to share her own wonderment more keenly: the injustice of it all – how was it possible?

Among the *cantigas de amigo* composed by men in Spain and Portugal, there are many touching plaints of a woman whose lover has left her. In some of these she also alludes, frankly and without vanity, to her own beauty.[58] I scarcely know this second feature elsewhere in medieval European love-lyric. What gives the Countess of Dia's song a deeper resonance, setting it apart even from the *cantigas*, is the way that, in the midst of perplexity – 'why have I been disprized?' – comes the conviction, 'but I *am* beautiful'. Both in the first and last strophes the woman speaks of 'ma beltatz'. And she compels us to see the whole problem with her eyes. Listening to the song we cannot for a moment doubt that her self-assessment is true, that she has every inner and outer quality which men admire and long for. How then could it be that the one man she loves so ardently,[59] so perfectly, wants her no more? By the time the song is over the poet has fully persuaded the listener of the pity of it; yet whether the heroine will persuade her imaginary listener is left open.

Martín de Riquer, who last edited this song, rightly called it 'comparable a las

Heroidas de Ovidio'.[60] The Countess' ways of articulating a passion in all its movements, of trying to rationalize irrational emotions, of retracing the steps of past love, caressing and goading, indeed bring us close to the world of the *Heroides*, where love is a subject capable not only of direct expressions of joy and pain, but also of finely developed argument. As children of the higher nobility often received a literary education, there is no reason why the Countess of Dia should not have had access to the *Heroides* (though it would be unsafe to assume that she had). If she knew them, it may well be that Ovid helped to give her song its more unusual epistolary qualities, with psychological and rhetorical dimensions that are rare among troubadour lyrics. At the same time, if there was an influence from the *Heroides*, it was no matter of simple imitation. Rather, the artistry of the Countess was such as to be capable of assimilating the realm of the *Heroides* freely and creatively, at Ovid's own imaginative level.

Thus Ovid's heroines seem to loom like exemplars at the close of our enquiry as at the opening. The women poets on whose witness we could draw belonged to the refined and learned milieux of the eleventh and twelfth centuries. The love-poetry that women of the people composed in this time is, inevitably, lost to us. Yet it is certain that they too composed, as well as recited and sang. We have one superbly revealing testimony to this, from another part of Europe. It is an ecclesiastical condemnation, which, while it uses some well-worn polemical expressions typical of its kind, also gives rare and arresting details. It comes from Iceland and relates to the end of the eleventh century, to the lifetime of Saint Jón, the first bishop of northern Iceland (†1121). His biographer tells:

There was a favourite game among the people – which is unseemly – that there should be an exchange of verses: a man addressing a woman, and a woman a man – disgraceful strophes, mocking and unfit to be heard. Bishop Jón had it discontinued – he utterly prohibited the practice. Poems or strophes of love-song (*mansaungs kvaethi etha vísur*) he would not hear recited or allow to be recited; nonetheless he did not altogether succeed in getting them stopped. It is said in this connection (*í frá sagt*) that he got to hear that Klaengr Thorsteinsson, who later became bishop in Skálaholt, and who at this time was a theological student, young in years, was reading the book that is called *Ovidius epistolarum*. In that book is contained a great love-song (*mansaungr mikill*). Jón prohibited Klaengr from reading books of this kind, and moreover declared that for any man it would be onerous enough to guard himself against sensual desire and illicit love, even without stimulating his mind towards it either with any customs or with verses of such a kind.[61]

The saga-writer uses the term 'love-song (*mansaungr*)' both of the customary verse exchanges between men and women of the people and of the *Heroides*. Did he, or the student Klaengr, or Saint Jón himself, perceive a real affinity between these two at first glance so disparate kinds of love-song – the improvised verses in which girls answered men in the vernacular, and Ovid's crafted symmetries, Helen answering the verses of Paris, Hero those of Leander, Cydippe those of Acontius? Perhaps for the Icelanders the link was merely one of erotic content, rather than that of poetic exchanges, in both popular and learned modes, whereby women answer the utterances of men. Yet it was precisely this link which intuitively the Continental women, from Constance to the Countess of Dia, made for themselves. They brought together something freshly improvised – in direct response to the verses that men in their world addressed to them – and something learnt: a range of artifice that could keep a heroine relatively safe from the real. The spontaneous movement of poetic answering, and the calculated movement of literary shaping, were the two constant and inseparable elements in their verse.[62]

5　Heloise

In the early 1130s, half a century after Constance had written her loving letter to Baudri of Bourgueil,[1] Heloise (*ca.* 1100–63) wrote her letters to Abelard. In Constance's lines, the hyperboles of Christian spiritual friendship, common since the Patristic period, are knowingly suffused with erotic colour. Or better, Constance elaborates a counterpoint between her protestations that the feeling and the life are chaste and her use of unchaste allusions and language to heighten her expressions of feeling. In showing her awareness of the incongruities, Constance introduces elements of humour, flirtation, and deliberate make-believe. She genuinely admires Baudri, who had taught her to compose Ovidian verse, and who had shown her how to study the pagan myths – to find a moral, or witty, allegoric meaning in them. She is fond of him, partly because of the way he pays her flattering attentions in his verse. The thought, 'in a different world we would be lovers', must have crossed her mind – indeed it seems latent in many turns of phrase in her letter. Yet here it is the *fiction* of eroticism which is also a guarantee of freedom, for Constance as for Baudri.

Constance wants Baudri to visit her if and when he can, and especially to continue writing to her. Since he has not come for a whole year, she brings accusing hints that he is being neglectful, or even disloyal. These moments might make one think of Heloise's first letter to Abelard – except that with Constance none of this is wholly in earnest. There is a sense in which her literary devices deliberately undermine any straightforward rendering of emotions. To say, with older scholars, that she was merely composing a literary exercise for Baudri is to say too little. Hers is a deftly calculated histrionic performance, in which the personal expression *is* the sum of the incongruous conventions, Patristic and Ovidian, modifying one another.

When we turn to Heloise, we can see that in a sense she, like Constance, writes her own *Heroides*. Her first two letters to Abelard express a heroine's affective states – vehement longing, the grief of abandonment, loving admiration *and* reproach of Abelard, even resentment of God, who has severed Abelard from her – a range wider and deeper than in the Epistles of Ovid, and incomparably more serious than in that of Constance.

It is possible, and legitimate, to consider these letters as works of high art, leaving in abeyance the question, how far and in what ways they are also biographical reality.[2] Heloise is evidently fully familiar with the literary past that Constance knew – the Ovidian tradition, as well as the letters of ardent Christian friendship and spiritual advice perfected by Jerome, writing to his circle of devoted women. The difference from Constance lies above all in the singlemindedness. Heloise's letters seem to bar incongruity; any possibility of humorous undercutting of the impassioned language is excluded. Rather, Heloise summons every resource she has – stylistic, intellectual and emotional – to express her experience (real and imagined) in the manner she deems most worthy. For in these Epistles, unlike Constance's, there is no playful posturing. The writer communicates what she feels she must.

From Heloise we have three letters to Abelard, preserved complete in seven of the nine manuscripts of their collected correspondence, and preserved also in the French translation of the Abelard-Heloise letters by Jean de Meun. We likewise have her *Problemata*, surviving in a unique manuscript, copied only towards 1400: this is a series of her questions, chiefly on problematic passages in Scripture, which she directed to Abelard with a letter introducing them, together with Abelard's replies. Finally, from the time after Abelard's death, we have a brief letter of hers to Peter the Venerable, the influential abbot of Cluny who gave protection and shelter to Abelard in his last years.[3]

Neither this letter nor that introducing the *Problemata* has ever been thought to be by anyone but Heloise. It is well known, by contrast, that many scholars have questioned the authenticity of her three letters in the collected correspondence. As the *Problemata* are closely linked with these letters, being, in Van den Eynde's words, their 'continuation and complement',[4] it is hard to see how one can consistently deny Heloise the letters to Abelard without also rejecting her share of the *Problemata*. The reason that this has never been challenged – one cannot but suspect – is because it contains nothing that could be thought unedifying. In other words, the doubts expressed about the three earlier letters may be motivated, even if largely unconsciously, by the doubters' disquiet at certain 'profane' passages encountered there.

But the letter-collection, insofar as it is a unified work, presents a further problem. Heloise outlived Abelard by twenty years, and it is possible that in those years she edited their correspondence to some extent, in order to leave it to posterity as a coherent testament and a just record of her former husband and herself. Yet one cannot rule out the possibility that someone other than, or later than, Heloise organized the letters as a collection, and, in so organizing, made certain editorial modifications both to her letters and to Abelard's. Even admitting this possibility, I still accept as substantially by Heloise the three letters (*Epp.* II, IV, VI in the collection)[5] which the manuscript tradition ascribes to her unanimously, as well as her parts of the sequel, the *Problemata* – where again we may reckon with an element of redaction in the formalized question-and-answer schema that follows her opening petition[6] – and the letter to Peter the Venerable. It is not possible to demonstrate definitively that such acceptance is well founded, yet it is based on what is still the simplest and soberest hypothesis regarding the texts and their transmission. By contrast, every attempt so far to attribute Heloise's letters to someone else has revealed itself full of fantastications – whether misreadings of the Latin, *a priori* assumptions about what an abbess could or could not have written, or additional postulates 'multiplied beyond necessity'.[7] Thus – to pause only at the most recent discussion of the matter – I think one can demonstrate that John Benton's attempt (*Trier 1980*) to ascribe Heloise's third letter to Abelard relies on methods and premises that reveal themselves to be questionable *on grounds of textual criticism alone* (see the Excursus below, pp. 140–3). This does not mean that everything in the Abelard–Heloise collection as transmitted is above suspicion. In particular, *Ep.* VIII, Abelard's *Regula* for Heloise and her nuns, which survives complete in only one of the nine manuscripts of the collection and does not occur in Jean de Meun's French version, still poses thorny textual problems.[8] But neither this nor the wider (and wilder) speculations about authenticity need impinge fatefully on a detailed attempt at a *lectura* of the letters of Heloise. In what follows they will be read not as historical source-material, but principally as works of imagination, shaped in a literary way. For they are that at least, whatever else they are besides.

The writing that we still have by Heloise is small compared with that of Dhuoda; in quantity it is perhaps a sixth of what remains of Hrotsvitha's work, little more than a hundredth of Hildegard's. While till now there has been scant close attention to Heloise's writing as such, there is a vast literature on the 'legend' of Heloise, and on the ever-fascinating theme 'Heloise and Abelard'. There can be no question of trying to add to this literature in the present context. Here only a few precise problems relating to Heloise's style and thought can be broached. I should like to concentrate especially on one that seems to me central to any attempt to assess Heloise as a writer: the problem of continuity. Heloise, whose first two extant letters, like the *cansos* of the Countess of Dia, are close to the most tragic elements in the *Heroides* – the laments of women loving hopelessly and forsakenly – goes on to letters and problems that in their acute spiritual gaze are close to some of Hildegard's finest letters. She passes from the expressive sphere of the *trobairitz* to that of the saint. What is the relation between the earlier and later thoughts that Heloise directs to Abelard? Can one see coherence in the nature and growth of the questioning in her writing?

Even if, as I hope to indicate, there is real continuity, the two first letters, in which Heloise dwells on her human love, the two which alone have given her a place in world literature, inevitably in some ways stand apart. They are both the most intimate and the most rhetorically brilliant. They move us because of their inner sorrow, but also because Heloise has effectively marshalled every device towards the intent of moving. To say that these are her most beautiful letters – in their unusual content as in their verbal artistry – is not, I believe, anachronistic or 'unmedieval'. It can be shown, for instance, that at least two early readers of the letters – Jean de Meun and Petrarch – responded more intensely to these two than to anything else in the collection. The asides and exclamations which Jean de Meun scatters in his French version, and Petrarch's marginal notes in the Latin manuscript he owned, are both more frequent in these two letters of Heloise than in the rest of the correspondence, and reveal more keenly emotional reactions than the two poet-readers allowed themselves elsewhere.[9] It is also because of these two letters, even more than the *Historia calamitatum*, that the historical figures of Abelard and Heloise captured the European imagination, almost as if they were a pair of lovers out of legend. There are perhaps only one or two truly comparable examples where writing has given historical lovers such a mythic dimension: thus Dante created the myth of Beatrice, Petrarch that of Laura. Here, however, it was the woman, not the man, who by her writing created loving myth out of harsh real events.

The highly-wrought verbal art of these letters is evident also at the start of Heloise's third letter (*Ep.* VI) – though much less so after that – and again in the letter with which she introduces her *Problemata*. Thus, in the indications that follow, diverse parts of Heloise's writing will be treated with diverse emphasis. Her daring stylistic flights need some comments on the nature and functions of their *ornatus*; but the later part of the third letter, and the *Problemata*, require principally a thematic discussion, to discover to what extent the motifs and pre-occupations link with those of the earlier writing.

On the distinctive technical features of Heloise's style, and their probable source, I shall summarize, and briefly add to, what I argued and documented in the Trier symposium on Abelard.[10] There an enquiry into Heloise's practice of prose rhythms showed, first, that at the ends of sentences she used certain kinds of cadence (in particular, *cursus tardus* and *cursus velox*) purposely: a statistical test that enables one to distinguish between the observed and the expected frequency of any possible cadence showed that Heloise's choice of these two types could not be fortuitous. Second, and more surprisingly, Heloise's proportion of 'slow' to 'swift' cadences was the opposite of that found in all the major northern French writers of her day: while they, if they used *cursus* in their prose, favoured swift cadences far more than slow, Heloise, though using both swift and slow rhythms deliberately in her sentence-endings, chose to conclude more than 25 per cent of her sentences with a *tardus*, as against 16 per cent with a *velox*.

Third, this particular distribution corresponds precisely to that chosen and diffused by a leading Italian teacher of letter-writing in the first years of the twelfth century, Adalbertus, whereas the French teachers of this art – at least all those traced till now – overwhelmingly preferred *velox* cadences to *tardus* ones. Fourth, the model epistles in Adalbertus' 'art of letter-writing' share with Heloise's letters not only their choice of sentence-endings but also, within sentences, their use of elaborate rhythmic parallelism in phrases and clauses, a parallelism that, especially when intense emotion is to be expressed, is heightened by frequent, often almost regular, rhymes. That is, it seems that Heloise was taught to compose in an Italianate style, one that may have been quite new in France at the time of her adolescence. While we cannot identify with certainty a precise treatise or teacher that Heloise knew, as too little is yet known about the first followers of Adalbertus, or about the dating and diffusion of their works (many of which, moreover, remain unedited), we can safely say that Heloise's letter-writing is technically of the 'Adalbertian' kind.

What of Abelard? The detailed evidence of a sample from his letters showed similar tendencies in *cursus* to those of Heloise, though they were not as marked (18 per cent of *tardus* cadences, for instance, to 16 of *velox*); so, too, his use of rhythmic parallelism and rhyme within sentences was less sustained than Heloise's.

This seems to warrant an inference that may cause many scholars surprise or even alarm. It has been tacitly or expressly assumed hitherto that, in their relationship, Heloise, some twenty years younger than Abelard, was in all respects the disciple and he the master – that he imparted knowledge to her while she absorbed it. And yet we know from the *Historia calamitatum* that Heloise, when Abelard first met her, was already 'supreme in the abundance of her literary knowledge (*per habundantiam litterarum erat suprema*, 285–6)', and that this had made her 'most renowned in the whole kingdom' of France (*in toto regno nominatissimam*, 288). This implies, I believe, that we should not imagine Abelard as giving Heloise her literary formation. Her stylistic training will almost certainly be something she had acquired before meeting Abelard. Indeed, unless they were both influenced by a common friend, Italian or Italian-trained (a notion for which we have no evidence, though it cannot be dismissed out of hand), it would seem that Abelard assimilated to quite an extent Heloise's habits in the epistolary style, rather than the other way round. Even though his letters do not show her distinctive features in the same fullness, it is demonstrable that his *tardus* and *velox* cadences are, like hers, deliberate, and that their proportion in his letters sets him too apart from the mainstream of the northern French writers who use *cursus*. It seems more plausible to assume that Abelard was influenced to some extent by Heloise's 'un-French' mannerisms, than that she should have derived these from him and then outdone him in their use. As we have no letters of Abelard's that can be dated before 1117, the year he met Heloise, this remains a hypothesis, yet it is the one that accords best with the stylistic facts that have emerged.

At all events, I think we should envisage between Abelard and Heloise a literary and intellectual partnership that was not wholly one-sided. If we ask, what did that partnership consist in, what did they read and discuss together in the time before their enforced separation, the best conjectures can be found among those texts that both he and she cite oftenest, and cite at times in such unexpected contexts that it gives the impression of spontaneous recollection – Ovid and Lucan, Horace and Persius, Cicero and Seneca, Augustine and Jerome. So, too, the parallels between Heloise's third letter and contributions to the *Problemata*, and works of Abelard's such as the *Sic et Non* and the *Ethica*, may be better explicable in terms of Abelard's and Heloise's shared pursuit of certain problems than in terms of her slavishly repeating things he had already set down in written form, or (as was recently suggested) of Abelard himself writing one of Heloise's letters and passing it off as hers. She who at seventeen was renowned in all France for her literary knowledge was assuredly capable, in her thirties, of writing independently.

Not only the details of rhythm and rhyme, but also the structural aspects (*dispositio*) of Heloise's first two letters to Abelard, were thought out with the utmost care. Each letter can be seen in terms of four principal movements,[11] each movement displaying its own distinctive register of effects. The first letter might, after the opening salutation, be demarcated as follows:

    I (4–67) The 'epistle to a friend'
    II (68–126) Abelard's obligation
    III (127–216) Heloise's description of her state of mind
    IV (217-75) Heloise's imprecations and reproaches

The superscription that precedes has its own subtlety:

To her lord, or better, her father; to her husband, or better, her brother; his handmaid, or better, his daughter; his wife, or better, his sister – to Abelard, Heloise.

Behind the verbal conjuring, that might seem superficial, lies the attempt to convey the gamut of relationships that she and Abelard have experienced. The salutation recalls the tyrannous, domineering aspect of their first encounters, the 'spiritual fatherhood' of the religious founder in their latest ones; it recalls their marriage, their equality of kinship in Christ, and last, their uniqueness.

The opening sentence in the letter itself raises a serious textual problem. I believe that Heloise's original wording there can be arrived at with the help of

Jean de Meun's rendering of this sentence (and Jean was probably using for his translation a Latin manuscript older than any of the extant ones). If Jean's version is correct, Heloise begins by saying:

Dearest one, your man has recently shown me your letter, which you sent to our friend for consolation.[12]

That is, Heloise, far from complaining that she had caught sight of the *Historia calamitatum* only by chance (*forte*), as the Latin manuscripts suggest, is acknowledging that Abelard had arranged for a copy to be sent her. The original had been written by Abelard for a mutual friend, with a view to consoling him for his griefs by recounting the incomparably greater griefs Abelard himself had lived through. It has been argued, notably by Mary McLaughlin, that the *Historia* was primarily a public 'open letter', not a private one – an attempt by Abelard at self-vindication, to prepare ecclesiastical opinion for his departure from Saint-Gildas and his return to the schools in Paris.[13] And it has usually been assumed that the friend who needed solace was a literary fiction of Abelard's, chiefly because the idea that Heloise saw the work fortuitously seemed so implausible. If this idea, however, goes back only to a textual error, the real existence of the friend for whom the *Historia* was first written remains perfectly possible. On the other hand, this would not preclude the possibility that Abelard had from the start the sense of a potential wider audience, or that his recounting of misfortunes also contained an element of self-defence, such as he might have wished to present more publicly.

The first movement of Heloise's letter, in which she meditates on this *epistola ad amicum* of Abelard's, shows many of her stylistic habits, and hints for the first time at motifs she will later extend. At the opening, as often elsewhere, she balances two thoughts of the kind 'the more . . . the more (*tanto . . . quanto*)': 'I began to read the letter the more ardently, as I embrace the writer the more lovingly.' Letter and writer are then contrasted as reality (*res*) against words and image (*verba, imago*): the writer cannot really return to her through a mere letter, and yet, if he is lost to her, she herself is lost, because her existence lies in him. This paradox does not become explicit at the opening – it is developed luxuriantly in later passages; here there is only the first faint sign of how absence could become presence.

Almost everything in Abelard's letter to his friend was 'full of gall and vinegar' – full, that is, of the two bitter drinks which, in the words of the Good Friday liturgy, were inflicted on the dying Christ. Abelard had frequently in the *Historia calamitatum* compared his own tribulations with those that Christ endured,[14] and Heloise seems to recall these comparisons as she writes of 'your unending crosses'.

She conjoins this expression with 'the pitiful story (*miserabilem historiam*) of our entry into monastic life'; yet in the whole of the reflection on Abelard's letter that follows, she leaves herself out of consideration and thinks fervently only from Abelard's standpoint. She is Abelard's totally committed partisan. It is the 'persecutions' of him by his teachers, the 'supreme betrayal' of his mutilation, the 'execrable envy' of his colleagues, the condemning of his 'glorious' book, *Theologia*,[15] that she insists upon.

No one could read that 'pitiful story' (the phrase recurs at 30) without weeping – she means, weeping for Abelard – and again the parallel constructions drive this home: 'it renewed my griefs the more abundantly, as it expressed each single thing the more diligently, and it increased them the more in that you told that your dangers were still increasing'. Abelard's sense that his life was in peril among the hostile Breton monks at Saint-Gildas plunges Heloise into mortal fear and anguish for him, and it is this more than anything else that makes her beseech him to write and console her. The words 'beseech' and 'alone', first sounded here (*obsecramus*, 39; *sole*, 41), recur almost like refrains after this point. Near the start Heloise speaks not for herself only, but in plurals that denote both her and the community of nuns at the Paraclete, the community that is Abelard's creation. Not till the end of the second movement does she set this decorum aside, and claim his debt to her alone, his 'one-and-only' (*unica* – the word that, at the opening and close of the letter, she also uses of him).

Solemnly Heloise alleges a precedent, the ancient *auctoritas* of Seneca, for the custom of writing letters of consolation. Throughout Heloise's writing, the pagan authors, the Church Fathers and the Bible are cited – sometimes at surprising length – in ways that make clear the heroic dimension in which she tries to set the particular thoughts and actions of Abelard and herself: their own lives will be lived worthily if they harmonize with such exemplars. Having quoted Seneca, Heloise makes the point personal in three parallel phrases. The third, which includes an 'I beseech (*obsecro*)' in parenthesis, is not quite parallel to the other two: it carries a hint of challenge and even reproach. Abelard can, thank God, be restored to her by letters:

> . . . in this at least
> you are not forbidden by any envy,
> you are not prevented by any hardship,
> you are not, I beseech, held back by any negligence.

The movement ends with a series of rhyming antitheses, evoking the effect of the *Historia calamitatum* on the friend and on herself. But the rhymes carry over into the opening of the next movement, urging Abelard to his obligation – a movement that begins with an imperative, and again an *obsecro*:[16]

cum eius intenderes consolationi,
nostre plurimum addidisti desolationi,
et dum eius mederi vulneribus cuperes,
nova quedam nobis vulnera doloris inflixisti
                et priora auxisti.
Sana, obsecro, ipsa que fecisti,
qui que alii fecerunt curare satagis.
Morem quidem amico et socio gessisti
et tam amicitie quam societatis debitum persolvisti,
sed maiore te debito nobis astrinxisti,
quas non tam amicas   quam amicissimas,
non tam socias   quam filias   convenit nominari,
vel si quod dulcius   et sanctius   vocabulum potest excogitari.

when you were intent upon his consolation,
you added greatly to our desolation,
and when you wanted to heal his wounds,
you inflicted as it were new wounds of grief on us,
        and increased the old.
Heal, I beseech, the wounds that you have caused,
you who are trying to heal wounds caused by others.
You have done right by a friend and comrade,
paying the debt of friendship and comradeship;
but you bound yourself to us by a greater debt,
we who must be called not friends but closest friends,
not comrades but daughters,
or any sweeter and holier name, if such can be conceived.

Though Heloise speaks in the plural – '*our* desolation' – her expression here begins to take on connotations that belong to the unique bond with her *unicus*. In the Ovidian language of love, love is an inflicted wound that only the beloved can heal, and the sweetest name conceivable is that of the person loved. Later Heloise, in a daring new modulation of these lines, shows what was here left unexpressed: though the name wife might seem holier and more valid (*sanctius ac validius*), that of concubine or whore always seemed sweeter (*dulcius*). So, too, in the thoughts that follow, everything that has an overt meaning in the monastic context likewise has a hidden one in that of love. A few examples: Abelard is 'solus' in relation to the Paraclete –

after God, you alone are the founder of this place,
you alone the constructor of this oratory,
you alone the builder of this community.

But a fourfold 'solus' recurs to bring out his bond with Heloise alone –

you who are alone my cause of grieving,
be alone in the grace of consoling.
You alone, indeed, can sadden or console me,[17]
and you alone owe me so much.

Again, at the Paraclete Abelard has planted 'tender plants', that need his 'frequent irrigation': the overt meaning is spiritual refreshment, yet one cannot help calling to mind the (somewhat later) model love-letter by the Italian rhetorician Boncompagno, where a neglected wife, whose husband has long been absent in the schools of Paris, laments that 'no rain or dew lights upon my field'.[18]

Heloise cites St Paul as *auctoritas* for the irrigation of the field of the mind, and in a series of parallel antitheses contrasts Abelard's undeserving plantation in Brittany with the deserving one that is truly his:

Quid tue debeas attende,
qui sic curam impendis aliene.

Think what you owe your own vine,
you who lavish such care on the alien one.

Abelard's monastery becomes almost a rival to her – and hers – for his care and affection. And here at last Heloise speaks of his debt to her alone: playing on Paul's phrase (1 Corinthians 7: 3), 'A husband shall render his wife his debt', she intimates that the sexual obligation, to which Paul alluded, culminates in the debt that she now claims, 'to be paid the more devotedly to your one-and-only one'.

The movement closes with a contrast between *auctoritas* and reality: the Church Fathers of old wrote letters 'of exhortation, or even consolation' to holy women – but you have disregarded this and not tried to console me, either by words when you were present or by a letter when absent. The long sentence, taking 'tanto ... quanto' (and 'eo ... quo') in its course, comes to a climax with 'you, the more indebted to me in that I have always, as is evident to all, embraced you with immoderate love'.

Again a phrase at the close of a movement, 'as is evident to all (*ut omnibus patet*)', prepares a dominant motif in the movement that follows. With expressions such as 'all men know' (127) and 'your betrayal, known everywhere' (128), Heloise as it were calls the outer world to witness: throughout the burning utterances that now emerge she affirms that her thoughts are no mere imaginings, but are evidently and objectively true.

Repeatedly, with words denoting command ('iubere', 'iussus', 'iussio'), Heloise hammers home the charge that she had become a nun only because Abelard compelled her to:

ad tuam statim iussionem tam habitum ipsa quam animum immutarem,
ut te tam corporis mei quam animi unicum possessorem ostenderem.

at once at your command I changed both my habit and my spirit,
to show that you were the unique owner of both my body and my spirit.

The gesture of abnegation is expressed in such poised symmetrical phrases, with her characteristic heavy idiom ('tam . . . quam') for pairing concepts. Heloise interprets this abnegation, which led her to transform or indeed destroy her life at Abelard's behest (*me ipsam pro iussu tuo perdere*), as an example of perfect friendship, in both the Christian and the Ciceronian sense. Ambrose, following Cicero, had exalted an ideal of wholly disinterested *amicitia*, in which each friend loves the other for no gain or advantage but for themselves alone.[19] This, she now claims, is what she fulfilled flawlessly in the time she and Abelard were lovers:

Nichil umquam (deus scit) in te nisi te requisivi:
te pure, non tua concupiscens.
Non matrimonii federa, non dotes aliquas expectavi,
non denique meas voluptates aut voluntates,
sed tuas, sicut ipse nosti, adimplere studui.

I never (God knows) looked for anything in you save you,
longing for you alone, not what was yours.
I expected no marriage-bond, no dowry,
it was not my ecstasies or my desires
that I tried to fulfil – as you know – but yours.

Abelard is her crown *auctoritas*: he himself, she reminds, had set out in the *Historia* the reasons why Heloise 'preferred love to marriage, freedom to a chain'. At that time her argument for free love, as Abelard reported it, was urgent in tone, fraught with anxiety, for then he was trying to overrule her, insisting upon marriage. Now, untied by circumstance, it becomes a triumphant affirmation: if Augustus offered her the world, 'it would seem to me dearer and worthier to be called your prostitute than his empress'. Once more a pair of comparatives ('karius . . . et dignius') qualifies the name that Heloise takes to herself: at first she had seen the sweetest name among the 'amicissimas . . . filias', then in the words 'concubina' and 'scortum', now in 'meretrix'.

The remainder of the movement consists of a series of justifications for this. It begins with a Boethian allusion: wealth and power such as an emperor has are a matter of Fortuna, not of his own quality of being (*virtus*).[20] Then Heloise reverts to, or better extends, the arguments of Cicero (who, writing *de amicitia*, had envisaged only friendship between men). In marriage, she argues – with profound originality – love must play precisely the rôle that friendship can in other relationships. Marriage for anything less than pure love is prostitution. Each partner must value the other, and cherish him or her, as the best on earth. Her 'authority' for this (again by way of Cicero) is the one *meretrix* of antiquity who was renowned as a *philosopha* – Aspasia,[21] the courtesan who was the mistress of Pericles. It is she who set up this free, disinterested ideal in the relation between a man and a woman, and in so doing the pagan hetaira, according to Heloise, showed her thoughts to be those of a saint (*sancta*).

Yet what Aspasia recommended, that each partner find his ideal in the other, could in all other couples be no more than a 'blissful delusion (*beata fallacia*)'; only for herself, Heloise concludes, was it 'manifest truth (*veritas manifesta*)'. She protests this in an exultant series of rhetorical questions, phrased with poetic symmetry, which together project the 'ideal Abelard':

Quis etenim regum aut philosophorum tuam exequare famam poterat?
Que te regio aut civitas seu villa videre non estuabat? . . .
Que regina vel prepotens femina gaudiis meis non invidebat vel thalamis?

Who ever, among kings or philosophers, could match your fame?
What region or city or village did not burn to see you? . . .
What queen or great lady did not envy my joys and my bed?

Then, more calmly, in rhythms closer to prose, Heloise singles out the qualities – so unlike those of other philosophers – that made Abelard irresistibly attractive: his gifts as love-poet and troubadour. In a hyperbole that echoes Ovid,[22] she claims these made him known throughout the world. Even the unlettered loved his melodies (the implication must be, that the words were in Latin, and the phrase 'metro vel rithmo' suggests that some of Abelard's love-poetry was in classical measures, some in accentual strophic forms). And she, the heroine of his love-songs, became envied by other women.

This thought leads to another bout of questions, rising to a crescendo. The exultation becomes tragic: 'Whom, of those who envied me then, would my calamity now . . . not move to pity?' Implicit is the motif of Fortuna and the savage reversal she has caused, which Heloise develops in a lyrical lament in her next letter. Here instead the questions lead back to moral analysis. First comes a word-play filled with that keenly serious wit which we associate especially with the Renaissance 'metaphysical' poets:

Que plurimum nocens,
plurimum, ut nosti, sum innocens.

I who, profoundly nocent,
am, as you know, profoundly innocent.

The argument defending this paradox continues in balanced antitheses, and continues by way of word-play. It is an argument Heloise shares with Abelard, indeed it was to become a cornerstone of Abelard's *Ethica*: the moral goodness or badness of any action can be judged not by its effect (*effectus*), but only by the state of mind (*affectus*) and the intentions of the doer. She summons Abelard to judge:

tuo examini   cuncta committo,
tuo per omnia   cedo testimonio.

I commit everything   to your scrutiny,
I yield in all things   to your testimony.

But at once the final movement, that of the imprecations and reproaches, opens with a ringing double challenge: 'Dic unum, si vales . . . dic, inquam, si vales . . .' ('Tell me one thing, if you can . . . tell me, I say, if you can . . .') Throughout the accusations, the contrast between pure and selfish friendship, love and lust, is held in tension. If Abelard has neglected Heloise, who had given herself totally to him, has he not failed in that ideal of *amicitia* which she fulfils? Was his no truthful love but only exploitation? Once more the outer world is in the wings, ready to try to judge, though Heloise's concern for objective truth means that the truth of intention must be found within him and her alone. Has he ceased to think of her because his sexual desire for her has ceased? –

This, belovedest, is not so much my conjecture as that of all,
    not so much a particular as a general,
    not so much a private as a public one.

Even the reproach is punctuated by the superlative 'belovedest (*dilectissime*)', and a moment later Heloise goes on to the thought, 'if only I could make up some pretexts for excusing you!' – where challenge, sorrow and reproach blend as they do for the deserted Phaedra or Medea in Ovid.

To reveal the full extent of her sacrifice in obeying Abelard, she insists it was in no way an act of submission to God:

In this I can expect no reward from God,
for whose love it is clear I have as yet done nothing . . .
as if you were thinking of Lot's wife, turning back,
you committed me to monastic habit and vows
before you committed yourself to God:
in this alone, I confess, that you trusted me so little,
I was overcome with grief and shame.
I would equally, God knows, have preceded or followed you
headlong to Vulcan's pit, at your command,
without the slightest wavering.
For my mind was not with me but with you;
now most of all, if not with you, it is nowhere –
without you it cannot be.
Let it be at peace with you, I beseech.

This is the climax both of the reproaches and the avowal of love. Here, uniquely, the biblical *auctoritas* works as a pseudo-exemplar: it is *as if* a moment in the Bible had sanctioned Abelard's shameful suspicion that Heloise might, left at liberty in the world, 'turn back' to worldly pleasure with another man. The denial of this becomes a soaring hyperbole, one such as some troubadours and *trouvères* were to use in their love-poetry in the decades after Heloise.[23] The lover would gladly go to hell to find his beloved (this may be a reflection of the Orpheus-motif in popular tradition); he would rather be in hell with her than in heaven without her (this relies upon – and defies – the specifically Christian concept of beatitude). But for a woman who loves her husband so greatly there was an exemplar in the ancient world, and I think Heloise alludes implicitly to that: it is Alcestis who was ready to go to hell for her husband's sake, and especially, was ready to precede him there, because he asked her to.[24]

From this affirmation of unqualified love Heloise passes to a measured, simple restatement in terms of Christian *amicitia*: in spirit, friends are one, each has existence in the other; so too, earlier in this letter, Heloise had spoken of the betrayal of Abelard 'taking myself away from myself, by taking you', and in her next letter she laments that she has not even Abelard's presence 'to restore me at times to myself'.[25] While these turns of phrase are familiar from a long tradition,[26] they are as if freshly rediscovered by her.

In the concluding sentences, that span from the imperative 'Memento, obsecro' (257) to the imperative 'Perpende, obsecro' (273), Heloise's justification of her perfect love ('I have kept nothing back for myself, unless to become yours now even more'), her reproaching and her imploring come together. Yet the imprecations at the close change in their emphasis: in her fierce desire for Abelard to write, Heloise at last dangles before him the possibility that his writing may, by refreshing her, make her 'more eager for the service of God' (268-9). At other moments in her next two letters, she seems again to think that she cannot serve God; but at this moment at least she knows that this half-promise is her most effective means of persuasion: it will prompt the kind of letter from Abelard that he still could write to her. At the close she is no longer analysing her emotions: she is talking his language, that of the monk and the spiritual director; for the first time in the correspondence she is making an effort to meet Abelard halfway.

Abelard's reply to this letter is aloof in tone. He defends himself from her charge of neglect by saying, he had never written to console her, or give her spiritual guidance, because he was sure she was too wise and holy to need that. She and her sisters are so devout, he claims, that it is they who could be helping him, by their prayers. These will be more acceptable in God's sight than any prayers of his own. He cites many *auctoritates*, from the Bible, Gregory the Great, and even from early Frankish history (Gregory of Tours), on the efficacy of prayers, and especially of the prayers of women.

As Heloise had turned from her community to her own unique bond with

Abelard, he makes a similar transition: 'But now to leave aside your holy convent . . . let me come to you alone, you whose holiness, I doubt not, prevails greatly before God, and who must most especially do for me all you can.'[27] Full of praises for Heloise, couched in biblical phrasing, he claims that her prayers for him will be the most effective of all. He ends by saying, in the Psalmist's phrase, 'if the Lord delivers me into the hands of my enemies' – that is, he explains, if the hostile monks in Brittany succeed in murdering me – then bring my corpse back to the Paraclete and pray for me in the sight of my tomb.

It is the facile assumption of Heloise's prayerful frame of mind, and the morbid thoughts anticipating his own violent death, that release the torrent of grief in Heloise's reply. Her second letter is on the one hand a bitter self-analysis, to prove to Abelard that she is not holy in her motives (and hence, that she cannot help him but desperately needs his help); on the other, it is a series of lamentations at having lost Abelard physically and at the prospect of losing him totally.

There can be no doubt that Heloise was shaken by Abelard's notion that his death might be imminent. Yet the lamentations are far from any direct 'shock-reaction': they have been thought through meticulously and endowed with form – even, as was to be expected, given Heloise's schooling, with artificial, quasi-poetic form. Here too one can perceive four principal movements, after a prelude in which Heloise protests against the nature of what Abelard had written. This prelude is followed by

    I (26–80) A double imprecation: 'Spare these words, my lord, I beseech . . .' (54) 'Spare us, then, I beseech . . .'

    II (81–152) A double lament: 'Oh I most wretched of wretched women . . .' (122) 'Oh wretched that I am . . .'

    III (153–247) Heloise's self-analysis

    IV (247–93) Heloise's *recusatio* – her rejection of Abelard's assessment of her piety

This time her salutation is brief: she takes up the word *unicus* with which she had concluded her first letter ('farewell, my one-and-only'), and opens with it: 'Unico suo post Christum   unica sua in Christo'. Abelard had begun by calling her his 'most beloved sister in Christ'; she begins by affirming the very thing that the letter reveals she can hardly bring herself to do – to set Abelard, her one-and-only, *after* Christ. Then at once she launches into reproaches: in his letter, Abelard has transgressed both in manner and matter – transgressed epistolary custom, and even 'the natural order of things', by setting her name before his in his salutation; and transgressed humanly, by writing a letter that, far from consoling, has brought her greater grief than ever. With sweeping hyperbole she writes as if not only she but her whole community could never outlive Abelard:

Oh dearest, what did you have in mind?
how could you bear to say it?
Let God never so forget his paltry handmaids
as to keep them alive after you;
let him never grant them that life
which would be more grievous than any death!

No, it is he who must celebrate the funerals of them all. (The unreal element in this outburst becomes clear if we compare the close of Heloise's third letter, where she herself dwells on the possibility that one day, after Abelard, the Paraclete might have another, less committed or less congenial, adviser.)[28]

The first imprecations ('Parce, obsecro'), after biblical and Senecan authority warning against the prognostication of evil,[29] consist of variations on the extravagant fantasies begun in the prelude, which now extend even to an imagined collective suttee: if Abelard died, then

the mind, insane, more angry as it were with God than at peace with him,
would not so much appease him by prayers as vex him by complaining . . .
and we would sooner hasten to follow you than bury you –
unable to bury, we would need burial by your side.[30]

Implicitly, Heloise's 'we' has more and more come to mean 'I'. And at last, with her second current of imprecations, she passes, as she had done in the first letter, to the grief his presage caused not only 'to us' but to his *unica*. By this, she argues, he makes it impossible for her to pray: 'Don't, I beseech, impede the service of God.' The movement closes with her citing some lines from Lucan, lines that Heloise calls Lucan's prayer to God, though indeed they were as much an outcry against God. Lucan, thinking of the portents of the civil war, exclaimed: why did you (God) have to inflict even more calamity upon suffering mankind? Why frighten them as well, by way of warning omens? –

Let it be sudden, what you have in store;
let man's mind be blind to future fate;
let him who is afraid at least have hope.[31]

She echoes the verses in her own words that follow: 'But what would I have left to hope for, if you were lost?' Lucan's motif of blindness to fate is transformed in Heloise's conceits about Fortuna. Here, at one of the most incandescent moments in the letters, she goes to elaborate lengths in stylizing language and imagery. The exclamation, 'Oh if it were lawful to be spoken, God cruel to me in every way!' – itself a figure of catachresis, that gains its impact by deliberately misapplying the word *crudelis* to the Christian God – is followed by the oxymoron 'oh inclement clemency!', and this by the sustained paradoxes about Boethius' blind goddess:

> Oh misfortuned Fortuna,
> who wasted every shaft of her pursuit on me,
> so that she has none left to rage at others!
> Against me she has emptied her full quiver –
> the dread of others now at her attacks is vain;
> even if she had still a single shaft,
> she would find no place left on me for a wound.
> In all her wounding she feared one thing only –
> that my torments might end in death;
> and though she does not cease to kill,
> she dreads my dying, while she hastens it.

As *crudelis* and *inclemens* are consciously inappropriate to the God of mercy, so the wounding arrows are (at least before *Hamlet*) inappropriate to Fortuna. It is Amor, not Fortuna, who wounds as archer, making those in love his quarry:[32] Heloise secretly acknowledges that the source of her tragedy is not Fortuna (or Lucan's *fatum*), but Amor – a love, however, whose doom was ordained by the Christian God.

In the symmetrical questions and parallelisms with which her lament (what I have called the second movement) now begins, we sense an onomatopoeic effect, as it were a depiction of the lurching motion of Fortuna's wheel:

> Quanto quippe altior   ascendentis gradus,
> tanto gravior   corruentis casus . . .
> Quam in te mihi   gloriam contulit!
> Quam in te mihi   ruinam intulit!

> The higher the degree of her who climbs,
> the more grievous the fall of her who is dashed down . . .
> What glory Fortuna brought me in you!
> What a downfall she inflicted upon me in you!

Heloise proceeds to defend her lament by argument: 'in us all the laws of justice have been overturned'. Here too this overturning (for she sees Abelard's mutilation as both a human and a divine injustice) is exemplified rhetorically, almost dramatically, by the carefully chosen figures of antithesis:

> What other men earn through adultery,
> that you incurred through marriage.
> What adulteresses bring upon their lechers,
> that your own wife brought upon you . . .
> The more you had made amends and, abasing yourself for me,
> had exalted me and all my family,
> the less had you made yourself prone to punishment,
> in the sight of God, and of those traitors.

In the second part of her *planctus* ('O me miseram . . .'), Heloise, seeing herself as the source of Abelard's fall, elaborates and justifies this extravagantly by claiming, with the customary biblical *auctoritates* that had been used for ascetic as for misogynistic argument, that women have always caused the ruin of the greatest men. Adam, Samson, Solomon, David, Job are adduced in turn; with Samson, Heloise even voices the thought, completely alien to the Fathers, that it was 'sorrow which at last forced Samson to destroy himself, along with the fall of his enemies'. In the act that was traditionally held to have been splendid, Samson delivering his people, Heloise sees a tragic aspect, the throwing away of a life that had failed.[33]

Heloise opens the third movement, that of her self-analysis, with a contrast between herself and all the *feminae fatales* of the Old Testament world: if she destroyed Abelard, it was not consentingly (*ex consensu*); her intention – which, as both she and Abelard upheld, alone determines the morality of actions – was innocent. And yet, she continues, she is not being punished unjustly (by the penance, *penitentia*, of living in a convent, without Abelard): this is God's way of chastizing the voluptuous bliss she had enjoyed (159–60). Where before she had seen only an overthrow of justice (*iura . . . perversa*, 98), she now attributes the *perversus . . . exitus* (163) to the wicked joys of the beginning of her love. If only by her penance she could make amends for these – but to Abelard, not to God, whom she still 'accuses of supreme cruelty (*summe crudelitatis arguo*)' towards her beloved:

Atque utinam   huius precipue commissi dignam
agere valeam   penitentiam . . .
et hoc tibi saltem modo,[34]   si non deo,   satisfaciam.

Again, relying on the premise that intention is all that counts in the value of deeds, she affirms she can go through the outer motions of religious contrition and penance, 'but it is most difficult to tear the mind away from longing for the greatest ecstasies'. She cites Job, Gregory and Ambrose as witnesses to the state of mind necessary for inner contrition, and sees within herself the reverse of that:

que cum ingemiscere debeam de commissis,
suspiro potius de amissis.

I who, when I should be moaning for my sins,
sooner sigh for what I have lost.

Even during the celebration of Mass, 'the phantasms of voluptuousness captivate'.[35]

The contrasts between the externals of pious observance and the spirit within were to be a central theme in Heloise's next letter. And there she cites the full context of St Augustine's argument that chastity is a mental, not physical, virtue. Here she only alludes to it, drawing a conclusion that, for herself, is negative: 'People proclaim me chaste, not perceiving that I am a hypocrite: they think of physical purity as a virtue, "though the virtue belongs not to the body but the mind".' Perhaps the outward semblance of the devout life 'seems in some sense laudable and acceptable to God . . . whatever the intention'. And yet, while it may be better than causing scandal, it cannot (as the Psalmist testifies) bring about the transition to positive good.

At the close of this movement, Heloise returns to a motif from her first letter: 'it was your command, not love of God, that drew me into the religious life'. Abelard too has been deceived by the façade of devoutness that she has kept up, for his sake and at his command – 'and so, commending yourself most specially to my prayers, you ask of me what I expect of you'. This brings on the forceful series of negative imperatives which dominate the final movement:

Do not, I beseech, presume such things of me,
lest you cease to help me by your praying.
Do not reckon me to be healthy,
lest you take away the grace of medicine.
Do not believe I am not in need,
lest you delay supporting my neediness.
Do not imagine I am strong,
lest I collapse before you stay my fall.

After buttressing these imperatives with authorities (Isaiah, Ezekiel and Solomon), a second wave of *recusatio* follows: 'Cease, I beseech, from praising me . . .', and this too is reinforced by biblical testimonies. They end in a final imperative, once more with 'obsecro': 'Always fear for me, I beseech, rather than trust me, so that I may always be helped by your solicitude. Now above all you should fear, when you have no more remedy for my sensual cravings.'

It is this fear of her own sensuality, which now can no longer find fulfilment with Abelard, that leads Heloise to claim in conclusion – with the *auctoritas* of St Jerome – that in the spiritual life she cannot ever aim high (and implicitly, that Abelard's high sentiments about her spirituality are misguided):

Non quero coronam victorie;
satis est mihi periculum vitare.
Tutius evitatur periculum
quam committitur bellum.
Quocumque me angulo celi deus collocet,
satis mihi faciet.

I do not seek the crown of victory –
avoiding danger is enough for me.
It's safer to avoid the danger

than to engage in combat.
In whatever corner of heaven God may set me,
I shall be satisfied.

That is, the most she can hope for is to reach heaven with Abelard's help, with his unfailing support and prayers. She will not march into a high seat in heaven like the champions of the ascetic life: she will slip in only as Abelard's *ancilla* – an *ancilla* who has tried to carry out with perfect fidelity the commands of her *dominus*.

The extent of the rhetorical and poetic shaping of these two letters will have become apparent even from the brief passages cited and translated. I should like to pause at the particular problem hinted at earlier: to what extent did Heloise have specifically the *Heroides* in mind as she wrote? To indicate an answer, I shall focus on only one of Ovid's Epistles, that of Briseis to Achilles (*Her.* III). There is naturally no question of any precise parallel of situation: Briseis, who had been Achilles' captive and concubine, is snatched away by Agamemnon, but still burns with love for her former *dominus*. Yet Briseis, more than any of Ovid's heroines, embodies the loving woman in the aspect of *ancilla*, she who longs to submit totally to the lord whom she admires and loves, and whom (even while she reproaches him for his neglect) she feels to be immeasurably above her.

Many of Briseis' phrases could have been evocative for Heloise as she wrote her first two letters. When we see her writing to Achilles:

> Tu dominus, tu vir, tu mihi frater eras (52)

> You were my lord, my husband, and my brother too

we are not far from Heloise's first salutation of Abelard (only the specifically Christian notion of spiritual fatherhood is lacking). When Briseis writes at the opening (5–8):

> Si mihi pauca queri de te dominoque viroque
>   fas est, de domino pauca viroque querar.
> Non, ego poscenti quod sum cito tradita regi,
>   culpa tua est – quamvis haec quoque culpa tua est

> If it is lawful for me to complain a little
>   of you, my lord and husband, I shall complain.
> That I was so soon handed over to the King
>   is not your fault – yet it also *is* your fault

it is hard not to recall Heloise's use of 'If it were lawful', in her outburst against the divine *Dominus*; and Briseis' paradox, 'guilt / no guilt' may well lie behind Heloise's 'nocens' / 'innocens'. And – in a different register – Abelard had indeed handed Heloise over to a King, not of her choosing, when he forced her to take the veil.

Briseis would sooner be swallowed up by the gaping earth than see Achilles abandon her totally – 'Devorer ante, precor, subito telluris hiatu' (63): here she foreshadows Heloise's determination not to outlive Abelard; even the paren- thetic 'precor' resembles Heloise's way of using 'obsecro'. But the most remarkable analogies are in the moments where Briseis declares herself happy to remain with Achilles as a concubine rather than a wife, provided he does not reject her altogether (69ff): 'I'll follow you, the victor, as a captive, not as a wife who is following her husband . . . I, your lowly servant, will card the wool I'm given . . .[36] Don't let your wife torment me, I beseech (deprecor) . . . Or I'll even endure that, as long as I am not spurned and abandoned . . . I did not want to pass for your wife, I who was often called to my lord's bed as a slave-girl.'

Technically, Heloise's prose, with its rhymes, rhythmic symmetries and cadences, was modern, not ancient: its movement, as I indicated, belongs with the Italian mode of letter-writing that was an innovation in the France of her youth; besides, her poetic prose has an openness and flexibility that take it far from the self-contained, 'closed' couplets in the Heroides. Yet even these few phrases of Briseis show, I think, that Ovid's verse-epistles were as much an imaginative reality for Heloise as they were, in other ways, for some of the women love-poets. Each writer could find there expressions rich in reverbera- tion for their own imaginings.

Abelard replied to Heloise's second letter much less calmly than to the first. Now he vehemently urges Heloise to suppress her passions, to cease 'your old and continual complaint against God',[37] and to sublimate the sensual longing. Taking up her own words from her first letter, on the nature of perfect human friendship, he claims that only God can be such a friend: 'What, I say, does he seek in you save you? He is the true friend, who desires you alone, not what is yours.' Yet Abelard also has an impulse parallel to that in Heloise's second letter. Where she had ended imploring him not to praise her ('Quiesce, obsecro, a laude mea', 261), he implores: 'Quiesce, obsecro, ab his dictis . . . ab his, obsecro, sicut dixi, quiesce querimoniis' (Cease, I beseech, from saying these things . . . as I told you, cease these complainings, I beseech).[38]

In this Heloise was once more ready – at whatever inner cost – to obey her dominus. That at least becomes clear in the much-discussed opening of her third letter. This time her salutation echoes a phrase Abelard had just used – 'remem- ber him who specially is yours (qui specialiter est tuus)' – and affectionately she outdoes it: 'Suo specialiter, sua singulariter'. With the second term, 'singulari- ter', a philosophical connotation is playfully added to the first: Heloise implies she is his with the concreteness that the singular individual has over and above its 'speciality', i.e. belonging to a species – though again the species (at least in terms of Abelard's dialectic) has no existence apart from its singulars. –

To him who is specially hers,
she who is uniquely his.

Lest perchance you could accuse me of disobedience in any way,
the curb of your command has been set
on my words, even of immoderate sorrow,
so that at least in writing
I may restrain myself from these,
though they are not just hard but impossible
to guard against in speech.
For nothing is less in our power than the mind . . .
So I shall hold back my hand from writing
what I cannot check my tongue from speaking –
if only the mind of her who is sorrowing thus
were as ready to obey as the hand of her who is writing!
Yet you can bring some remedy for that sorrow
even if you cannot remove it totally.
For as one nail drives out another,[39]
so a new thought shuts out the old . . .
All of us, then, handmaids of Christ
and your daughters in Christ,
imploringly ask two things now of your paternal care . . .

The two things are, a discussion by Abelard of the origin and nature of the nun's way of life, and a new Rule to be set down by Abelard for his Paraclete to follow.

Heloise was still to write to Abelard of many things, yet she never again (as far as we know) brought up in writing her 'old and continual complaint against God'. Overtly, all she discusses in the rest of her third letter and in the *Problemata* has to do with spiritual advice, questions on details of the monastic life and on problems encountered in her biblical reading. Was this only an outward compliance with Abelard's command, or could she finally bring her mind to obey as well? In the text just cited she seems to say, she longs to be able to, but has not yet attained this.

As Heloise never reverts to the question, scholars have been deeply divided in their speculations. They have tended to project two very different images: one, a rebellious, passionate heroine, who never submitted ultimately in her mind to the Christian 'system', but who pretended outwardly, for Abelard's sake, to acquiesce in it; the other image is that of a latterday Mary Magdalen, whose repentance for her sensuality we can allegedly discover in Heloise's later letters: that is, her writing at such length about the monastic life is interpreted as evidence that she had become truly converted to it.

Neither image – the unrepentant *amoureuse* or the edifying convert – is, I believe, warranted by Heloise's surviving texts. Both images are the product of a kind of bigoted apriorism, whether of the Romantic or the clerical variety. If one looks for a certain slant in the text of the letters, it is only too easy to persuade oneself that the slant is there. For some, that Heloise never again mentions her sensual thoughts, which at their last mention she still clung to fondly ('suspiro de amissis'), suggests that she never came to feel contrite about them; for others, her silence about contrition is seen as a kind of *aposiopesis*: that is, Heloise would here be relying consciously on the rhetorical device of 'cutting-off' and leaving a difficult conclusion tacit; she then goes on, it is claimed, to further writing such as no one who was merely maintaining a façade of piety would be likely to set down.

The theory of *aposiopesis* has been advanced first and foremost by Peter von Moos,[40] and I believe it is plausible. Yet it becomes plausible only if we reject von Moos's accompanying theory – that the collection of eight letters was shaped as an exemplary work, showing the religious conversion first of Abelard and then of Heloise. If the letter-collection were meant (even in part) as an *exemplum* of conversion, the one thing for which the figure *aposiopesis* could *not* be used would be the conversion itself, since this would leave the intention of the work unclear and thus make the *exemplum* lose all force and value. In such a genre and such a context, 'cutting-off' could be nothing but incongruity. I believe we should discard the notion that the correspondence was meant as an *exemplum*, since this prevents the full perception of its individualities. It is only insofar as the surviving letters – even if they were in some measure edited by another person – still represent an individual exchange between two living people, that we can envisage that exchange leaving certain vital matters unspoken. Then the 'thoughts that do often lie too deep for tears' would not have needed outright expression in writing, as the letters would have been complemented by real life. The *aposiopesis* that would be a glaring rhetorical fault in an *exemplum* could also be a device of sensitive tact in an intimate statement.

According to von Moos, the only alternative to Heloise's 'exemplary' conversion is 'the anachronistic legend . . . in which Heloise, possessed by a grandiose, demonically self-destructive passion, persisted till the end of her life in the unforgivable sin against the Holy Ghost'.[41] 'Such an Heloise', he adds, 'could never have been exemplary for medieval people.' This last is true, if also a tautology. But do we really need to choose between an *exemplum* and a 'Gothick' novelettish fantasy? (Incidentally, Heloise in the *Problemata* asks Abelard about the nature of the sin against the Holy Ghost – see below, p. 137 – and, at least in Abelard's view, this sin has nothing whatever to do with 'self-destructive passion'.)

Clearly Heloise did not *think* she was being demonic or committing an unforgivable sin. This is evident even at the climax of her most openly passionate letter: 'In whatever corner of heaven God may set me, I shall be satisfied.' Yet this does not warrant our assuming that she repented in the edifying, Mary Magdalen sense. Rather, it could mean that she was seeking a standard of integrity for herself which she saw as different from a conventional religious one. The reason for the difference would have been, at least in part, that Abelard had, at two crucial moments – marriage, and the convent – forced her into patterns of life she had not chosen, and which were against her conscience. What kind of *regula* is existentially valid for a Christian soul that has been forced into such 'hypocrisy' by her husband and spiritual director? The complexity of this question – and of Heloise's varied endeavours to answer it well – cannot be circumscribed by the trite alternatives repentance/lack of repentance, conversion/inability to be converted. It is a measure of this complexity that Heloise's third letter and the *Problemata* show us a woman who, even though she had been forced into taking the veil, had also developed a willing, serious concern with every aspect of womanly monastic life.

In asking about the origins of and authority for the nun's profession, Heloise enquires into the *raison d'être* of the women living at the Paraclete. In asking for a fresh Rule, composed by Abelard, expressly for these women and for herself, she is seeking a pattern of guidance less extrinsic than what was handed down by the Fathers, who had generally prescribed monastic practices with only the needs of men in mind. To show why the Rule of St Benedict, which men and women alike professed in western Europe, was inadequate to the requirements of women, Heloise begins with a touch of humour: many of the directions on clothing for monks are physically unsuitable for women – what is to become of the 'woollen garments worn next to the skin' at menstruation?[42] Other aspects of the commonly followed Benedictine Rule are theologically inappropriate (since a male abbot, for instance, can have priestly functions such as an abbess cannot); others again are morally inept. Thus Benedict's magnanimous notions of how a monastery should give hospitality to men visitors could be dangerous for women to copy: 'Oh how easily the cohabitation of men and women together can lead to the ruin of souls!' We may conjecture that in her exclamation Heloise recalls her own seduction by Abelard, when she first lived under one roof with him (*domo una, Hist. cal.* 332). She cites Ovid as *auctoritas* for how readily festive meals with men could lead to sex; yet even women guests, she adds, could well become go-betweens.

Then she turns, troubled, to the verse in St James's Epistle, 'Whoever observes the whole law but offends in one single point becomes guilty of offence in all', a verse she persuades Abelard to explain to her in the *Problemata*.[43]

Here she asks merely, if some of the male-oriented prescriptions of Benedict are impossible for us women to follow, does James's verse imply that everything else we do towards following the Rule is valueless? Behind Heloise's question, quite possibly, lies the further thought – if I cannot bring my own *animus* to obey, does it mean that everything else I do to lead a fitting religious life is fruitless?

Yet of her own accord, after mentioning further practical difficulties, Heloise here reaches at least a provisional solution: 'discretion, the mother of all virtues, and reason, the moderator of all things good', must surely be the principles by which specific actions are to be tested, by nuns as by monks. Moreover, even the Benedictine Rule, so ill-adapted to nuns as it stands, has a *discretio* of its own, which shows itself in a certain inbuilt relativism, as when it makes special provisions for the very young and the very old, for the sick or the weak. What particular provisions, then, would Abelard, with his reason and discretion, make for women, 'whose weak and infirm nature is especially well known' (244, 1)?

It would be much, Heloise argues, if we women could equal even religious laymen – not to speak of monks – in our observance. Yet according to Chrysostom, the duties of layfolk too are severe (except that sexual abstinence is not required of them). If in our religious way of life we could rise to fulfilling the Gospel precepts, would there be any need to devise more arduous ascetic norms? Would not the attempt to fulfil such norms and fall short of them be far worse than not trying to mount too high? The passage Heloise cites in support of this, from a letter of Jerome to Eustochium, makes clear that again she has sexual temptations in mind: we can see the whole passage as a development of the thought at the end of her second letter:

I do not seek the crown of victory –
avoiding danger is enough for me.

It is also because of the sexual perils, Heloise continues, that canon law, taking account of our infirmity, has decreed that deaconesses should not be ordained before the age of forty. As Abelard once states that 'deaconess (*diaconissa*)' is synonymous with 'abbess (*abbatissa*)',[44] this sentence of Heloise's raises a problem. She cannot have been more than about twenty-nine when she became abbess of the Paraclete. In his *Regula* for her Abelard even quotes St Paul saying that a *diaconissa* should be a widow, at least sixty years of age, though there Abelard also seems, with some of his provisions, to adapt his notion of the rôle of abbess to Heloise herself: a woman who has known a man, he says, is more suitable than a virgin; she should excel the others in her convent both in life and learning, and her age should give promise of maturity.[45]

Taking up again the theme of how far outward acts of austerity are appropriate to women, Heloise alludes to the Augustinian canons, who are allowed to eat meat and to wear linen: 'it would not be considered little, would it, if our weakness could match their virtue?' Whenever Heloise speaks of womanly *infirmitas* in a monastic context (that is, whenever she is not referring to sexual weaknesses), her tone suggests a certain impatience with external prescription. It is not heroic, in her eyes, to abstain from specific foods or from wine, and, compared with the problem of living an inner rule with integrity, such things are trivial. Each time she alludes to womanly weakness, it is difficult not to recall her own unquenched strength, in acquiescing without losing heart in the life that Abelard had compelled her to live. In the light of the opening of the third letter, all Heloise's subsequent references to womanly weakness seem to have an edge of tragic irony: for, whatever she may say of frailty, Heloise shows herself to be in a mould as brave as Lucan's Cornelia.[46] And yet, in the context of monastic minutiae, she returns continually to that *infirmitas* or *fragilitas*. It is probably a concession to Abelard – not so much to acknowledge a masculine stereotype concerning women as to provide an opening for him to say something opportune, in his rôle as founder of the Paraclete.

The suggestion that, as women, they might aim to equal the observances of the (relatively unascetic) Augustinians, continues:

But that we may the more safely and easily be allowed any kind of food, Nature herself has protected our sex with a greater power of sobriety. It is indeed known that women can be sustained with less nourishment, and at much less expense, than men, and medicine bears witness that they are not so easily intoxicated.

Citing Aristotle (by way of Macrobius) in support of this, she concludes:

Consider, therefore, how much more safely and aptly any kind of food and drink may be allowed our nature and infirmity.

Besides, it is better to take on modest monastic vows and surpass them in performance than to aim at a more ambitious discipline and fall short of it, as many men do. Benedict himself (she adds, citing him) saw his own Rule as a set of minimal ordinances rather than as counsels of perfection.

This passage is followed in the extant manuscripts (and in Jean de Meun) by a page of diatribe against wine, beginning 'What, moreover, is so contrary to religion and monastic peace [as wine]?', citing condemnations of wine from the Bible, Jerome, and the *Lives of the Fathers* ('wine is Satan'), and concluding sadly that even Benedict was unable to ban wine totally, much as he would have liked to.

Then, with a request for a flexible and humane regulation as regards the eating of meat (248, 1), the tone of *ratio* and *discretio* returns. This request also links in sense with the earlier discussion of temperateness; the invective against wine that comes between breaks into the argument quite illogically. The same wine-passage recurs almost verbatim, with identical quotations, in Abelard's *Regula*[47] – and there it seems equally quixotic and misplaced, since in the remainder of his argument Abelard aims, precisely, to *allow* a modest amount of wine at the Paraclete, not to ban wine as something diabolical. What the provenance of this incongruous wine-diatribe might be, and how it came to be slipped into two different places in the Abelard–Heloise manuscripts, would repay detailed investigation.

Heloise, at all events, would like to see at the Paraclete a supple, tolerant ruling on all aspects of nourishment and clothing. For – she insists once more – these are external matters, 'common as much to the reprobate as to the elect, to hypocrites as to the truly religious' (248, 2). This phrase clearly echoes and refers to what she had said in her second letter about *hypocrisis*: 'they obtain no merit in the sight of God, the things that are common to the reprobate and the elect alike: they are the things done externally, which none who are holy perform as zealously as hypocrites do'.[48] Again, not what is done but the intention is of decisive importance.

With a row of quotations from St Paul Heloise supports this: 'The kingdom of God is not eating and drinking but justice and peace and joy in the Holy Spirit . . . All things indeed are pure.' It makes sense to abstain from a particular food only if it is a question of not causing offence to others. If anyone looked simply to ascetic externals, he would place John the Baptist higher than Christ in holiness.

Heloise sets this last paradox in the context of a long quotation from St Augustine, one she had already alluded to in her second letter: 'Continence is a virtue not of the body but the mind.'[49] There she had been thinking specifically of the mind's consent to sensual fantasies; now, returning to Augustine's own broader frame of reference, she points the distinction between abstinence of any kind as a mental disposition (*habitus*), and on the other hand the outer practice, which inevitably is tied to circumstance. Only virtues of the mind obtain merit in God's sight, and true Christians are concerned only with the inner man. But the same also applies negatively, to the question of guilt: the intention of adultery, or murder, is as sinful as the act itself.

Thus Heloise comes to repeat, with only minor variation, the words by which, in her first letter, she had challenged Abelard to judge the innocence of her intentions at the time of their marriage: 'So what must be weighed is not so much what things are done as the state of mind with which they are done.'

Yet what applied then to Abelard's wife applies equally now to the abbess of his monastic foundation. In a superb juxtaposition, Heloise cites the Psalmist (Psalm 55: 12) – 'within me, God, are your vows, which I shall give back as praises' – and Persius (1 7): 'Don't look outside yourself.' The pagan poet and the Old Testament prophet express two aspects of the single goal Heloise has set herself.

She is not saying this, she adds, in order to reject bodily works (252, 1), only to see them in proportion; she is defending not idleness but the inner serenity with which Mary sat listening to the words of Christ (Luke 10: 39). This leads Heloise to further thoughts about divine reading for the nuns: Abelard is to judge what is best for them as regards reading the Psalter, or, during night vigils, the Gospels. And the letter concludes with phrases that endow with a new harmony words Heloise had used in the first movement of her first letter (see above, p. 115):

On you, my lord, it is incumbent, as long as you live,
to establish what we should adhere to, in perpetuity:
you indeed, after God, are the founder of this place,
you, through God, are the planter of our community,
you, with God, the preceptor of our religious life.

In her earlier phrasing there had been no mention of God: the words had expressed only Heloise's unrelenting human dependence on Abelard. Now they express her readiness to accept the converted Abelard, Abelard in his relation to God. The letter concludes: 'Speak to us and we shall hear. Farewell.'

It was this openness that led Abelard to a new flood of creative activity for the sake of Heloise and the Paraclete: not only did he write, as requested, about the origin of nuns and about prescriptions for them, and later answer Heloise's *Problemata*, but many of his major works in the last years of his life are explicitly for his former wife and her community: a treatise on the Creation, a collection of homilies, a book of 133 hymns, composed for every part of the Church year, and (as has only recently been shown) extensive other liturgical compositions, which still await full publication.[50] There is also a long, idealistic letter-treatise to the Paraclete 'on the study of literature';[51] and it is hard to imagine the first recipients of the brilliant cycle of six lyrical laments on Old Testament themes, the *Planctus*, being anywhere but at the Paraclete.

Heloise in her third letter submits all her thoughts modestly to Abelard for advice and judgment – yet she also shows her own masterly decisiveness about all that matters if women's life in a convent is to be more than petty outward forms. For all her references to womanly weakness, she reveals her introspective fortitude: Persius' Stoic device, which she quotes, is exemplified in the movement of her thought.

While Abelard wrote so many and such varied works for the Paraclete, the *Problemata* still hold a unique place: for in these Abelard is not simply addressing Heloise and her nuns but entering into a dialogue with them. About the genesis of that dialogue much remains uncertain. The opening letter, by Heloise, indicates that it was she who took the initiative; the last words in that letter – 'we shall set down the problems and send them to be resolved as they occur to us day by day, not keeping to the order [of appearance of such matters] in the Bible' – suggest that the questions (and presumably the answers too) were actually dispatched in written form, rather than that the work as a whole represents a stylized report of oral discussions. If the *Problemata* stem from *ca.* 1135, a messenger could well have travelled with questions from the Paraclete to Saint-Gildas, or quite possibly only to Paris, if Abelard (recorded as teaching again in Paris in 1136) had already returned there. Nonetheless, we must not imagine forty-two 'special deliveries', one for each *Problema*: internal evidence alone shows that some were, from the start, in groups.[52] To whom the final redaction of the work as a miscellany of questions is to be ascribed must remain open.

In her introduction Heloise returns, at least for an extended passage, to the parallelistic rhymed prose she had last used at the opening of her third letter. She begins with the precedent of Jerome writing to Marcella about the scriptural questions that Marcella raised, and the expression Heloise uses – 'your wisdom knows this better than does my simplicity (*vestra melius prudencia quam mea sinplicitas novit*)'[53] – takes us back to a similar moment in her first letter: there too she had mentioned the exemplar of the Fathers writing to holy women, adding (117) 'Your excellence knows this better than my littleness (*tua melius excellentia quam nostra parvitas novit*)'. Then it had been a matter of persuading Abelard to write at all; now the relation between Jerome and Marcella portends something more complex: Marcella – as Heloise's quotation from Jerome insists – was no passive pupil, she wanted not just answers but reasoned answers, she was 'not so much a disciple as a critic'. Because of this, Heloise adds by way of another quotation, Jerome proposed her as a *magistra* for other women. These quotations reflect both the rôle Heloise will play in the *Problemata* and her task as instructress at the Paraclete.

Then comes Heloise's passage of heightened prose, laden with rhymes:

Yet to what end do I tell this, beloved of many
but most beloved of us?
These are not learned instances, but admonitions,
which will make you remember what you owe
and make you less sluggish in paying your debt.
Christ's handmaids, your daughters in spirit,
whom you gathered in your own oratory,
enlisting them in divine service,
you always used to exhort copiously
to concentrate on the divine words

and devote time to holy reading . . .
My sisters and I,
much aroused by those admonitions,
obeying you in this, too, as best we can,
as we concentrate on this study,
seized by that love of learning
of which Jerome somewhere says
'Love the knowledge of the Bible and you won't love the body's vices' –
we are troubled by many problems
that slow our reading down . . .
So, sending some little questions
as disciples to our teacher,
as daughters to our father,
we ask imploringly,
asking we implore,
that you do not disdain to bend to solve them,
you at whose admonition,
or rather at whose command,
we specially embarked upon this study.[54]

Central is the quotation from a letter of Jerome (*Ep.* 125), to a young scholar, Rusticus, about to become a monk, in which the study of Scripture is commended as a remedy against physical cravings.[55] Heloise's eagerness to follow that counsel can well be seen in the light of the unceasing sensual reveries that she had evoked in her second letter, and in the light of the phrase here, 'obeying you in this, too, as best we can' – that is, it is not just a matter of her outward compliance with Abelard's command (*iussus*) about scriptural reading, but her attempt to obey him more deeply, trying to banish certain thoughts from her *animus*.

Yet in the whole of this letter Heloise again speaks in plurals – overtly at least in the name of her community, not just her own. The 'debt' Abelard owes now is not so much that of husband to wife as that of the founder to his foundation. There is, however, a very personal moment hidden in the passage: when Abelard in his first letter to Heloise had warned her of his 'anxiety about greater danger', among the Breton monks, he had besought her and her nuns to pray for him, using the word-play 'Supplicando itaque postulo, postulando supplico' ('And so, imploring, I demand, demanding I implore').[56] Heloise, by imitating this formulaic play here ('supplicando rogamus, rogando supplicamus'), assuredly brings the former occasion to mind. If Abelard was already safely installed again in Paris, there may even be a lighthearted note in her allusion: now the appeal is not anguished, there is no danger to Abelard's life, but only her keen longing to carry out his injunctions as perfectly as possible.

While it would be excessive to suspect personal reverberations throughout the questions relating to biblical passages that follow this letter, one can see at least in some instances that Heloise's 'problem' was no purely abstract exegetic one, such as she could have resolved on her own by looking at a standard commentary, but that she was troubled by the human implications of a number of biblical sentences and episodes, and that it was to clarify and resolve this disquiet that she consulted Abelard himself rather than works of reference.[57]

The verse in James's Epistle (*Problem* 2), already cited in her third letter, is a good instance – and Abelard in his answer stresses the full rigour of its implication: the law is one, and to offend in any aspect of it means to transgress absolutely. Other passages relate to the paradoxes of forgiveness – the greater joy in heaven over the converted sinner than over all the just (11), or the 'irremissible sin against the Holy Spirit' (13). The scriptural allusions to this sin, says Heloise, 'move us as they move many people'. For is not any sin against Christ also a sin against the Spirit? How then – she means – can any sin at all be forgiven? But Abelard in his answer claims that there is only one specific sin against the Holy Spirit: to call that Spirit malignant, while knowing this to be a lie.

Only the last of the forty-two *Problems* does not arise directly out of a scriptural passage. Heloise asks 'Whether anyone could sin in what they do if it has been conceded, or even commanded, by their lord'. The last word (*dominus*) seems to refer not to God (which would orient the question to the fateful divine commands that occur at times in the Bible) but to the husband as the lord of his wife, and in particular to Abelard himself.[58] Abelard at least tries to answer the question in terms of conjugal obligations and guilt. Yet the greater part of his lengthy answer is not his own, but a choice of quotations from Augustine's *De bono coniugali*, the treatise from which Heloise had already cited other passages, both in her second and third letters. Here the teaching of Augustine is used to declare that a woman, in marriage, is justified in giving in to her lord's sexual demands, and he to hers, provided the demands are not against nature. If the couple make love in order to bear children, there can be no question at all of sin; if they make love out of sheer sensual desire, it is a 'pardonable fault (*culpa venialis*)'. The 'debt' between husband and wife is a permanently binding one: it would be wrong for either partner to make a unilateral declaration of continence, for 'each has power over the other's body'.

In these quotations, that Abelard set down with scarcely a personal note, Heloise would have found many thoughts relating to her preoccupations in the earlier letters: her consent to marrying Abelard, her yielding to his sexual demands, her own sexual cravings, and her own later consent to live continently, again at his command. All these have to do with the implications of that binding debt of wife and husband to each other which Augustine discusses. But Heloise had claimed a further debt, as strong and inescapable as the older one between husband and wife, one that, as intellectual and teacher and abbot, Abelard could still fulfil for her: 'quid debeas recorderis / et debitum solvere non pigriteris'. It is this debt – a transformation of the sexual one about which Augustine had written – which she so ardently, in the letter opening the *Problemata*, urges Abelard to pay, and pay without reluctance or procrastination.

At first, if we look back to Heloise's earlier letters from the vantage of the third letter and the *Problemata*, the dominant impression may be of discontinuity. In those earlier letters the frequent allusions to the outer world ('noverunt omnes') suggest that Heloise's prose, consummate in artifice, is directed not only to Abelard but, at least half-consciously, to other readers and to succeeding generations.[59] The later writing, in a sense, is more private than the so-called 'personal' letters – it concerns only Abelard and the Paraclete, whereas in the first two letters we see Heloise determined publicly to set a particular human record straight. She commends Abelard for not having, in the *Historia calamitatum*, glossed over some of the less comfortable truths in that record, such as the reasons why she had argued against marriage;[60] yet she still feels he has not told the complete truth about her. Against his edifying picture of her near the close of the *Historia*[61] – the abbess whom bishops love as a daughter and the layfolk as a sister, whose holiness is evident to all who meet her, she sets the unedifying, disturbing picture of one who has to keep up a façade, who cannot feel any true religious impulse but still harbours resentment against God (a resentment such as, in the fictional sphere, Wolfram von Eschenbach was to portray in his hero Parzival). She wants the world to know her one day not just as the abbess who had once been Abelard's concubine (which everyone 'knew', inasmuch as the world knows such things), but as one whose sufferings in real life had gone beyond those of Ovid's fictive heroines, and equally as one who, even to the brink of the impossible, tried to obey the *dominus* whom she loved.

It is under this last aspect that the continuity in her writing begins to be perceptible. Heloise's passion for lucid truth manifests itself in different ways in all her writing. In the most troubling way, perhaps, in her initial reaction to the *Historia calamitatum*. If Abelard had persuaded himself that she had become nun-like in spirit, because everyone said how good an abbess she was, Heloise wanted to shake his complacent delusion, and wanted not only him but posterity to realize that there was another side to the picture: that one can obey the command of one's lord outwardly, but not lie about the emotions that remain alive within. Outer simulation, in order not to give scandal, is acceptable to the conscience; an inner hypocrisy would be intolerable.

Yet Heloise also, as abbess, wanted to shake complacencies of another kind. Here her eye for what is truthful, by the standard not just of abstract but of personal knowledge, is equally limpid: she wanted a pattern of monastic observance that would reflect inner integrity, and thus would discard in the externals all that is stultifying and ill-fitting in the existing monastic Rules. So, too (as we learn from Abelard's Preface to his *Hymnarius*),[62] she wanted new hymns for the Paraclete, because the text of so many of the older ones was garbled: what point would there be in singing things that sound vaguely pious but do not give full sense? The same impulse spurs the *Problemata*: what point is there in going on with Bible study if one simply passes over the apparent inconsistencies in the Gospel accounts of the resurrection, for instance,[63] or the seemingly repugnant implications of certain sentences that one is taught to believe are divinely inspired?[64] Thus the continuity in Heloise's writing lies especially in her ceaseless quest for complete and honest understanding – of her years with Abelard and of her present state of mind, of the monastic way of life and of the text of Scripture. In the earlier as in the later letters, what mattered to her supremely was arriving at a standard of truth that went beyond outer conformities and involved the assenting mind: 'non que fiunt, sed quo animo fiunt'.

In Heloise's writing we can also see almost a *summa* of motifs and techniques that were glimpsed separately in the women writers considered so far. In Berthgyth, we saw rhythmic, rhymed prose express a longing that hovered between human clinging and spiritual friendship; in Dhuoda, the tender, affectionate practicality, and the search for ideals of conduct not imposed from without, but harmonizing with a life that was sensed to be unique; in Hrotsvitha, the virtuoso style and the subtle consciousness of a woman's rôle, always conceding womanly weakness while displaying strength; in the women who wrote personal poetry, the varied expressions of desire and of love's sorrows. At the same time, it is the extent to which Heloise's writing reveals her as committed to a man, to Abelard, that also sets it apart from the writing of all the others.

EXCURSUS: DID ABELARD WRITE HELOISE'S THIRD LETTER?

My purpose here is to examine the most recent arguments by which John Benton (*Trier 1980*) claims to 'demonstrate' or 'support the theory of Abelardian authorship' of the third letter ascribed to Heloise (*Ep.* VI in the collection). The points in Benton's discussion that concern me are the following:

Ep. VI contains a long excerpt (over 275 words) from St Augustine's *De Bono Coniugali* which is with one exception word for word the same as that which appears in the *Sic et Non* (q. 130. cc. 6–9). The omissions are the same, the placement of *item* is identical, and the texts agree in reproducing a notable error in the transmission of what Augustine wrote. At the beginning of the passage Augustine wrote *Virtutes autem animi aliquando in opere manifestantur*, and consequently Fr Muckle amended the text of 'Heloise' to read *opere* rather than the *corpore* given by all the manuscripts. The emendation should be rejected, however, for all the manuscripts of *Sic et Non* which give the extract also read *corpore*. The only difference between the text of *Ep.* VI and the *Sic et Non* is that towards the end the letter reads *qui non poterat non promebat*, rather than *qui poterat non promebat*, an error which remains inexplicable. But this second error, rather than creating a stumbling block, has its value, for it demonstrates, should anyone want a demonstration, that the *Sic et Non* or the Abelardian *fichier* from which it was drawn was the source of *Ep.* VI, rather than that a letter sent by Heloise or a common source lay behind the passage in *Sic et Non*.

. . . the author of the letter gives no indication that the passage is borrowed from another work. Such a procedure is common for Abelard, who presumably felt that authorities he had collected were 'his', to be used as he wished, though if Heloise were writing with her finger running down the page of *Sic et Non*, we might expect her to acknowledge the borrowing.

. . . there can be absolutely no doubt that this and several other passages in the correspondence are taken word for word, omission for omission, from the *Sic et Non* or Abelard's *fichier* of quotations, for the variants can be accounted for in no other way.[1]

This passage conflates many dubious assumptions, which it may be helpful to try to isolate. First, the two textual errors that Benton mentions are of completely different kinds. The earlier one follows a sentence of Augustine's contrasting the virtues of *body* and soul: 'Continentia quippe non corporis, sed animi virtus est.' Hence it is understandable that the next sentence should have been read 'But the virtues of the spirit are sometimes manifest in the *body* . . .' (rather than, 'manifest in action'): this gives good sense in the context. There are two principal ways to account for the reading 'corpore', neither of which can be ruled out: (a) though none of the sixteen manuscripts or two early printings used for the critical edition of Augustine's treatise have the reading 'corpore' for 'opere' here (CSEL XLI 219, line 1), it may have stood in the manuscript used by the author(s) of *Sic et Non* and *Ep.* VI; (b) the reading could be a scribal slip in these two works, under the influence of 'corporis' in the previous sentence cited, but a slip that is more likely to go back to the author(s) than to a later copyist. *Sic et Non* and the *Letters* have completely separate textual transmission, and it seems unnecessary to postulate that two scribes will have perpetrated 'corpore' independently.

The second error in the Augustine quotation (found only in all seven manuscripts of *Ep.* VI, and in none of the five of *Sic et Non* that contain the passage)[2] gives no sense whatever: it is purely scribal. In the discussion of continence as a latent habit, Augustine's sense requires 'he who could [be continent] did not display [that continence,] even though he possessed it (*qui poterat non promebat, sed tamen habebat*)'; the opposite, which we read in *Ep.* VI – 'he who could *not* be continent did not display his continence (*qui non poterat non promebat*)' – being simply absurd. Yet the insertion of this extra 'not' is far from 'inexplicable', as Benton claims. Under the influence of the 'non' before 'promebat', the further 'non' could be written in error by anyone thinking ahead – by Abelard, or Heloise, or a copyist – as easily as, for instance, in modern English we might write in error: 'I am *not* saying not only . . .' This error demonstrates nothing about priority or sources. It demonstrates only that a scribal error of the simplest kind (anticipating a *non*) occurred in a manuscript that lies behind the extant manuscripts of the letters, including the one that was used by Jean de Meun (who translates the double *non*, and thereby also inadvertently gives nonsense).[3]

The relation between the two passages, in *Ep.* VI and *Sic et Non*, 'can be accounted for in no other way', says Benton, than that '*Sic et Non* or Abelard's *fichier* of quotations' is the source. This *fichier* is itself a questionable and perhaps anachronistic assumption. Let me suggest a few alternatives. How did Abelard – or Heloise – gather quotations? Many times, as is well known, the letters ascribed to Heloise, and her portion of the *Problemata*, cite the same or similar passages as Abelard does. The most natural basic assumption is that they read certain texts together at one stage of their lives, and that, when they were separated, they still read texts in the same manuscripts, exchanging these (or sometimes perhaps making copies for each other) when necessary. That Abelard should have provided as learned a community as Heloise's a building but no books is hard to imagine (and indeed at the opening of *Ep.* III he mentions sending a *psalterium* that Heloise had requested). Lucan, Cicero, Seneca, Jerome, much of Augustine – it is easy to see how these authors pervade the writings ascribed to both Abelard and Heloise. If there was a *fichier* – or should one say a commonplace-book, in which quotations were stored by topic? – many possibilities remain open: it could have been kept jointly, added to jointly, or even copied out by one of the two for the other. But it is also possible that the codices Abelard and Heloise had in common were marked by both of them, so that particular passages, and links between passages, would be signalled in the margins. Then either Abelard or Heloise could make use of these signals in their writing.

These are only conjectured possibilities, but I believe none of them should be eliminated. What underlies Benton's argumentation, however (though it never becomes wholly explicit), is the notion that in all that Abelard and Heloise shared intellectually, Abelard was exclusively the giver, the active partner. And this is purest prejudice. There is no plausible reason, for instance, why Heloise should not have found this passage in *De bono coniugali* for Abelard, even years before the correspondence, rather than vice versa. Whether one or other of them found it first, or they found it while reading together, it seems anachronistic to suppose that either would lay claim to 'copyright', or would feel the need to acknowledge borrowing a quotation discovered or cited by the other. If there *were* a 'cross-reference' to *Sic et Non* in *Ep.* VI, this would make me really suspicious that a later redactor had been at work.

Finally, Benton completely ignores the two contexts of the Augustinian quotation. In *Sic et Non* it is one of the texts adduced in the discussion of whether any sexual intercourse can be free of guilt; in the letter, it is to provide an *auctoritas* for the difference between virtue (of any kind, not just sexual) and its outward display.

The only occasion where the repetition of quotations poses a serious problem is where the context is closely similar. And here I must illustrate briefly from the relations between *Ep.* VI (Heloise's third letter) and *Ep.* VIII (the *Regula* for the nuns), of which even Benton believes that 'much (though not necessarily all) was composed by Abelard', though he adds that it 'may have been shortened by a *remanieur*'.[4] In four pages of the best available edition of the *Regula* (ed. McLaughlin, pp. 269–72), no fewer than 63 lines are virtually identical with 64 lines in *Ep.* VI.[5] These include a set of quotations, some quite lengthy – from Paul, Jerome to Eustochium, Proverbs, Ecclesiasticus, Jerome to Nepotian, the *Vitae Patrum*, and Macrobius' *Saturnalia* (a remarkable excerpt of nine lines). All the abridgements and *item*'s likewise coincide. But most important, the contexts coincide: the writer of *Ep.* VI has raised the question of nuns taking wine, and has adduced all these quotations; and the writer of *Ep.* VIII, offering counsel, just gives these same quotations back!

To maintain that Abelard wrote *Ep.* VI, pretending to seek advice, and then in *Ep.* VIII, instead of discussing the propositions set out in the earlier letter, simply parroted all these once more, would be an insult to his intelligence. Moreover, there is an evident lack of coherence in the context in both letters, because in both, as was noted above (p. 132), paragraphs where a modest tolerance of wine is defended seem to alternate without rhyme or reason with others where 'wine is Satan'. Before a full study of the textual problems is undertaken, one can only say that in the portions shared by *Epp.* VI and VIII there is a strong likelihood of contamination, and that some passages, which do not seem to fit into either argument, may well have been interpolated. *Ep.* VIII poses special problems of transmission, since it survives complete in only one of the nine manuscripts that contain the collection of letters. As for *Ep.* VI, even if we must reckon with the later insertion of an ill-fitting diatribe against wine, with its own *auctoritates*, it is safe to say that no reason of weight has yet been advanced for attributing the remainder of this letter to anyone other than the person to whom all the manuscripts assign it: Heloise.

6   Hildegard of Bingen

On ne peut écrire que les yeux grands ouverts et ce que l'on voit n'est autre que
ce que l'on apprend à mesure que l'on avance, confiant, ou que l'on recule,
effrayé.

Edmond Jabès, Le Livre des Ressemblances

I

Hildegard of Bingen still confronts us, after eight centuries, as an overpowering,
electrifying presence – and in many ways an enigmatic one. Compared with
what earlier and later women writers have left us, the volume of her work is
vast. In its range that work is unique. In the Middle Ages only Avicenna is in
some ways comparable: cosmology, ethics, medicine and mystical poetry were
among the fields conquered by both the eleventh-century Persian master and the
twelfth-century 'Rhenish sibyl'.[1] In more recent centuries, Goethe – who saw
and was astonished by the illuminated *Scivias* manuscript in Wiesbaden[2] – shows
perhaps most affinity to that combination of poetic, scientific and mystic
impulses, that freedom with images and ideas, which characterized Hildegard.

To sketch the ways in which Hildegard understood herself and the world
around her, we have in a sense too many materials, and of too diverse kinds, at
our disposal. The finest studies of her work in the past have given primacy to her
trilogy of allegorical visions.[3] Here instead I shall focus first on the twelve
principal autobiographic passages that are still preserved in Hildegard's *Vita* in
the form in which she set them down. To complement these, certain moments
in which Hildegard's personality emerges vividly in her letters will be chosen,
with special stress on letters that are not yet published. At the same time, to convey something of Hildegard's wider outlook, I shall turn to the work known as
Causae et curae. Even though this (surviving imperfectly in a unique manuscript)
is only a fragment of what was conceived as a larger synthesis, a book of 'the
subtleties of the natures of diverse creatures',[4] it can reveal certain things about
Hildegard's way of looking with more immediacy than can the visionary works.
Historians of science (Thorndike, Singer and others)[5] have quarried in *Causae et
curae* for curious physical notions; the 'autobiographic' element in the work has
never been discussed or even surmised.

Born in the Rhineland in 1098, Hildegard was the last of ten children of a
noble family. The first extensive autobiographic note cited in the *Vita* tells
something of her childhood, and of the way she found her vocation and won
through to recognition:[6]

Wisdom teaches in the light of love, and bids me tell how I was brought into this my gift of vision . . . 'Hear these words, human creature, and tell them not according to yourself but according to me, and, taught by me, speak of yourself like this. – In my first formation, when in my mother's womb God raised me up with the breath of life, he fixed this vision in my soul. For, in the eleven hundredth year after Christ's incarnation, the teaching of the apostles and the burning justice which he had set in Christians and spiritual people began to grow sluggish and irresolute. In that period I was born, and my parents, amid sighs, vowed me to God. And in the third year of my life I saw so great a brightness that my soul trembled; yet because of my infant condition I could express nothing of it. But in my eighth year I was offered to God, given over to a spiritual way of life, and till my fifteenth I saw many things, speaking of a number of them in a simple way, so that those who heard me wondered from where they might have come or from whom they might be.

Then I too grew amazed at myself, that whenever I saw these things deep in my soul I still retained outer sight, and that I heard this said of no other human being. And, as best I could, I concealed the vision I saw in my soul. I was ignorant of much in the outer world, because of the frequent illness that I suffered, from the time of my mother's milk right up to now: it wore my body out and made my powers fail.

Exhausted by all this, I asked a nurse of mine if she saw anything save external objects. 'Nothing', she answered, for she saw none of those others. Then, seized with great fear, I did not dare reveal it to anyone; yet nonetheless, speaking or composing, I used to make many affirmations about future events, and when I was fully perfused by this vision I would say many things that were unfathomable (*aliena*) to whose who listened. But if the force of the vision – in which I made an exhibition of myself more childish than befitted my age – subsided a little, I blushed profusely and often wept, and many times I should gladly have kept silent, had I been allowed. And still, because of the fear I had of other people, I did not tell anyone *how* I saw. But a certain high-born woman, to whom I had been entrusted for education, noted this and disclosed it to a monk whom she knew.

. . . After her death, I kept seeing in this way till my fortieth year. Then in that same vision I was forced by a great pressure (*pressura*) of pains to manifest what I had seen and heard. But I was very much afraid, and blushed to utter what I had so long kept silent. However, at that time my veins and marrow became full of that strength which I had always lacked in my infancy and youth.

I intimated this to a monk who was my *magister* . . . Astonished, he bade me write these things down secretly, till he could see what they were and what their source might be. Then, realizing that they came from God, he indicated this to his abbot, and from that time on he worked at this [writing down] with me, with great eagerness.

In that same [experience of] vision I understood the writings of the prophets, the Gospels, the works of other holy men, and those of certain philosophers, without any human instruction, and I expounded certain things based on these, though I scarcely had literary understanding, inasmuch as a woman who was not learned had been my teacher. But I also brought forth songs with their melody, in praise of God and the saints, without being taught by anyone, and I sang them too, even though I had never learnt either musical notation or any kind of singing.

When these occurrences were brought up and discussed at an audience in Mainz Cathedral, everyone said they stemmed from God, and from that gift of prophecy which the prophets of old had proclaimed. Then my writings were brought to Pope Eugene, when he was in Trier. With joy he had them read out in the presence of many people, and read them for himself, and, with great trust in God's grace, sending me his blessing with a letter, he bade me commit whatever I saw or heard in my vision to writing, more comprehensively than hitherto.'

Because of her abnormal gift, Hildegard saw herself as called – notwithstanding all her inner fears and uncertainties – to the rôle of prophet. That, late in life, she felt impelled to tell of herself and her visionary experience, she sees as a summons made to her by Sapientia – the beautiful womanly divine emanation celebrated in the 'Sapiential' books in the Old Testament.[7] She senses that it is not merely her own personal testimony, but Sapientia speaking through her. The prophet sees herself as timid in her own right, daring insofar as she is Sapientia's mouthpiece. This, more than anything else, underlies the blend of diffidence and assurance in Hildegard's account of her rôle. She was born providentially, at a critical moment of Christian world-history. This could easily sound overweening, yet Hildegard is convinced that Sapientia bids her affirm it. She had been aware of her 'talent', her *visio*, from earliest childhood, and it remained with her for the whole of her life.

Hildegard uses *visio* to designate three related things: her peculiar faculty or capacity of vision; her experience of this faculty; and the content of her experience, all that she sees in her *visio*. Her mode of vision is most unusual: she sees 'in the soul' while still fully exercising, and remaining aware of, the powers of normal perception.

Richard of St Victor, the mystic from Scotland who was Hildegard's contemporary, in his commentary on the Apocalypse of John distinguished four kinds of vision:[8] two outer and two inner, the first two being physical, the others spiritual. The least of the four, physical sight (1), contains no hidden significance; but a second kind of bodily vision, though physical, also contains a force of hidden meaning (2). It was in this mode, for instance, that Moses beheld the burning bush (Exodus 3: 2–4). Of the two modes of spiritual vision, one is that of the eyes of the heart, when the human spirit, illuminated by the Holy Ghost, is led through the likenesses of visible things, and through images presented as figures and signs, to the knowledge of invisible ones (3). This is what Dionysius had called symbolic vision. The second, which Dionysius had called anagogic vision, occurs when the human spirit, through inner aspiration, is raised to the contemplation of the celestial without the mediation of any visible figures (4).

Hildegard's *visio* is clearly of Richard's third kind rather than his fourth. Throughout her visionary trilogy she sees, with an inner eye, images presented as figures and signs. And these lead her to understanding of a spiritual kind: mostly in that she is enlightened by the divine voice she hears in her *visio*, which explains to her the figural or allegoric meaning of the images she beholds. What is exceptional in Hildegard, and what she herself felt to be unique, is that this

146

mode of vision was for her absolutely concurrent with physical sight. There was not the least suspension of her normal faculties: her insights had nothing to do with dream or daydream or trance or hallucination or *extasis* (a word that she, like a number of twelfth-century writers, uses only in a pejorative sense). What Hildegard wants to stress is that, with all that she saw in her soul, she remained physically lucid throughout.

At the same time her *visio* was, she felt, linked in a mysterious way with her recurrent bodily afflictions. When, after describing both her *visio* and her ravaging illness, Hildegard begins the next sentence 'Exhausted by all this . . . (*His valde fatigata . . .*)', it is not clear whether she means, exhausted by illness or exhausted by her *visio*. The ambiguity may even be deliberate: the gift or blessing of *visio* may also have been so great a strain that it was at the same time the chief source of her sickness. (Conversely, the sickness may have been a necessary condition of the *visio*.) Singer, analysing various passages in which Hildegard describes both her symptoms and her mode of vision, as well as some components of the *Scivias* visions themselves – the falling stars, the concentric luminous circles, the many evocations of dazzling or blinding lights – concluded that Hildegard suffered from frequent migraine or 'scintillating scotoma'.[9] A diagnosis of this kind can indeed be accepted, even if Singer in his formulation did not sufficiently distinguish between the pathological basis of the visions and the distinctive intellectual qualities of what Hildegard said about them. Hildegard did not simply suffer such disturbances: she made something imaginatively and spiritually fecund out of them.

The next lines in Hildegard's notes display something of the same mixture of fear and pride as Hrotsvitha had shown. She is aware of a gift that sets her apart, a gift that in her case even allows her to foretell future events; at the same time she is afraid of staking any claims, and of making herself seem presumptuous or ridiculous. Where with Hrotsvitha it was perhaps no more than a normal bashfulness, together with partly true, partly affected, modesty, with Hildegard it seems to have been an intense, even morbid, fear of the outer world – a world which, she acutely observes, her constant illnesses had made her less capable of coping with in the ways that ordinary people could.

Like Hrotsvitha again, Hildegard is in a kind of limbo of unease till she and her gift are approved and accepted by the 'greater', masculine world. Till then, the temptation to hide or dissemble or abandon their talent was acute in both. The first step in confidence for each of them is with a loved woman teacher, an abbess of high birth – Gerberga in Hrotsvitha's case, Jutta of Sponheim in Hildegard's. Through the teachers, a few men come to know about the young prodigies; but it is only much later that the inner pressure not to remain concealed gains the ascendant in them. Hildegard's *pressura* to reveal her visions was accompanied by an exultant sense of physical strength, such as she had never known in her long years of ailment. The monk in whom she confided, Volmar – after satisfying himself that here was no case of hubris or of demonic delusion – gladly became, with his abbot's permission, her helper and secretary.[10]

The nature and extent of Volmar's help has been much discussed. In his fundamental study Herwegen argued, with detailed reference to the sources, that while Hildegard welcomed the grammatical and syntactic improvements Volmar could furnish, she allowed no changes in vocabulary or content: however strange her wording and imagery could be, they had to remain intact, because given to her prophetically. I believe Herwegen's conclusions are still broadly valid: only with Hildegard's last major work, the *Liber divinorum operum*, and some of the very late writings, is the textual situation more complex.[11] Hildegard claimed her prophetic gift as the direct source not only of what she wrote but also of her intuitive mastery of the Scriptures and of theological and philosophic works: she could penetrate their difficulties readily, even though her schooling had been quite rudimentary, her command of Latin had remained in many ways uncertain, and she had had no specialist training in philosophy or theology. In the same way her gift of musical composition and performance was intuitive, not dependent on the study of written music or of singing.[12]

In her fortieth year, then, Hildegard felt an irresistible *pressura* to keep her gifts hidden no longer. We may conjecture that the fact that the previous year, 1136, the sisters on the Disibodenberg had elected Hildegard as their abbess, to succeed her beloved former teacher Jutta, filled her with greater confidence than she had known before; then for the first time she felt a surge of health. The decade 1137–47 saw her progressive acceptance in the more powerful male world around her – first in the ambience of the archbishop of Mainz, then in that of the pope himself, just as Hrotsvitha's progress was (as I argued) from writing, at first chiefly for her own satisfaction, in an aristocratic community of learned women, to finding acceptance in the more grandly aspiring world of the Ottonian court.

The synod of Trier – November 1147 to February 1148 – saw the papal ratification of Hildegard's visionary writing, and implicitly of the prophetic rôle which impelled her to write. Earlier in 1147, on that same journey through northern Europe, Pope Eugene had given his approval to another profoundly original work – the *Cosmographia* of Bernard Silvestris.[13] That both the *Cosmographia* and *Scivias* (the second still 'work in progress', not completed till 1151) were given the blessing of this pope is of special importance in terms of twelfth-century intellectual history. Two writers who showed such daring in their cosmological conceptions and formulations could so easily, had it not been for Pope Eugene, have been persecuted, the works called in question and condemned by council or synod, as happened with Abelard, William of Conches, or Gilbert

148

of Poitiers. St Bernard, who was active in the attempts to condemn these three, had himself in 1147 been approached by Hildegard for encouragement in the completing of *Scivias*, and had approved her task (though in a brief, and one must admit somewhat perfunctory, letter);[14] he was also among those present when Pope Eugene declared himself for Hildegard at Trier. The following year another Frenchman, Odo of Paris, who had likewise been at Trier, wrote to Hildegard praising the originality of her songs, and asking her whether, through her *visio*, she could pronounce on the correctness or otherwise of one of the central theses of Gilbert of Poitiers, which was about to be discussed at Gilbert's hearing at the Council of Reims: were God's 'fatherhood' and 'godhead' identical with God?[15] That is, Odo credited Hildegard with a means of judging different from and superior to normal methods of metaphysical enquiry.

From 1147 onwards Hildegard, her prophetic rôle endorsed, is often appealed to for counsel, and often volunteers it, among the secular and religious leaders of her day. Her correspondents include three popes (Anastasius IV and Hadrian IV as well as Eugene III), monarchs (Conrad III, Frederick Barbarossa, Henry II of England, Eleanor of Aquitaine, and the Byzantine Empress Irene), as well as a host of lesser dignitaries. She undertakes preaching journeys, addressing sermons to monks in their abbeys, to bishops and clergy at their synods, as well as to the laity in towns. She attempts to exorcize. In a word, as prophet Hildegard assumed without serious opposition many high sacerdotal functions which in general the Church had seen, and continued to see, as male prerogatives. Always she distinguishes between herself in her own right, the 'poor little womanly figure (*paupercula feminea forma*)', and what the divine voice, or the living light, expresses through her. When she admonishes, warns, or castigates, it is always in the name of that light and that voice, not in her own.

Thus she is able to write Emperor Frederick both a letter holding up to him a mirror of princely conduct, and later (probably in 1164, when for the second time Frederick set up his own anti-pope) a ferocious warning: he is behaving 'childishly, like one whose mode of life is insane (*velut parvulum et velut insane viventem*)'.[16] She explains the nature of the prophet's task beautifully in a letter to Elisabeth of Schönau, whose own visions were of an ecstatic kind. Here Hildegard expresses herself gently, yet her words carry a hint of reproachful admonition:

Those who long to perfect the works of God ... should leave heavenly things to him who is heavenly; for they are exiles, ignorant of the celestial, only singing the hiddenness of God, in the same way as a trumpet only brings forth sounds but does not cause them: another must blow into it, for the sound to emerge. So too I, lying low in pusillanimity of fear, at times resound a little, like a small trumpet-note from the living brightness.[17]

The tension that this inner duality entailed showed itself physically in the ever-recurring migraines and related ailments; then, in the years 1150–1, the tension was exacerbated by two events in which Hildegard was certain she had received prophetic knowledge of God's will, but where keen human resistance was shown. In 1150 it was a question of fighting for the independence of her community – of allowing the sisters to move some 30 kilometres away from the Disibodenberg, to the Rupertsberg on the Rhine. Here, after bitter opposition from the Disibodenberg monks, on grounds of prestige and finance as well as of personal attachment, Hildegard at last had her way. The following year she was faced with the desire for independence of Richardis, the nun whom she loved best. There, despite impassioned appeals to archbishops, to members of Richardis' high-born family, and even to Pope Eugene, Hildegard failed.

II

Her own reflections on the two events, which survive in the *Vita*, deserve to be quoted:[18]

At one time, because of a dimming of my eyes, I could see no light; I was weighed down in body by such a weight that I could not get up, but lay there assailed by the most intense pains. I suffered in this way because I had not divulged the vision I had been shown, that with my girls (*cum puellis meis*) I should move from the Disibodenberg, where I had been vowed to God, to another place. I was afflicted till I named the place where I am now. At once I regained my sight and had things easier, though I still did not recover fully from my sickness. But my abbot, and the monks and the populace in that province, when they realized what the move implied – that we wanted to go from fertile fields and vineyards and the loveliness of that spot to parched places where there were no amenities – were all amazed. And they intrigued so that this should not come about: they were determined to oppose us. What is more, they said I was deluded by some vain fantasy. When I heard this, my heart was crushed, and my body and veins dried up. Then, lying in bed for many days, I heard a mighty voice forbidding me to utter or to write anything more in that place about my vision.

Then a noble marchioness, who was known to us, approached the archbishop of Mainz and laid all this before him and before other wise counsellors. They said that no place could be hallowed except through good deeds, so that it seemed right that we should go ahead. And thus, by the archbishop's permission, with a vast escort of our kinsfolk and of other men, in reverence of God we came to the Rupertsberg. Then the ancient deceiver put me to the ordeal of great mockery, in that many people said: 'What's all this – so many hidden truths revealed to this foolish, unlearned woman, even though there are many brave and wise men around? Surely this will come to nothing!' For many people wondered whether my revelation stemmed from God, or from the parchedness (*inaquositas*) of aerial spirits, that often seduced human beings.

So I stayed in that place with twenty girls of noble and wealthy parentage, and we found no habitation or inhabitant there, save for one old man and his wife and children. Such great misfortunes and such pressure of toil befell me, it was as if a stormcloud covered the sun – so that, sighing and weeping copiously, I said: 'Oh, oh, God confounds no one who trusts in him!' Then God showed me his grace again, as when the clouds recede and the sun bursts forth, or when a mother offers her weeping child milk, restoring its joy after tears.

Then in true vision I saw that these tribulations had come to me according to the exemplar of Moses, for when he led the children of Israel from Egypt through the Red Sea into the desert, they, murmuring against God, caused great affliction to Moses too, even though God lit them on their way with wondrous signs. So God let me be oppressed in some measure by the common people, by my relatives, and by some of the women who had remained with me, when they lacked essential things (except inasmuch as, through God's grace, they were given to us as alms). For just as the children of Israel plagued Moses, so these people, shaking their heads over me, said: 'What good is it for well-born and wealthy girls to pass from a place where they lacked nothing into such penury?' But we were waiting for the grace of God, who had shown us this spot, to come to our aid.

After the pressure of such grief, he rained that bounty upon us. For many, who had previously despised us and called us a parched useless thing, came from every side to help us, filling us with blessings. And many rich people buried their dead on our land, with due honour . . .

Nonetheless, God did not want me to remain steadily in complete security: this he had shown me since infancy in all my concerns, sending me no carefree joy as regards this life, through which my mind could become overbearing. For when I was writing my book *Scivias*, I deeply cherished a nobly-born young girl, daughter of the marchioness I mentioned, just as Paul cherished Timothy. She had bound herself to me in loving friendship in every way, and showed compassion for my illnesses, till I had finished the book. But then, because of her family's distinction, she hankered after an appointment of more repute: she wanted to be named abbess of some splendid church. She pursued this not for the sake of God but for worldly honour. When she had left me, going to another region far away from us, she soon afterwards lost her life and the renown of her appointment.

Some other noble girls, too, acted in similar fashion, separating themselves from me. Some of them later lived such irresponsible lives that many people said, their actions showed that they sinned against the Holy Spirit, and against the person who spoke from out of the Spirit. But I and those who loved me wondered why such great persecution came upon me, and why God did not bring me comfort, since I did not wish to persevere in sins but longed to perfect good works with his help. Amid all this I completed my book *Scivias*, as God willed.

Nearly thirty years before Hildegard's move to the Rupertsberg, Abelard had confronted problems which were in many aspects similar, and which he sketches in his *Historia calamitatum* in ways that are often close to Hildegard's.[19] Abbot Adam of Saint-Denis was as reluctant to let Abelard free himself from the great royal monastery as Abbot Kuno was to release Hildegard from the Disibodenberg. Abelard, like Hildegard, achieved release only after encountering various intrigues, by appealing to high authority – to the bishop of Meaux and the king of France – as Hildegard appealed to the archbishop of Mainz and the marchioness of Stade. The place in which he won freedom is described, like hers, as full of physical hardship: at the barren site that was to become Abelard's foundation, the Paraclete, the students who followed him, 'leaving spacious dwellings, built themselves small huts; instead of living on delicate foods, they ate wild herbs and coarse bread; instead of soft beds they used thatch and straw'. And later, when the Paraclete was made into a refuge for Heloise and her nuns, Abelard expresses the same sense as Hildegard of a miraculous change for the better, a sudden advent of wealth and plenty where before there was want:

Heloise and her nuns at first endured a life of privation there – for a time they were desolate – but in a short while the gaze of divine mercy gave them comfort . . . and made people all around merciful and helpful to them. And God knows, their earthly commodities were multiplied more in one year, I think, than I could have achieved in a hundred, had I stayed.[20]

Nonetheless, neither Abelard nor Hildegard won complete inner security. He suffered the disloyalties and slanders (and even violence) of the monks at his new abbey, Saint-Gildas; Hildegard too was beset by what she took to be disloyalty among her community – those who complained of the discomforts of the new settlement, those who left it for a less demanding life; most of all she was overcome by the departure of her much-loved Richardis, a defection to which Hildegard attributes only unworthy motives. And just as Abelard tells laconically of the abbot of Saint-Denis, who had refused his plea for permanent release, 'Departing in such obstinacy, he died a few days later', so too Hildegard mentions Richardis' sudden early death as if it had been a consequence of her stubbornness. It is not the crude and ferocious way in which, in the seventh century, St Valerius branded those who opposed his will to live in solitude – saying for instance of Bishop Isidore of Asturias, who tried to get the saint to assume some public responsibility at the Council of Toledo:

. . . through the true judgement of almighty God, he suddenly fell into the pool which he had opened as a trap for me. It left me unharmed, while endless hell swallowed him.[21]

Still, in Abelard's words as in Hildegard's, the sense that God's judgment showed itself in their favour, after their own wish had been thwarted, seems implicit.

And yet Hildegard's account has an element relating to her particular situation that is different from Abelard's. She is a woman, and she claims to have received prophetic illumination: she is disbelieved and mocked on both counts. So too in one of Hildegard's lyrical sequences for St Ursula: she pictures Ursula shouting out her longing to race through the heavens and join the divine Sun, and causing scandal by her mystical utterances –

> so that men said:
> 'What simple, girlish ignorance!
> She does not know what she is saying.'[22]

This detail – which has no parallel in the hagiographic sources about Ursula – suggests that the sequence, which may indeed have been composed in the very years of the events which caused Hildegard such turmoil, contains a personal projection, that Hildegard sees this saint in a special way as *figura* and aspiration for herself.

Yet she is again like Abelard in that she continually applies parallels from Old Testament characters to her own destiny. She leads her little band to the Rupertsberg in the way Moses led the Israelites to the wilderness, and is grumbled at as Moses was. In the next note 'in scripto suo', the exemplars continue. Now her struggle is for administrative and financial independence for her new foundation. On account of this, she says, she suffered hostility like Joshua, she was envied like Joseph by his brothers; and as God came to Joshua's and Joseph's aid, so did he to hers. The details of the conflict are recorded not in the *Vita* but near the beginning of a didactic letter, explaining the Athanasian Creed to her daughters on the Rupertsberg. She fought the monks, she there tells, not only on the question of property, but on that of keeping with them the monk Volmar, who had long been her provost and secretary, and who strictly should have remained in his own cloister. The Disibodenberg monks, even after they had been made to let Hildegard and her twenty sisters move, were not happy to see the disappearance of the endowments which these women (all from prominent families) had brought with them to the monastery; nor did they wish to lose one of their ablest confrères:[23]

At God's behest I made my way back to the mountain of blessed Disibodus, from where, with permission, I had seceded. And I made my petition in the presence of all those living in the cloister: that our site, and the domains donated with that site, should no longer be tied to them . . .

And in accordance with what I perceived in my true vision, I said to the Father Abbot: 'The serene light says: You shall be father to our provost, and father of the salvation of the souls of the daughters of my mystic garden.[24] But their alms do not belong to you or to your brothers – your cloister should be a refuge for these women. If you are determined to go on with your perverse proposals, raging against us, you will be like the Amalekites, and like Antiochus, of whom it was written that he despoiled the Temple of the Lord.[25] If some of you, unworthy ones, said to yourselves: Let's take some of their freeholds away – then I WHO AM[26] say: You are the worst of robbers. And if you try to take away the shepherd of spiritual medicine [i.e. Provost Volmar], then again I say, you are sons of Belial, and in this do not look to the justice of God. So that same justice will destroy you.'

And when I, poor little creature (*paupercula forma*), had with these words petitioned the abbot and his confrères for the freehold of the site and domains of my daughters, they all granted it to me, entering the transfer in a codex.

In the same way as the Rupertsberg, Abelard's Paraclete, when it was made over to women through his gift, had to have its independence officially secured: a papal *privilegium* (1131) confirmed in perpetuity for Heloise and her nuns the possession of all property connected with the foundation.

III

On the Disibodenberg, Hildegard launched not so much a petition (though she calls it that) as a fulmination. Even more in her other ordeal at this time, the loss of Richardis, where in the end she did not get her way, we sense that Hildegard could use her prophetic persona savagely and overbearingly. In her first letter about this, where she appeals to the marchioness, mother of Richardis and grand-mother of Adelheid (who likewise wanted to leave the Rupertsberg and accept a more prominent appointment as an abbess), there is as yet no attempt to legislate in the name of the God of Moses, only a sense of human anguish – quickly followed, however, by a vehement conviction of being in the right:[27]

I beseech you and urge you not to trouble my soul so deeply that you bring bitter tears to my eyes and wound my heart with dire wounds, on account of my most loving daughters Richardis and Adelheid. I see them now glowing in the dawn and graced with pearls of virtues. So take care lest by your will, your advice and connivance, their senses and their souls be moved away from the sublimity of that grace. For the position of abbess, that you desire for them, is surely, surely, surely not compatible with God (*certe, certe, certe non est cum deo*), or with the salvation of their souls.

Nonetheless, the two girls accepted nomination as abbesses. With Adelheid, there is no record of further resistance by Hildegard; but she did not give Richardis leave to take up her new task. When the archbishop of Mainz wrote to Hildegard demanding (with even a hint of threat) that she now yield and release Richardis, she answered, claiming to speak with the voice of God, in unbridled denunciation of the archbishop himself. By insisting on this office for Richardis, he shows he is nothing but a simoniac:

The lucid fountain who is not deceitful but is just says: the reasons that have been alleged for the appointment of this girl are unavailing in the sight of God, because I, the high and deep and encompassing one, who am a piercing light, did not lay down or choose those reasons: they were perpetrated in the conniving audacity of ignorant hearts . . . The spirit of God, full of zeal, says: pastors, lament and mourn at this time, because you do not know what you do, when you squander offices, whose source is God, for financial gain and to please the foolishness of wicked men, who have no fear of God. Then your malicious curses and threatening words must not be heeded . . .

Arise, because your days are short, and remember that Nebuchadnezzar fell and that his crown perished. And many others fell who rashly raised themselves up to heaven. Ah, you ember, why do you not grow red with shame at flying up when you should be fading?[28]

For Hildegard, losing Richardis meant losing her close collaborator and losing the disciple whom she admired most and to whom she was most deeply attached. Was it simply arrogant possessiveness that impelled her to speak as prophet here, so as to try and overthrow the archbishop's decision? Her broader invective, against clergy motivated by financial gain, implies that there had been some-

154

thing irregular about Richardis' election. This could perhaps be corroborated by considering that the marchioness' grand-daughter, Adelheid, was at almost the same date (1152) elected abbess of the illustrious foundation Gandersheim, making this move at a time when she was probably still of schoolgirl age and certainly too young to have taken her monastic vows on the Rupertsberg. This suggests that those who elected Adelheid – and possibly those who elected Richardis, too – may have been influenced less by the suitability of the two girls than by a hope of rich endowments from the von Stade family in return for these elections. (Adelheid's mother had married exaltedly three times, and had been Queen of Denmark.)

With Richardis, however, the matter is more complex: Hildegard in the *Vita* passage intimates that Richardis herself was eager for a position that she felt befitted her high worldly rank. Possibly the primitive conditions on the Rupertsberg, in the first year after the move, irked her, possibly she came to feel oppressed by Hildegard's dominance – many contributing elements can be surmised, though none proved.

Hildegard's conviction, which comes out so strongly in the letter to the marchioness, that any acceptance of such dignities for reasons other than idealistic ones is evil and imperils the soul, sounds wholly genuine, however much her own impassioned obduracy may have played a part in her seeing it that way. She next appealed to Richardis' brother, Archbishop Hartwig, whose diocese, Bremen, included his sister's new abbey:

Dear friend, I greatly cherish your soul, more than your family. Now hear me, prostrate in tears and misfortune before your feet, for my soul is deeply sad, because a horrible man (*horribilis homo*) has overthrown my advice and will.

Here Hildegard seems to accuse even her beloved Richardis of having deliberately bought her office:

If one of restless mind seeks preferment, longing to be master, striving lustfully for power rather than looking to the will of God, such a one is a marauding wolf in person . . . That is simony.

Yet a moment later the chief blame is laid on Abbot Kuno of the Disibodenberg:

Thus it was not necessary for our abbot to predetermine a holy soul, bedazed in sense and ignorant, into these actions and into such irresponsibility of mental blindness. If our daughter had remained at peace, God would have prepared her for the intention of his glory. So I beg you . . . send my beloved daughter back to me! For I shan't ignore an election that stems from God, nor contradict her, wherever it may be . . . I ask it, so that I may be consoled through her, and she through me. What God has commanded I do not oppose. May God give you blessing from the dew of heaven, and may all the choirs of angels bless you, if you hear me, God's handmaiden, and accomplish God's will in this issue.[29]

Hildegard's accusations, taken together, are somewhat confusing. At times they are levelled at Richardis herself, at times against her family, at others against the abbot of the Disibodenberg or the archbishop of Mainz. In a word, Hildegard felt there was a conspiracy against her. And quite possibly this was no mere persecution-fantasy. The von Stade family clearly had a whole network of influential connections in the Church throughout Germany. Yet they would scarcely have taken advantage of these had they not been prompted by Richardis' own desire to leave. Hildegard, unwilling to accept this, in her doting attachment, made an exhibition of herself in a way she never did (though she had feared to) in her early visions.

In her letter to Hartwig, once more, Hildegard does not claim outright to be speaking as God's mouthpiece. And yet she is never less than certain that she knows the will of God; doing God's will and doing her will are seen as identical. There is a frightening hint of megalomania here. It does not seem to have escaped Pope Eugene, to whom Hildegard wrote in a last attempt to quash Richardis' abbacy. The text of her appeal to him does not survive, but Eugene's answer,[30] while full of praise for Hildegard, 'so kindled by the fire of divine love', also contains a hint of warning: it is those who are great who often greatly fall. 'Reflect then, my daughter, because that serpent of old who cast the first man out of paradise longs to destroy the great, such as Job . . .' Then, almost as if it were an afterthought, he turns to her petition, and he evades it: only if there were no adequate scope for practising the Benedictine Rule in Richardis' new abbey, Bassum, should she be returned to Hildegard. (As Bassum was at that moment a more renowned Benedictine foundation than the Rupertsberg, this was a wholly hypothetical alternative.) The archbishop of Mainz was to judge whether Bassum was monastically suitable. This was in effect to confirm his earlier decision against Hildegard.

It is a token of Hildegard's greatness that, faced with this defeat, she not only tried to resign herself to it but to find fruitful meaning in it. Thus she wrote, 'to the maiden Richardis':

1 Daughter, hear me, your mother in the spirit, saying to you: My grief rises up. Grief kills the great trust and solace that I found in a human being. From now on I shall say: 'It is good to set one's hope in the Lord, better than to set it in the world's mighty ones.' That is, man ought to look to the one on high, the living one, quite unshaded by any love or feeble trust such as the dark sublunary air offers for a brief time. One who beholds God thus raises the eyes like an eagle to the sun. And because of this one should not look to a high personage, who fails as flowers fall.

2 I fell short of this, because of love for a noble person. Now I tell you, whenever I have sinned in this way, God has made that sin clear to me in some experiences of anguish or of pain – and this has now happened on account of you, as you yourself know.

3 Now, again, I say: Woe is me, your mother, woe is me, daughter – why have you

abandoned me like an orphan? I loved the nobility of your conduct, your wisdom and chastity, your soul and the whole of your life, so much that many said: What are you doing?
4 Now let all who have a sorrow like my sorrow mourn with me – all who have ever, in the love of God, had such high love in heart and mind for a human being as I for you – for one snatched away from them in a single moment, as you were from me.
5 But may the angel of God precede you, and the son of God protect you, and his mother guard you. Be mindful of your poor mother Hildegard, that your happiness may not fail.

The language Hildegard uses in this letter is both intimate and heavy with biblical echoes. These can heighten, but also modify, what she is saying; they make the letter suprapersonal as well as personal. Both aspects are vital to what is essentially a harsh confrontation between transcendent love and the love of the heart.

The opening words, 'Daughter, hear me (*Audi me, filia*)', echo a verse in Psalm 44 that, by its continuation – which will have been present to Richardis' mind as to Hildegard's – suggests an implicit claim greater than Hildegard spells out:

> Daughter, hear me and see, and incline your ear,
> and forget your people and your father's house –
> then the King will desire your glorious beauty . . .

That is, Hildegard by her choice of opening suggests it is only by heeding her and turning her back on the world of her own family that Richardis will become a bride of the heavenly King. So too she does not address Richardis as an equal, an abbess like herself: she is still 'the maiden', the spiritual daughter, who must listen to her mother. Yet what the mother now brings forth is not a command but a *planctus*. She expresses her sense of betrayal citing the words of Psalm 117:9 ('Bonum est sperare in Domino quam sperare in principibus'), which contrast the steadfastness of God's love with the fickleness of human hopes. All human attachments, Hildegard concludes, are by their nature mutable, and should be surmounted in singleminded contemplation of the changeless one. Isaiah (40: 7–8) contrasts the human lot – to wither like a flower - with the word of God, which remains forever. Yet the echo from the Epistle of James (1: 11) is perhaps even more pertinent here, James who says of a rich person, 'the flower falls, the beauty of its aspect has perished'.

From meditation on the two kinds of attachment (1), Hildegard passes to introspection (2). All that drew her to Richardis was of necessity transitory, and her clinging to that transitoriness was the source of her suffering: it carried its own nemesis within. And yet this second 'movement', of changed awareness (*anagnorisis*), is also parallel with the third, which is an outbreak of renewed lament. The closeness of the two impulses is reflected in the parallelism of wording ('Nunc tibi dico . . . Nunc iterum dico'). In the complaint that follows (3), biblical echoes again evoke the love of God in contrast to human love. But the connotations pull in two directions: the words 'why have you abandoned me (*quare me dereliquisti*)' are the Psalmist's anguished reproach of God (Psalm 21: 2), yet here they are capped by the words 'like an orphan (*sicut orphanam*)', recalling the moment in John (13: 18) when Christ promises his disciples that, after leaving them to go back to the Father, 'I shall not abandon you like orphans – I shall come to you.'

Amid her grieving Hildegard claims the human loftiness of the love she felt – and a moment later acknowledges that, long before herself, others had perceived this was a hopeless attachment. This leads into a final threnody (4), summoning fellow-mourners, in the words of Jeremiah's lamentation (1: 12):

> Oh all of you who pass by the wayside,
> take heed and see if there is a sorrow like my sorrow . . .

In Jeremiah the words are spoken by a feminine projection, Jerusalem. The context there has many reverberations that enrich the letter: 'the *domina* of peoples has become like a widow . . . there is none to solace her among all her dear ones . . . she has sinned and therefore has become unstable . . . moaning and turning away . . . she has been cast down violently, having no comforter'. And yet there is perhaps an even greater audacity in Hildegard's echo of Jeremiah, for in the medieval Good Friday liturgy the words were seen as spoken not by Jerusalem but figurally by Christ in the Passion.

At the close (5), lament resolves itself in calm and loving valediction. Here Hildegard brings together the thought of Christ's mother and of herself, the 'wretched mother' of Richardis. Now, parted from her unhappy former spiritual mother, Richardis shall have a greater, heavenly mother to watch over her. Yet (again the term that springs to mind is from the Aristotelian dynamic of tragedy) a *peripeteia* has been accomplished: Hildegard has moved from the confident opening summons, 'hear me, your mother in the spirit (*matrem tuam in spiritu*)', to a dejected close – 'be mindful of your poor mother (*esto memor misere matris tue*)'. At the same time the last words – 'that your happiness may not fail (*ut non deficiat felicitas tua*)' – suggest that, even if no human attachment can or should endure, this should not exempt anyone from lovingly remembering one's fellow-being 'in the love of God'.

After Richardis' sudden death her brother Hartwig wrote again to Hildegard, telling her that at the end, weeping, with all her heart she longed to return:

So I ask you with all my power, if I am worthy to ask, that you love her as much as she loved you. And if she seems to have failed in any way – since this was due to me, not to her – that at least you consider the tears she shed for having left your convent, tears that many people witnessed. And if death had not prevented her, she would have come to you – the permission had only just been given.[31]

Hildegard answers this letter with a superb flight of magnanimity, sublimation and forgiveness:

Full divine love (*plena caritas*) was in my soul towards her, for in the mightiest vision the living light taught me to love her (*ipsam amare*). Listen: God kept her so jealously that worldly delight could not embrace her: she fought against it, even though she rose like a flower in the beauty and glory and symphony of this world . . .

So my soul has great confidence in her, though the world loved her beautiful looks and her prudence, while she lived in the body. But God loved her more. Thus God did not wish to give his beloved to a rival lover, that is, to the world . . .

So I also expel from my heart that pain you caused me regarding this my daughter.[32]

Hildegard here uses of Richardis a kind of hyperbole more familiar in the love-poetry of the following century. Thus in the *Vita Nuova*, after Beatrice's death, Dante claims 'it was only her great benignity' that took her from the world: 'a sweet desire came to [God] to summon so great a perfection: he made her come to him, from here below, because he saw that this wretched life was unworthy of so noble a creature'.[33] So too, even before her death, an angel in the divine intellect cries out to have Beatrice in 'heaven, which has no defect save for not having her: heaven begs her of its Lord'.[34] Dante also, like Hildegard, echoed Jeremiah's lamenting words to express grief in the dimension of human love: 'Oh you who pass along the road of Love, attend and see if there is any sorrow heavy as mine.'[35] There is a touching incongruity in Hildegard's allusion to Richardis' prudence – she who in life had accused Richardis so vehemently of mental blindness (*obcecatio mentis*), in her longing for independence. Yet if this letter suggests that, at however great an inner cost, Hildegard had arrived at a comprehending acceptance of the young woman who had wanted to carve out her own life rather than remain a disciple, there is the troubling consideration that the succinct and unsympathetic note preserved in the *Vita* represents Hildegard's later reflections. She made these notes probably after the *Liber divinorum operum* (completed 1173/4), which is their last point of reference. Even if some notes had been compiled intermittently in earlier years, it is unlikely that any were set down as early as Richardis' death (29 October 1152). It seems as though, later in her life, it was what had rankled then with Hildegard that came once more to plague her thoughts.

IV

In the next autobiographic note in the *Vita*, Hildegard, describing her recurring illnesses, speaks of 'aerial torments' that pervaded her body, drying up the veins with their blood, the flesh with its humoral juice (*livor*), the marrow with the bones. An 'aerial fire' was burning in her womb. She lay motionless on a coarse cloth (*cilicium*) on the ground, and all gathered round her, convinced she was about to die. Hildegard believed it was 'aerial spirits' who were causing these afflictions. At the same time she heard a good angel, one of Michael's host, inviting her to die and so regain heaven. He summons her in language akin to that of the invitations in the Song of Songs; yet whilst there the beloved bride is called dove (*columba*), Hildegard (who dares to gaze at the divine Sun, like the eagle in the bestiary tradition) is called – or sees herself as – *aquila*: 'Ah, ah my eagle, why do you sleep in knowledge? Rise from your doubt, you are known! Oh gem full of splendour, every eagle shall behold you. The world shall mourn, but heavenly life shall rejoice. And so, in the dawn, fly up to the sun! Rise, rise, come eat and drink!' Again the closest parallel in imaginative situation is the one already cited from the *Vita Nuova* – the angel calling to Beatrice to join the heavenly throng. And just as God answers in Dante's canzone, so here the angelic host answers the first angel, declaring that heaven has not yet sanctioned this hope.

Malignant aerial spirits, Hildegard saw in this *visio*, also attacked some of her noble daughters in the convent, and meshed them in a net of vanities. When she tried to recall them to a holier life, some, who looked at her with fierce eyes (*torvis luminibus me aspicientes*),[36] also slandered her in secret, saying that the form of monastic life she wanted to impose was intolerable. Other sisters took Hildegard's part, she relates, as Daniel took Susanna's, and in the midst of these conflicts God revealed her second visionary work, the *Liber vitae meritorum*, and allowed her to complete it (1158–63).

At the close of this *Liber*, Hildegard not only sets forth once more, with eloquent images, her awareness of her prophetic task, but she adds a curse on any future person who might add to or cut away any word she has written – a curse that, in Christian Latin, Gregory of Tours had been the first to call down upon later generations.[37] As with Gregory, the integrity and inviolability of her written text is of supreme importance to Hildegard – but with her this is grounded specifically in her sense that throughout writing she has been God's instrument: of herself she writes:

> She lives and does not live, she perceives the things formed of dust and does not perceive them, and utters God's miracles not of herself but being touched by them, even as a string touched by a lutanist emits a sound not of itself but by his touch . . . Therefore, if anyone of his own accord perversely add anything to these writings that goes beyond their clear intent, he deserves to be exposed to the punishments here described; or if anyone perversely remove any passage from them, he deserves to be banned from the joys that are here shown.[38]

Then, in the elaborate, mysterious vision that next follows in the *Vita*, this awareness of her own work as an entity with its unique claims extends (I would argue) to an intimation of the qualities of her life and work as a whole. –

In vision I saw three towers, by means of which Wisdom opened certain hidden things up
for me. The first tower had three rooms. In the first room were nobly-born girls together
with some others, who in burning love listened to God's words coming from my mouth –
they had a kind of ceaseless hunger for that. In the second were some steadfast and wise
women, who embraced God's truth in their hearts and words, saying 'Oh, how long will
this remain with us?' They never wearied of that. In the third room were brave armed men
from the common people, who, advancing ardently towards us, were led to marvel at the
miracles of the first two rooms, and loved them with great longing. They came forward
frequently, in the way that common people seek the protection of a prince, to guard them
against their enemies, in a firm and mighty tower.
   In the second tower there were also three rooms. Two of them had become arid in dryness, and that dryness took the form of a dense fog. And those who were in these rooms
said with one voice: 'What are these things, and from where, which that woman utters as
if they were from God? It's hard for us to live differently from our forefathers or the people
of our time. So let's turn to those who know us, since we cannot persevere in anything else.'
Thus they turned back to the common people – they were of no use in this tower, or in the
first . . . But in the third room of this tower were common people who, with many kinds
of love, cherished the words of God that I brought forth from my true vision, and supported
me in my tribulations, even as the publicans clung to Christ.
   The third tower had three ramparts. The first was wooden, the second decked with
flashing stones, the third was a hedge. But a further building was hidden from me in my
vision, so that I learnt nothing about it at the time. Yet in the true light I heard that the
future writing which will be set down concerning it will be mightier and more excellent
than the preceding ones.

The structuring of a vision by telling of diverse buildings and parts of buildings, of people who welcome a divine message in diverse ways and others who
reject it, was something Hildegard had learnt from the second-century prophetic
treatise *Pastor Hermas*.[39] But where Hermas explains most details in allegoric
terms, and Hildegard often follows him in this technique, here she makes no
attempt at interpreting her vision: all is left enigmatic. And yet her meticulous
differentiation of details is unlikely to be arbitrary invention. The whole mode
of presentation suggests that an allegorical meaning was intended, but is missing
(at least among the autobiographic notes that have survived), though it is also
possible that Hildegard at the time of receiving this *visio* was not yet fully conscious of its precise further significance. No interpretation, to my knowledge,
has ever been proposed. The one I would suggest – though very tentatively –
takes its cue from the close of the vision. The building which is still hidden from
Hildegard, but which – she hears – will stimulate writing mightier and more
excellent than the others, would seem to be a glimmering intuition of her last
major work, *Liber divinorum operum*. This is indeed grander in design than her
other visionary writings and could be called her masterpiece. If this hypothesis is
correct, it indicates some possible interpretations for the earlier part of the vision

of the towers. The first tower, with its three rooms, could then stand symbolically for *Scivias*, with its three books. Her words reach her fellow-nuns, younger
and older, in the first two rooms, but also go out to the populace, to those
among them who acknowledge Hildegard as prophet and are ready to see her
as their *princeps*. Does the linking of the common people with the third room
perhaps imply that it was especially the third book of *Scivias*, in particular the
lyrical and dialogued parts near the close, which ordinary people could come to
love (even without knowing Latin), in the form of songs in the *Symphonia* and
of dramatic action in the *Ordo Virtutum*? – that it was principally these which
brought the unlearned to admire Hildegard and all she stood for?

The next tower would presumably refer in some way to the *Liber vitae
meritorum*. That two of its three rooms are arid and filled with fog could then
perhaps reflect that in this work, with its wide-ranging images of vices and
virtues, the chief emphasis – till near the close – is on evil and sin, and the
penalties for these, rather than on the joyous rewards. Yet here there is no exact
correspondence of rooms with books: the *Liber vitae meritorum*, at least in the
form in which it survives in all the earliest manuscripts, is divided into six books,
not three, hence the specific interpretation must remain open. The same holds of
the third tower, with its three ramparts. Yet this tower could well be an image
for Hildegard's scientific treatise, the *Subtilitates naturarum diversarum creaturarum*.
This comprehended both the so-called *Causae et curae* and *Physica* – texts that
originally belonged to a work which, according to Hildegard's explicit testimony, formed a single, larger whole.[40] In particular, three parts of the *Physica*
– the books on trees, on precious stones, and on plants – might correspond to the
triple rampart – wooden, gemmed, and hedged – of this tower.

The conviction that her greatest work was still to come increases in the next
'showing' preserved in Hildegard's *Vita*. This is remarkable in being the only
time she describes a vision accompanied by loss of normal consciousness. Her
note about the three towers, and the fourth, still unfinished, edifice, continues:

At last in the time that followed I saw a mystic and wondrous vision, such that all my womb
was convulsed and my body's sensory powers were extinguished, because my knowledge
was transmuted into another mode, as if I no longer knew myself. And from God's inspiration as it were drops of gentle rain splashed into the knowledge of my soul.

She compares this moment to the one in which St John received the inspiration
'In the beginning was the Word . . .' Reflecting on the nature of that Word,
'sucking its revelation' as John had done ('revelationem suxit'), leads her to see
the complementarity of human and divine:

Man, with every creature, is a handiwork of God. But man is also the worker (*operarius*)
of divinity, and the shading (*obumbratio*) of the mysteries of divine being.

The vision showed Hildegard how to explain the Prologue of John: 'And I saw that this explanation had to be the beginning of another piece of writing, which had not yet been manifested, in which many investigations of the creations of the divine mystery would have to be pursued.' This is now an unequivocal forward reference to the *Liber divinorum operum*, where the first book has as its climax an interpretation of the Prologue of John.[41]

V

The visionary insight into how to interpret John's Prologue, which came to Hildegard about 1167, was followed by another half-year of mortal sickness, first brought on – she writes – by the blowing of the south wind (*de flatu australis venti*), that 'Föhn' which even in present-day Germany is still seen as a source of malaises of every kind, physical and psychological. It is during this sickness that she hears of Sigewize, a young noblewoman living on the lower Rhine, who is being assailed by a demon. Hildegard was reflecting on and longing to know (*cogitante et scire volente*) the exact way in which a demon can affect human beings. In her vision she sees that it cannot 'enter' a person (*non intrat*); yet she believes it can envelop and shadow humans 'with a smoke of darkness (*fumo nigredinis*)'. That is, it can besiege or 'obsess' a person (*obsidere*), though there is no question of demonic 'possession (*possessio*)'.[42] God tolerates the demons' causing various disasters in the world: they can vomit up a plague (*pestilentiam evomunt*), they can cause floods and wars and hostilities and evils among mankind. Their effects, in short, can be material and immaterial: their dark smoke, it would seem, has baleful results very similar to those widely attributed to the 'Föhn'.

Hildegard is asked to help Sigewize, because the demon (speaking, the context suggests, with the young woman's voice), had cried out that only a certain *vetula* on the upper Rhine could do so. The ironic reference is elaborated by Theodoric, author of the third book of the *Vita*, which also includes Hildegard's own notes on the episode: according to Theodoric, the *vetula* is named, derisively, not Hildegardis but Scrumpilgardis ('Wrinklegard'). It seems prudent, however, to discount any details given by Theodoric that are not corroborated in Hildegard's own words, for he, concerned to attribute miraculous powers to her, such as she herself never claimed, embellishes his account with many details that patently derive from a less-than-scrupulous hagiographic tradition. What emerges from Hildegard's account is that, after her initial refusal, on grounds of being too unwell, she tried to cure the young woman by devising an elaborate mimetic scenario for her – an *ordo* in many ways comparable to her play, *Ordo Virtutum* – to drive the demon away. A good part of the text of this eloquent and ingenious attempt at shock-therapy survives.[43] Nonetheless, Hildegard makes clear that it had only a passing effect on the patient, not a durable one. So the abbot of Brauweiler, where the scenario had been performed, pleaded with Hildegard to receive Sigewize and try to help her in person.[44] Though she and the Rupertsberg nuns were terrified at the prospect ('multum exterrite fuimus'), they accepted her, and weeks of communal prayer and ascetic practices resulted, first in a physical spasm, then in Sigewize's gradual convalescence ('de die in diem', P.L. 197, 183 A). It is noteworthy that, though Theodoric's part of the *Vita* is packed with fantasizing miracle-tales, Hildegard herself pretends to nothing beyond having assisted the woman's cure by means of prayer, and by letting the demon 'express himself' through her: we might say, she helped Sigewize's recovery by allowing her to voice openly all her religious fixations and woes, and even her 'demonic' rage, when Hildegard argued against some of her utterances.

The last two autobiographic notes preserved in the *Vita* take us to the period 1170–4. Another grievous illness followed the liberation (*liberatio*) of Sigewize. In it, Hildegard sees 'evil spirits mocking my sickness, cackling at it, saying "Hah, she will die, and her friends will weep, those with whom she confounds us!" Yet I did not see the departure of my soul towards being. I suffered this sickness more than forty days and nights.'

In her vision it was shown to her that she was obliged to undertake another voyage as preacher. 'As long as I neglected these journeys that God commanded me to make, for fear of people, the pains in my body increased. They did not cease till I obeyed – as happened to Jonah, who was fiercely afflicted till he bent himself to obedience.'

For her assent, she was rewarded in her *visio* with the consolation of 'the fairest and most loving man' (*pulcherrimus et amantissimus vir* – the identification with Christ is not made explicit),

. . . such that the look of him perfused all my womb with a balmlike perfume. Then I exulted with great and immeasurable joy, and longed to go on gazing forever. And he commanded those who afflicted me to depart from me, saying: 'Away, I do not want you to torment her any more!' They, departing with great howls, cried out: 'Woe that we ever came here, as we leave confounded!' At once, at the man's words, the sickness that had troubled me, like waters stirred to a flood by tempestuous winds, left me, and I recovered strength.

Hildegard was now well enough, too, to fulfil a request of her former monastery, that she write the life of Disibodus, its patron saint. The same renewed health, she concludes, enabled her to write – that is, complete – the *Liber divinorum operum* (1173/4). For personal testimonies about the last years of her life we must resort to letters.

This last pair of showings has been invested with new kinds of literary stylization. It would seem that Hildegard, refusing here as always to demarcate material and immaterial phenomena, interprets all her illnesses in retrospect as attacks from demons – just as, in early Christian tradition, the nocturnal afflictions and temptations that beset the mind had been both bad dreams and phantoms of the night (*somnia / et noctium phantasmata*).[45] Instinctively, when she gives her demons words, Hildegard resorts to a lower or comic register of speech, including the vernacular exclamations of disgust and disappointment, 'Wach!' and 'Ach!' (So too in Hrotsvitha's writings, evil, about to be confounded, always showed itself as comic and grotesque.) At the same time, Hildegard does not let this lowering of tone affect the central experience: implicitly, with 'forty days and nights', she compares her sickness with Christ's time in the wilderness; explicitly, her dolorous resistance and hard-won obedience to a divine command are likened to Jonah's; and the evocation of the solace of 'the most loving man' relies on the language of the Song of Songs.

VI

Tengswindis, *magistra* of a foundation of canonesses on the Rhine, wrote Hildegard a letter that was both an (overtly polite) enquiry and a challenge.[46] The fame of Hildegard's holy life and wondrous visionary gift, she says, had reached her; yet rumours of a more disquieting kind had also come. Was it true that on festive days Hildegard's nuns wore rings, veils, and tiaras studded with symbolic images? 'We believe you wear all these for love of the heavenly Bridegroom, even though it is right for women (*mulieres*) to adorn themselves modestly.'

Besides, Tengswindis is amazed that Hildegard admits into her fellowship only women who are of high birth. 'Still, we know you are doing this on some reasonable ground (*rationabili causa*), not unaware that in the earliest Church (*in primitiva ecclesia*) the Lord chose fishermen, the lowly and the poor.' She reminds Hildegard of the words of St Peter ('God is no respecter of persons') and of St Paul ('not many who are mighty, not many who are nobly born . . .').

The blandness with which Tengswindis supposes unimpeachable motives behind Hildegard's two innovations becomes, I believe, more palpably ironic near the close, in a request for further illumination:

Such novelty in your practice incomparably excels the minute measure of our littleness, and arouses no small wonderment (*admiratio*) in us. Thus we, so exiguous (*tantillule*), rejoicing inwardly at your advances, have resolved to send our letter to your holiness,[47] beseeching humbly and most devoutly – so that our religious observance may be enhanced by the authority of such a one – that your dignity do not disdain to write back to us in the near future.

In her reply,[48] Hildegard begins by distinguishing between the rôles of married woman and virgin. The first should not flaunt herself: since the Fall, woman has been exposed to danger, precisely because she is so beautiful a divine creation:

The form of woman flashed and radiated in the primordial root . . . both by being an artifact of the finger of God and by her own sublime beauty. Oh how wondrous a being you are, you who laid your foundations in the sun and who have conquered the earth!

Over against this hymn to womanhood Hildegard sets St Paul's notion of woman's submission to her husband in modesty and fidelity. Woman has known winter – she cannot rise proudly in the flower of perpetual spring; she must not demand the exaltation of a tiara or gold, 'except at the wish of her husband, so that, in harmonious measure, she may give him delight'.

The *virgo*, by contrast, can still, even after the Fall, lay claim to that never-fading spring: 'She remains in the simplicity and beautiful integrity of paradise.' It is right for her, 'by licence and by revelation in the mystic breath of God's finger', to have bridal splendour.

Hildegard's answer to the second point, the 'élitism' of her convent, deserves close attention. It is God who holds the 'scrutiny (*scrutinium*)' of diverse classes,[49] 'so that the lesser order does not mount above the higher, as did Satan and the first man'. What farmer would put oxen, asses, sheep and goats in a single enclosure? – they would all scatter. So there must be differentiation among people, 'lest those of diverse estates, herded into the same flock, scatter themselves in the pride of self-assertion and the ignominy of being different . . . tearing one another with hate, when the higher rank sets upon the lower and the lower mounts above the higher.' God ranked his angels in nine hierarchies – and he loves them all.

Hildegard is convinced that this view is based on a correct assessment of human limitations, that it is 'realistic', and that such realism on earth has its sanction in heaven: 'For it is good that man should not catch hold of a mountain, which he cannot move, but rather should stay in a valley, learning gradually what he can master. These things are said by the living brightness, not by man.'

The eleventh and twelfth centuries, as Georges Duby has shown in an admirable recent book, saw the philosophic and political elaboration of a myth of classes, of *les trois ordres*, in Christian Europe.[50] Yet Tengswindis in her letter was clearly, in terms of the original Christian message, right. By her allusions to the Christ of the Gospels, and to Peter and Paul, she succinctly showed that the myth of classes was not compatible with *primitiva ecclesia*. Hildegard's analogies, in effect, rest on a fallacy: for there are different *species* of animals (and, to the theologian, of angels), but not of human beings.

That Hildegard claims her fallacy, and all else she says in her reply to Tengswindis, as the word of God (the letter opens with the words, 'The living fountain says . . .'), is not perhaps a particular act of hubris, but the obverse of her frequent admission that in her own right, without the sense of divinity speaking to her and through her, she would not dare pronounce on anything. Here she has deluded herself into thinking that the political myth of the ruling class of her day is a divine truth: deluded in the sense that she imagines this myth to be consistent with the teachings of Christ, about which in principle she has no doubts whatever, but which she had not consulted on this point. She is here in full accord with the dominant social beliefs of her class and time (just as, from the twelfth century to the fourteenth, we know of only the fewest people who believed, or argued, that crusading was an activity irreconcilable with Christ's teachings). Is it anachronistic to say that Hildegard could and should have done better? I think not: both because of the amount that *is* freshly and daringly thought out in the course of her writings, and even more, because of the very existence of Tengswindis' letter.

We know almost nothing else about Tengswindis.[51] What is perhaps most surprising is that her letter emanated not from a regular convent but from a foundation for canonesses – as these were almost invariably, by their statutes, aristocratic communities, founded and maintained by the greatest families of the empire. It was rare indeed for nunneries to be so exclusive. Yet Tengswindis' assured and witty, well-documented plea for human equality in a Christian society comes out of precisely such an enclave of privilege.

The highly-wrought diadems worn by the women on the Rupertsberg also aroused the curiosity of the ardent Walloon monk, Guibert of Gembloux (1124/5–1213/14), who began as Hildegard's far-off admirer and became her last intimate friend. As a complete stranger he wrote her two letters full of excited reverence and full of questions. Does she dictate her visions in Latin or in German? Does she forget them after they are written down? Does her understanding of Scripture come through literary instruction or sheer inspiration? Does she see her visions during sleep, in the form of dreams, or awake, in ecstasy (*excessus mentis*)? (He seems not to reckon with any other possibility.) What is the exact meaning of the title of her book, *Scivias*? Has she written other books as well? And what about those tiaras? Are they due to a divine revelation, rather than to a taste for finery?[52]

After two such letters, Hildegard wrote a long answer, one that so overwhelmed Guibert that he moved heaven and earth – or better, bent every conventual regulation – to be able to emigrate to the Rupertsberg and spend the rest of his days in Hildegard's company. This he enjoyed for just over two years – from June 1177, till her death (17 September 1179). As Hildegard's and Guibert's mother-tongues were very different, all their conversations must have been in Latin.

The letter of Hildegard's that prompted Guibert to seek his life with her contains some of her most explicit and most beautiful self-revelations. It was to a stranger, though one whose devotedness she sensed in his letters, that she revealed for the first – and only – time that her vision comprised two modes, one of which was far rarer, more intense and more blissful than the other. She defines her experience in comparison with that of St Paul and St John: they 'mounted in soul and drained the cup of wisdom from God: holding themselves to be nothing, they have become heaven's pillars'. The contrast with herself seems all too apparent:

Then how could it be that I, poor little creature, should not know myself? God works where he wills – to the glory of his name, not that of earthbound man. But I am always filled with a trembling fear, as I do not know for certain of any single capacity in me. Yet I stretch out my hands to God, so that, like a feather which lacks all weight and strength and flies through the wind, I may be borne up by him. And I cannot [see] perfectly the things that I see in my bodily condition and in my invisible soul – for in these two man is defective.

Since my infancy, however, when I was not yet strong in my bones and nerves and veins, I have always seen this vision in my soul, even till now, when I am more than seventy years old. And as God wills, in this vision my spirit mounts upwards, into the height of the firmament and into changing air, and dilates itself among different nations, even though they are in far-off regions and places remote from me. And because I see these things in such a manner, for this reason I also behold them in changing forms of clouds and other created things. But I hear them not with my physical ears, nor with my heart's thoughts, nor do I perceive them by bringing any of my five senses to bear – but only in my soul, my physical eyes open, so that I never suffer their failing in loss of consciousness (*extasis*); no, I see these things wakefully, day and night. And I am constantly oppressed by illnesses, and so enmeshed in intense pains that they threaten to bring on my death; but so far God has stayed me.

The brightness that I see is not spatial, yet it is far, far more lucent than a cloud that envelops the sun. I cannot contemplate height or length or breadth in it;[53] and I call it 'the shadow of the living brightness'. And as sun, moon and stars appear [mirrored] in water, so Scriptures, discourses, virtues, and some works of men take form for me and are reflected radiant in this brightness.

Whatever I have seen or learnt in this vision, I retain the memory of it for a long time, in such a way that, because I have at some time seen and heard it, I can remember it; and I see, hear and know simultaneously, and learn what I know as if in a moment. But what I do not see I do not know, for I am not learned. And the things I write are those I see and hear through the vision, nor do I set down words other than those that I hear; I utter them in unpolished Latin, just as I hear them through the vision, for in it I am not taught to write as philosophers write. And the words I see and hear through the vision are not like words that come from human lips, but like a sparkling flame and a cloud moved in pure air. Moreover, I cannot know the form of this brightness in any way, just as I cannot gaze completely at the sphere of the sun.

And in that same brightness I sometimes, not often, see another light, which I call 'the living light'; when and how I see it, I cannot express; and for the time I do see it, all sadness and all anguish is taken from me, so that then I have the air of an innocent young girl and not of a little old woman.

168

Yet because of the constant illness that I suffer, I at times weary of expressing the words and the visions that are shown me; nonetheless, when my soul, tasting, sees those things, I am transformed to act so differently that, as I said, I consign all pain and affliction to oblivion. And what I see and hear in the vision then, my soul drains as from a fountain – yet the fountain stays full and never drainable.

But my soul at no time lacks the brightness called 'shadow of the living brightness'. I see it as if I were gazing at a starless firmament within a lucent cloud. And there I see the things I often declare, and those which I give as answers to the people who ask me, from out of the blaze of the living light.[54]

It was in my vision, also, that I saw that my first book of visions should be called *Scivias* ['Know-ways'], because it was made known by way of the living brightness, not drawn from other teaching. As for [your question about] tiaras: I saw that all the ranks of the Church have bright emblems in accord with the heavenly brightness, yet virginity has no bright emblem – nothing but a black veil and an image of the cross. So I saw that this would be the emblem of virginity: that a virgin's head would be covered with a white veil, because of the radiant-white robe that human beings had in paradise, and lost. On her head would be a circlet (*rota*) with three colours conjoined into one – an image of the Trinity – and four roundels attached: the one on the forehead showing the lamb of God, that on the right a cherub, that on the left an angel, and on the back a human being – all these inclining towards the [figure of the] Trinity. This emblem, granted to me, will proclaim blessings to God,[55] because he had clothed the first man in radiant brightness.

As in the letter to Tengswindis, Hildegard alludes to the notion (common in early Patristic thought)[56] that virginity is a continuing image on earth of the paradisal state. But her development of this here shows that she invests the notion with high 'courtly' significance. If her community of virgins can be an image of paradise, if even on earth they are queens of the divine Bridegroom, then they must manifest joy as a permanent quality of their being. Troubadours had spoken of joy in just this way, as a necessary condition of the true chivalric lover. In Hildegard's counterpart fantasy in the divine sphere, the black veil, suggestive of the servant-girl (*ancilla*), is replaced by the joyous white one, and by the tiara that betokens a *domina*. The imagery on the tiara itself reveals that her maidenly élite displays a convergence of the human, the angelic, and the divine. It is from the standpoint of this spiritualized courtly joy, also, that the cultivation on the Rupertsberg of lyric drama, vocal and (as we shall see) instrumental music becomes fully comprehensible. In one of her last and profoundest letters Hildegard explains music as man's attempt to recapture the lost paradise.[57]

The radiant, half-celestial woman, whom Hildegard longs to see incarnate in the women around her, appears also in some of the allegorical contexts that she creates. Thus for instance in a letter to Werner of Kirchheim, the head of a community whom Hildegard addressed in 1170, in the course of her last preaching journey, she makes an original fusion of feminine images from *Pastor Hermas* and Boethius' *Consolatio Philosophiae*:[58]

Lying long in my bed of sickness, in the 1170th year of the Lord's incarnation, I saw – awake in body and spirit – a most beautiful image of womanly form, most peerless in gentleness, most dear in her delights. Her beauty was so great that the human mind could not fathom it, and her height reached from earth as far as heaven. Her face shone with the greatest radiance, and her eye gazed heavenward. She was dressed in the purest white silk, and enfolded by a cloak studded with precious gems – emerald, sapphire and pearls; her sandals were of onyx. Yet her face was covered in dust, her dress was torn on the right side, her cloak had lost its elegant beauty and her sandals were muddied. And she cried out . . . 'The foxes have their lairs, and the birds of the sky their nests, but I have no helper or consoler, no staff on which to lean or be supported by.'

The allegory Hildegard unfolds shows that, as in *Pastor Hermas*, this woman, who is both radiant with youth and (as the last words cited imply) weak with age, is Ecclesia. At the same time, like Philosophia at the opening of Boethius' *Consolatio*, her height reaches to heaven, and her dress is torn. Though so beautiful, Ecclesia has been maltreated and humiliated – not by false philosophers, as in Boethius, but here, as we soon learn, by unworthy priests.

Yet there is another such image in Hildegard's letters where womanly perfection and beauty, both in face and dress, remain untarnished. It is Hildegard's vision of heavenly Love (*Caritas*). Love, for Hildegard, is a girl (*puella*) with dazzling brightness streaming from her face; her cloak is whiter than snow and brighter than stars – and this cloak has no need of gems; her shoes are gold – not dark as onyx, like Ecclesia's. She holds the sun and moon, and embraces them; she has a sapphire image of a human being on her breast. 'And all creation called this girl *domina*.'[59]

In the letter, the allegory unfolded from this vision is about creation and redemption; the details become as tradition-bound as those with Ecclesia had been. It is when we see these images in relation not only to their allegories but to that image of the bride of God which Hildegard wanted to embody in her disciples, that certain aspects of her thought cohere in an unexpected way. In paradise, the first woman was created – Hildegard tells us in *Causae et curae* – as the embodiment of the love that Adam felt. Eve, that is, was initially, in her paradisal state, the glorious *puella* whom Hildegard describes in her vision. And insofar as the virgin brides on the Rupertsberg could still re-enact that paradisal state, they could manifest something of the splendour of this *puella*. That, probably, is also why Hildegard (in the wake of Gregory of Nyssa, Scotus Eriugena and others[60]) decided that the paradisal love was so sublime that it was free of any carnal element. She who wrote so openly about women's sexuality in the context of medicine nonetheless retained an asexual concept of love in her ideal realm. Implicitly this tended to Manichaean fantasy – for it would follow that it was the sensual aspect of love which rendered it unparadisal and tainted. I shall return to this problem below (VII).

Hildegard was the first of the women mystics who personified Love as a consummately beautiful womanly apparition. It is probably not through her direct influence that 'Lady Love' (*Minne*, *Amour*) becomes a protagonist in the writings of Mechthild, Hadewijch, and Marguerite Porete in the following century: there we must reckon with the convergence of diverse impulses – especially from vernacular personifications of human love, from the 'Sapiential' books of the Old Testament, and from Boethius. What Hildegard shows, however, is the extraordinary imaginative potential that was latent in a certain allegorical tradition. Even if her descriptions of Caritas and Ecclesia turn into elaborately constructed explications, they begin in something that she sees; and in telling what she sees, Hildegard informs these images with a vivacity that gives them momentarily the compelling power of myths. She does not disclose the identity of her figures at first: she captivates by infusing a sense of mystery in the descriptions. The allegoresis that nearly always (except in her lyrics) follows, roots the images again in a more conventional exegetic past. Thus in the allegorizing letters (as also in the one to Tengswindis) divergent and indeed contradictory impulses, towards unpredictable and towards predictable insights, can be traced in Hildegard's outlook.

VII

To gain an impression of Hildegard's way of understanding the spiritual and physical universe, it is necessary to consider some of these contradictory impulses more fully. Here I shall concentrate on the two least-known sources: the series of unpublished letters in the Berlin manuscript, and certain key passages in *Causae et curae* (printed in 1903, in an often decried but never yet replaced edition).

Causae et curae takes us to the root of what is unreconciled in Hildegard's thought. As a medical writer, her whole inclination is to look at human beings in their empirical reality: they are organisms that can be accounted for in terms of physical principles. Not that she demarcates physical principles in any irrevocable way from metaphysical ones. Yet whenever she is writing of the human being (rather than of the soul or spirit), Hildegard's emphasis tends to be what in later periods would be called a materialist and deterministic one. The same holds true, for instance, and in a similar way, of the scientific and especially the medical writings of Avicenna. Yet Hildegard, like Avicenna, is also a committed mystic, one for whom the transcending of the physical world is of supreme importance. This, for both thinkers, was a source of keen tension: in the words of Marlowe's Faustus – 'O Ile leape up to my God: who pulles me downe?' Because they have a biologically oriented approach, the tension seldom breaks out, for either Hildegard or Avicenna, in a simplistic conflict between a higher, immaterial principle and a material body prone to what is base – even though expressions reminiscent of this model do tend to occur. The biological emphasis, however, made the whole notion of a separable immaterial soul problematic, and – at least when one was speaking as a scientist – impossible. So one of the few ways open to the scientist–mystic of transcending the physically conditioned (or even fully determined) world, of leaping up to God, was by exploring – or creating – a psychological condition that is the inner counterpart of Manichaean myths.[61] The concept of the soul rising victoriously over its irremediably corrupt body is then transfigured: the divine realm – which does not necessarily exclude the physical – rises, conquering that of Lucifer. At the same time Hildegard (again like her Persian predecessor) longs to withdraw from outright Manichaeism: in the last resort she wants to say, Lucifer has no veritable realm that is his own.

These disparate impulses are evident near the opening of *Causae et curae*. Here, and in the complementary *Physica*, even when Hildegard's thought comes close to that of her visionary writings, she never presents anything as revelation; here it is never 'the living light told me . . .', but rather her own, and perhaps her most personal, series of attempts to apprehend the cosmos. –

When Lucifer stretched himself out towards nothingness, the beginning of his stretching produced evil, and soon this evil, without radiance or light, flamed up in itself through jealousy of God,[62] whirling and turning like a wheel (*ut rota*), and showed ignited darkness in itself. And thus evil fell away from good; neither did good touch evil nor evil good.

Yet God remained whole like a wheel (*ut rota*) . . . Now this wheel is somewhere, and is full of something. For if the wheel had nothing but an outer rim, it would be empty. And if perchance an outsider came and wanted to work there, this cannot be, for two craftsmen cannot exercise their craft in one and the same wheel. Oh humans, look at the human being! For it contains heaven and earth and other creatures in itself, and is one form, and all things hide in it.

This is what fatherhood is like. In what way? The round of the wheel is fatherhood, the fullness of the wheel is divinity. All things are in it and all stem from it, and beyond it there is no creator. Lucifer, however, is not whole, but divided in dispersion, since he wanted to be what he should not. For when God made the world, he had in his age-old plan that he wanted to become human.

And he made the elements of the world, and they are in man, and man operates with them.[63]

The fluctuations of outlook are notable. At first there are two wheels – that of Lucifer and that of God, one evil, one good. Each is autonomous, neither impinges upon the other. This comes close indeed to Manichaean myth. Yet in the next paragraph the emphasis seems the very opposite of Manichaean: God is the outer part of a human wheel, that he fills with divinity, a wheel which, by being human, also comprises the rest of creation. The wheel is full, is perfect:

there is no room for an outsider, a Lucifer, to act in it. This seems a thoroughly optimistic affirmation of man, and of a cosmos directly and completely informed with divinity.

In the third paragraph cited, the optimism goes still further: now Lucifer is not regarded as having a wheel of his own at all – he is fragmented. He wanted to be what he should not: that is, he wanted to be God. But God, too, wanted to become something other, namely human, and his wish was fulfilled. The wheel that is simultaneously divine, human and elemental emerged.

It is possible to read *Causae et curae* sorting its component parts in two divisions. On the one hand, the greater part of the work tends to a 'positive' orientation. There the natural, fertile world is affirmed; creation is accounted for on materialist lines; psychological and spiritual phenomena are explained with the help of a physical determinism that at times also has overtones of astrology; human sexuality is acknowledged without moral censure; human characters are established physiologically, without value-judgments. Contrasting with these are the 'negative' moments in the work, where the Manichaean impulses become strong. Then the whole cosmos is regarded as inexorably tainted by the Fall, Lucifer is seen as having won an autonomous realm in which he has dominion. This expresses itself particularly in the domain of sexuality, which in its existent form is a direct result of corruption and of the Fall. The primordial corruption displays its effects in three of the four possible human temperaments: only the sanguine still gives a reminiscence of the well-balanced nature of prelapsarian man, the other three – choleric, phlegmatic, and melancholic – betray that man is doomed to imperfection and frustration. The initial inner harmony is irretrievably lost, and it was that loss which caused a lack of outer harmony. Yet these attitudes – though they occur repeatedly – represent a much smaller proportion in the whole.

Near the opening, the two kinds of statement can be found starkly juxtaposed. On the one hand the affirmation of a fecund universe:

The sun in its circle is whole and full, and never fails; he sends his light into the moon when she comes near him, as a man sends his sperm into a woman.

On the other, a mythical static universe which became cankered and was lost:

Before Adam's Fall the firmament was immobile and was not whirled about, but after the Fall it began to be moved and whirled. Yet after the last day it will again stand immobile, as it was in the primal creation before Adam's Fall.

On the one hand there is harmonious parallelism:

For just as body and soul exist together and are strengthened by each other, so too are firmament and planets – they cherish and strengthen each other mutually. As the soul vivifies and consolidates the body, so too sun, moon and the other planets cherish and strengthen the firmament with their fire. For the firmament is as it were man's head, sun, moon and stars are as the eyes, air as the hearing, the winds are as smell, dew as taste, the sides of the world are as arms and as touch. And the other creatures that are in the world are as the belly; but the earth is as the heart . . .

And yet this last parallel again leads towards a Manichaean type of fantasy – an unrelenting rivalry between the creating God and the envious Lucifer:

The abyss is as it were the foot and the walk of man. Thus when the devil hurtled down from heaven – he who wanted to sit and reign and who was unable to create and fashion any creature – God at once made the firmament, so that Lucifer would see and understand what things and what great ones God could fashion and create. Then too he set sun, moon and stars into the firmament, that from these Lucifer would see and recognize how great a glory and splendour he had lost.

In its main lines, Hildegard's theory of creation in *Causae et curae*, the theory underlying her varied medical and sexual insights in the work, is a naturalistic one. Without too great an anachronism we could call hers a materialist cosmogony. Certainly the Christian God is brought in at various points in the argument – yet nothing that is said of him has any intrinsic connection with the theory as such. Thus in the following chapter it is the elemental components, rather than any miraculous, 'supernatural' action, which are crucial to the divine experiment:

That there are only four elements:[64] There cannot be more than four, or fewer. They consist of two kinds: upper and lower. The upper are celestial, the lower terrestrial. The things that live in the upper ones are impalpable and are made of fire and air; those that move in the lower are palpable, formed bodies, and consist of water and mud.

For spirits are fiery and airy, but man is watery and muddy. When God created man, the mud from which he was formed was stuck together with water, and God put a fiery and airy breath of life into that form.

Later, by contrast, Hildegard seems to allow the orthodox Christian notion of God infusing the soul in the human body. Yet even there her language is of a materialist tendency: 'the living wind, which is the soul, enters this bodily shape by the will of the almighty God, and strengthens it and makes it alive and goes about in it everywhere, as a worm that weaves silk is covered and enveloped in the silk as in a house'.

Even though Hildegard here alludes to 'the will of the almighty God', the soul, in her earlier discussion, is thought of specifically in physical elemental terms: 'The soul is fiery, windy and humid, and it occupies the whole heart of man. The liver heats the heart, the lung covers it . . .' Most of all the soul is envisaged as the highest element: 'the soul is fire, which penetrates the whole body and vivifies the human being'. At the same time, three of the four elements are seen as the sources of man's 'spiritual' condition – of his affective and intellectual aspects as well as of his power of movement: 'Man draws his sensuality and desire from fire; from air he draws thoughts and their power to roam; from water, knowledge and motion.'

Adam had a greater mode of cognition, but this too was brought about by physical means: it was through the 'cooking' of his powers (*viribus coctus*), while he slept, that he awoke as a prophet of heavenly things, endowed with all earthly knowledge and art. His knowledge is evoked also in a sexual metaphor: God gave Adam all creatures, that he might penetrate them with virile force (*virili vi eas penetraret*). He knew them (*scivit et cognovit*), 'for man himself is every creature'. Here the ultimately Aristotelian conception, of the knower uniting with what he knows, and the image of man as *summa* of all creation, blend remarkably with the biblical usage in which 'to know' has a sexual force.

Hildegard's *rota*, however, comprehends not only man and the physical world, but the presence of divinity. Though she has so keenly naturalizing a notion of the human soul, she also affirms the orthodox belief that such a soul can exist separately from its body after death – till the end of time, when they are reunited. Are these two viewpoints compatible? Hildegard believes them to be so, because for her the temporary separateness of the soul is as nothing to the triumphant reintegration of the *rota* that she envisages:

After the last day the soul will desire its dress from God, to draw that dress to itself . . . so too God has drawn to himself his dress, which was eternally hidden in him. And in this way God and man are one, as soul and body . . . As each thing has its shadow, so too man is the shadow of God, and this shadow is the showing of creation, and man is thus the showing of the almighty God in all his miracles . . . Thus the whole celestial harmony is the mirror of divinity, and man the mirror of all God's miracles.

Nonetheless, Hildegard also has moments where she seems to succumb to a fully Manichaean model for understanding the human soul. In a section headed 'Concerning the contrariety of soul and flesh' we read:

The soul is a breath striving towards the good, but the body strives towards sins; and rarely and at times hardly at all can the soul restrain the body from sinning; just as the sun cannot prevent little worms from coming out of the earth to the place that he is warming in his splendour and heat.

A similar tension exists in Hildegard's accounts of sex. There are 'medical' passages filled with an enraptured feeling for the beauty of the sexual act:

When a woman is making love with a man, a sense of heat in her brain, which brings with it sensual delight, communicates the taste of that delight during the act and summons forth the emission of the man's seed. And when the seed has fallen into its place, that vehement heat descending from her brain draws the seed to itself and holds it, and soon the woman's sexual organs contract, and all the parts that are ready to open up during the time of menstruation now close, in the same way as a strong man can hold something enclosed in his fist.

Not every detail in the attempted description is clear, but Hildegard seems to be thinking of two phenomena – vaginal contractions, and the squeezing of the man's organ by the woman's vaginal muscles – as the consummate physical expressions of a woman's passionateness, of that *delectatio* which begins in her brain and brings the man to his climax.

There are also 'metaphysical' passages that move in this direction, that try to project a wholly positive theology of sex. The beauty of the act is exemplified in the archetypal love-union:

When God created Adam, Adam experienced a sense of great love in the sleep that God instilled in him. And God gave a form to that love of the man, and so woman is the man's love. And as soon as woman was formed God gave man the power of creating, that through his love – which is woman – he might procreate children. When Adam gazed at Eve, he was entirely filled with wisdom, for he saw in her the mother of the children to come. And when she gazed at Adam, it was as if she were gazing into heaven, or as the human soul strives upwards, longing for heavenly things – for her hope was fixed in him. And so there will be and must be one and the same love in man and woman, and no other.

The man's love, compared with the woman's, is a heat of ardour like a fire on blazing mountains, which can hardly be put out, whilst hers is a wood-fire that is easily quenched; but the woman's love, compared with the man's, is like a sweet warmth proceeding from the sun, which brings forth fruits . . .

Then, suddenly, falls the Manichaean shadow: the love-making before the Fall was sweeter, because it was gentle rather than fiercely passionate:

But the great love that was in Adam when Eve came forth from him, and the sweetness of the sleep with which he then slept, were turned in his transgression into a contrary mode of sweetness. And so, because a man still feels this great sweetness in himself, and is like a stag thirsting for the fountain, he races swiftly to the woman and she to him – she like a threshing-floor pounded by his many strokes and brought to heat when the grains are threshed inside her.[65]

Even here Hildegard does not write with distaste: the love-making she now evokes is still beautiful, though the *dulcedo* is of another kind. What seems inconsistent is that, in the first, ideal picture, she had evoked the man's ardour as something intense, like a mountain-fire, whereas now it seems as though Hildegard imagines the primordial love to have been devoid of ardour – 'as sweet as balm, as soft as air, as gentle'. And there are indeed a number of other passages of Manichaean inclination that bear this out. At times it sounds as if the human sexual impulse as such is a taint and a direct result of the Fall:

When man transgressed God's command, he was changed both in body and mind. For the purity of his blood was turned into another mode, so that, instead of purity, he now ejects the spume of semen. If man had remained in paradise, he would have stayed in an immutable and perfect state. But all these things, after his transgression, were turned into another and bitter mode. For man's blood, burning in the ardour and heat of lust, ejects a spume from itself that we call semen, as a pot placed on the fire brings up foam from the water because of the flame's heat.

In the same way, the innate heavenly gift of melodiousness was lost:

Adam before his Fall sang like an angel and knew every kind of music . . . Just as, at his Fall, the holy and chaste manner of begetting children was transmuted into another mode of physical delight, so too the voice singing heavenly joys, which Adam had, was turned to a contrary mode of laughing and guffawing.

Here the implication is unmistakable: the 'other mode of physical delight' is unholy and unchaste. Manichaean fabulation has, for the moment, gained the ascendancy.

It is the naturalistic outlook in Hildegard which leads her to trying to account for human beings by physiological determinism. Thus, in love-making, the strength of the feeling of love in the man and the woman, and the strength of the man's semen, together determine the sex *and character* of the child. In the midst of expounding this, there is one brief nod in the direction of the Christian Creator, and scriptural authority is alleged to confirm the 'biological' account:

When the man approaches the woman, releasing powerful semen and in a true cherishing love for the woman, and she too has a true love for the man in that same hour, then a male child is conceived, for so it was ordained by God. Nor can it be otherwise, because Adam was formed of clay, which is a stronger material than flesh. And this male child will be prudent and virtuous . . .

But if the woman's love is lacking in that hour . . . and if the man's semen is strong, a male child will still be born, because the man's cherishing love predominates. But that male child will be feeble and not virtuous . . .

If the man's semen is thin, and yet he cherishes the woman lovingly and she him, then a virtuous female child is procreated . . .

If the man's semen is powerful but neither the man nor the woman cherish each other lovingly, a male child is procreated . . . but he will be bitter with his parents' bitterness; and if the man's semen is thin and there is no cherishing love on either side in that hour, a girl of bitter temperament is born.

The reference to the time of love-making would seem to have astrological implications: it is the particular hour that determines the result; and the strength of love, it is here assumed, could change from one hour to the next. In a later passage, it is specifically the moon that conditions the birth of children, both because the strength of the man's semen varies in accordance with the moon and because the weakness of the semen at certain times in the lunar month entails a biological deficiency – an innate lack of physical and moral *virtus* – in the child conceived at such a time:

The blood in every human being increases and diminishes according to the waxing and waning of the moon . . . When, as the moon waxes, the blood in human beings is increased, then both men and women are fertile for bearing fruit – for generating children – since then . . . the man's semen is powerful and robust; and in the waning of the moon, when human blood also wanes, the man's semen is feeble and without strength, like dregs . . . If a woman conceives a child then, whether boy or girl, it will be infirm and feeble and not virtuous.

At the close of *Causae et curae*, in its surviving form, comes a far more elaborate lunar characterology, based on the day of the moon when a child is conceived. As the genuineness of the earlier passages has never been called in doubt, it is difficult to follow Schipperges in seeing this whole later section as an interpolation, 'diametrically opposed to all other pronouncements of Hildegard's'.[66] To give two examples of the procedure in this section:

One who is conceived on the first day after the new moon, when it receives its splendour from the sun, if a boy he will be proud and hard, and love no man except one who fears and honours him. He readily takes vengeance on people, [seizing] their fortune and all they possess. Yet he will be healthy in body and have no great sicknesses, though he will not grow very old. If a girl is born, she will always covet being honoured, and will be loved more by outsiders than by her household; and she is wicked in private, and always falls in love with strangers and newcomers, but is bad to her household and neglects them. She is physically healthy, though if an illness seizes her she gets very ill, almost to the point of death, and does not live long . . .

One who is conceived on the eighteenth day after the new moon, if a boy he will be a thief, and have such a longing to steal that he will in fact be discovered thieving; and owner-ship of land will be denied him, so that he wants to have almost nothing of his own of fields or vineyards or such things, but always to take away from others what is not his; and he is healthy in body, and as such will live long. If a girl is born, she will be astute and will behave foxily, and say almost nothing of what she has in her heart, but because of her evil habits she will deceive men by her talk, and bring honourable men to their deaths if she can. She is healthy in body, but sometimes plagued by insanity, and of herself she can live long; but behaviour such as that of this man or woman is troubling to God.

The character-traits in the majority of these lunar sketches are not flattering. The emphasis is always predictive: for each day an answer is given concerning the boy or girl conceived – how healthy will they be? how long will they live? If their state of health and length of life are physically determined, then how far are their personalities determined too? At times it sounds as if Hildegard thinks in terms of conditioning and inclinations rather than of complete determinism, at others not: the kleptomaniac cannot help stealing, yet his behaviour also offends God. Of those conceived on the twentieth day after the new moon Hildegard says categorically that the boy will become 'a bandit and homicide, and take delight in this', the girl, 'a poisoner, who gladly destroys men, and she will easily become lunatic, and will live long'. The medical, or pseudo-medical, context seems to preclude the questions of human will and responsibility, such as are crucial to Hildegard's *Liber vitae meritorum*. Here the sense of physical–medical laws, the heady excitement at the thought that complete predictability might be possible, lead Hildegard to indulging in the part of the 'Rhenish sibyl'. As we shall see again among the Berlin letters, her prodigious gifts and magnetism led to her being besieged for advice; and pleas for intellectual or spiritual guidance, or for medical help, were often scarcely separable from more naïve demands for predictions, both about the here and the beyond. Hildegard assented to such pleas in varied ways, adapting herself often, it would seem, to the expectations of her correspondent. We do not know what she will have included in her complete *Subtilitates* – both *Causae et curae* and the related 'Berlin fragment' are too haphazardly assembled to give much help in ascertaining this. Thus theoretically the elaborate and fanciful lunar characterology at the close of *Causae et curae* might be an interpolation, and yet there is no cogent evidence, internal or external, in favour of this.

Another passage from this closing section, however, which is likewise rejected by Schipperges as inauthentic, seems to me to bear the clear stamp of Hildegard's thought, and to be a fine example of the 'materialist' orientation in her work. It concerns the concept of purgatory:[67]

There are some unquenchable fires in the air, which are kindled through diverse actions of men; for these fires, which should have been for human glory, become punitive fires through men's evil deeds. So they descend to some places on earth, and there congregate, where too some rivers rise and flow forth, that draw heat and ardour from those fires, so that also by God's judgement some souls are tested in the fires and in the waters. But some streams from these waters at times flow into diverse regions among men – streams that are always hot, because they derive from the unquenchable fires. There are also some parts of the earth on which at times fire descends by divine vengeance, as is written: 'he rained coals of fire upon them, and the spirit of the storms is a part of their chalice'. And the earth and mountains and stones which that fire has touched will always remain burning, till the last day; and in the places that burn thus, streams sometimes rise that are hot with the same fire and flow warm. And men too, sometimes, by their art, brought streams to those burning places, in order to get warm through them . . . And these waters do not harm the men who use them for bathing in, but make them healthy, for the heat of the streams assuages the excessive heat in human beings and consumes their disordered humours.

Purgatorial fires are here described and explained naturalistically (with the same approach as, in the previous generation, the Chartres philosophers William of Conches and Thierry would have used).[68] They are physical fires and fire-heated rivers that descend into the realms men inhabit. The last sentences cited re-establish the link with the medical tradition of taking hot baths for therapeutic effect. Purgatorial fires and boiling streams of divine chastisement are thus set on the same level of perception as volcanoes and thermal springs. Divine, human and natural forces can all play a rôle in bringing such phenomena about. There is a natural 'purgatorial' effect, which is medically beneficial, as well as a divinely intended moral one – and the two effects are, in the last resort, not different in kind.

One other notable instance of materialist analysis, earlier in *Causae et curae*, takes us back to the question of the physical determination of human character. Hildegard tries to work out the implications for personality of the four humoral temperaments, with a vividness and richness of detail unparalleled in earlier medical or physiognomic tradition.[69] What is particularly new and startling in her procedure is that she interprets the four humours fundamentally in terms of sexual behaviour, and that she gives a separate detailed account for four temperaments of women as well as for those of men. Such predictive physiological sketches of women are not previously attested. –

(*De sanguinea*) Some women are inclined to plumpness, and have soft and delectable flesh and slender veins, and well-constituted blood free of impurities ... And these have a clear and light colouring, and in love's embraces are themselves lovable; they are subtle in arts, and show self-restraint in their disposition. At menstruation they suffer only a moderate loss of blood, and their womb is well developed for childbearing, so they are fertile and can take in the man's seed. Yet they do not bear many children, and if they are without husbands, so that they remain childless, they easily have physical pains; but if they have husbands, they are well.

(*De flecmatica*) There are other women whose flesh does not develop as much, because they have thick veins and healthy, whitish blood (though it does contain a little impurity, which is the source of its light colour). They have severe features, and are darkish in colouring; they are vigorous and practical, and have a somewhat mannish disposition. At menstruation their menstrual blood flows neither too little nor too abundantly. And because they have thick veins they are very fertile and conceive easily, for their womb and all their inner organs, too, are well developed. They attract men and make men pursue them, and so men love them well. If they want to stay away from men, they can do so without being affected by it badly, though they are slightly affected. However, if they do avoid making love with men they will become difficult and unpleasant in their behaviour. But if they go with men and do not wish to avoid men's love-making, they will be unbridled and over-lascivious, according to men's report. And because they are to some extent mannish on account of the vital force (*viriditas*, lit. 'greenness') within them, a little down sometimes grows on their chin ...

(*De colerica*) There are other women who have slender flesh but big bones, moderately sized veins and dense red blood. They are pallid in colouring, prudent and benevolent, and men show them reverence and are afraid of them. They suffer much loss of blood in menstruation; their womb is well developed and they are fertile. And men like their conduct, yet flee from them and avoid them to some extent, for they can interest men but not make men desire them. If they do get married, they are chaste, they remain loyal wives and live healthily with their husbands; and if they are unmarried, they tend to be ailing – as much because they do not know to what man they might pledge their womanly loyalty as because they lack a husband ...

(*De melancolica*) But there are other women who have gaunt flesh and thick veins and moderately sized bones; their blood is more lead-coloured[70] than sanguine, and their colouring is as it were blended with grey and black. They are changeable and free-roaming in their thoughts, and wearisomely wasted away in affliction; they also have little power of resistance, so that at times they are worn out by melancholy. They suffer much loss of blood in menstruation, and they are sterile, because they have a weak and fragile womb. So they cannot lodge or retain or warm a man's seed, and thus they are also healthier, stronger and happier without husbands than with them – especially because, if they lie with their husbands, they will tend to feel weak afterwards. But men turn away from them and shun them, because they do not speak to men affectionately, and love them only a little. If for some hour they experience sexual joy, it quickly passes in them. Yet some such women, if they unite with robust and sanguine husbands, can at times, when they reach a fair age, such as fifty, bear at least one child . . . If their menopause comes before the just age, they will sometimes suffer gout or swellings of the legs, or will incur an insanity which their melancholy arouses, or else back-ache or a kidney-ailment . . . If they are not helped in their illness, so that they are not freed from it either by God's help or by medicine, they will quickly die.

While the idea that the particular physical blend (*krasis*) of humours conditions character is of long standing in the West, and certain writers such as Vindician and Bede had characterized 'temperaments' (sanguine, phlegmatic, choleric and melancholic) in a way that orthodox Galenic medicine would not have sanctioned,[71] Hildegard's portraits can scarcely be accounted for by the influence of one or more earlier theories. We must, I believe, reckon with a degree of free invention, as well as with the literary systematization here of popular images, or stereotypes, that had not previously surfaced in a learned context.

For Hildegard, then, the epitome of the 'sanguine' woman is the delicate and attractive lady, well-nurtured (the phrase 'subtle in arts' gives a hint of her privileged background), serene, able to show her love physically and to take delight in love-making. She is romantic, and basically uncomplicated; it is a misfortune if she does not marry and have children. The 'phlegmatic' evokes for Hildegard a more sombre, coarse-grained type – her dark colouring suggests she works outdoors and is no lady of leisure. She has cruder sexual instincts and cravings than the other, she is sturdy and commonsensical, and can also be fierce and domineering.

The 'choleric' woman is seen by Hildegard as laudable rather than lovable. She commands respect by her discreet and helpful behaviour, she is loyal and virtuous, yet somehow cold. After the gentle châtelaine and the smouldering, earthy working woman, we might say, comes the austere headmistress.

What of the last, the 'melancholic' type? She is described at greater length than the others. She is complicated and highly strung; she has more ups and downs than the rest, and is prone to suffer more both in body and mind than they. She is neither physically nor mentally suited to marriage. She has a quite different cast of mind from the others: she is *vaga in cogitationibus* – free-roaming in her thoughts. She is (to adapt today's typology) the neurotic – or the intellectual.

While Hildegard in her medical orientation projects these four temperaments as if they were all on the same plane, she also, in her quasi-Manichaean moments, has a very different interpretation of melancholy. Then it is no longer one physiologically-based tendency among others, but a curse resulting from Adam's guilt. Before the Fall, human beings were naturally sanguine; but 'when splendour was quenched in Adam, the black bile (*melancolia*) curdled in his blood, whereby sadness and despair arose in him'. 'This melancholy is black and bitter and breathes forth every evil, and at times brings sickness to the brain and heart . . . It is natural to every human being, through the first suggestion of the devil.'

Thus melancholy is both the tragic aspect of human existence since Adam and (when Hildegard writes as physiologist) a tendency particularly acute in men and women of a certain humoral 'complexion'. In men, according to Hildegard, it expresses itself far more grimly than in women: they become not only bitter and mean, but show a cold, vicious sensuality that is barren of love. Hildegard does not explicitly compare her two uses of the term, yet we could conclude from what she says that those who are melancholic by temperament are the ones who will experience the tragic condition of fallen man more intensely than others, the ones most prone to be maladjusted by it.

Hildegard, I submit, understood herself as a melancholic woman. If we juxtapose with her description of the type another key passage in *Causae et curae* (cited below), and relate these passages to all she tells us of herself in the autobiographic notes in the *Vita*, the implied diagnosis is clear. Shortly before her character-sketches, she had made a distinction between the two 'precellent' *humores* (sanguine and phlegmatic), which she also calls the *phlegmata*, and the two following (choleric and melancholic), which she calls *livores*. For human beings – at least since Eden – these four must all be well tempered if they are to achieve physical and mental health. And yet there can be rare exceptions, where the person is unbalanced, but beneficially so:

If one of the *livores* extends itself beyond measure in superfluity in any human being, the *humores* cannot be at peace in him, save only in those human beings whom God's grace has infused, either in strength, like Samson, or in wisdom, like Solomon, or in prophecy, like Jeremiah, or certain pagans such as Plato and those like him. And where others in such cases go mad, these will in this situation be bravest in excellence through the grace of God, for this grace allows them to be in a certain changeable condition, so that they are now ill, now well, now afraid, now strong, now in sadness, now in joy. And God brings about the relief in them, so that when they are ill he makes them well, when fearful, he makes them strong, when sad, he makes them joyful.

The passage refers to both the choleric and the melancholic *livor*. Samson is an outstanding example of the first: Hildegard notes in choleric men their virility, their mighty limbs, their sexual exuberance and the strength of all their passions – 'they direct their eyes like arrows at the women they love . . . their thoughts are like a blast of tempests'.[72] The others – Solomon, Jeremiah, Plato and those like him – are, in Hildegard's view, those who could most easily go mad, but who, by a special grace, can also be the abnormally gifted ones.[73] The fluctuations of mind, oscillating between illness and revival, fear and a sense of firm purpose, belong with the portrait of the melancholic, and with Hildegard's self-portrait. Here she is implicitly placing herself at the side of those melancholics to whom God gave an overwhelming grace, as of wisdom or prophecy, making them both 'unbalanced' and exceptional. Solomon, for Hildegard, was the author of both the bitter Ecclesiastes and the ardently joyful Song of Songs – these, we might say, were his oscillations. In Jeremiah, grief and prophecy were inseparable. As for Plato, it is not certain what traditions Hildegard knew. (I have found no clear indication, for instance, that she had read the Latin *Timaeus*.) But at least in Augustine's *City of God* she will have found a memorable tribute to Plato's exceptionality ('excellentissima gloria claruit, qua omnino ceteros obscuraret'), as well as praises of 'those like him' – the *Platonici* – for their many 'prophetic' anticipations of Christian beliefs. She may also have known from one of Jerome's letters (*Ep.* 53, 1) an anecdote about how God could make the virtuous philosopher strong, so that, 'captured by pirates and sold to a most cruel tyrant . . . imprisoned, chained and enslaved, Plato still was greater than the man who bought him'.

This accords well with Hildegard's thoughts: that where others might go mad, a man like Plato 'will in this situation be bravest in excellence through the grace of God'. Beyond this, Hildegard's notion of Plato's psychological make-up, brilliant but unstable, may be entirely her own surmise. In the legends and anecdotes concerning Plato, assembled and discussed by Novotný and by Riginos, I have found nothing comparable, save for an isolated testimony, in an eleventh-century Arabic life of Plato (by al-Mubashshir ibn Fātiq), that Plato wept incessantly – a testimony that is very unlikely to have reached northern Europe by Hildegard's lifetime.[74]

VIII

The Berlin manuscript Lat. Qu. 674 contains a series of fifty-six letters by Hildegard, of which the great majority, uniquely preserved here, have remained unknown.[75] With one exception, the letters' opening salutations are omitted in this collection: the copyist was not concerned with their personal or historical aspects, but wished to make of each letter a small treatise or homily. Thus he or she[76] furnished nearly every piece in the collection with a title intended to stress what was exemplary, to give the contents an evident spiritual application: these titles often fit the actual subject-matter poorly. It is only occasionally possible to deduce to whom the letters were originally addressed.[77] What we have, then, is a varied group of examples of Hildegard's writing, some more formal and some less, ranging from detached exposition to personal advice and impassioned appeals. Now and then, too, we find autobiographic details and reflections not known to us from other sources.

The third letter in the series offers a fine example of the self-contained meditation. It is possible that the copyist excerpted this from a longer letter – omitting more, that is, than the initial greeting – yet it is not necessary to assume this. Hildegard's correspondents frequently asked her to clarify scriptural passages for them, and in many complete letters published from other manuscripts, including some that reply to such requests, she plunges into an answer without preliminaries. –

'The mountains ascend and the fields descend to the place you have established for them.' That is: the ascent of the mountain means God's might, and the descent of the field means his potential; and in these two parts he places and divides all things, for he has set the heaven into the height, and his own light – that is, the earth – beneath him, and has ordained this placing in the whole of creation. Pride contradicted this, and claimed the likeness of equality with God, which cannot be; so it was accounted as naught by him – for if a man were without his wings of arms and hands, the human form which is in him would be accounted as naught. The godhead prepared heaven and all its hidden places, and built up all creatures in their lands, and the earth sustains them. But Pride's effort at building lacks both head and wings, and Pride can scarcely stand even on one foot, and cannot walk.

That it lacks head and wings means it is without God; nor has it any possibility of standing upright, but always falls, and sets up each of its works mendaciously, in nothing but a word. Without the body of truth, it is trying to stand on one foot – which means a lie – but he who has two feet cannot walk on one. So let all the faithful flee from Pride, which always consists in lying, for it cannot be called craftsman either in bronze or earthenware. So it builds nothing, either in heavenly or earthly things, but is the destroyer and despoiler of what is built – for it lost heaven and deceived man, as Scripture tells.

This letter shows in small compass some of Hildegard's characteristic themes, qualities and techniques. More than any other twelfth-century writer known to me, she returns ever again to the theme of the war in heaven, God against Lucifer, the epitome of pride. She sees this war as the universe's primal threat, and in so doing she inevitably invests it with something of the quality of Manichaean myth: insofar as Lucifer was not a puny rebel but a towering one, insofar as the battle was a real issue and no foregone conclusion, Lucifer was indeed on a par with the victorious God.

She begins with an original allegorization of a verse from Psalm 103, the high hymnic praise of the creator of the cosmos. The mountains that rise signify his might, as exercised; the fields sloping downwards, his latent capacity. These – the actual and the latent powers – Hildegard sees as together responsible for the making of heaven and earth. Implicitly, the mountains are now heaven, the fields earth; yet by an extraordinary identification – swift and to my knowledge without parallel – Hildegard also equates earth with the divine light. Perhaps she was stimulated by the phrase in Psalm 108, 'Amictus lumine sicut vestimento' – 'clothed with light as with a garment' – and extended this by seeing the earth as God's garment: not one that he wears, but that he spreads beneath him.[78] Later, when she says 'the earth sustains' all creatures, we see how apt it is that here the earth should also mean God's light. The phrase, 'has ordained this placing in the whole of creation (*atque hoc in omni creatura fecit*)', is again compressed and enigmatic, but it may suggest that the dividing into a heavenly and an earthly aspect extends to all that God brings forth.

Then Hildegard turns to Lucifer's rebellion, though here the rebel is simply called Superbia: he is Pride personified. Pride is a rival builder, who is set at naught (or, reduced to nothingness). Pride then loses its essential character, as an armless man (note the striking phrase, 'without the *wings* of arms and hands', with its angel connotations) lacks essential human features.

The condition of Pride – headless, wingless and limping – is finally made into a moral allegory. Yet the closing sentences, touching on its nature as a moral fault, again imply a cosmological mythic perspective: there was a rival builder, but he was as unsuccessful in the ageless medium of bronze as in the earthly one of clay; he could not fashion any building, but only ravage those already built. The challenger was essentially destructive, not creative – what he achieved was nothing, merely negative effects. And this gives new meaning to Hildegard's opening allegory: both actually and potentially, the world is filled with the work of the victorious builder.

Nonetheless, Lucifer remained active in that world. After the war in heaven came the primordial temptation on earth, and a number of the Berlin letters dwell on themes of human temptation, on the 'replay' of that first encounter in the here and now. The most touching and personal is one where Hildegard's primary reference is to herself:

God is wondrous and invisible, and man cannot know or fathom his hidden mysteries by any capacity of his own. But the devil, through his first deception, laid waste what was celestial in man, by serpentine deceit; yet God wanted to save a new being. So too it often happens when some inspiration proceeds from the living light – which is God – touching the breath of man's soul; if that person glories unfittingly, or rises higher than he can, soon the serpent makes mockery of that; so let what proceeds from truth be heard, and what from lying be removed – but removed mercifully, since no one is in so great a perfection that he is not in some respects a liar: as David says in the Holy Spirit, 'every man is a liar'.

The expression 'the living light' makes clear that Hildegard is reflecting especially on her own experience. The words *inspiratio* and *spiramen* – 'inspiration' and the 'breath' of the soul – are symptomatic of her steady refusal to sever the abstract and the physical.[79] Is she herself free of vaingloriousness and excessive ambition? Can any prophet be sure that he or she is transmitting only what is divine in inspiration, and is leaving it untarnished? Even a prophet should not be heard uncritically, but compassionately: Hildegard says it by alluding to a moment when David in the Psalms (115: 10–11) felt shame at his own pronouncements: 'I was utterly humiliated; beside myself, I said: everyone lies...'

The temptation to rise higher than one's capacities is something of which Hildegard also warns a fellow-abbess, in one of the longest letters in the Berlin collection. It is the only letter where the salutation is preserved: 'To the lady abbess H, Hildegard'. I believe we can identify the correspondent as Hazzecha, abbess of Krauftal (in the diocese of Strasbourg), who in two letters already known[80] shows an almost pathetic craving for and dependence on Hildegard's advice. She is quite unable to cope with her unruly convent, and is longing to escape this responsibility by turning instead to a hermit's life (*solitaria vita*). Hildegard is convinced that this is no true solution: Hazzecha is too unsteady to persevere in such a goal (*propter vicissitudinem*), and 'then your end will be far worse than your beginning' (cf. Matthew 12: 45). Besides, we should 'not spurn other sinners, who are like ourselves', we should not seek with restless heart to reject reasonable human solutions in favour of others 'that we consider more advantageous and more fitting'.[81] These thoughts, and the allusion to Matthew, recur in the unpublished letter, where Hildegard is replying, it would seem, to a further suggestion of Hazzecha's: she had now conceived the plan of taking two of her most loyal adherents away with her, either to set up a hermitage in some remote place or else to go on pilgrimage. Hildegard urges her not to yield to such impulses of flying to spiritual goals that are beyond her, rather to resign herself to the less delightful burden that is truly hers – to make all well again within her convent:

To the lady abbess H, Hildegard. In true vision I saw and heard these words:
Daughter of God, you that in God's love call me – poor little creature – mother, learn to have discretion, which, in heavenly things and earthly, is the mother of us all, since by this the soul is directed, and the body nurtured in appropriate restraint. A person who, amid sighs of repentance, remembers sins committed – thinking, speaking, acting at the devil's prompting – should embrace her mother, Discretion, and be submissive to her, and in true humility and obedience should correct her sins, in the way that her teachers advise. Indeed, as the fruit of the earth is harmed by a freak rainstorm, and as from untilled earth sprout no true fruits, but useless weeds, so a person who toils more than her body can bear is rendered useless in her spirit by ill-judged toil and ill-judged abstinence.
When the blackest of birds – the devil – senses that someone wants to banish illicit longings and cease from sins, it curls itself into the fasting, prayers and abstinence of that person, like a viper into its den; suggestively it says to her: 'Your sins can't be wiped out unless you trample down your body with tears and grief, and with such immense labours that it withers totally.' So, living hopeless and joyless, that person's senses often fail, she is fettered by

grievous sickness, and thus, despoiled of the quality of holiness by the devil's deceit, she leaves what she began without discretion unfinished, and in this way her last condition will be worse than the earlier one.

Also, let one who is bound in obedience, in accord with Christ's example, take utmost care not to choose something in a self-willed way, trusting more in herself than in the good advice of others – lest she be overcome by the Pride that tumbled from **heaven**, by wanting to be better than others who are good, reckoning that to be good and holy which is decided by herself. For of herself she can know this, that she should not acquiesce in her own will, since she exists in two natures – body and soul – and these discord, as what pleases the one displeases the other. This being so in human beings, how can they, their soul unharmed, consent to their own will, which belongs to the body? But the person who, for fear and love of God, despises her own will, and submits herself to the precepts, instruction and rule of her teachers, offering example to others in true humility of good works – she makes herself a living tabernacle in the heavenly Jerusalem; the Holy Spirit rests on her.

Dearest daughter, I cannot see that it will help you and your two dependants to seek a forest or a recluse's cell or a pilgrimage to Rome, since you are already marked with the seal of Christ, with which you journey to the heavenly Jerusalem. For if you embark on a greater effort than you can endure, through the devil's deceit – as I said – you will fall.

In the love of Christ, too, I tell you that it is not my wont to speak of the end or the achievements of people, or of what will befall them; but the things I am taught by the Holy Spirit in the vision of my soul – though I am untaught – these I speak and write. As for the men whom you commended to me, in my prayers I gladly commend them to the grace of God. I'll also gladly pray to God for you, that he free you from everything that is ill-suited to you, and that he guard you from future ills. And may you perfect the efforts of holy works with such blessed discretion that, strengthened by the radiance of pure holiness and kindled by the ardour of true love of God, you may attain the supreme bliss. May you live in it forever.

The keynote of the letter is Discretio. In *Scivias* (III 6, 34), this personified virtue is described as 'the most skilled sifter (*sollertissima cribratrix*) of all things', she who, 'in the breast of human minds, contains all that is apt and fitting, even in their most minute counsels and arts'. Discretio, we might say, is Hildegard's counterpart in the spiritual sphere to the troubadour ideal of courtly *mezura*.[82] In the twelfth-century Latin epics composed at about the time of Hildegard's death, John of Hauvilla's hero, Architrenius, marries Moderantia, whose beauties are elaborated wittily and lovingly, and again, when the virtues fight on behalf of the 'new man' at the close of Alan of Lille's *Anticlaudianus*, Moderantia conquers Excessus. In the two epics the emphasis is this-worldly: it is a quest for a decorous, as well as morally acceptable, goal. And for Hildegard too there is a question of decorum: there can be excesses of piety (or pietism), when what is 'apt and fitting' is a more earthbound task.

Most unusual in the letter, perhaps, is Hildegard's theory of will, with which she buttresses her dissuasion of Hazzecha. For her, it seems here, human *voluntas* is to be seen wholly negatively: it belongs to the body, not the soul, and body and soul are forever at war. This last notion is characteristically Pauline; yet the implication in Hildegard's argument – that will is on the side of the body, and that this is the wrong side – is another instance of her unconscious Manichaeism. Not that she always uses *voluntas* in a bad sense, or associates it only with the body. In *Scivias*, for instance, she frequently speaks of good will, of will in the human soul, and naturally also of the will of God (*voluntas dei*).[83] In her *Expositio Evangeliorum*, the phrase in the Prologue of John – 'born not of the will of flesh, nor of the will of man' – is taken to refer to the sexual desire of the woman and the man respectively: this brings forth children, but does not of itself show them to be children of God. Rather, it points to the purely natural aspect of child-bearing: 'the children are curdled like cheese'.[84] Returning to the passage from John in the *Liber divinorum operum*, however, Hildegard adds: 'but man is perfected by flesh and spirit'.[85]

Nonetheless, it would be wrong to minimize the pejorative use of *voluntas*, and the moments of pessimism about the human body, in Hildegard's thought. Thus for instance, in a letter to a nun who had renounced her monastic life, Hildegard sees the issue in black and white: the woman can again put on her heavenly dress, and so be saved, or else remain in the power of her own sensuality and, by rejecting her immortal – that is, monastic – dress, lose all hope of reaching heaven. Her correspondent has alleged that she took the nun's veil unwillingly, and Hildegard replies to this with the astounding analogy, that infants too are baptized resisting. This would mean that, in the matter of taking monastic vows, the question of assent is irrelevant. In complete contrast to Heloise, Hildegard assumes that the act – the baptism or the vow – is all-important, and that intention counts for nothing. It looks as if for her the human will, belonging to the baser part, the body, is there only to be subjugated. There is a simple fallacy here, which escaped Hildegard: a desire *for* the virginal life (such as she depicts so beautifully in St Ursula) would be meaningless unless a valid alternative desire were also possible. –

Daughter of Adam, take heed – for in your falling you behave like Adam, who showed contempt for his Lord and listened to the foulest worm; thus he flung his honour and his angelic dress behind him, and, in place of paradise, received Gehenna as heirloom! So too did you, when you took off the heavenly dress you had put on, and looked to the ostentation of this world, which you had renounced before – even though you would like to excuse yourself by saying that you stepped into that dress unwillingly, But think: the struggling infant is submerged in baptism, and, even if he weeps and howls, still becomes a Christian...

Remember too that younger son who, receiving his inheritance from his father, went off into a distant region, and there, living riotously, wasted it all, and was driven to such need that he herded pigs and craved the husks that were their food, and no one gave them to him. So too you now, overwhelmed by physical delights and unchaste love, are enjoying your inheritance, which is meant to bring peace and plenty, today; but surely days that are alien and not yours will swiftly come upon you. Then your enemies will surround you from all

188

sides, and they will tear your poor soul out of your body and drag it with them to the land of pitch and sulphur, the land of death . . .

Therefore, dear daughter, I implore you to put on Christ again, whom you had taken off, and on bended knee fly to God, that he reawaken you from death to life before the day of your passing. For your days are short.

Even Hildegard's dramatic expression, that Adam 'received Gehenna as heirloom', would not have stood up to rigorous theological analysis: Adam did not suffer the damnation with which Hildegard is threatening the wayward nun; to claim the contrary would be to deny Christ's deliverance of Adam in the harrowing of hell.

Again, writing to a man who was beset by his sensuality, Hildegard uses the dualistic language of the battle of flesh against spirit. And yet what she does with this language is distinctive. Her opening phrase – 'Oh son of God, in your life you are like that soil which brings useful and useless plants to germination' – acknowledges that the heavenly impulses and their frustration through earthly desires are rooted in the same human being. But she continues: 'and so, neglect-ing . . . the desires of your heavenly soul, you most often do what your body demands'. Then, with the next lines, Hildegard uses an extraordinary figure of catachresis: This man should become 'a most brave knight of the true Solomon, gloriously clad in the mightiest armour, fighting manfully and untiringly, in valour and constancy, against your physical craving and delectation'.

The 'true Solomon' is a traditional *figura* for Christ; but to recall Solomon at all in this particular context, of sensuality to be mastered, is to ensure that the delectations of the first Solomon are not forgotten. The *figura* is consciously filled with its double capacity, as if to say, it is through a deeper cognizance of the sensual demands that the sensual failings can be dominated, the nature of the true Solomon imprinted on the cravings of the earlier, weak one.

In another letter, to a young nobleman, Hildegard tries to elaborate an ideal that is both courtly and spiritual. Ignoble behaviour, she says, goes against the honour of a royal court: the primary meaning would seem to be literal, and her correspondent may well have been a courtier of Henry and Eleanor, or else of Frederick Barbarossa. It is certain at least that Hildegard is projecting an image of gracious behaviour for someone in the secular life. And yet by *regalis curia* she may also be alluding to the court of heaven, whose honour is likewise tarnished by conduct that is base in courts on earth:

Your eyes see clear when with good striving you look to God and your knowledge is wakeful, when you restrain yourself amid the baseness of this world and your mind flies aloft, when you flee the vices of the deceiving devil and the scurrility and vanity of the vagaries of human conduct. In your thoughts, however, take great care to flee from churlish behaviour, which is ignorant of the renown of a royal court – namely anger and vengeance, which suppress measured and honourable action.

For in the vision of my soul I saw you looking towards a high mountain, to see a most beautiful girl, whose face seemed supremely elegant and whose robes were radiantly white; yet you could not see their rich beauty as perfectly as you longed to do. This fairest girl is the flowering of the restraint of a pure mind.

Set that girl in the chamber of your mind, and she will make for you an emerald column in a window of the heavenly Jerusalem – a window that, fashioned of noblest stones, topaz and sapphire, below, and of purest gold studded with every kind of precious gem above, appears gleaming and lucent as a mirror; thus also many people, looking at their faces in that window, will recognize the foulness of their aspect, the ignominy of their conduct, in that reflection.

As Hildegard had commended Discretio to Abbess Hazzecha and her two disciples, so here, for the young man, she sets up an ideal of Continentia, which is another Christian counterpart to the chivalric *mezura*, now adapted to his particular problems and condition. Noble behaviour, Hildegard argues, while embracing a courtly ideal, also implicitly comprehends a higher one: it 'flies aloft'. In a base world, the truly noble man must show restraint;[86] anger and vengeance are uncourtly, a negation of the beauty of composed behaviour.

Hildegard hints that the young man has not escaped these vices entirely, and so designs for him her talisman of Continentia. She is not like the motherly figure, Continentia, with children clustering round her, whom Augustine evoked in the scene of his conversion (though Hildegard may well have recalled this image)[87]; nor is she merely the expression of sexual restraint (though this is certainly included); rather, she embodies *mezura* in its most exalted and complete sense.

Hildegard tries to make the image alluring for her correspondent: she conjures up a girl not only of consummate beauty but of the highest elegance (that is, beauty in its most aristocratic aspect). She is far away on a mountain-top, and he cannot yet see all her beauty fully – perhaps because some blemish of churlishness still prevents his eyes from seeing with total clarity, with that clearsightedness which Hildegard, at the opening of the letter, had identified with virtuous seeing; perhaps, too, because the *puella* has something of the mysterious attraction of the *amor de lonh* of romances.

And yet she can be won and possessed. The last image is complex and subtle. A fabulously wrought window of the heavenly Jerusalem can become a mirror of human conduct, which shows the flaws in beauty and nobility of him who looks at himself there. The mirror-window, that is, serves as a conscience. But the lovely girl, Continentia, has set an emerald column in that window: no explanatory allegory is added, but I think the sense of that pillar as measurer, or *regula*, in the window of self-awareness is clear. It is set there by one's own most beautiful and most elegant ideal of behaviour (the *puella*). This seems to be the implication in Hildegard's delicate blending of courtly and homiletic thoughts.

Hildegard has here transformed imaginings and values of the aristocratic world into which she was born, to make of them a strategy for guiding her correspondent. Similarly, she can adapt her medical lore – her characterology for instance – in a wholly individual way, so as to console and advise another friend, an abbot:

The secret mysteries of God cannot be comprehended or known by anything that has its source through the Beginning. And yet all his judgements are just, because there is no emptiness in him: he is as he was and is. But even as man consists of elements, and the elements are conjoined, and none is of any avail of itself without another, so too the modes of behaviour of men are unequal, even though they arise from one and the same breath of life.

There are four modes of behaviour among men: some are hard, some airy, some stormy, some fiery.

One who has the hard mode is sharp in everything, and in none of his affairs does he heed anyone else, but reckons all that is his for himself alone, and takes pleasure in that.

And as for one who has the airy mode, his mind is always wavering; and yet he fears God and restrains himself as regards sinning, because he is not pleased with what he does.

Those who have the stormy mode are not wise, but compound all they do with foolishness; they are not improved by words of wisdom, but shudder at them indignantly.

And those who have the fiery mode aspire to everything worldly and alienate themselves from spiritual people; they shun peace and, wherever they see it, strike at it with some worldly ambition . . .

But God gathers to himself some of all those who have such modes of behaviour – when, growing aware, they turn what goes against their souls' salvation back towards God: those who at last fear him, as happened in the case of Saul and many others.

This four-part division of human *mores* is not strictly based on the elements or complexions. It is Hildegard's free variation on traditional tetrads. It is also (unlike a number of passages in *Causae et curae* that deal with the same problem) essentially optimistic: here no type of person is, by virtue of his temperament, fated to be an enemy of God. Yet this is also Hildegard's way of 'explaining' to the abbot the source of his particular human difficulties: he himself is of the airy mode, and his sickness is bound up with the dominance of that mode in him, whereas his flock are hard, stormy, and fiery types. He feels oppressed by them, they give him no comfort – that is, there is a clash of temperaments that cannot be resolved in human terms. Yet the sickness can also be his 'purgation', Hildegard concludes, turning the medical concept into a spiritual one.

In a similar way, Hildegard uses her expertise to advise a man who had asked her for help against nightmares. She 'accounts for' these in two distinct – but for her complementary – ways. On the one hand they have a specific medical cause in a humoral maladjustment, on the other she sees them as a malevolent disturbance worked by demons. The remedy she suggests is reading the Prologue of John's Gospel at night, hand on heart, together with a prayer composed by herself. The use of John's Prologue in this way can be abundantly paralleled in twelfth-century *adiurationes* of demons. It is employed in formulae for bringing about fair weather, it is used apotropaically, to ward off dangers and fiends; it is read over a woman in labour, if the birth is difficult; and especially in the earlier period it is used in a ritual *ad purificandam mulierem*, after giving birth.[88] There too the use was apotropaic: till purified, the woman was still hedged with demonic powers. The German translation of the Prologue of John inserted in the Codex Buranus[89] may likewise have been used quasi-magically, to secure celestial aid. –

Servant of God, you who are outstanding in Christ's service, do not fear the oppressiveness that terrifies you in your sleep: it arises in you through your sanguine humours being stirred by a melancholy temperament (*complexio*). That is why your sleep is burdened, and most often the visions in your dreams are not true, because the ancient deceiver, though he does not harm your senses, nonetheless by his deception troubles you in this. Yet it is by God's dispensation that you are punished by such pressure, that, through your fear, carnal desire may be curbed in you. Each night, placing your hand on your heart, read the Gospel 'In the beginning was the Word' with devout intention, and then say these words:

'Almighty Lord God . . . free me from this harrowing disquiet, and defend me from all ambushes of airy spirits.'

Finally there is a group of letters where, in order to offer solace, Hildegard takes advantage of her reputation for divinatory powers. In one, she addresses a widow, who (it would appear) had written to her enquiring about the lot of her husband in the otherworld, and asking Hildegard to prognosticate for her as well. That this widow is sent an answer in Latin suggests she was one of the high-born, privileged laity who had received a clerical education.

Hildegard's reply is curious.[90] At first it seems full of disclaimers: in the vision of her soul she sees many of God's *mirabilia*, and the deep and difficult parts of the Scriptures; but her *visio* is not a crystal ball. And yet, in the very next lines, it seems to become just that. Suddenly Hildegard claims to have seen the exact condition of the dead husband in the otherworld, and to have special knowledge of his hidden thoughts and intentions, ones he had not revealed or carried out in life. So, too, while beginning with a disavowal of any knowledge of the widow's future fate, she works her way (by a series of unexceptionably pious injunctions) to a hint, at the close of the letter, that she knows this outcome also – knows that both the woman and her husband will at last attain heaven.

The letter that follows this one in the manuscript, though it begins with a capital, has no heading, and hence was not recognized as separate by Degering in his description.[91] But this letter is to a *pastor*, and begins 'O mitis pater'. As before, Hildegard denies that she has any advance knowledge of human 'outcomes (*eventus*)', or of what will befall human beings. She, 'poor little untaught womanly form' can know nothing save what she is taught in her vision. The next sentence – 'So I too shall gladly pray for that matron, that she may be ruled by God's grace in body and soul, and that God may bring her the seemly joy of an heir' – suggests that here likewise she had been asked to prognosticate: will this woman be able to have a child?

Then she turns to the *pastor*, who had made or transmitted this request, and reverts to her familiar theme of *discretio*: he is one who fails in this virtue, because he is too severe with his flock.

A page later, in the shortest letter in the Berlin collection, Hildegard declares to a man whom she addresses only as 'servant of God' (he could be a layman or one of the lower-ranking clergy), that she does know the fate of a particular soul in the next life. This time there are no disclaimers, nor is there a reference here to her vision: she simply alleges that she knows:

Servant of God, this soul about which you ask is not yet freed from its purgation of suffering: so pray for it lovingly to God, and rejoice that God has reckoned it in the number of blessed souls. May the Holy Spirit kindle you with his grace and confirm you in his service.

If this letter is complete as it stands, it suggests that Hildegard at times was not above a simple piece of fortune-telling, however pious in intent.

IX

In conclusion I wish to draw special attention to two letters of a more complex kind. The first is again unpublished, and is one of the few in the Berlin collection where I believe we can identify the correspondent and thereby win new insights into Hildegard's life and method of work. The second, to the prelates of Mainz, is perhaps her greatest letter.

In 1173 Hildegard's beloved secretary Volmar died. Hildegard then wrote to her friend Ludwig in Trier (who had become abbot of St Eucharius in 1168), lamenting that, because of Volmar's death, she, 'lonely as an orphan', had not yet been able to finish her new book, the *Liber divinorum operum*. But 'soon, when it is completed and copied, I shall show it to you for correction'.[92] This 'key letter', as Schrader and Führkötter called it in their edition and commentary, survives uniquely in the Berlin manuscript. But there is a second letter in this manuscript, still unconsidered, which in my view should be understood as following up that promise: it is the 'covering letter', that is, with which Hildegard despatched the copy of her last major work.[93] –

The sun arises at dawn and, from the place where it is set, perfuses all the clouds with its brightness by beholding them, and rules and lights up all creatures by its ardour, running its course to twilight: in the same way God has made the whole of creation – which is man – and then has vivified and lit it with the breath of life.

For as the earliest dawn rises with damp cold and changing cloud-shapes, so man in his childhood has damp coldness, since his flesh is still growing and his bones are not yet filled with marrow, nor is his blood yet sparkling in full redness. But, as the third hour of the day begins to grow hot in the sun's course, so he too, chewing different foods, acquires their taste, and at the same time learns to walk. When childhood is over, man in youth becomes daring, joyful and serene, making his own plans for what he would like to begin, so that if, turning to the right side, he chooses the good in the sun's light, he will become fruitful in good deeds; but if, pursuing evil, he inclines down to the left side, he will grow black and most foul in sin. But when, accomplishing his course of action, he arrives at the ninth hour, he will falter and dry up in flesh and marrow, and in the other forces with which he advanced as he grew. So too the highest craftsman has drawn up the ages of the world, ordered in time from dawn to twilight.

But you, father, who are so named after the Father, reflect on how you began, and how you proceeded in life: for in your childhood you were foolish, and in youth you were filled with joyous assurance. Meanwhile you have embarked on an adventure of the unicorn – unknown to you in your youth – and this indeed was my writing, which often carries echoes of the mortal dress of the son of God, who, loving a maidenly nature, resting in it like the unicorn in the maiden's lap, gathered the whole Church to himself with the sweetest sound of fairest believing.

Remember too, loyal father, what you often used to hear from a poor little womanly creature soft in form, about that dress of the son of God; and, because my helper has been taken away by the highest Judge, I now am entrusting what I have written to you, asking imploringly that you preserve it carefully, and look over it, correcting it lovingly, that your name too may be written in the book of life,[94] imitating the blessed Gregory in this, who, despite the burden of his Roman episcopate, never ceased composing, impelled by the lute-like sound of the infusion of the Holy Spirit.

Put on celestial armour like a noble knight, washing away the deeds of foolishness of your youth, and toil strenuously in the noonday in the angelic robe of your monk's habit, before the day declines, so that you may be welcomed joyously in the heavenly tents into the angels' company.

It is an elaborate letter in thought and language. Here, late in life, we see how Hildegard had acquired the power to construct complex, fluent and fluid sentences, apparently quite unaided: she was just then without a secretary, and the text shows no trace of reworking by another hand. At first she makes a series of interleaving parallels between macrocosm and microcosm. The day in the outer world, from the first dawn to nightfall, is like the ages of man, from childhood to senescence. As the sun lights up the world from dawn to twilight, God lights it up with the breath of life. But as 'the whole of creation . . . is man', human life also epitomizes that divine light-giving breath. The hours of the human day are both stages of human life and ages of the world.

When Hildegard applies these thoughts to her friend, it is of special interest that she stresses the courtly temperament of his youth – 'audax, letus et serenus . . . letam securitatem habebas'. It is the perfect Latin equivalent to the complex notion celebrated by the Minnesinger – Hoher Mut – that joyous assurance and élan which characterize the disposition of a splendid young lover. Yet the noon-day of life is another time of day, and by then a definitive choice must have been made. Hildegard plays on the 'Pythagorean' topos of choosing between the right path and the left.[95] The way she does so is perhaps closest to that of Chrétien de Troyes, who, some five years after this letter of 1174, brought religious allusions into his development of the theme in the Prologue of *Perceval*:

The left hand . . . signifies vaingloriousness, which comes from false hypocrisy. And the right? It means charity, who does not vaunt her good deeds, but hides herself so well that none knows their existence save he whose name is God and charity.[96]

The abbot's life is one 'day' – of the sun's course, and of God's – still far from complete. His courtly youth has turned into another, sublimated metaphoric form of chivalric action – the pursuit of the unicorn. Hildegard, by a playful conceit, suggests that for him this has been his engagement in her writings: he hunts and finds Christ the unicorn hiding in her maidenly lap. As she confirms in the Epilogue of *Liber divinorum operum*, after Ludwig had helped her in its last stages: 'he knew me and my visions well, before this'.[97]

Reminding him of their close friendship, in which she, 'poor little womanly creature, soft in form', had been his instructress, she at last comes back to the favour she is asking him: to read carefully in manuscript her last, enormous book. She shows she is aware that (because of its size and difficulty) this may prove a burden on him, but asks it nonetheless: 'toil strenuously in the noonday'. It can be a penance for his adolescent follies, it can gain merit for him in heaven; she even suggests it may be his particular way of winning a place in heaven. She also warns, more practically: be careful not to lose the manuscript! If, as I believe, what she sent to Trier with this letter was the still-uncorrected Gent codex, it will have been especially precious in that no other fair copy had yet been made. (Presumably Hildegard had at least her rough notes, on wax tablets, in the convent.)

The letter, remarkable in its scope, ranges between earnestness and humour, between highly-wrought, high-flown analogies and metaphors and informal, personal requests, filled with a blithe awareness of the fascination she could exercise. Here motifs that were part of the medieval Platonic *koinê* – the sym-metry of macrocosm and microcosm, the *bivium* of human existence – are alluded to lightheartedly and given a wholly personal modulation. Hildegard does not argue in the manner of her contemporaries, *Platonem diligentes*, such as William of Conches or Gilbert of Poitiers. Here as so often she expounds her thoughts uniquely. In her way of doing so she is not so much a Platonist as a figure comparable to Plato's own creation, the priestess Diotima, in the *Symposium*.

X

In the year before her death, Hildegard, eighty years old, faced the bitterest conflict she had ever known, one that nearly spelt tragic destruction for herself and her community. She had agreed in 1178 to let a nobleman be buried in the consecrated ground at the Rupertsberg. Twice in the *Vita* notes she mentions the endowments that came to her foundation because 'many wealthy people buried members of their family there, with due honour'; even a rich philosopher, who had visited Hildegard full of scepticism about her visions, had been wholly won over by her and had asked to have his sepulchre in their midst.[98] But the unnamed nobleman who was buried on the Rupertsberg in 1178 was someone who had once been excommunicated, though before his death he had become reconciled with the Church. The prelates of Mainz, however, in the name of their archbishop (who was away in Italy, engaged in mediation between Emperor Frederick Barbarossa and Pope Alexander III), alleging that this man died excommunicate, ordered Hildegard to have his corpse dug up and cast away. The penalty for not doing so was that she and her nuns would themselves be excommunicated, no longer able to hear mass, receive the eucharist, or sing the divine office.

Hildegard defied the interdict. The 'protocol' of her canonization – witnesses' reports taken down in the years 1233–7, and surviving in their original manuscript[99] – tells that she responded by making the sign of the cross over the tomb with her *baculus* (the staff that was an emblem of her authority as abbess), and wiping away all traces that could have led to the grave's being identified and desecrated.[100] She took upon herself and her community to live in public shame, deprived of the sacraments that were the source of grace in their lives. Why did she choose to disobey in this way? Could it have been because to exhume the body meant to forgo some great endowment for the Rupertsberg, or because she respected an aristocratic family more than the clergy of Mainz? Her letters offer no basis for such suspicions. Hildegard was ready to endure humiliation and spiritual rejection because her living light – here we might paraphrase, her conscience – told her that to obey the prelates, to violate the body buried in holy ground, would be to disobey God. The first part of her letter to the Mainz prelates shows a situation most truly comparable with that of Antigone: to obey the human law set up by a Creon, that a corpse should be sacrilegiously degraded, is to flout a greater law, a divine light and command that can be clearly perceived within the soul. Whatever the human cost, this must not – and for one like Hildegard, or Antigone, cannot – be contravened:[101]

In the vision that was fixed within my soul, by God the craftsman, before I came forth in my birth, I was compelled to write this, on account of the fetter by which we have been

bound by our superiors, because of a dead man who, at the direction of his priest, was
buried without calumny in our midst. When, a few days after his burial, we were ordered
by our superiors to fling him out of the cemetery, I, seized with no little terror at this order,
looked to the true light, as is my wont. And, my eyes wakeful, I saw in my soul that, if we
followed their command and exposed the corpse, such an expulsion would threaten our
home with great danger, like a vast blackness – it would envelop us like a dark cloud that
looms before tempests and thunderstorms . . .

So we did not dare expose him . . . not at all because we make light of the advice of
honourable men or of our prelates' command, but lest we seem to injure Christ's sacraments
– with which the man was blessed while still alive – by women's savagery. Yet, so as not to
be wholly disobedient, we have till now ceased singing the songs of divine praises, in
accordance with the interdict, and have abstained from partaking of the body of the Lord . . .

While I and all my sisters were afflicted with great bitterness through this, and oppressed
by a huge sadness . . . I heard in my vision that I was guilty in that I had not come with all
humility and devotion before my superiors, to ask their leave to receive communion, most
of all since we were not at fault in accepting the body of that man.

The later part of the letter goes far beyond this. The interdict had specifically
forbidden music in the convent. We know how much music meant to
Hildegard, composer of the 'Symphony of the harmony of heavenly revelations', and we can imagine how keenly this ban will have affected her humanly.
But now, reflecting on its implications, she sees the music – both vocal and
(as here emerges) instrumental – of her convent in a symbolic way. She works
out her own philosophy of music: music becomes not only the *musica mundana*,
the cosmic harmony familiar from Boethius' *De musica*, [102] but a way of understanding history – Adam and Lucifer, the Old Testament prophets and the New
Testament Church – and a way in which human beings can still incarnate
heavenly beauty in an earthly mode. The symbolism then turns into micro-
cosmic allegory – music is the human body and soul, and the principles with
which they are informed – an allegory that is dynamic and in no way forced,
arising effortlessly out of Hildegard's pattern of thoughts and images. Her sentences themselves here are like melismas – huge arclike rhythmic phrases,
controlled more subtly and perfectly than ever before in her prose. And in the
midst of these she, once more an Antigone, can warn the Creons of her world:
it may be they who are flouting the highest law, the law that comprehends the
heavenly harmony. –

I also beheld something about the fact that, obeying you, we have till now ceased to celebrate the divine office in song, reading it only in a low voice: I heard a voice from the living
light tell of the diverse kinds of praises, of which David says in the Psalms: 'Praise him in
the call of the trumpet, praise him on psaltery and lute, praise him on the tambour and in
dancing, praise him on strings and on organ, praise him on resonant cymbals, praise him
on cymbals of jubilation – let every spirit praise the Lord!'

In these words outer realities teach us about inner ones – namely how, in accordance with
the material composition and quality of instruments, we can best transform and shape the

performance of our inner being towards praises of the Creator. If we strive for this lovingly, we recall how man sought the voice of the living spirit, which Adam lost through disobedience – he who, still innocent before his fault, had no little kinship with the sounds of the angels' praises . . .

But in order that mankind should recall that divine sweetness and praise by which, with the angels, Adam was made jubilant in God before he fell, instead of recalling Adam in his banishment, and that mankind too might be stirred to that sweet praise, the holy prophets – taught by the same spirit, which they had received – not only composed psalms and canticles, to be sung to kindle the devotion of listeners; but also they invented musical instruments of diverse kinds with this in view, by which the songs could be expressed in multitudinous sounds, so that listeners, aroused and made adept outwardly, might be nurtured within by the forms and qualities of the instruments, as by the meaning of the words performed with them.

Eager and wise men imitated the holy prophets, inventing human kinds of harmonized melody (*organa*) by their art, so that they could sing in the delight of their soul; and they adapted their singing to [the notation indicated by] the bending of the finger-joints,[103] as it were recalling that Adam was formed by the finger of God, which is the Holy Spirit, and that in Adam's voice before he fell there was the sound of every harmony and the sweetness of the whole art of music. And if Adam had remained in the condition in which he was formed, human frailty could never endure the power and the resonance of that voice.[104] But when his deceiver, the devil, heard that man had begun to sing through divine inspiration, and that he would be transformed through this to remembering the sweetness of the songs in the heavenly land – seeing the machinations of his cunning going awry, he became so terrified that . . . he has not ceased to trouble or destroy the affirmation and beauty and sweetness of divine praise and of the hymns of the spirit. So you and all prelates must use the greatest vigilance before stopping, by a decree, the mouth of any assembly of people singing to God . . . you must always beware lest in your judgement you are ensnared by Satan, who drew man out of the celestial harmony and the delights of paradise . . .

And because at times, when hearing some melody, a human being often sighs and moans, recalling the nature of the heavenly harmony, the prophet David, subtly contemplating the profound nature of the spirit, and knowing that the human soul is symphonic (*symphonialis*), exhorts us in his psalm to proclaim the Lord on the lute and play for him on the ten-stringed psaltery: he wants to refer his lute, which sounds lower, to the body's control; the psaltery, which sounds higher, to the spirit's striving; its ten chords, to the fulfilment of the Law.[105]

The human soul is symphonic, and any symphony of voices and instruments on earth, which is directed heavenwards, is a means of reintegration, of bringing the lost human–heavenly condition alive again. I would also suggest that Hildegard's concept *symphonia* can illuminate, and at least implicitly harmonize, the otherwise unreconciled aspects of her picture of the cosmos. Like Avicenna, she worked with two models of understanding. This became particularly noticeable in the analysis of moments in *Causae et curae*. The one model, underlying her medical discussions, was full of materialist perceptions. The elements were the ultimate constituents not only of physical objects but of the soul, of all the motions of human thought, feeling and knowledge. They conditioned human character by their various combinations or 'complexions'. The other model of understanding loomed up whenever Hildegard thought of a direct bond between man and God. The only way man has of knowing and loving God is by transcending the physically conditioned world, by overcoming his fallen physical state, freeing his higher self – by cultivating a psychological condition, that is, which has its counterpart macrocosmically in the Manichaean myths. In *Causae et curae* the two approaches jostle each other and are not resolved. It is here, in the letter of the eighty-year-old visionary on the philosophy of music, that we glimpse the kind of reconciliation which she saw as possible and which she might have worked out fully had she lived.

For a *symphonia* is something that is of necessity both material and immaterial. The voices are human, the instruments fashioned and played by human beings on earth, not just by angels. Earthly music emerges from the earthly – yet is not earthbound. It 'leaps up to God' – not by overcoming its physical components, but in the act of affirming them. Faustus, Marlowe's embodiment of the dualist, cried out 'Who pulles me downe?' Hildegard too knows that a Mephistophilis can 'destroy the affirmation and beauty and sweetness of divine praise'. And yet she also declares that the human musician, and listener to music, survive, because, whatever an envious Satan or a Creon-like prelate might achieve, the capacity to hear the symphony and to produce it are innate, and hence remain. The symphony manifests itself whenever the community assemble their instruments and voices to project them heavenward, but also inwardly, in the accord of each soul with its body, orchestrated by the divine Law.

The prelates paid no heed to this letter, and persisted with their interdict; but in March 1179, six months before Hildegard's death, the archbishop of Mainz wrote to her from Rome and made it possible for the ban to be lifted. For him it turned on a legalistic question – if reliable witnesses could be found to testify that the buried man had made his peace with the Church, then his corpse need not be disinterred. For Hildegard, by contrast, it was a question of the primacy of conscience, of her living light. Towards the beginning of her letter she also argued that she was not technically at fault; towards the close we sense that this consideration is hardly even relevant any longer: what she will not tolerate is any affront to that symphony of the heavenly and the earthly which had become consubstantial with her way of grasping truth.

What, in the last resort, is our image of this fiery soul? Much could be said on the adverse side. The unshakeable strength and conviction could be seen as stubbornness, combativeness, and a naked will to dominate. It may well have been so, for instance, when Hildegard refused to let go her much-loved companion Richardis, defending her human possessiveness by arguments that ostensibly turned on purely spiritual issues. There, and on certain other occasions of conflict, one might suspect a megalomanic tendency: that Hildegard could use the device of saying 'the living light told me . . .' in order to give herself, in any controversial question, an unchallengeable stand.

So too she could use her illness, like her visionary gift, as a weapon, though more especially in a negative way, in order to have an unanswerable excuse for not yielding to the importunacy of others when she did not want to. Thus when opposition was raised to her decision to move away from the Disibodenberg, Hildegard took to her bed and heard a voice telling her to cease writing and speaking there. In human terms, it was rather as if she had gone on strike. Similarly, when at first she was reluctant to get involved with helping the 'obsessed' woman, Sigewize, in person, her outlet was, she was too ill to do so.[106]

Finally, one cannot ignore what today might be called Hildegard's snobbishness, but what is perhaps best seen as her partisanship for feudal against Christian values, in refusing to admit women who were not well-born as nuns in her convent. When her colleague Tengswindis questioned this exclusiveness, appealing to New Testament ideals, Hildegard countered by appealing to her living light, which showed her that class-distinctions had been divinely ordained.

In various ways, in short, Hildegard could blind herself. Nonetheless she remains not just a captivating but an indelibly attractive person. First in her originality. Her frankness with people is matched by the way she approaches every field and every problem as if for the first time. While she claims that her learning is rudimentary and her command of language faulty, she writes a Latin that is as forceful and colourful, and at times as subtle and brilliant, as any in the twelfth century; and her learning is often so astounding that (as she gives no source-references) it still sets countless problems to determine all she had read. Her use of language reflects intimately both her febrile vitality and her exultant sense of the beauty of the physical world, the beauty of music, the beauty that is possible in men and women. Bounded in the nutshell of the Rupertsberg, she counts herself a queen of infinite space – though she too has bad dreams. The torments, conflicts, nightmares are evoked as intensely as the rays of the living light.

While she is clearly of mystical disposition – her sense of the divine presence is the lodestar of her life – she is never in cloudcuckooland. Her medical writing shows her attempts, restless yet full of empathy, to understand all that is human: human bodies, their sexuality, their ailments, the vagaries of character; so too her letters often show shrewdness, compassion, and helpfulness in practical matters.

Despite her constant illness – or perhaps because of it, in that it impelled her to concentrate, when well, on what mattered most to her – Hildegard never lost her smouldering energy. She could plan and carry out her visionary trilogy on an immense scale, think about medicine and nature, poetry and music, and the great problems of Church and State in her time. There is scarcely a field to which she did not bring her individual contribution. She rediscovers the cosmos – and the Christian revelation, from the fall of the angels to the Judgement – for herself, in her *visio* of the living light. She rediscovers existentially, uninhibitedly.

Her approach to every problem – human, scientific, artistic, or theological – was her own. She took nothing ready-made. Her conviction that she *saw* the answers to the problems in her waking vision meant that she did not have to defer to established answers. Often we see she does not give a damn about these, however powerful their proponents. Many times she expresses herself courteously and modestly; yet when it comes to asserting what she believes to be right, she will do it bravely, outfacing all opposition. She has no qualms about speaking out against Barbarossa, when she felt he was shaming the Church, or about warning or denouncing any of the mighty in the Church's hierarchy itself. Yet (except perhaps in the matter of Richardis) her utterances are calmly considered and not strident. She moves in the world of great rulers, ecclesiastical and temporal, with a superb assurance, which owes perhaps as much to her privileged birth as to her awareness of her rôle as prophet. At the same time the many expressions of her sense of frailty and helplessness – 'paupercula feminea forma' – while they become formulaic, are no empty formulas. They are truthful, at times anguished, admissions that without her unique gift or grace she would be nothing. A melancholic woman by her own reckoning, she oscillates between rapturous praise of womankind – 'o feminea forma, quam gloriosa es!' – and a despairing sense of woman's weakness.

In her letters the commanding tones alternate with expressions of great fondness and gentleness. She is capable of showing strong attachment to people. Perhaps this always shaded to some extent into possessiveness; yet it is clear that for instance the men who helped her with her writing – Volmar, Gottfried (who began the *Vita*), Ludwig of Trier and Guibert of Gembloux – felt bound to her in steady friendship as well as admiration. And that she was not abandoned by her nuns in 1178, when they were excommunicated along with her because of her magnificent defiance, suggests that, after the storms of the earlier years, she could count on fierce loyalty from those who had remained with her. In her campaign against the interdict I believe there was far more than a point of honour at stake: Hildegard saw that what matters is the spirit of laws and not their letter. She was ready even to cut herself off from the Church rather than endure an outrage to the corpse of a man to whom, while he lived, she had pledged her care; nothing would let her conscience be crushed by clerical legalism.

She was daunting and eccentric; stupendous in her powers of thought and expression; lovable in her warmth and never-wearying freshness in everything she tackled.

Hildegard of Bingen died in 1179. The 120 years that followed her death saw an astounding proliferation of writings by religious women, Latin and vernacular, prose and verse. Some of the high imaginative achievements of this period – the lyrics of Hadewijch of Antwerp, or Mechthild of Magdeburg's *Flowing Light of Godhead*, with its haunting transitions from prose to rhyming free verse, from inner dialogues to dramatically shaped scenes – have received expert and sensitive treatment in recent decades.[1] The work of one woman, however, has remained largely unknown. This is Marguerite Porete – the most neglected of the great writers of the thirteenth century. Marguerite wrote her book of poetic prose, dialogue and lyric about 1285–95. The full title that she gave it was *The mirror of simple annihilated souls, who dwell only in will and desire of Love* (*Le mirouer des simples ames anienties et qui seulement demourent en vouloir et desir d'Amour*). Marguerite's vision of divine desire and love will be interpreted in some detail in the later part of this chapter.

One characteristic is shared by Marguerite and a number of the thirteenth-century women writers: they belonged not to traditional foundations for nuns or canonesses, but to the new and in many ways freer communities of the time,[2] of which the *béguinages* were the most numerous, especially in northern Europe. In such communities, women were less sheltered – and often less privileged – than in the older ones; they were encouraged to tasks that involved the outer world, such as caring for the poor and the sick. Yet the new generations of women writers do not look at the outer world: indeed their most marked common feature is a greatly increased subjectivity.[3]

As Hildegard had projected a vision of Love (*Caritas*) in the figure of a sublimely beautiful celestial *Domina*, so too a womanly divine emanation, *Minne* or *Amour*, occurs – and often becomes a protagonist – in many of the thirteenth-century women's writings. But where Hildegard oriented her vision of Love wholly towards a theological allegory of the incarnation and redemption, the appearances of *Minne–Amour* are occasions for dialogue with the soul of the writer, for a series of exchanges which, while they touch on many of the major Christian beliefs, have their *raison d'être* in their detailed evocation of the writer's inner life, her hopes and despairs, fears and sorrows, moments of ecstatic fulfilment and aching emptiness. Where Hildegard used visions in order to show her individual map of the Christian cosmos, the thirteenth-century women show the map of a soul in solitude, however intensely that soul may be pervaded by Christian presences.

But the most striking difference between Hildegard and the succeeding generations is this. Hildegard's daring was always – except in her two physical treatises – circumscribed by her affirmation that she wrote in the name of the 'living light', not in her own. This meant that, once her prophetic gift had been officially acknowledged as genuine (the papal sanction, as we saw, was given even before her first major work was complete), her utterances were almost beyond challenge.[4] When she spoke out against powerful church authorities, or against Emperor Frederick Barbarossa, it was with the prophet's impunity. The thirteenth-century women speak in their own name. They are not prophets, but passionate, often anguished, minds. The beauty of their writing is bound up with their vulnerability.

To characterize what is new in sensibility, I should like, before turning to Marguerite Porete and her *Miroir*, to focus on certain testimonies that would seem – at least on the surface – to be of a very different kind. The first, which shows an outlook shaped chiefly by human love, is a record, little more than five pages long, of the thoughts of an unlettered peasant girl in Provence, who was widowed at the age of nineteen. Her name was Grazida Lizier.

Grazida is one of the villagers, from Montaillou and neighbouring regions, whose beliefs and thoughts about themselves and their world were recorded in lengthy interrogations by the Cathar-hunting bishop of Pamiers, Jacques Fournier, who later became Pope Benedict XII. The full transcripts of the interrogations were printed in 1965 by Jean Duvernoy, though for complete precision it is still necessary to go back to the manuscript and cite and translate the texts from there.[5] Many of the most striking utterances of people from Montaillou have meanwhile become well known through the eloquent presentation of their community by Emmanuel Le Roy Ladurie.[6] Yet with some of the more outstanding depositions, something important remains to be done even after Ladurie's admirable panorama: it is to retrace the lines of thought and the integrity of thought in such testimonies, considering their movements and complexities, their inner contradictions even, but not isolating sentences or phrases atomistically, as Ladurie tended to do for the sake of his synthesis. For Grazida and several of her contemporaries have something not only profound but coherent to say; and if we give the closest attention to their words, as these emerge through the painfully awkward Latin of the official record, we can see, I would argue, that what she and certain others wanted to present is a way of looking that is often far removed both from the Christian and the Cathar commonplaces that were current in their surroundings. Though it has reached literary record only by an accident of history – the mad inquisitorial zeal of Jacques Fournier – it survives, and it belongs with the most individual moments of medieval self-expression.

Grazida was born at Montaillou in 1297/8. Her mother, Fabrisse,[7] had married into a Cathar family; but she had been brutally thrown out of her home by her husband, Pons, because she did not become one of his sect. Being illegitimate, she had no family to take her part or to return to; she then made her living as keeper of the local tavern. When Grazida was twenty-one years old, she was called before the inquisitor, not only as a Cathar suspect but also because she had been the mistress of the libertine rector of Montaillou, Pierre Clergue, who was both Cathar and informer. What Grazida told the inquisitor was as follows:[8]

Seven years ago, or thereabouts, in summer, Pierre Clergue came to my mother's house – she was out reaping – and incited me to let him make love with me. I consented; I was still a virgin then, fourteen years old I think, or perhaps fifteen. He took me in the barn where the straw is kept, but not at all violently. Afterwards he made love with me often, till the next January, and this always in my mother's house. She knew, and tolerated it. It was mostly in the daytime.

Then in January he gave me in marriage to Pierre Lizier, my late husband. And after that he still often lay with me, in the four years my husband was alive: my husband knew about it, and did not put up resistance. When he asked me about our love-making, I said yes, it was true, and he told me to take care it should be with no other man. But Pierre and I never made love when he was at home, only when he was out.

I didn't know Pierre Clergue was, or was said to be, a cousin of my mother, Fabrisse: I had never heard anyone say so,[9] I didn't know she was related to him by blood in any way. Had I known she was a cousin of his – though an illegitimate one – I would not have let Pierre near me. Because it gave me joy and him also when we made love, I did not think that with him I was sinning.

At the time we made love together, both before I was married and after, as our love-making in all that time gave joy to us both, I did not think I sinned, nor does it seem so to me now. But now there'd be no joy in it for me – so, if I were to make love with him now, I believe it would be a sin.

When I was married and made love with the priest Pierre, it did seem more proper to make love with my husband – all the same it seemed to me, and I still believe, it was as little sin with Pierre as with my husband. Did I have any qualms at the time, or think that such deeds might displease God? No I had none, and did not think my lying with Pierre should displease any living being, since it gave joy to us both.

If my husband had forbidden it? Supposing he had – even though he never did – I still would not have thought it a sin, because of the shared joy of love. If any man whatever lies with any woman (unless she is related to him by blood), whether she's a virgin or has been seduced, whether in marriage or outside it – all such coupling of men and women gives displeasure to God, and yet I still do not think the partners sin, insofar as their joy is mutual. Does it displease God more when the partners are married than when they are not? I think it displeases him more when they are unmarried lovers.

I don't know, but I've heard it said that there is a paradise, and I believe it; I've also heard there is a hell, but that I don't believe, though I won't urge it is untrue. I believe there is a paradise, for it is something good, as I've heard tell; I don't believe in hell (though I don't argue against it), for that is something evil, as people say. I've often heard that we shall rise again after death – I don't believe that, though I don't discredit it.

I still believe it is no sin when love-making brings joy to both partners. I have believed that ever since Pierre first knew me. No one taught me these ideas except myself. I haven't taught them to others – no one has ever asked me about them.

I believe God made those things that are helpful to man, and useful too for the created world – such as human beings, the animals men eat or are carried about on – for instance oxen, sheep, goats, horses, mules – and the edible fruits of the earth and of trees. But I don't think God made wolves, flies, mosquitoes, and such things as are harmful to man; nor do I think he made the devil, for that is something evil, and God made nothing evil.

The remainder of Grazida's testimony should be assessed with more reserve as evidence of how she understood herself and her world. She was imprisoned 'seven weeks and more', because the bishop and his assistant thought 'she had not confessed the truth fully'. Clearly they had hoped she would inculpate Pierre Clergue as a heretic. In the interrogation that took place after her imprisonment, Grazida told something of Pierre's cynical talk about women. (The record claims she confessed it 'freely and spontaneously, not in fear of or through force of torture' – as if her imprisonment had not constituted duress!) –

Between the time that Pierre took my virginity and when he gave me to my husband – I don't remember the day – I was standing at the door of the Balle family's house in Montaillou, with Fabrisse my mother, and Pierre was making his way to the castle and stayed with us a little while, and we had a lighthearted conversation[10] about sensual sinning. He said that to lie with a woman was no sin as long as it gave her pleasure; also that one woman was as good as another – it was as much sin with one as with another. After that he at once went up towards the castle of Montaillou. Did he say such things to me at other times? Not that I can remember. Nor did he tell me there was no hell, or that the devil made some things in this world. It was because of his words that I believed extramarital love was no sin, and that I was not sinning with him. But I did not believe him that it was as much sin with one woman as with another – no, I always thought it was a more grievous sin to make love with kindred than with other, unrelated women. I once told him that I'd learnt that my mother Fabrisse was his cousin by blood, and he answered that this wasn't known, since Fabrisse's mother had been the [natural] daughter of Guillaume Clergue, the brother of his own father, Pons.

I did not want to admit that he taught me these errors about sexual sin, because when I was first summoned I came with Alazaïs Adémar, who could not walk well or manage well in company; and on the way she said to me that the rector of Montaillou had done many good things for me, and had given me in marriage. I should say nothing bad about him, even if I swore to tell the truth, for it's a hard task to rehabilitate anyone's character: it was no sin not to tell, I was to remain firm and constant. She also said she was afraid that if I told the truth about the rector and his brothers, they would kill me or otherwise maltreat me.

The last part of the record consists simply of Grazida's recantation and formal acceptance of orthodox beliefs in the form that the bishop instructed her in these.

Several points need elucidation. In her second questioning Grazida admits Pierre had undermined for her the teaching with which she had been brought up, that extramarital love was sinful. It would indeed be astonishing if, when she first met him, a man perhaps in his late thirties, she had already, at the age of fourteen or fifteen, possessed a fully-thought-out view of her own and had not been susceptible to his persuasive talk. Yet it is important not to blur the distinction between his promiscuous attitude and her unswervingly idealistic conviction. For Grazida it is uniquely the quality of shared joy between two lovers which frees love-making from all taint. The only possible external impediment to love that she can see is consanguinity (this is clearly a vestige, that she still acknowledges, of her orthodox upbringing). Such an outlook, and the assumptions underlying it, are so different from those of Pierre Clergue, that nothing in Grazida's second avowal prevents us from fully accepting her statement in the first: 'No one taught me these ideas except myself.' If at the beginning of their affair Pierre had relaxed her traditional beliefs, he was too shallow ever to arrive at Grazida's own.

He looks at love-making from the coarse standpoint of the conquering male who 'pleasures' a woman ('no sin as long as it gives her pleasure'); she is concerned with tenderness, with the mutual giving of joy. Both of them have the sense that God is to some extent displeased by any human sexual pleasure, whether in marriage or outside it. This could still be affirmed – with appropriate qualifications – by the most orthodox theologians, around 1300 as in earlier centuries.[11] The sexual pleasure in marriage was only venially, or minimally, culpable if love-making was directed purely to the goal of producing children: this would still have been a widespread 'orthodox' view. It is because of some such teaching that Grazida admits that love within marriage displeases God less than love outside it. For Pierre, the sensualist mouthing Cathar doctrines, by contrast, the notion of God's displeasure at sex is so strong that all love-making is equally tainted, so that, if there is to be sex at all, any further distinctions become irrelevant: total licence and conjugal love are on the same level.

As a Cathar, however slippery a one, Pierre will also have accepted the belief that the devil, a black counterpart of God, created the material world. So too he will have accepted the existence of a hell in which all human beings who did not – at least very shortly before death – renounce the material world would be punished.[12] It was (except for the 'perfect' Cathars, who made their renunciation earlier) a question of living as one pleased but repenting in the nick of time. Here too the ways in which Grazida differentiates her convictions from both orthodox Christian and orthodox Cathar belief are exceptional and touching. From the side of Christian thought she has learnt the idea that existence and goodness are coterminous. Evil has no being of its own, it must be understood as the frustration or privation of existence, of the good that alone truly has being.

So if hell is defined as something evil, hell does not exist. (Instinctively she here joins the Christian Platonic tradition – Origen, Gregory of Nyssa, Scotus Eriugena – for whom an eternal place of torment is inconceivable.[13]) Nor does she see Satan as creating the evil things in the world: again, if Satan is defined as an evil being, that is a self-contradiction and there can be no Satan.[14]

This is bound up with Grazida's strangest affirmation: that God made the good and useful things in the created world, but not wolves, flies, mosquitoes... Who then made these? Grazida has cut herself off from the easy Cathar answer, that the evil Satan made them (as well, according to the Cathars, as making all other bodily things) – for her, the evil Satan does not exist. Unfortunately, she attempts no answer of her own – or rather, her interrogators, hunting down Cathars, were probably not interested enough in her private world-view to ask her about this detail and record it. Yet one can perhaps reconstruct. For Grazida, the problem of the existence of wolves and mosquitoes is precisely of the kind that orthodox, non-Cathar theologians faced when discussing the existence of physical evils – earthquakes, for instance, or the diseases that cause the deaths of young children, or any physical source of misfortune that cannot be blamed upon a human will. Such evils exist: they are not illusions, any more than wolves are; how then can they be reconciled with belief in a good and all-powerful God, who 'made nothing evil'? Of God's goodness Grazida had no doubt, any more than the most pious theologian had. And like such a theologian, she would probably have tried to define God's omnipotence in such a way that it deliberately left a certain space of freedom for the physical as for the mental sphere, even knowing that all such freedoms can go awry – that wolves can bite, the earth be convulsed, and men kill one another.

But it is also quite possible that Grazida had no developed answer ready for this question. We might most aptly see her as indulging in a piece of myth-making of her own. Intuitively, the object of this was to bridge her two perceptions – of the human condition, and of God and the world. The human condition is good if people love each other, if their joy in love is mutual. To this goodness corresponds, in the macrocosm, the goodness of a God who can create good things, because these have being, but not evil ones, because evil is nothing but privation of what is good. He can create paradise, but not hell or Satan. Yet Grazida's paradise would seem to be an earthly paradise: she does not find she can believe the orthodox notion that mankind will rise again after death. So her 'myth' – that God created none of the things which are harmful to men (even though she is equally sure that no evil creator exists who could have done so) – is above all, we might say, her expression of an ideal: a paradise of lovers who give each other equal bliss in love, and who need fear no harmful intruder from the realms outside them.

Grazida's projection of a world, of a myth and an ideal, is unparalleled: it

cannot, without falsification, be assimilated or reduced to other notions preva-
lent in her time and place.[15] What is individual in her thought was stimulated by
her attempt to understand herself and set up a goal for herself – one that could
not be adopted ready-made, because she had been placed, by Pierre Clergue, in
a unique situation. If her mother or husband had forbidden her love-affair or
had tried to punish her for it, it would have been easier for her to fall back on
conventional attitudes – whether of the repentant fallen woman or the defiant
mal mariée. It was their connivance and tolerance that created an existential
problem. If one feels, even vaguely, as Grazida felt, that it is more fitting to make
love with one's husband than with the roistering local priest, and yet all the joy
of love one has ever known, since the beginning in early adolescence, is bound
up with that lover, who clearly – however cynically he may talk at times – also
experiences an intense happiness that answers hers: what standard of integrity is
one to aspire to? There a complaisant mother and husband leave Grazida in the
lurch; at the same time, she knows that to think like the village Don Juan would
be for her an unbearable betrayal of what is beautiful. It is because of what she
knows is beautiful, through her experience, that Grazida feels impelled to think
out her own macrocosm, onto which she projects that inner beauty. Here she
proceeds eclectically: she can accept the goodness of the Christian God, but not
the ugly fantasies of Christian theologians about devil and hell, any more than
she can accept the Cathar fantasy that an evil being made the physical world. For
in the last resort her ideal world is grounded in the physical, the only world she
knows by experience, which she loves in her physical loving. Examining her
conscience to see how far she can accept the tenets of her (orthodox, though not
strict) upbringing, she still feels the force of a taboo such as that against incest,
or of the notion that conjugal love is the least culpable fulfilment of one's sexual
passions. On the other hand, common sense prevents Grazida from believing in
a general resurrection. So, being unable to create the larger ideal out of such
'otherworldly' elements, what can she do but create it out of the most intensely
lived elements of beauty that she knows? Beyond what she knows for herself is a
God who, even if displeased, still pardons true lovers, who creates the 'things
that are helpful to man', and who creates paradise. Why paradise? Grazida's
reasoning – 'for it is something good' – may conceal an argument like that with
which Gaunilo resisted St Anselm's proof of the existence of God:[16] if paradise
is perfect, then its perfections must include the perfection of existing.

In the record of Grazida's thoughts I would distinguish three principal
elements. One is the erotic: Grazida's reflections on the quality of human love,
on what is good in it, and hence, in the last resort, not unacceptable to the good
creator, God. The next is her scepticism about the 'otherworld' aspects of
Christian and Cathar belief: about hell, or Satan, or the general resurrection.

The third, which to some extent bridges the other two, is her myth-making. The God who creates paradise but not wolves – wolves that emerge not because they are the fabrication of some evil genius, but perhaps simply because the good God did not actively intervene to prevent their emergence – is Grazida's private myth. It is one for which I think it unlikely that she had a model, or even an indirect learned source: it seems to spring so naturally from her unusual attempts at understanding, and at finding something to live by.

Among the other women of and near Montaillou who were interrogated, Grazida's reflections on the nature and quality of the erotic relation are hard to parallel. Scepticism about the Christian realm of the spirit, on the other hand, is abundantly testified. It is not – or at least not primarily – Cathar in inspiration. It is an instinctive suspicion, often based on common-sense considerations and analogies, at times also inspired by distrust and dislike of the clergy. This scepticism could as easily extend to Cathar beliefs (such as metempsychosis) as to Christian ones (such as the real presence of Christ in the sacrament).[17]

Myth-making, too, is found frequently among the women – though often it is clear that they are adopting prevailing myths rather than individually fashioning new ones. Yet the myths do not derive in any simple way from things that male priests or Cathar leaders had propounded to them. Often they go completely against Cathar as well as Christian teaching. Most persistently attested among the village women (much more than among the men) is Grazida's belief in an ultimate existence – not necessarily otherworldly – in which no one is damned. This is equally far from Cathar dualism and from the dualizing tendency in Christianity. It is a popular, perhaps wholly intuitive, rendering of the theological myth, apocatastasis.[18] It represents a quest for an integrated worldview, for the complete overcoming of dualism.

These three elements of thought – erotic, sceptical, and mythopoeic – have their counterparts in the manifestoes of sacred love among women at this time. That writers such as Angela of Foligno and Marguerite Porete should use a language of spiritual eroticism is not surprising: the mystical tradition of such language in previous centuries is well known and has been richly documented.[19] More unusual, and corresponding to the human scepticism, is what I would call an element of mystic nihilism. This could be said to transcend orthodox Christian beliefs (as the language of pseudo-Dionysius had traditionally done), but also, in a new and more startling way, to dismiss them. Once more a kind of myth-making, a series of fresh conscious fabulations, is evolved to help bridge the erotic and nihilistic impulses in this spiritual realm.

If we look at what other women of the Montaillou region say about lovemaking, it is clear, for instance, that Mengarde Buscalh's outlook is very different from that of Grazida Lizier. She too is approached by Pierre Clergue, who with her (as with several other women) resorts to ruses and messengers in order to lure her to him. Both before and after becoming his mistress, Mengarde is convinced – whatever he might say – that making love with him is sinful (even though she is unrelated to him and, being a widow, is 'free').[20] She never admits to experiencing any joy with him: she was simply browbeaten by his male arrogance, and afraid of him. She resists him, and then, when her resistance is broken by his threats and blustering, she submits passively, still gnawed by guilt:

Six years ago or so, around Easter, Pierre Clergue, the rector of Montaillou, sent a boy over to me in Prades, who told me that he wished me to come to his house in Montaillou, because the procurator or justice of his Lordship the Count was there. I went with the boy, and found the rector on his balcony. Finding no one else with him, I asked him why he'd made me come. He answered that for a long time he had loved me passionately, and wanted to make love with me. When I told him I would not give in to him in this, as it's a great sin, since I was a widow, he answered that it was no sin at all, except with one's mother or sister. I told him that it was the devil making him speak when he said such love-making was not sinful. Then he threatened me, and even said: 'And how dare you contradict me in this, when there's no woman I cannot have, if only I pursue her as much as I've pursued you?' Then I said that, seeing it was so, I'd be content to let him do his will with me. And there and then he took me, and afterwards again, in the same place, another time.[21] Later on, he even took me three times in my house, to which he came by night. And, having perpetrated his sin, he went away.

The detached expressions suggest that, in Mengarde's own eyes, she was little more than the object on which the rector imposed his desires.

Yet Mengarde, who had none of Grazida's erotic optimism, resembles her in another trait. While she is attracted theoretically to the Cathar myth of *consolamen* and *endura* – whereby a person ritually received into the sect before dying, if he takes no food or drink after the rite but starves to death, ascends to heaven at once in perfect purity – she finds that, with her own infant, the impulse of human love and pity is too strong to let him die in pain:

When my mother-in-law became a Cathar, I had a sick child, a boy two or three months old, and Guillaume Buscalh said to me: 'Would you like us to have one of those good men receive your child into their sect, if he begins to dwindle into death – for, if he's received by them and dies, he'd be an angel of God?' And when I asked him 'What should I do about the child after he's been received by the Cathars?' he told me that then I must not give the boy milk or anything else, just let him die like that. Hearing this, I said I'd never stop giving him my breast as long as he was alive. For, as he was a Christian, and had no sin except from me,[22] I thought that if I lost him God would take him . . . And because of this the boy was not received, though it would have pleased me if he had been, if only I could have suckled him afterwards.

For Mengarde as for Grazida, it is the existential truth that counts supremely. However powerful myths may be, they are as nothing in the face of the individually recognized inner *regula*.

A similar situation occurred with another woman, Sybille Peire. Sixteen years before her interrogation, she and her husband, griefstricken at having lost a daughter, welcomed the gentle, saintly Cathar Pierre Authié, and his son Jacques, and listened to their myths, which she recounts as follows:[23]

The heavenly father in the beginning made all spirits and souls in heaven, and they remained with him there. Then the devil went to the gate of paradise, wanting to enter, and could not. He remained at that gate for a thousand years. After that he entered paradise by a fraud, and, once inside, persuaded spirits and souls made by the heavenly father that all was not well with them, since they were subject to that father,[24] but if they wanted to follow him and come to his world, he would give them possessions – fields, vineyards, gold and silver, wives, and other good things of this visible world.

At his persuasion, the misguided spirits and souls in heaven followed the devil, and all who accepted that persuasive course[25] fell from heaven. So many fell, nine days and nine nights – they fell like the small rain. Then the heavenly father, seeing himself almost deserted by spirits and souls, arose from his throne and put his foot over the hole through which they were falling, and said of those who remained that if they moved to any extent[26] from then onwards, they would never have peace or rest. And to those falling he said: 'Go for a time, for now.' If he had said 'from now on', none of them would be saved or would return to heaven. But because he said 'for now', that is, for some time, all those spirits will return to heaven: in such a way, however, that bishops and other great clerics – since their spirits were counsellors and gave the advice to move out of heaven – will return there with great difficulty and belatedly; but the spirits or souls of simple folk, because they consented to leave heaven on impulse and as it were deceived by others, will return there swiftly and with ease . . .

After the world's end all this visible earth will be full of fire, sulphur and pitch, and will be burnt up – and this is what is called hell. But all human souls will then be in paradise, and in heaven one soul will have as great a good as the next, and all will be one, and the soul will love any soul whatever as much as the soul of its own father or mother or children.

Clearly these myths helped to answer many of the bereft Sybille's existential needs at that moment. They were optimistic myths, promising final bliss to all, and at the same time they were egalitarian, favouring especially the have-nots of the world and mocking the presumptions of the high and mighty clergy. The contrast is almost that which Sybille's northern contemporary, Marguerite Porete, makes between the 'Little Church', authoritarian and tainted, and the invisible 'Great Church', the loving commonalty of simple souls.[27] The clergy's myth of hell, their powerful weapon, is here dismissed by means of a naturalizing explanation – it is simply a physical cataclysm that will take place, it will leave unscathed the paradisal assembly of souls. And these will be free and equal, united in love. Sybille herself will then be lovingly reunited with her dead child.

Nonetheless later, when she had another child dying – a daughter, Jacotte, less than a year old – Sybille could not face the real-life inhumanity of sending her straight to paradise by denying her milk and food. Sooner did she endure the upbraidings and even hatred of her husband and his friends. It caused her to measure the myths against her inner convictions, and to find the myths wanting:

'I had thought that all their teaching was true . . . and I remained in that conviction for a year or so, till they told me I must not suckle my daughter.'[28]

For other women, the myth of apocatastasis offers consolation in a homely, familiar way. It is administered to them almost as a therapy by a man, Arnaud de Monesple, who is a medium, a messenger of souls. When two women, Guillemette Bathégan and Mengarde Pomiès, whose daughters had died, consult him, he gives them neither a cosmological fable nor a belief of Christian or Cathar colouring, but a mélange of folklore and pietism that he gauges (no doubt correctly) will help them to readjust:

. . . he said the dead do no other penance than to walk at night from church to church, keeping vigil. And when I said, they must surely suffer when it's cold, he said the dead seek a house or place where there's a lot of wood, and warm themselves at a fire, making the wood fire themselves. He told me that my daughter Fabrisse had come to me and found me in my bed. And later the man told me, as a message from her, to have a mass celebrated for her, and to put half a pound of oil in a lamp that burnt in front of Mary's altar.

. . . When he claimed that she walked well, and as merrily as the other women, I said, 'And how could my daughter walk as quickly as the others, since she died heavily pregnant?' And he answered, 'Your daughter is beautiful and strong . . . at the coming feast of All Saints she will go to rest. No soul of a grown man or woman enters paradise itself before Judgment day, only the souls of children who die before they are seven go at once into God's glory . . . Later, at the Judgment, all will be saved, so that no soul of man or woman will perish or be condemned.' I answered: 'Please God that no one be condemned!'

To Mengarde de Pomiès Arnaud explains that souls, when freed from their wanderings, go to rest in the earthly paradise, till the last day. Nonetheless the message that he passes on to her is in the last resort an affirmation of earthly existence so strong that it seems almost as if the medium were secretly a sceptic:

Your daughter will soon come and kiss you in your bed, and from then on you will sleep better . . . She says to tell you you should try to eat and drink as best you can, and to see that you live in the present world as fully as you can, because there is no life so good or so precious as the present one.[29]

Many varieties of scepticism are attested among the women of Montaillou: Jacotte Carot at the mill, who was said to swear 'By the flower of this flour, there'll never be a world except this one!'[30] or Guillemette Benet, who argues:

I can't see anything come out of men or women when they die. For if I saw their soul, or anything at all, coming out, I'd know that the soul existed. But as I see nothing, I can't make out what it is, that soul . . . When men die, one only sees them expire, and their last breath is nothing but wind.[31]

For the châtelaine of the village, Béatrice de Lagleize, scepticism about the real presence of God in the sacrament is blended with satire of clerical gluttony: 'Do you believe that what the priests handle on the altar is the body of the Lord?

Surely if it were, and even if it were as big as a mountain, the priests alone would by now have eaten it all up!'[32]

But there is another woman, the prosperous farmer's wife Aude Fauré, whose disbelief in the 'real presence' has a spiritual intensity of quite a different kind, and whose ideas have not yet been fully or correctly understood.[33] Her thoughts may indeed be fittingly compared with those of Marguerite Porete, for, together with a keen longing to believe and to be one with God, Aude is again and again plunged into the experience of nothingness. Yet for her that nothingness does not bring mystic discovery of the God beyond being – it means a nightmare of atheism. Not theoretical atheism, such as has been familiar since the world of the Encyclopédistes, but that neurotic, tormented atheism which Otloh of St Emmeram had lived and recounted in the eleventh century,[34] and which made Aude's nearest family – her husband and aunt – treat her savagely and as an outcast.

Like Grazida, Aude stresses that she has not been brought to think as she does by others: all her thoughts are her own:

No man or woman has led me to it. I think it came over me because of the persistence of a sin I had not confessed.[35] I've never mixed with heretics or talked with them – I've never even seen one, as far as I know.

I did not confess or reveal my error to a priest or anyone else till recently, when I was grievously ill and told my husband, Guillaume, and [my aunt] Ermengarde Garaude, of Merviel. First to my husband I said: 'My lord, how can it be that I cannot believe in our Lord?' And he reproached me, saying: 'What, you accursed creature, are you in your right mind?' And I answered, 'Yes.' And he said that if I hadn't confessed this I must do so at once, for otherwise I could not stay with him but he would cast me out . . .

'Alas,[36] aunt, how can it be that I cannot believe in God, and can't even believe that the host the chaplain raises on the altar is Christ's body?' And Ermengarde reproached me fiercely, and told me many things to induce me to believe.

She told Aude, in particular, an edifying anecdote – a miracle-story about the host, that brought belief to a woman who had scoffed – one of many such *exempla* as were used in sermons for encouragement or warning. And Aude was longing to assent to that anecdote, longing not to be cut off from the world of 'right-thinking people' around her. 'Dear aunt, you have such good words, you have comforted me so well.'

Yet, according to Ermengarde's own testimony, she also tried shock-therapy on her niece: 'How now, mistress Treachery – it cannot be (Christ's body)!'[37] . . . Take care you don't bring us heresy from elsewhere – don't shame this place!' The village priest even claims that the aunt shouted at the sick and desperate young woman: 'Get out – to the fire with you, to the fire!'[38] As she wavers between such ferocities and gently teaching Aude some touching improvised prayers, in order to help her believe – 'Lord, send me a tear from the water that flowed from your side, that I may wash my heart clean of all ugliness' – so Aude herself fluctuates between fantasies that she will be damned and other fantasies, which she thinks are sacrilegious, but which come upon her irresistibly, precisely at the moment, the elevation of the host, that was held most sacred – just as erotic thoughts crowded Heloise's mind at the same moment:[39]

. . , one day as I was going to the church of the Holy Cross to hear mass, I heard some women – I don't recall their names – saying that a woman had given birth on the roadside, in the village of Merviel: she could not reach a homestead in time. Hearing this, I thought of the disgusting afterbirth that women expel in childbearing, and whenever I saw the body of the Lord raised on the altar I kept thinking, because of that afterbirth, that the host was something polluted. That's why I could no longer believe it was the body of Christ.

Aude is less detailed about her atheism – her failure to believe in God's existence – though on four occasions she distinguishes this from her more limited affliction, her disbelief in Christ's presence in the host. It would be too easy to dismiss her thought of the host as a woman's placenta as a mere obsession: rather, it was one symptom of a more complex and far-reaching malaise of scepticism. This was not a malaise for which any rational or lasting remedy was available to Aude, at least in Merviel. The only remedy the villagers could think of was greater trust in God: the nurse who, when Aude became ill, was hired to look after her youngest child, was convinced that, if Aude's make-believe could become intense enough, it would revert to true belief:

I said to the nurse: 'You have just received the body of Christ – do you believe that what you took is really that?' She answered that she believed it firmly. And I said: 'How can it be that I cannot believe?' The nurse then said to me: 'My lady, you will return to God. Only believe firmly enough that it *is* Christ's body.' And I asked her to beseech God to put belief in my heart, and when she did, as best she might, our maid Guillemette came in, and I said: 'Guillemette, start praying, and ask the Blessed Virgin of Montgauzy[40] to illuminate me, so that I can truly believe in God.' She did so, kneeling down. And at once I was illuminated and believed firmly in God, and I still do.

Despite this affirmation, we learn from Aude's subsequent testimony that a few hours later that day she had a relapse, which expressed itself in a frenzy of remorse. Two women, Alazaïs and Raymonde, who had seen her with the nurse earlier in the day, were visiting Aude that evening:

They found me in the hall of my house, lying on a couch, disfiguring myself and delirious, and saying 'Holy Mary, help me!' And when they said 'In heaven's name, lady, why are you in such a state, what is wrong with you?' I said, 'I did not make a good confession.' And Raymonde said, 'Oh my lady, and what sins have *you* committed? You've never done anything but good, and you're the mainstay of all the poor people in this valley.' And I answered: 'Look, this is how it is: even now I cannot believe in God!' Then they comforted me, and told me to put my trust in God.

The anguished oscillations between doubt of God and renewed attempts at faith will presumably have continued. Aude's atheism is in a sense an aspect of her religious hypersensitiveness. This too was true of Otloh of St Emmeram who, nearly two centuries earlier, had recorded his writhing efforts to overcome disbelief, and thereby to recover sanity, to feel at one again with that monastic world which was his life. Aude likewise longs to return to normality, to overcome the humiliation of her disbelief, for only through this, she knows, can she be re-accepted by her family and village, and regain her self-respect. She asks the bishop–inquisitor:

Impose any penance on me that you wish, I'm ready to receive it and perform it, however harsh – but let it not be a public penance, or such as would bring me to the world's shame and scorn.

The bishop, with uncharacteristic gentleness, sentenced her to nothing but a vast programme of religious observance: pilgrimages and fasts, confessions and communions, at a rate far beyond that of the most zealously devout Christians of the time. Whether this programme was a refuge, or at least distraction, for Aude, or made her lacerate herself still more within, we have no means of knowing.

It was a religious hypersensitiveness such as Aude's that also lay behind the more outrageous mystic utterances of an Angela of Foligno or Marguerite Porete. But whereas Aude, like Otloh before her, strove with all her heart to re-conform to the thoughts of those around her, Angela and Marguerite boldly distanced themselves from those thoughts more and more. For Angela this distancing took a form that was akin to the rhetoricians' 'topoi of outdoing' – yet hers was an existential outdoing even more than a rhetorical one. Thus the love-mysticism based on the Song of Songs, in which the loving soul becomes Christ's beloved bride, is invested by Angela with graphic physical detail of a kind not previously known. Many holy women had meditated on the loving surrender of the bride; but Angela acts it out:

Standing beside the cross, I stripped myself of all my clothing and offered myself wholly to him. And though I was full of fear (*cum timore*), I promised him to remain chaste in every part of my body, charging each part in turn . . . On the one hand I was afraid to promise, on the other the fire of love compelled me – I could not do otherwise.[41]

So too, many contemplatives had been among those who, in the words of Matthew (19: 29), 'have abandoned home, brothers or sisters, father or mother, wife or children' for the sake of Christ. Yet the antinomy between love of family and love of Christ had never been as cruelly – indeed manically – affirmed as by Angela:

Then I began to send away my better clothes, and provisions, and kerchiefs. Yet still I was full of shame and it was painful, for I still did not feel [heavenly] love, and I was living with my husband . . . Then it happened, as God willed, that at that time my mother died – she had been a great impediment to me. And then, a short while afterwards, my husband died and all my children too. And because I had begun on that way [of divine love], and had asked God that they should die, I had great solace from their deaths.[42]

This cruel quality extends to Angela's fantasies of bliss with Christ. She sees herself as a Bacchante: both ardent devourer and humiliated victim. She swings violently between joy and sorrow:

While I was praying, and awake, Christ showed himself to me on the cross more clearly . . . And then he called me, and told me to place my mouth on the wound on his side. And it seemed to me that I saw and drank his blood, freshly flowing . . .[43] And I asked God to let me shed the whole of my blood, for his love, as he had done for me. And I determined, for love of him, that I wanted all my limbs to suffer death – not as in his passion, but more vilely . . . And I could not think out a death as vile as I longed for . . .

I had many and beautiful dreams, and was comforted by them . . . And I felt the greatest joy at the things I'd seen in dreams, but grieved deeply that I had lost them. And still it delights me, when I remember . . .

Then I reached so much greater a blaze of love that, if I heard anyone speaking of God, I screamed. And even if someone had stood over me with an axe to kill me, I would not have been able to stop.[44]

The first time such a fit of screaming came over her, Angela goes on to say, was when she tried to sell her country property, the best piece of land that she had, in order to give the price of it to the poor. Later, as her outbursts of screaming came upon her more often, irresistibly –

. . . when people said I was afflicted by a demon, in that I could not do otherwise, and I was deeply ashamed, then I too said in the same way, perhaps I *was* sick and afflicted by a demon.[45]

This account of a spiritual journey, to the brink of mental collapse, is preserved substantially in Angela's own words, set down by the friar who was her confessor. It would seem that at the beginning there was an element of intense make-believe, of playing a part – Angela undressing before the sculpture of Christ so as to offer her body to him, the outer gestures of the wanton woman symbolizing a total chastity, the rejection of her human husband in favour of the divine lover. She indulges increasingly in fantasies – drinking blood from Christ's side, shedding blood for him in a humiliating death, the axe poised over her as she screams with ardour at hearing the name of God – and at last, after her defiant claims to a wisdom that is foolishness to the world, she experiences a poignant self-doubt: 'perhaps I *was* sick'. Subjectively Angela was vulnerable, yet she was not persecuted for her fervid thoughts and fantasies, as many of the women of Montaillou were persecuted. In the same decade as Grazida Lizier was imprisoned for over a year, Angela of Foligno, revered by Franciscan advisers in her lifetime, became the object of a cult. However extravagant her emotional utterances, Angela did not lay claim to any new belief, any idea that challenged the prevailing world-picture of theologians in her time. Her innovations were startling; yet they were confined, we might say, to the form in which she experienced and retold accepted spiritual realities; she did not impinge upon their content. Thus one can begin to understand why her memorial, her book, was unfailingly treasured, whilst the far greater book of her contemporary, Marguerite Porete, led to Marguerite's being atrociously put to death.

Like Angela, Marguerite tells of divine love and how she experiences it; like hers, Marguerite's language to evoke that love can be provocative and deliberately shocking. The reason she was persecuted and condemned, however, had little to do with this. It was rather that, unlike Angela, she laid claim to new perceptions of the divine realm, and of the Church. So too, in a sense, had Hildegard of Bingen – yet Hildegard had advanced such thoughts only in her recognized function as messenger of the divine light. Here Marguerite showed a fateful audacity: like Hildegard, she castigated those in all ranks of the clergy who failed to welcome her unique insights; but where Hildegard did this with a prophet's safe-conduct, Marguerite did so of her own accord, speaking only in the name of the 'simple souls', the 'free souls' – an invisible ideal community to which she aspired to belong, and which she was certain should guide and judge the 'Little Church' that is established on earth, Sainte Eglise la Petite.

Marguerite's work was publicly condemned at Valenciennes (probably her native city) around 1300, but this did not shake her convictions or lead her to renounce them. The free souls, she believed, must never be cowed by Sainte Eglise la Petite. Because of her persistence she was imprisoned, tried and executed, publicly burnt in Paris on 1 June 1310, at the instigation of the archbishop of Paris and the papal inquisitor. A contemporary witness tells that her nobility of bearing and her devotion as she went to die made many who were present weep.[46] Marguerite's killers also demanded the surrender of all copies of her book: to retain one meant becoming excommunicate. And yet they were powerless to prevent the *Miroir* from being cherished. Though only one manuscript of the French original is known to have been saved, the existence of five medieval translations – two Latin, two Italian, and one English[47] – bears eloquent witness to the continuing spell that Marguerite cast in the fourteenth and fifteenth centuries. This contrasts sadly with the forgottenness of the *Miroir* today, though in one very recent literary history (1978) there is a hopeful sign: Kurt Ruh mentions the *Miroir* in the context of Mechthild and Hadewijch, and rightly affirms Marguerite's work, like theirs, 'a religious testimony of incomparable originality'.[48] The *Miroir* should also be seen as a text of fundamental importance in relation to the movement, or group of movements, known as the 'Free Spirit' (*secta spiritus libertatis*), and much remains to be done by historians to ascertain its rôle there.[49] But in the present chapter it is some aspects of the *Miroir*'s 'incomparable originality', as an imaginative construction and an expression of self-awareness, that I should like to evoke and assess.

The lyrical and the quasi-dramatic passages are integral to the construction. In her extended complex dialogues Marguerite never dispenses with narrative transitions – in this she is closer, for instance, to Ramón Lull than to Mechthild. Yet as in Mechthild's *Fliessendes Licht*, spontaneous dramatic tension can arise in the interchanges and conflicts between Marguerite's projections of inner and celestial forces, and among these forces (again as in Mechthild) Lady Love takes the lead. A further likeness lies in what we might call the lyrical continuum, which, in the *Miroir* as in the *Fliessendes Licht*, extends from rhythmic prose, filled with parallelism and homoioteleuta, to more sustained rhymed passages, to fully poetic forms. But where in Mechthild these always remained free, or irregular, Marguerite on two occasions uses a 'bound' form – once a canzone, and once a rondeau. The canzone is her Prologue, her first 'manifesto'; the rondeau comes near the close, and is perhaps the most perfect crystallization of her thoughts. The other lyrical passages occur at high points, at the most daring or climactic moments, throughout the work, and the conclusion of the first version (seventeen further chapters were added later, after the 'Explicit'), the 'finale' of nearly a hundred verses that opens with the rondeau, is purely lyrical. In the course of the *Miroir*, on the other hand, there are many 'border' passages where it may always remain debatable whether a prose or a verse printing gives a more illuminating picture of the rhythm and movement of thought. This is only natural, as the prose continually reaches out into free-flowing, even over-flowing, lyrical modulations. For the lyrical element, we might say, is Marguerite's truest element. It is not so much that she chooses to write lyrically, like the composers of religious *laude* or *caroles* for instance, in order to fulfil certain expectations for performance, or to attain effects known to be possible in this or that form; rather, it is a vital aspect of the way her imagination moves. She floats into lyrical moments and out of them again, back into prose dialogue, which then, gaining fresh intensity and with it fresh symmetry, hovers once more on the brink of lyricism.

To comprehend Marguerite's erotic depiction of divine love, let us begin with her fable of Alexander:

Once upon a time there was a maiden, a king's daughter, of great heart and gentleness, and of fine spirit too; she lived in a foreign land. It came to pass that she heard tell of the great courtliness and nobility of King Alexander, and at once in intent she loved him, because of the great renown of his noble excellence. Yet this maiden was so far from the great lord in whom she had spontaneously set her love, she could neither see him nor possess him.

Because of this she was often disconsolate within herself, since no love save this contented her. And when she saw that this far-off love, which was so close to her, or inside her, was so far outside, she thought she would solace her unease by somehow imagining the looks of her friend, for whose sake she was so often rent in heart. Then she had an image painted, which portrayed the semblance of the king she loved, as close as she could get to portraying the way she loved him, in the affection of the love that held her; and by means of this image, together with her other practices (*usages*), she dreamt the king himself.[50]

The image of the far-off beloved is familiar from romances and lyrics of human love, as is the exaltation of the state of longing. The mystical tradition, too, had made use of the image of Christ as a chivalric lover, whose beloved is the human soul. What is unusual here is the way Marguerite shows how love can create its own dimension – 'more distant than stars and nearer than the eye' – and its own reality. Is this a purely subjective fabrication of the loving soul? The conclusion Marguerite draws from her fable suggests otherwise: her book, she says, *is* her image of the noblest King, the far-off heavenly one. But the princess was not given her loved image by Alexander, whereas 'to make me remember him, he gave me this book, which in some aspects represents his love (*qui represente en aucuns usages l'amour de lui mesmes*)'.[51]

Again the word *usages* occurs, bridging subjective and objective experience – just as 'l'amour de lui mesmes' means both the love that comes from the King and the love felt for him by the soul. In the earlier context, the *usages* that helped the soul to dream her King meant all the cultivation of her love that she undertook (figuratively, we might say, all her practices of prayer and meditation). And in a sense, in the second context, it is these same practices which not only represent the love she feels but which become transformed into signs of *his* love, his caring for her.

Nonetheless, in the course of the work the subjective note predominates. The princess cannot really tell whether Alexander loves her in return, or whether his love for her is simply her own creation:

She is alone in love . . . She is the phoenix, which is alone. For this soul is solitary in love, slaking herself with herself.

. . . all that this soul has within her from God, by gift of divine grace, seems to her nothing; at the same time what she loves, which is inside her, is what he will not give to anyone but her. And understanding it in this way, this soul has all and has nothing, she knows all and knows nothing.[52]

At times this state is imagined as an unchanging bliss:

Such a soul, said Love, swims in the sea of joy – that is, in the sea of delights flowing and streaming down from the godhead. She feels no joy, for she herself is joy, and swims and floats in joy without feeling any joy, for she inhabits joy and joy inhabits her.[53]

Yet the same soul also imagines a series of tests in which her lover treats her with callous cruelty, to gauge how complete is her amorous submission to him. It is only after extravagant unconditional surrender to each of his cruelties that the soul imagines him giving her an unconditional reward. In this scene the fantasies of heartless deception go beyond any comparable motifs known to me in the world of profane romances. After many declarations of torments that she would gladly accept if they were her beloved's will, Marguerite says:[54]

What if he were to ask me what I would do, if I knew he would prefer me to love another more than himself? And at this my senses failed . . . Then he asked what I would do if it could happen that he might love another more than me. And here my senses failed – I did not know what to answer, what to wish, or what to hide. Beyond this, he asked what I would do . . . if he might wish for someone other than himself to love me more than he. And again my senses failed . . . And I said, overcome, how could it be that I should love another more than him, and that he love another more than me, or that another love me better than he? And there I fainted . . . And still I could have no peace unless he had my answer. I loved myself with him so much that I could not answer lightly . . . And yet I had to answer, if I did not want to lose both myself and him.

The ambiguity of the subjective and objective love becomes deliberate in the lines that follow:

I said to him of him, that he wanted to test me in all points. Alas, what did I say? Indeed I did not speak a word. The heart all alone waged this battle over him, and it answered in anguish of death that it wanted to abandon its love, by which it had lived.

Here the wording of the French – 'que il se vouloit despartir de son amour, dont il avoit vesqu' – allows equally for the other possibility, that the phrases refer to the lover – the heart protesting that *he* wants to abandon his love, by which he had lived.

Finally Marguerite replies:

If I possessed the same as you do, together with the created world you gave me – if in this way, sire, I would be equal to you . . . since you would wish, unconditionally, these three things that are so grievous for me to bear and to grant . . . I would wish them, and never wish for anything again. And so, sire, my will takes leave in saying this. And because of this my will is a martyr and my love a martyr: you have brought them to martyrdom . . .

Thereupon the Land of Freedom showed itself. There Justice came to me, who asked me in what way I wanted her to spare me. And I answered . . . in no way. Then Mercy came after her, who asked me what help I wanted from her, and I answered . . . I wanted no more help . . . Then Love came after me, filled with goodness, Love who had so often driven me mad and at last killed me . . . and she said:

> Beloved, what do you want of me?
> I contain all that was, and that is, and that shall be,
> I am filled with the all.
> Take of me all you please –
> if you want all of myself, I'll not say no.
> Tell me, beloved, what you want of me –

I am Love, who am filled with the all:
what you want,
we want, beloved –
tell us your desire nakedly.

At its climax the scene is transmuted into lyric, the echoing lines setting up a movement as of a serene dance.

The impulses of intuitive scepticism – about life after death, about hell, about the presence of God in the host, even about God's existence – that we encountered among the unlettered women in Provence have strange analogues, in another register, in the moments of mystic nihilism that surface many times in Marguerite's *Miroir*:

This soul, said Love, does not take account of shame or honour, of poverty or riches, ease or unease, love or hate, hell or paradise . . . If anyone were to ask such free souls . . . if they would wish to be in paradise, they would say no. Besides, with what would they wish it? They have no will at all, and if they were to wish for anything, that would mean severing themselves from Love . . . For that one all alone is my God of whom one cannot utter a word, of whom all those in paradise cannot attain a single atom, no matter how much knowledge they have of him . . . And so I say, and it is truth, that one can give me nothing, nothing that could be . . . Ah what a sweet insight this is! In God's name, understand it fully, for paradise is nothing other than this understanding.[55]

Clearly Marguerite was familiar with the Dionysian paradoxes of the unknown God, especially the 'hymn of Hierotheus' in the *Divine Names*,[56] just as she was familiar with the Pauline paradox, 'having nothing and possessing all things'. Yet she seems to stretch both the objective and the subjective paradox – the divine nothingness, and the sense of finding perfect bliss in emptiness – with an unmatched intense daring.

For this high insight Marguerite also uses the image of dwelling on the plain of Truth (*le plain de Verité*),[57] spontaneously rediscovering the image, ἀληθείας πεδίον, so vital in Plato's *Phaedrus*, the text of which had not yet been restored to the Latin West. So too, the enigma in Plato's *Symposium* concerning the birth of Love – child of the god Plenty and the goddess Poverty, Love who like his mother is always needy, always in distress[58] – finds an historically mysterious parallel in Marguerite's most astonishing argument for the coincidence of all and nothing, good and evil, and (within herself) endless plenty and endless neediness. Here she not merely flings down the paradoxes but seems to delight in demonstrating them, in a sublime parody of dialectic method:

God has nowhere to put his goodness, if not in me . . . no place to put himself entire, if not in me. And by this means I am the exemplar of salvation, and what is more, I am the salvation itself of every creature, and the glory of God . . . For I am the sum of all evils. For if of my own nature I contain what is evil, then I am all evil . . . Now if I am all evil, and he is all goodness, and one must give alms to the poorest being, or else one takes away

what is hers by right, and God can do no wrong, for otherwise he would undo himself –
then I am his goodness, because of my neediness . . . I need to have the whole of his goodness, that my evil may be staunched: my poverty cannot make do with less. And his goodness, being powerful and prevailing, could not endure my begging, and I would perforce
have to beg if he did not give me all his goodness . . . So it is clearly evident that I am the
praise of God forever, and the salvation of human creatures – for the salvation of any
creature is nothing but knowing the goodness of God . . . Nor can I ever lose his goodness,
since I can never lose my evil.[59]

Grazida Lizier's ideal of human love and her innate scepticism about much of
the Christian (and Cathar) realm of the spirit were brought together, as we saw,
by her private and keenly individual myth-making. So too, in the *Miroir*, the
erotically described adventures with Lady Amour and with God, and the
mysteries of nothingness, are bridged at times by pieces of deliberate sustained
fabling on Marguerite's part. A striking instance, and one that especially shocked
many churchmen in her day (as the Latin list of thirty censured passages from
her work makes plain),[60] is the dramatic scene she invents where the loving soul
bids farewell to the virtues. If the soul is wholly caught up in love, then she is all
one with God – or, Marguerite would equally say, she is annihilated in the
divine nothingness. Then the virtues of the Christian spirit seem to that soul like
shadowy forms from a past life, forms that can be dismissed, because now they
could only disturb the experience of oneness. Thus when Love declares that the
soul 'can tell the Virtues that she has been a long time and many a day in their
service', she replies – and her answer, mounting in intensity as well as calm,
turns from speech into song –

I admit it, Lady Love: there was a time when I was bound to them, but now is another
time – your courtly grace has freed me from serving them. So now I can indeed say and
sing to them:

Virtues, I take leave of you   for evermore:
I'll have a freer heart for that –   more joyful, too.
Your service is too unremitting –   indeed I know.

For a time I set my heart on you   inseverably,
you know that to you I was   surrendered totally;
so I used to be your slave –   now I am free . . .

I suffered many a torment thus,   bore many a pain:
it is a marvel second to none   that I escaped alive.

Yet since it is so, I am unconcerned: I am severed from you,
for which I thank the God on high –   the day is good to me . . .

I have quit your tyrannies;   now I am at peace.[61]

Allied to this fantasy – or we might say, projecting it into another, social
dimension – is the myth of Holy Church the Little and Holy Church the Great.
Here Marguerite is developing in her own way ideas that had long been in the

air, ideas that first received a truly memorable embodiment in the late twelfth century, with Joachim of Fiore's projection of *Ecclesia spiritualis*.[62] Marguerite's greater Church, or Church of the spirit, is, like Joachim's, the ideal assembly of free souls, divinely loving and hence united in God. Yet what she stresses more than Joachim, and what gives her fabling about the two Churches a particular edge of daring, or even hubris, is her sense that the greater Church judges and overrides the lesser, which is the empirical Christian assembly on earth. In Joachim, we might say, the lesser Church is superseded by the greater, but in the sense of being transformed into it.[63] There is an historical succession: the age of the Son passes into that of the Spirit, which becomes the age of freedom, of *Ecclesia spiritualis*. For Marguerite, it is more as if in history the two Churches co-exist, and the ideal one must measure and correct the claims of the actual.

Where is that ideal assembly to be found? –

... few people know where such souls are, but there must be some, through the just goodness of Love, to uphold the faith of Holy Church ...

Oh Holy Trinity, said Faith, Hope and Charity, where are such soaring souls as those of which this book tells? Who are they, where are they, what do they do? Teach us this through Lady Love, who knows all things – then those who are shocked at hearing this book will be pacified. For Holy Church, if she heard it read, would be amazed at it ...

True, said Love, Holy Church the Little[64] would be, she who is governed by Reason; but never Holy Church the Great, who is governed by us ...

Now tell me, said Love to the three divine virtues, why do you ask who these souls are, and where, and what they do? Without fail, if you don't know, then nothing God has created could ever find them. Where they are, all three of you know, for you are with them in all their movements in time, for you three ennoble them. And what they do, you also know. But who they are – to speak of their value and their dignity – neither you know nor they themselves. Thus Holy Church cannot know.

Speaking of the free souls, Lady Love asks almost scornfully:

How could Holy Church know these queens, these royal daughters, sisters and brides of the King? Holy Church could know them perfectly only if she were in their souls. And nothing created enters into their souls – only God, who created those souls, is there. So none can know such souls save God, who is inside them.[65]

Gradually it becomes clear that what Marguerite envisions is an élite of divine love. Just as poets of human love had set their hopes in a small ideal group of 'noble hearts' (Gottfried's *edele herzen*, Guido Guinizelli's *cuori gentili*),[66] so Marguerite sets hers in this invisible Church which for her surpasses the visible and is the veritable one:

You Holy Church beneath this Holy Church, said Love, truly such souls are properly called 'Holy Church', for they sustain and teach and nourish all of Holy Church – never they themselves, said Love, but the whole Trinity in their midst ...

Oh Holy Church beneath this Holy Church, said Love, what will you say of these
souls . . .?

We want to say, said Holy Church the Little, that such souls are above us in life, for
Love dwells in them and Reason dwells in us.[67]

The myth of this aristocracy of love is even exploited symbolically in its social
connotations:

This soul has its share of refined nobility . . . She replies to none if she does not wish to,
if he is not of her lineage: for a nobleman would not deign to reply to a churl if the churl
challenged him.[68]

But Marguerite (who in prison did not deign to reply to her inquisitors) is
herself a challenger. The antinomy between Love and Reason – the life-force
of the invisible Church against that of the lesser, visible one – is present from the
outset of her work. In the lyrical Prologue,[69] she enters the lists as Love's
champion against Reason:

> Theologians and other clerks,
> you won't understand this book
> – however bright your wits –
> if you do not meet it humbly,
> and in this way Love and Faith
> make you surmount Reason:
> they are the mistresses of Reason's house.
>
> Reason herself proclaims to us
> in the thirteenth chapter
> of this book, unashamed,
> that Love and Faith make her live:
> she never frees herself from them –
> they have sovereignty over her,
> and she must do obeisance.
>
> So bring low your sciences
> which are founded by Reason,
> and put all your trust
> in the sciences conferred by Love,
> that are lit up by Faith –
> and then you'll understand this book,
> which by Love makes the soul live.

There is even a fantasy, in the course of the work, in which the soul and Lady
Love watch Reason die. Only when Reason is dead does Love begin to take her
rival's part.[70] St Paul had championed a wisdom that is foolishness to the heathen,
and an ideal of *caritas* that transcends all knowledge and all faith. Again, the
surmounting of reason by love is a familiar element in many moments of the
Christian mystical tradition. Nonetheless, Marguerite's formulations have a

polemical edge that makes them distinctive: she is not thinking primarily of St Paul or St Bernard, but rather of what she sees – admittedly without nuance or specific detail – as the limitations of the Parisian Scholastics of her own day.

Marguerite's spiritual eroticism and nihilism, and her myth-making in the spiritual realm, all lead us to the existential question: did she understand herself as one of the free souls? The answer is not easy or unequivocal. I would signal especially two moments early in the book that have a bearing on it. At one moment Amour claims that the free soul is so absorbed in love of God that it would not even notice the needs of its neighbours, could not even imagine that all might not be well with them:[71]

Yet if this soul, who is set so high, could help her neighbours, she would help them in their need with all her power. But the thoughts of such souls are so divine that they never pause to such an extent among passing[72] or created things that they might conceive of any unease in them, since God is, beyond comprehension, good.

A moment later, this notion of sovereign indifference towards fellow-beings is modified:

If such souls possessed anything, and they knew that others might have greater need of it than they, such souls would never keep it back, even if they were certain that bread and corn and other sustenance would never grow again on earth.

Here, notwithstanding her affirmation of a God good beyond comprehension, Marguerite shows she is aware of such things as human neediness and hunger. There seems to be a touching naïveness about her formulation – for how would a 'free' soul know even of such possibilities save by concerning herself affectionately with 'passing or created things', and 'conceiving of unease' in them? Is the implication, then, that Marguerite, who does understand this, has no claim to be a free soul? Later on that page we read:

Whoever it may be who speaks of God, as much as he wants and to whom he wants and wherever he wants to speak, must in no way doubt but must know beyond any doubt, said this [free] soul, that he has never experienced the true kernel of divine love.

This could be taken as Marguerite's manifest self-disqualification. Yet would that mean that she, who devotes a whole book to speaking of her unfathomable God, and of joining him in a love-union that is also a leap into the unfathomable, is simply writing wildly of what she has not experienced? Rather, she is like the princess in her first fable, experiencing her love of the never-seen Alexander by means of the portrait she conceives, which is simply a picture of the way she loves him and longs for him. As a writer, Marguerite is making the blind leap of creating the free soul, the loved ideal; in a similar way, she imagines the free souls making a blind leap, into the loved nothingness.

At the same time, we might see another possibility: that it is not Marguerite herself who is telling of God. The motive for her putting almost everything in her book in the mouths of projections – the free soul, Lady Love, Reason, Holy Church the Little, and the rest – might be to intimate that it is not she who is speaking; and this would leave open the possibility that she is, or is becoming, the free soul she aspires to be.

In her opening poetic Prologue Marguerite had declared the need to approach her book with humility; on the other hand, she often invests her personifications with a heady arrogance which it is hard to dissociate entirely from her, the individual imagination behind these projections. The impassioned and at times soaring quality of her work is inseparable from her conviction that she personally has found a 'plain of Truth' inaccessible to the wise and powerful who propound truths in the visible Church. Where Hildegard saw the *lux vivens* as the supremely objective reality, which visited her and showed her truths, and hence never presented that light as being her own, Marguerite's projection of free souls was a subjective challenge – to portray for herself the image that she did not know, the image she could never know for sure to be more than her own infatuated illusion; but equally it was an objective challenge, flung at the 'Little Church' of her time. Thus the close of the *Miroir* (in its first version) is a blend of lyric epithalamium of divine love and topical polemic, such as medieval poetry had not known before. The Trinity implores the soul to guard her secrets:[73]

> I beg you, dear daughter, let be:
> no cleric in the world is great enough
> to speak with you of this . . .

> I beg you, dear daughter,
> my sister and my beloved,[74]
> in Love's name, if you will,
> do not wish to say more
> about the secrets
> that you know:
> by these others would damn themselves,
> there where you will be saved,
> since Reason and Desire rule them,
> and Fear and Will.
> But know, my chosen daughter,
> that the others *are* granted paradise.

> Paradise? said the chosen one –
> you do not give them something different?
> Then murderers shall as easily have it,
> if they will cry mercy!
> Nonetheless
> I'll say no more of this,
> since you wish it so.

With these words, the soul resolves to begin her 'farewell song of *Fine Amour*'. After a brief transition, the cycle of lyrical farewell opens, with the rondeau:

> *Thinking is no more use to me,*
> *nor work, nor verbal skill:*
> Love draws me up so loftily
> *– thinking is no more use to me –*
> with her godlike glances,
> that I've no other goal.
> *Thinking is no more use to me,*
> *nor work, nor verbal skill.*

Then come renewed praises of the divine *Amis* – but soon among these a note of challenge is heard again:

> Beloved, what will béguines say,   and the pious throng,
> when they hear the excellence   of your divine song?
> Béguines say that I am wrong,   priest and clerk and preacher,
> Austins and Carmelites   and the Friars Minor,
> wrong in writing of the being   of this noble Love.
> I am not – no slight to their reason,   that makes them tell me this:
> surely Desire, Will and Fear   rob them of cognizance,
>   rob them of the flood
> and union of the highest   light of the ardour
>   of divine Love.[75]

The concluding lyric, limpid and concentrated, suggests that, in the subjective abnegation, the objective reality of the divine beloved has been found, and that with this all exacerbation is resolved in serene absorption:

> I've said that I will love him –
> I lie, it is not I:
> it's he alone who loves me –
> he is, and I am naught.
> And I need nothing
> save what he wills
> and that he prevails.
> He is fullness
> and with this I am filled:
> this is the divine kernel
> and loyal love.

The last words allude to the moment where Marguerite had discounted herself as a free soul: by speaking of God at all she showed herself to be one who 'has never experienced the true kernel of divine love'. But her book is also her portrait of Alexander: by painting the way she loved him, the loving woman dreamt the king himself.

227

Grazida Lizier's testimony and Marguerite Porete's are two of the most moving expressions of love by medieval women that have come down to us. At the beginning of the fourteenth century, they caused Grazida to be imprisoned, and Marguerite to be put to death, by the men – Christian at least in name – who ruled the official Church of the day. We can see why the declarations of these two women kindled anger: being first and foremost statements of personal belief, made with complete integrity, they could not help being, at the same time, protests against Sainte Eglise la Petite.

For a while, in the early stages of the Cathar movement, it had looked as if women were being invited to a rôle other than that of the subjugated. Among the 'perfect' Cathars men and women had been proclaimed equal in every aspect of religious life – preaching, cult, and the charge of a community.[76] Yet well before 1300 these Cathar ideals had given way before a renewed male dominance. The movement came to assume the features of the feudal society and Church against which it had struggled. Thus the truly 'free souls' had yet again to find their own way: no organized form of thought had room for their aspirations. Grazida's affirmations are no more an expression of Cathar doctrines than Marguerite's are of official Christian ones.

And yet, against seemingly impossible odds, the spirit of such women was not crushed. However savagely the authoritarian Church tried to suppress them, their beliefs lived on irresistibly – Grazida's, indeed, only through the record that her persecutor kept of them. Across the centuries, such testimonies remain a wonder and an inspiration.

TEXTS

Hildegard of Bingen

Autobiographic passages preserved in the *Vita*

I

6vb Sapiencia quoque in lumine caritatis docet et iubet me dicere quomodo in hanc visionem constituta sim.[1] Et ego verba hec non dico de me, sed vera Sapiencia dicit ista de me, et sic loquitur ad me: 'Audi, o homo, verba hec, et dic ea non secundum te, sed secundum me – et, docta per me, hoc modo dic de te. –

In prima formatione mea, cum deus in utero matris mee spiraculo vite suscitavit me, visionem istam infixit anime mee. Nam post incarnationem Christi anno millesimo centesimo, doctrina apostolorum 7ra et ardens iusticia quam in Christianis et spiritualibus constitu-/erat tardare cepit et in hesitationem vertebatur. Illis temporibus nata sum, et parentes mei cum suspiriis deo me vovebant. Ac tercio etatis mee anno tantum lumen vidi quod anima mea contremuit; sed pre infancia de his nichil proferre potui. In octavo autem anno meo in spiritualem conversationem deo oblata sum, et usque in quintum decimum annum fui multa videns, et plura simpliciter loquens – ita quod et admirabantur qui hec audierunt, unde venirent et a quo essent.

Tunc et ego in me ipsa admirata sum, quod cum infra in anima mea[2] hec vidi, exteriorem etiam visum habui, et quod hoc de nullo homine audivi; atque visionem quam in anima mea[3] vidi quantum potui zelavi;[4] multaque exteriora ignoravi, de frequenti egritudine quam a lacte matris mee huc usque passa sum, que carnem meam maceravit, et ex qua vires mee defecerunt.

His valde fatigata, a quadam nutrice mea quesivi, si aliqua exceptis exterioribus videret; et "nichil" michi inde respondit, quoniam nichil horum videbat. Tunc, magno timore correpta, non ausa eram hec cuiquam manifestare; sed tamen plura loquendo, dictando, de futuris solebam enarrare. Et quando hac visione pleniter perfundebar, multa que audientibus aliena erant loquebar; sed cum vis visionis aliquantum 7rb cessit, in / qua me plus secundum mores infantis quam secundum annos etatis mee exhibui, valde erubui, et sepe flevi, et multociens libenter tacuissem si michi licuisset. Pre timore autem quem ad homines habebam, quomodo viderem nulli dicere audebam; sed quedam nobilis femina, cui in disciplinam[5] eram subdita, hec notavit et cuidam sibi noto monacho aperuit.

Eidem femine deus per graciam suam quasi rivulum ex multis aquis infudit, ita quod corpori suo in vigiliis, ieiuniis,[6] et ceteris bonis operibus quietem non tribuit, quousque bono fine presentem vitam finivit, cuius etiam merita deus per quedam pulchra ostendit signa. Post cuius finem ita permansi videns, in quadragesimum etatis mee annum.

Tunc in eadem visione magna pressura dolorum coacta sum palam manifestare que videram et audieram; sed valde timui et erubui proferre que tamdiu silueram. Vene autem et medulle mee tunc plene virium erant, in quibus ab infancia et iuventute mea defectum habebam.

Ista cuidam monacho magistro meo intimavi, qui bone conversacionis et diligentis intencionis ac veluti peregrinus a sciscitationibus 7va morum multorum hominum erat, unde / et eadem miracula libenter audiebat. Qui admirans michi iniunxit, ut ea absconse[7] scriberem, donec videret que et unde essent. Intelligens autem quod a deo essent, abbati suo intimavit, magnoque desiderio deinceps in his mecum laboravit.

In eadem visione scripta prophetarum, ewangeliorum, et aliorum sanctorum, et[8] quorumdam philosophorum, sine ulla humana doctrina intellexi, ac quedam ex illis exposui, cum vix noticiam litterarum haberem, sicut indocta mulier me docuerat. Sed et cantum cum melodia in laude dei et sanctorum absque doctrina ullius hominis protuli, et cantavi, cum nunquam vel neumam vel cantum aliquem didicissem.

Hec ad audienciam Moguntine ecclesie allata cum essent et discussa, omnes ex deo esse dixerunt, et ex prophecia quam olim prophete prophetaverant. Deinde scripta mea Eugenio pape, cum Treberi esset, sunt allata,[9] qui ea gratanter coram plurimis legi fecit, ac per se ipsum legit. Multumque de gracia dei confidens, benedictionemque suam cum litteris michi mittens, precepit, ut ea que in visione[10] viderem vel audirem scriptis adtencius conmendarem.'

II

8va Quodam[1] tempore ex caligine oculorum nullum lumen videbam, tantoque pondere corporis deprimebar quod, sublevari non valens, in doloribus maximis occupata iacebam. Que ideo passa sum, quia non 8vb manifestavi visionem que michi osten-/sa fuit, quod de loco in quo deo oblata fueram in alium cum puellis meis moveri deberem. Hec tamdiu sustinui, donec locum in quo nunc sum nominavi, et ilico visu recepto levius quidem habui, sed tamen infirmitate nondum ad plenum carui. Abbas autem meus, et fratres, et populus eiusdem provincie, cum percepissent de hac mutatione quid hoc esset – quod de pinguedine agrorum et vinearum, et de amenitate loci illius, ad inaquosa, ubi nulla essent commoda, ire vellemus – mirum habuerunt, et ne hoc fieret, sed ut nobis resisterent, invicem[2] conspiraverunt. Me quoque quadam vanitate deceptam esse dicebant. Cumque hec audissem, cor meum contritum est, et caro mea et vene aruerunt, et per dies plurimos lecto decumbens, vocem magnam audivi, me prohibentem ne quaquam[3] amplius in loco illo de visione hac proferrem vel scriberem.

Tunc quedam nobilis marchionissa, nobis nota, archiepiscopum Moguntinum adiit: ei[4] hec omnia aliisque sapientibus manifestavit. Qui dixerunt quod nullus locus nisi per bona opera sanctificaretur, unde et hoc ut fieret conveniens videretur. Itaque permissione archiepiscopi, cum magno comitatu proximorum nostrorum et aliorum hominum, in reverencia dei ad locum istum venimus. /

9ra Tunc antiquus deceptor per multas irrisiones me excribravit, ita quod multi dixerunt: Quid est hoc, quod huic stulte et indocte femine tot mysteria revelantur, cum multi fortes et[5] sapientes viri sint? In dispersionem itaque vertetur! Multi enim de revelatione ammirabantur, utrum a deo esset, an de inaquositate aeriorum spirituum, qui multos seducunt.

Et ita in isto loco cum viginti puellis nobilibus et de divitibus parentibus natis mansi, nullamque habitationem seu habitatorem hic invenimus, excepto veterano[6] quodam et uxore eius ac filiis. Tanta quoque adversitas tribulationum et pressura laborum super me cecidit, velut cum tempestuosa nubes solem obtegit, ita quod valde suspirans et lacrimas fundens dixi: O o deus nullum confundit, qui in ipsum confidit! Sed iterum deus graciam suam michi adhibuit, quemadmodum cum sol recedentibus nubibus apparet, et veluti[7] cum mater flenti infanti lac prebet, unde ille post fletum gaudet.

Tunc in vera visione vidi, quod tribulationes iste in exemplo Moysi super me venissent, quia cum ille filios Israhel de Egypto trans mare 9rb rubrum duceret in desertum, contra deum murmu-/rantes, Moysen quoque valde afflixerunt, quamvis eos deus mirificis signis illustrasset. Ita deus aliqua parte me affligi permisit, a communi populo, a propinquis meis, et ab aliquantis que mecum manserunt, cum eis necessaria defuerunt, nisi quantum nobis per graciam dei in elemosinis dabatur. Quia sicut filii Israhel Moysen afflixerunt, ita et isti super me caput moventes dixerunt: Quid prodest quod nobiles et divites puelle de loco in quo eis nichil defuit in tantam penuriam devenerunt? Nos vero graciam dei nobis succurrere expectabamus, qui hunc locum nobis ostenderat.

Post pressuram doloris huius, graciam suam deus super nos pluit.

Nam multi qui nos prius contempnentes inaquosam inutilitatem nominaverunt, venerunt ad nos undique adiuvantes et benedictionibus nos replentes. Multi etiam divites mortuos suos in honore apud nos sepelierunt. Plurimi quoque, visionem hanc in fide cognoscentes, magno desiderio ad nos venerunt, sicut per prophetam dictum est: Venient ad te ⟨. . .⟩ qui detrahebant tibi [Isaiah 60: 14]. Tunc spiritus meus revixit, et que prius / in dolore fleveram, nunc, quia deus in oblivionem me non duxisset, pre gaudio flevi, cum locum istum extollendo et multis utilibus rebus et edificiis multiplicando confirmavit.

9va

Sed tamen deus noluit quod in plena securitate constanter perseverarem, sicut ab infancia mea in omnibus causis meis fecerat, cum nullam securitatem gaudii vite istius michi dimisit, per quod mens mea elevari posset. Nam, cum librum Scivias scriberem, quandam nobilem puellam – supradicte marchionisse filiam – in plena karitate habebam, sicut Paulus Thimotheum; que in diligenti amicicia in omnibus his se michi coniunxerat, et in passionibus meis michi condoluit, donec ipsum librum complevi. Sed post hec, propter eleganciam generis sui, ad dignitatem maioris nominis se inclinavit, ut mater cuiusdam sublimis ecclesie nominaretur; quod tamen non secundum deum, sed secundum honorem seculi huius quesivit. Hec in alia quadam regione, a nobis remota, postquam a me recessit, vitam presentem cum nomine dignitatis cito perdidit.

Alie etiam quedam nobiles puelle similiter fecerunt, se a me separantes; ex quibus quedam postea tam negligenter vivebant, / quod multi dixerunt, quia opera eorum ostenderent quod in spiritum sanctum et in hominem qui de spiritu sancto loquebatur peccassent. Ego autem et diligentes me admirabamur cur tanta persecutio super me veniret, et deus consolationem michi non adhiberet, cum in peccatis perseverare non vellem, sed bona opera deo adiuvante perficere desiderarem. In his librum Scivias complevi, sicut deus voluit.

9vb

III

10vb

In lectum egritudinis quodam tempore me deus stravit et aeriis penis totum corpus meum infudit, ita quod vene cum sanguine, caro cum livore, medulle[1] cum ossibus in me aruerunt, velut anima mea a corpore eximi deberet. In isto strepitu triginta dies fui, ita quod ex calore aerii ignis venter meus fervebat. Unde quidam hanc egritudinem pro pena computabant. Virtus quoque spiritus mei carni mee infixa deficit, nec ex hac vita translata, nec pleniter fui in ea. Corpus etiam meum inmutatum sternebatur in terram super cilicium, nec tamen vidi finem meum, cum et prelati mei, filie, et proximi cum planctu magno venirent, ut meum obitum[2] viderent.

11ra At ego in vera visione aciem magnam angelorum, / humano intellectui innumerabilem, per hos dies interdum vidi – qui de exercitu illo erant qui cum Michael contra drachonem pugnabant – et hii sustinebant quid de me deus fieri iuberet. Sed unus fortis ex eis clamabat ad me, dicens: Ei, ei, aquila! quare dormis in sciencia? Surge de dubitatione. Cognosceris! O gemma in splendore, omnes aquile videbunt te; sed mundus lugebit, vita autem eterna gaudebit. Et ideo aurora ad solem surge. Surge, surge – comede et bibe! Mox acies tota clamabat voce sonora: Vox gaudii, nuncii siluerunt; nondum venit tempus transeundi. Puella, ergo, surge!

Statim corpus meum et sensus mei ad presentem vitam mutabantur. Quod filie mee, que prius fleverant, cernentes, de terra me levatam[3] in lectum reposuerunt, et sic pristinas vires recepi. Penalis autem infirmitas a me pleniter non recessit, sed tantum spiritus meus de die in diem plus quam prius in me confortabatur . . .

12va Ad veram vero[4] visionem aspiciebam, magna sollicitudine, quomodo
12vb aerii spiritus contra nos pugnarent, vidique quod idem / spiritus quasdam nobiles filias meas per diversas vanitates quasi in rete perplexerant. At ego per ostensionem dei eis hoc innotui, ipsasque verbis sanctarum scripturarum et regulari disciplina bonaque conversatione circumfodi et munivi. Sed quedam ex eis, torvis luminibus me aspicientes, verbis occulte me laniabant, dicentes quod importabilem strepitum regularis discipline, quo eas constringere vellem, sufferre non possent.

Sed deus in aliis bonis sapientibusque sororibus, que in omnibus michi astiterant,[5] solacium adhibuit – sicut in Susanna factum est, quam deus per Danielem a falsis testimoniis liberavit. Quamvis autem huiusmodi tribulationibus frequenter fatigarer, tamen Librum vite meritorum – divinitus michi revelatum – per graciam dei ad finem perduxi.

IV

14rb Tres turres in visione aspiciebam, per quas Sapiencia quedam occulta michi manifestavit. Prima tria habebat habitacula. In primo, nobiles puelle cum[1] quibusdam aliis erant, que in ardenti karitate verba dei ex ore meo audiebant, atque in hoc quasi esuriem semper habebant. Sed in secundo alie quedam stabiles et sapientes fuerunt, que in cordibus et verbis suis veritatem dei amplectabantur, dicentes: O quamdiu ista

14va nobiscum perseverabunt? Et ex hoc fatigate non sunt. In tercio / vero habitaculo fortes armati ex communi populo erant, qui, vehemens ad nos iter facientes, in admirationem de predictis miraculis ducti sunt, magnoque desiderio ea amaverunt; et hoc sepe faciebant, sicut communis populus in firma et forti turri alicuius principis defensionem querit, ut ab inimicis muniatur.

In secunda vero turri tria habitacula erant, quorum duo arida in siccitate fuerunt, et eadem siccitas quasi densa nebula apparebat. Et ⟨qui⟩² in his duobus habitaculis fuerunt, in unum consencientes, dixerunt: Que et unde sunt ista, que hec quasi de deo loquitur? Durum est nobis aliter vivere quam qui nos precesserunt, aut qui adhuc vivunt. Quapropter ad illos qui nos cognoscunt convertemur, quia in aliis perseverare non possumus. Sicque ad prefatum communem populum se convertebant, et nec in illo³ nec in prefata turri ullius utilitatis erant. Et in vera visione audivi vocem ad ipsos dicentem: 'Omne regnum in se ipsum divisum desolabitur, et domus supra domum cadet' [Luke 11: 17]. In tercio autem eiusdem turris habitaculo communis populus fuit,

14vb qui / multiplici amore verba dei que de vera visione proferebam dilexit, ac in tribulationibus michi astitit, quemadmodum et⁴ publicani Christo adheserunt.

Sed et tercia turris tria propugnacula habebat, quorum primum ligneum fuit, secundum ex fulgentibus lapidibus ornatum, tercium de sepi factum. Aliud autem edificium in visione michi occultatum est, ita quod verba de eo nunc non didici;⁵ sed in vero lumine audivi quod futura scriptura que de illo exarabitur forcior et excellencior precedencium erit.⁶

Subsequenti demum tempore mysticam et mirificam visionem vidi, ita quod omnia viscera mea concussa sunt, et sensualitas corporis mei extincta est, quoniam sciencia mea in alium modum conversa est, quasi me nescirem. Et de dei inspiratione in scienciam anime mee quasi gutte suavis pluvie spargebantur, quia et spiritus sanctus Iohannem ewangelistam imbuit, cum de pectore Iesu profundissimam revelationem suxit – ubi sensus ipsius sancta divinitate ita tactus est, quod absconsa mysteria

15ra et opera ape-/ruit: In principio, inquiens, erat verbum [John 1: 1], et cetera. Nam verbum quod ante creaturas sine inicio fuit, et quod post eas sine fine erit, omnes creaturas procedere iussit, et opus suum in ea similitudine produxit – sicut faber opus suum fulminare facit – quia quod⁷ ante evum in predestinatione sua fuit, modo visibiliter apparuit.

Unde et homo opus dei cum omni creatura est. Sed et homo operarius divinitatis, et obumbratio mysteriorum eius⁸ esse; atque in omnibus sanctam trinitatem revelare debet, quem[9] deus ad ymaginem et similitudinem suam fecit. Sicut enim Lucifer in malignitate sua deum dispergere non potuit, ita nec statum hominis destruere valebit,[10] quamvis in primo homine id temptaverit. Omnem itaque dictatum et verba ewangelii huius, quod de inicio operis dei est, predicta visio me docuit et me explanare fecit. Vidique quod eadem explanatio inicium alterius scripture, que necdum manifestata erat, esse deberet – in qua multe scrutationes creaturarum divini mysterii querende essent.

V

18vb 〈P〉ostea quam me visio docuit dictatum et verba ewangelii Iohannis, in lectum egritudinis decidi, de cuius pondere nullomodo me levare potui. Hec de flatu australis venti in me afflata est, unde corpus meum tantis doloribus conterebatur, quod anima vix sustinebat. Post dimidium annum idem flatus corpus meum ita perforavit, quod in tanto agone fui, quasi anima mea de hac vita transire deberet. Tunc alius

19ra ventosus flatus aquarum huic / calori se admiscuit, unde caro mea aliqua parte refrigerabatur, ne ex toto combureretur. Sic per integrum annum afflicta sum, sed tamen in vera visione vidi quod vita mea in temporali cursu necdum finiretur,[1] sed adhuc aliquantum protraheretur.

Interea michi relatum est quod in inferioribus Reni partibus, a nobis remotis, quedam nobilis femina a diabolo esset obsessa. Nuncii quoque de hac ad me sepius venerunt. At ego in vera visione vidi quod ipsa permissione dei quadam nigredine et fumo diabolice conglobositatis obsessa erat et obumbrata, que totam sensualitatem rationalis anime illius opprimebat, nec eam elevato intellectu suspirare permittebat – velut umbra hominis aut alterius rei, vel fumus, opposita obtegit et perfundit; unde hec rectos sensus et actus perdebat, et inconveniencia sepius clamabat et faciebat. Sed cum hoc malum iussione dei in illa adtenuabatur, tunc lenius[2] gravabatur.

Et me cogitante et scire volente quomodo diabolica forma hominem intraret, vidi et responsum audivi, quod diabolus in forma sua hominem

19rb ut est[3] non intrat, sed eum um-/bra et fumo nigredinis sue obumbrat et obtegit. Si enim forma illius hominem intraret, cicius membra[4] eius solverentur[5] quam stipula a vento dispergatur. Quapropter deus non permittit quod hominem in forma sua intret, sed supradictis perfundens, ad insaniam et inconveniencia evertit, et per eum quasi per fenestram vociferatur, et menbra illius exterius movet, cum tamen in eis in forma sua interius non sit . . . Quoniam vero deus populum per istos purgare

19va vult, permissione et iussione eius stuporem in aere / commovent, ac

per spumam aeris pestilenciam evomunt, atque inundationes et pericula
in aquis faciunt; bella excitant, adversitates et mala producunt . . .

Cumque mulier illa per plurima loca ad sanctos esset deducta, spiritus
qui eam oppresserat, devictus meritis sanctorum et votis populorum,
vociferabatur quod in superioribus Reni partibus vetula quedam esset

19vb per cuius consilium expellendus foret. Quod / amici eius percipientes,
octavo anno fatigationis sue ad nos eam, sicut dominus voluit, per-
duxerunt . . .

22ra De adventu mulieris[6] multum exterrite fuimus: quomodo eam
videre vel audire possemus, de qua plurimus populus per tot tempora
erat commotus? Sed deus rorem suavitatis sue super nos pluit, et
absque horrore et tremore in habitacula sororum, absque adiutorio
virorum, eam locavimus, et deinceps nec pro horrore nec pro confusione qua demon supervenientes pro peccatis confudit, nec pro
irrisoriis vel turpibus verbis quibus nos superare voluit, nec pro pessimo
flatu suo ei ullatenus cessimus.

22rb Et vidi quod in ipsa muliere tres cruciatus pas-/sus est: primum cum
illa de loco ad locum sanctorum ducta est. Secundum cum communis
populus elemosinas pro ea dabat. Tercium cum per orationes spiritualium ex gracia dei abire compulsus est. Itaque a Purificatione sancte
Marie nos et comprovinciales nostri, utriusque sexus, ieiuniis, orationibus, elemosinis et corporum castigacionibus usque in sabbatum pasche
pro ipsa laboravimus.

Interim, per dei potenciam coactus, inmundus spiritus multa de
salute baptismi, de sacramento corporis Christi, de periculo ex-
communicatorum, de perditione Chatharorum et his similium, ad
confusionem sui, ad gloriam Christi, coram populo – quamvis invitus –
protulit, unde multi fortiores ad fidem, multi promptiores effecti sunt
ad peccatorum emendationem. Sed ubi illum falsa proferre in vera
visione vidi, statim illum[7] redargui, unde mox conticescens[8] dentibus
in me frendebat; loqui vero illum propter populum non prohibui, cum
vera proferebat.

Denique sabbato sancto, cum fons baptismatis consecraretur per

22va flatum sacerdotis quem in fontem[9] mittit, cum / verbis que spiritus
sanctus racionalitati hominis et doctoribus ecclesie infudit, quoniam in
prima creatione spiritus domini[10] aquas movit – sicut scriptum est,
'spiritus domini ferebatur super aquas' [Genesis 1: 2] – mulier illa
presens ibi erat, atque timore magno correpta[11] ita contremuit, quod
terram pedibus perfodit, et de horribili spiritu qui eam obpresserat
sufflatum sepe emisit. Mox in vera visione vidi et audivi quod vis

altissimi, que sanctum baptisma obumbraverat et semper obumbrat, ad
diabolicam conglobositatem qua femina illa fatigabatur dixit: Vade,
Sathanas, de tabernaculo corporis mulieris huius, et da in eo locum
spiritui sancto!

Tunc inmundus spiritus per verecundiam[12] femine cum egestione
horribiliter egressus est, et ipsa liberata est, ac deinceps sana in sensibus
anime et corporis permansit, quamdiu in presenti seculo vixit.

VI

23ra Post hec, nimirum[1] post mulieris illius liberationem, magna egritudo
iterum invasit me, ita quod vene mee cum sanguine, ossa cum medullis
emarcuerunt, et viscera mea infra[2] me distracta sunt, totumque corpus[3]
ita elanguit, sicut herbe viriditatem suam in hyeme perdunt. Et vidi
quod nequam spiritus inde irridebant, chachinnando dicentes: Wach!
ista morietur, et amici eius flebunt,[4] cum quibus nos confundit![5] Ego
autem exitum anime mee ad esse[6] non vidi.

Infirmitatem autem istam plus quam quadraginta dies et noctes
paciebar. Inter hec in vera visione michi ostensum fuit quod quasdam
congregationes spiritualium hominum – virorum ac mulierum –
23rb inviserem, eisque / verba que deus michi ostenderet aperte manifestarem.
Quod dum tandem facere temptarem, nec vires corporis haberem,
infirmitas mea aliquantum[7] lenita est; et preceptum dei exequens,
dissensiones quas quidam inter se habebant sedavi. Has vias quas michi
deus[8] precepit cum negligerem propter populi timorem, dolores
corporis sunt michi aucmentati,[9] nec cessabant quousque obedivi – sicut
et Ione contigit, qui valde afflictus fuit quousque ad obedienciam se
reclinavit.

VII

Pulcherrimus et[1] amantissimus vir in visione veritatis michi apparuit,
qui tante consolationis fuit quod omnia viscera mea velut odore
balsami eius aspectus perfudit. Tunc gaudio magno et inestimabili
23va exultabam, semperque prospicere[2] / desiderabam. Et ipse his qui me
afflixerunt precepit ut a me discederent, dicens: Abscedite, quia nolo ut
eam amplius[3] sic torqueatis! Qui magno[4] ululatu recedentes clamabant:
Ach quod huc venimus, quia confusi recedimus!

Mox egritudo, que me inquietaverat velut aque per procellosos
ventos inundatione commoventur, ad verba viri me dereliquit, et vires
recepi – quemadmodum peregrinus, cum ad patriam revertitur,
possessiones suas recolligit – atque vene cum sanguine, ossa cum

medullis in me reparata sunt, quasi de morte suscitata fuissem. At ego tacui paciencia, silui in mansuetudine; et sicut pariens post laborem, ita loquebar post dolorem.

Post hec[5] ab abbate meo et fratribus humillima instancia et devotione coacta sum, ut vitam sancti Dysibodi, cui prius oblata eram, ut deus vellet scriberem – quia nichil certi inde haberent. Et, oratione cum invocatione spiritus sancti premissa, ad veram Sapientiam in vera visione commo-/nita prospexi, ac secundum quod ipsa me docuit vitam et merita ipsius sancti conscripsi. Deinde Librum divinorum operum scripsi, in quo, ut omnipotens deus michi infudit altitudinem, profunditatem et latitudinem[6] firmamenti, vidi et quomodo sol et luna, stelle et cetera in illo constituta sunt.

23vb

B: Berlin, Staatsbibl. Lat. Qu. 674, fols. 1ra–24vb
R: Wiesbaden, Hess. Landesbibl. 2 ('Riesenkodex'), fols. 317ra–327vb

I   1 sum R   2 mea *om.* R   3 mea *om.* R   4 celavi (*orthogr. variant only*) R
5 disciplina R   6 in ieiuniis R   7 absconsa R   8 et *om.* R   9 allata sunt R
10 visionem R

II   1 inquit *before* tempore BR (*the words preceding the heading* Visio secunda *were* Audi ipsam ita scribentem)   2 in invicem R   3 nequaquam B ne quicquam R   4 et *expunged* B et ei R   5 ac R   6 veternano (*orthogr.*) R
7 velut (*orthogr.*) R

III   1 medulla R   2 obitum meum R   3 levantes R   4 ergo R   5 astiterunt R

IV   1 cum cum (*the first expunged*) B   2 qui R (*om.* B)   3 illa B illo R   4 et *om.* R   5 dici R   6 *Since Hildegard's text continues without break here, the intervening rubric* (De septima visione . . .) *has been omitted*   7 quod quia B quia quod R   8 dei R   9 *scil.* ille quem   10 potuit *expunged before* valebit B

V   1 finietur R   2 levius R   3 ut est hominem R   4 umbra B   5 solveretur B
6 inquit *before* mulieris BR   7 illum statim R   8 contiscescens (*orthogr.*) R
9 fonte R   10 super *del. before* aquas B   11 correpto R   12 per verecunda loca R

VI   1 inquit *before* nimirum BR (*the words* nimirum . . . liberationem *may be Theodoric's explanatory gloss*)   2 intra R   3 corpus meum R   4 *corr. from* flabunt B   5 confudit R   6 adesse (*one word*) R; *but cf. Berlin Fragment* (ed. Schipperges) 632–3: Deus ignis omnia vivencia ad esse incendit, que ita incensa in esse ardent . . .   7 aliquantulum R   8 d.m. R   9 dolores m.c.s.a. R

VII   1 inquit *before* et BR   2 eum prospicere R   3 amplius eam R   4 cum magno R   5 *The rubric before* Post hec (Quod rogata . . . ostensam sibi) *has been omitted*   6 altitudinem, profunditatem et latitudinem: *see below p.* 309 *n* 53

References in the margins above are to folio and column in B, the manuscript chosen as base for these passages and corrected with the help of R. The text differs in many minor and some major details from that in P.L. 197. The correspondences are as follows. I: 102 C – 104 B; II: 106 A – 108 A; III: 109 D – 113 A; IV: 115 C – 116 D; V: 122 C – 124 A, 125 D – 126 D; VI: 127 B–D; VII: 127 D – 128 C.

I also collated a third manuscript of the *Vita*: Bruxelles, Bibl. royale 5527–34, s. XII/XIII, fols. 191va–209ra, from Gembloux. Its very substantial divergences from both B and R did not seem to lead any nearer to Hildegard's original wording. The impression was rather of a slightly later hand – perhaps Guibert's – attempting to make Hildegard's notes more 'literary'. A fourth manuscript of the *Vita*, Bruxelles Bibl. royale 5387–96, s. XIII in., fols. 156v–175v, also from Gembloux, of which I collated only sample passages, appears to have been copied from 5527–34. While a future critical edition of the *Vita* would warrant a full conspectus of variants from the Gembloux manuscripts – or even a separate transcription of the Gembloux text – they would have burdened the apparatus here disproportionately.

Passages from *Causae et curae*

I God and Lucifer

1 b Cum enim ille [Lucifer] ad nichilum se extendit, inceptio extensionis eius malum produxit, et mox malum hoc, absque claritate et absque luce, in semetipso per zelum dei exarsit, ut rota se circumferens et circumvolvens, et ignitas tenebras in se ostendit. Et sic malum a bono declinavit, nec bonum tetigit malum, nec malum bonum.

Deus autem integer ut rota permansit, et pater in bonitate, quia paternitas ipsius bonitate ipsius plena est, et ita iustissima et benignissima et firmissima atque fortissima est paternitas, et de hac mensura sicut rota ponitur. Nunc alicubi rota est, et ipsa alicuius rei plena est. Quod si rota illa nichil aliud preter exteriorem circulum haberet, vacua

2 a foret. Et si forte alienus superveniret / et ibi operari vellet, hoc esse non posset. Nam in rota una duo fabri res suas constituere non possunt. O homo, aspice hominem! Homo enim celum et terram atque alias facturas in se habet, et forma una est, et in ipso omnia latent.

De paternitate.

Sic paternitas est. Quomodo? Circulus rote paternitas est, plenitudo rote deitas est. In ipsa, et ex ipsa, sunt omnia, et preter eam creator non est. Lucifer autem integer non est, sed in dispersione divisus est, cum esse voluit quod esse non debuit. Cum enim deus mundum fecit, in antiquo consilio habuit quod homo fieri voluit . . .

Et elementa mundi deus fecit, et ipsa in homine sunt, et homo cum illis operatur.

2 Macrocosm and microcosm

6 a   Et sol in circulo suo integer est et plenus et non deficit, et lumen suum in lunam mittit, cum ad eum accedit, ut vir semen suum in feminam mittit . . .

6 b   Sed et postquam luna repletur, ita quod velud mulier pregnans efficitur, lumen suum emittit et stellis tradit, et ita stelle lucidiores efficiuntur . . .

7 b   Ante casum Ade firmamentum immobile fuit, et non circum-volvebatur; post casum autem eius cepit moveri et circumvolvi. Sed
8 a   post novissimum diem inmobile stabit, ut in / prima creatione ante casum Ade fuit . . .

Sicut enim corpus et anima simul sunt, et ab invicem confirmantur, ita etiam firmamentum et planete sunt, et ab invicem mutuo foventur et confirmantur. Sed et sicut anima corpus vivificat et consolidat, sic eciam sol, luna et ceteri planete firmamentum cum igne suo fovent et confirmant. Nam firmamentum est velud capud hominis, sol, luna et
8 b   stelle ut oculi, aer ut auditus, venti ve-/lud odoratus, ros ut gustus, latera mundi ut brachia et ut tactus. Et alie creature que sunt in mundo sunt ut venter, terra autem ut cor, quia quemadmodum cor superiora et inferiora corporis[1] continet, ita etiam et terra aquis illis que super eam fluunt est ut arida, aquis vero que sub ea sunt est obstaculum, ne ⟨in⟩ contrarium[2] modum erumpant.

De Luciferi casu et firmamenti creatione.

Abyssus autem est velud pedes, et ut incessus hominis. Cum igitur dyabolus de celo corruit, qui sedere et regnare voluit et qui nullam creaturam creare et facere potuit, deus firmamentum statim fecit, ut ille videret et intelligeret que et quanta deus facere et creare posset. Tunc eciam solem, lunam et stellas in firmamentum posuit, ut dyabolus in eis videret et cognosceret quantum decorem et splendorem perdidisset.

3 Elements and man

30 a   Quod quatuor sunt elementa tantum:

Plura igitur, vel pauciora, quam quatuor[3] esse non possunt. Et ex duobus generibus consta⟨n⟩t:[4] superiorum et inferiorum. Nam superi-
30 b   ora sunt celestia, inferiora vero terestria, / et que in superioribus vivunt inpalpabilia sunt, et ex igne et aere sunt. Que vero in inferioribus versantur, palpabilia et formata corpora sunt, et ex aqua et limo constant.

De anima et spiritibus.

Spiritus enim ignei et aerei sunt, homo autem aquosus et limosus est.

De Ade creatione.

Nam cum deus hominem crearet, limus per aquam conglutinatus est, ex quo homo formatus est. Misitque deus in formam illam spiraculum vite igneum et aereum . . .

31 a Anima autem ignea, ventosa et humida est, et totum cor hominis possidet. Iecur vero cor calefacit, pulmo illud tegit . . .

31 b Et anima ignis est, qui totum corpus penetrat et hominem vivificat . . .

32 a Et homo de igne sensualitatem et desiderium trahit, de aere autem cogitationes et vagationem, de aqua vero scientiam et motionem.

De Ade vivificatione.

Adam enim cum terra fuit, ignis eum excitavit, et aer eum suscitavit,[5] et aqua eum perfudit, quod totus movebatur. Tunc deus soporem in eum misit, et in hiis viribus coctus est, ita quod caro eius per ignem estuabat, et quod per aerem spiravit, et quod sicut molendinum aqua in eo circuivit, qui postquam evigilavit propheta celestium fuit, et sciens in omni vi creature et in omni arte erat.

De Ade prophecia.

33 a Et deus omnes creaturas illi dedit, / quatinus virili vi eas penetraret, quoniam illas scivit et cognovit. Nam ipse homo omnis creatura est, et spiramen vite in eo est, quod finem vite non habet.

4 The human soul

47 b Anima autem sine corpore vivit, et post novissimum diem indumentum suum a deo desiderat, ut sibi illud attrahat; et ita etiam deus, qui ante evum et in evo vita sine principio fuit, in constituto tempore indumentum suum, quod eternaliter in ipso latuit, sibi attraxit. Et hoc modo deus et homo unum sunt, ut anima et corpus, quoniam deus hominem ad ymaginem et ad similitudinem suam fecit [Genesis 1: 26]; ut autem queque res umbram habet, sic eciam homo umbra dei est, et umbra

48 a ostensio facture est, et homo omnipotentis / dei in omnibus miraculis suis ostensio est: ipseque umbra est, quia inicium habet. Deus autem nec inicium nec finem habet. Unde omnis celestis armonia speculum divinitatis est, et homo speculum omnium miraculorum est dei.

62 b Sed et anima est spiraculum ad bona tendens, caro autem ad peccata, et raro et vix corpus interdum continere potest quin peccet, sicut et sol vermiculis resistere non valet, quin de terra in illo loco exeant, quem ipse in splendore et calore suo calefacit.

5 Sexuality

78 a   Sed cum mulier in coniunctione viri est, tunc calor cerebri eius, qui delectationem in se habet, gustum eiusdem delectationis in eadem coniunctione prenunciat, et seminis effusionem. Et postquam semen in locum suum ceciderit, predictus fortissimus calor cerebri illud sibi

78 b   attrahit et tenet, / et mox eciam renes eiusdem mulieris contrahuntur, et omnia membra que in menstruo tempore ad apertionem parata sunt modo ita clauduntur, quemadmodum fortis vir rem aliquam in manu sua claudit.

104 a   Cum ergo deus Adam creavit, Adam dilectionem magnam in sopore habebat, cum deus soporem in ipsum misit. Et deus fecit formam ad dilectionem viri, et sic femina dilectio viri est. Et mox cum femina formata est, virtutem illam creationis deus viro dedit, ut dilectione sua – que femina est – filios procrearet. Cum enim Adam inspexit Evam, totus sapiencia impletus est, quia matrem per quam filios procreare debebat inspexit. Cum autem Eva inspexit Adam, sic eum inspexit quasi in celum videret, et ut anima sursum tendit que celestia desiderat, quoniam spes eius erat ad virum. Et ideo una dilectio erit, et esse debet, viri et femine, et non aliena. /

104 b   Sed dilectio viri ad dilectionem femine in calore ardoris est velut ignis ardencium moncium, qui difficile extingui posset, ad ignem lignorum, qui[6] facile extinguitur. Dilectio autem femine ad dilectionem viri ut suavis calor de sole procedens, qui fructus producit, ad ardentissimum ignem lignorum, quoniam et ipsa suaviter in prole fructus profert.

  Magna autem dilectio que in Adam erat cum Eva de ipso exivit, et dulcedo soporis illius, qua tunc dormivit, in transgressione eius in contrarium modum dulcedinis versa est. Et ideo quia vir hanc magnam dulcedinem in se sentit et habet, ut cervus ad fontem, sic ipse ad feminam currit, et femina ad ipsum in similitudine horrei[7] aree, que multis ictibus percutitur, et ad calorem perducitur, cum grana in e*a*[8] excuciuntur.

23 b   De Ade casu.

  Deus ita creavit hominem quod omnia animalia ad servitutem eius subiecta sunt. Sed cum homo preceptum dei transgressus est, mutatus est eciam tam corpore quam mente. Nam puritas sanguinis eius in alium modum versus est, ita quod pro puritate spumam seminis eicit.

Si enim homo in paradyso mansisset, in inmutabili et perfecto statu perstitisset. Sed hec omnia post transgressionem in alium et amarum modum versa *sunt*.[9]

De spermate.

24 a   Nam sanguis hominis, in ardore et / calore libidinis fervens, spumam de se eicit, quod nos semen dicimus, velud olla aliqua ad ignem posita spumam de fervore ignis de aqua emittit.

114 a   Adam quoque ante prevaricationem angelicum carmen et omne genus musicorum sciebat, et vocem habebat sonantem ut vox monochordi sonat . . .

Nam sicut in prevaricatione Ade sancta et casta natura prolem gignendi in alium modum delectacionis carnis mutata est, ita eciam et vox supernorum gaudiorum, quam idem Adam habebat, in contrarium modum risus et cacynnorum versa est.

6 The sexual act and predictability

25 b   De conceptus diversitate.

Nunc autem cum vir in effusione fortis seminis sui, et in recto amore caritatis quam* ad mulierem habet, ad ipsam accedit, muliere quoque rectum amorem ad virum tunc in eadem hora habente, masculus concipitur, quia sic a deo ordinatum est, nec aliter fieri potest quin masculus concipiatur, quoniam et Adam formatus est de limo, qui fortior materia est quam caro. Et hic masculus prudens et virtuosus erit, quia sic in forti semine, ac in recto amore caritatis utrorumque, quem ad invicem habent, conceptus est.

Si autem hic amor deest in muliere ad virum, ita quod tantum vir rectum amorem caritatis in ipsa hora ad mulierem habet, et non mulier ad virum, et si semen viri forte est, masculus tamen concipitur, quia amor caritatis viri superexcellit, sed idem masculus debilis erit et non virtuosus, quoniam hic amor in muliere ad virum defuit.

Quoniam si semen viri tenue est, qui tamen amorem caritatis ad mulierem habet, et ipsa eundem amorem ad illum, ibi femina virtuosa procreatur . . .

Sed si semen viri forte est, sed tamen nec vir ad mulierem nec mulier
26 a   ad / virum amorem caritatis habet, masculus inde procreatur, quia tamen semen forte fuit, sed amarus ex amaritudine parentum; vel si semen viri tenue est, et neuter ad alterum amorem caritatis in ipsa hora tenet, femina nascitur amare complexionis.

57 a   Sanguis enim in quolibet homine secundum incrementum et detrimentum lune crescit et minuitur . . .

De tempore gignitionis. /

57 b   Et cum in incremento lune sanguis in homine sic augetur, tunc homo etiam, scilicet tam femina quam vir, fertilis est ad fructum, videlicet ad generandum prolem, quia in augmento lune, cum eciam augmentum sanguinis hominis est, forte et robustum est semen hominis; et in detrimento lune, cum eciam detrimentum sanguinis est in homine, semen hominis debilis et absque fortitudine est, velud feces sunt, et ideo tunc magis defectus est ad prolem propagandam. Quod si tunc aliqua mulier prolem conceperit, sive masculus sive femina fuerit, hic homo infirmus et debilis et non virtuosus erit.

177 b   Luna prima.

Sed homo qui in prima luna concipitur, cum ipsa de sole splendorem suum recipit, si masculus est, superbus et durus erit, nec ullum hominem amat nisi illum qui eum timet et honorat, ac homines libenter 'verrechet' – et substantiam eorum et omnia que possident; sed sanus in

178 a   corpore est, nec magnas infirmitates habebit, sed non / multum senex erit. Si vero femina est, honorari semper appetit, et ab extraneis plus quam a domesticis semper amatur, et apud se ipsam impia est, et alienos et novos adventantes homines semper amat, sed circa domesticos mala est et illos negligit; et in corpore sana est, sed si infirmitas eam apprehenderit, tunc valde infirmatur, et fere usque ad mortem, et diu non vivit . . .

180 ab   Qui in octavadecima luna concipitur: / Si masculus est, fur erit et cupiditatem furandi habet, et ita reperietur fur, et proprietas terre ei abstrahitur, ita quod fere nichil proprium de terra querit habere, scilicet nec agros nec vineas nec similia, sed semper aliis auferre que sua non sunt; et in corpore sanus est, et per se diu vivet. Si vero femina est, astuta erit, et vulpinos mores habebit, et nichil fere loquitur sicut in corde habet, sed propter nequiciam morum suorum in loquela sua homines decipit, et probos homines ad mortem perducit, si poterit; et sana est in corpore, sed per insaniam interdum fatigatur; et diu per se vivere potest – sed isti mores, tam masculi quam femine, deo molesti sunt.

7 Purgatorial fires

176 a De purgatoriis penis.

Quidam etiam inextinguibiles ignes in aere sunt, qui de diversis operibus hominum incenduntur, quoniam qui illis ad gloriam esse debeba⟨n⟩t,[10] ex malis operibus eorum ipsis ad penales ignes fiunt, et ita in aliqua loca terrarum descendunt, et ibi congregantur, ubi etiam aliqua flumina oriuntur et effluunt, que calorem et ardorem ex eisdem ignibus contrahunt, ita quod etiam iuditio dei quedam anime in ipsis
176 b ignibus et in ipsis aquis / examinantur.

Sed quidam rivuli ex eisdem aquis aliquando in diversas terras inter homines fluunt, qui semper calidi sunt, quia de inextinguibilibus ignibus exeunt. Sed et quedam partes terrarum sunt super quas deus divina ultione aliquando ignis descendit, ut scriptum est: 'pluit super eos carbones ignis, et spiritus procellarum pars calicis eorum' [Psalm 10: 7]. Et terra et montes et lapides, quos ignis ille tetigit, in igne semper ardebunt, usque ad novissimum diem; atque in illis locis qui sic ardent, rivuli interdum oriuntur qui de eodem igne semper calidi sunt et calidi fluunt.

Sed et homines interdum arte sua ad eadem loca aliquando quosdam rivulos ducebant, ut ex eis calefierent, qui per eadem loca fluentes, et ardorem ibi accipientes, deinde calidi effluebant. Et aque iste homines illos qui balneis in eis utuntur interdum non ledunt sed eis sanitatem conferunt, quia calor earum iniustum ardorem qui in illis est conpescit et malos humores in eis consumit.

8 The four temperaments of women

64 b De sanguinea.

Quedam autem femine pinguis nature sunt, et molles et deliciosa⟨s⟩[11] carnes habent, et graciles venas, atque rectum sanguinem absque tabe. Et quoniam vene earum graciles sunt, ideo minus sanguinis in se habent, atque caro earum tanto plus crescit, et tanto plus sanguine permixta est; et iste claram et albam faciem habent, et in amplexione amoris sunt et amabiles, atque in artibus subtiles, et per se ipsas[12] in animo suo continentes; et modice effluentem sanguinem in rivulis menstrui temporis patiuntur; atque vasculum matricis earum fortiter positum est ad pariendum, unde eciam fecunde sunt et virile semen concipere possunt, sed tamen plurimos pueros non generant, et si iste absque maritis sunt, ita quod prolem non pariunt, facile dolent in
65 a corpore, si autem / maritos habent, sane sunt. Quod si gutte sanguinis

in menstruo tempore ante naturale tempus in istis clauduntur, ita quod non effluunt, tunc interdum aut melancolice erunt, aut dolorem lateris pacientur, aut vermis in carne earum crescet, aut effluentes glandes, que scrofule dicuntur, in eis erumpent, aut lepra – que tamen moderata est – in eis crescet.

De flecmatica.[13]

Sed quedam alie femine sunt, quarum carnes non multum crescunt, quia grossas venas habent, et aliquantum sanum sanguinem et album, sed modicum veneni in se continentem, unde album colorem contrahit. Et severam faciem et subnigri coloris habent, et strennue et utiles sunt. Ac aliquantum virilem animum tenent, atque nec nimis parum, nec nimis multum, sed moderate effluentes rivulos sanguinis in menstruo tempore sustinent.

Et quoniam grossas venas habent, plurimum fecunde sunt in prole, et facile concipiunt, quia eciam matrix et omnia viscera earum fortiter posita sunt. Sed viros attrahunt, et eos post se ducunt, et ideo viri eas amant. Quod si a viris se continere volunt, se continere a coniunctione eorum[14] possunt, nec inde multum – quamvis parum – debilitantur. Sed tamen si viros in coniunctione devitaverint, difficiles et graves in moribus suis erunt. Si autem cum viris fuerint, ita quod se a coniunc-
65 b tione eorum continere noluerint, incontinentes et superflue – / secundum viros – in libidine erunt.

Et quod eciam aliquantum viriles sunt, propter viriditatem quam in se habent, aliquantum lanuginis circa mentum interdum emittunt. Si autem rivulus sanguinis in menstruo tempore ante naturale tempus in eis strangulatur, tunc interdum aut insaniam capitis – que est frenesis – incurrunt, aut splenetice aut ydropice erunt, aut extantes carnes, que semper in ulceribus sunt, in eis crescunt, aut in aliquo membro suo supercrescentem carnem – velud quedam pustula in aliqua arbore vel in aliquo pomo est – emittent.

De colerica.

Alie autem quedam femine sunt, que tenues carnes sed grossa ossa habent, et moderatas venas, et spissum ac rubeum sanguinem; et pallidi coloris in facie sunt, et prudentes sunt ac benivolenciam tenent, et eis reverencia ab hominibus exhibetur, et timentur; sed plurimum sanguinem in menstruis paciuntur, et matrix in eis fortiter posita est, ac fecunde sunt. Et viri mores earum amant, sed tamen eas aliquantum devitando fugiunt, quoniam ipse illos alliciendo[15] post se non trahunt. Quod si in coniunctione maritorum sunt, caste sunt, et fidem uxorum illis servant, atque cum eis sane sunt in corpore. Sed si maritis caruerint,

dolebunt in corpore et debiles erunt – tam de hoc quod nesciunt cui
66 a homini / femineam fidem servare possint quam de hoc quod maritos
non habent.

Et si fluenta menstrui temporis prius quam iustum sit in eis cessa-
verint, facile paralitice erunt, et in humoribus suis diffluunt, ita quod in
eisdem humoribus suis infirme erunt, aut quod in iecore dolebunt, aut
quod etiam facile nigrum tumorem dragunculi incurrunt, aut quod
ubera earum de cancro ingrossantur.

— De melancolica.

Sed alie quedam femine sunt, que macres carnes habent, et grossas
venas, ac moderata ossa, et sanguinem magis livosum quam sanguineum,
et que eciam faciem velud glauco et nigro colore permixtam habent; et
iste eciam ventose, et vage in cogitationibus suis sunt, et tediose in
molestia tabescentes, et sunt eciam diffluentis nature, ita quod eciam
interdum melancolia fatigantur.

Sed et plurimum sanguinem in menstruo tempore patiuntur; et
steriles sunt, quia debilem et fragilem matricem habent, unde semen
viri nec concipere, nec retinere, nec calefacere possunt, et ideo eciam
saniores, fortiores et letiores sunt absque maritis quam cum eis –
quoniam si cum maritis fuerint, debiles reddentur. Sed viri ab eis
declinant, et eas fugiunt, quia ipse viros affabiliter non allocuntur, et
quoniam viros modice diligunt. Et si iste ad horam aliquam delecta-
66 b tionem / carnis habuerint, cito tamen in eis deficit. Sed quedam ex hiis,
si cum robustis et sanguineis maritis fuerint, tunc interdum – cum ad
fortem etatem, velud quinquaginta annorum, pervenerint – saltem
infantem unum pariunt.

Si autem cum aliis maritis fuerint, quorum natura debilis est, tunc ab
illis non concipiunt, sed steriles permanebunt. Quod si menstrua in eis
defecerint antequam iustum secundum naturam feminarum fuerit, tunc
aliquando podagram, aut intumencia crura, habebunt, aut insaniam
capitis – quam melancolia excitat[16] – incurrent, aut dolorem dorsi et
renum, aut cito corpore intumescent, quoniam tabes, et fetitas illa que
per menstrua in corporibus earum purgari debuit, in eis obstruse
remanent; et si istis in infirmitate non succurritur, ita quod ab ea per
adiutorium dei, seu per medicinam, liberate non fuerint, cito morientur.

9 Unbalanced and exceptional people

37 a Cum autem quilibet humor modum suum excedit, homo ille in
periculo est. Sed cum aliquis livor predictorum modum suum iniuste
transierit, sufficientes vires non habet ut supereminentes sibi humores

vincat, nisi aut a subsequente livore – si precedens est – instigetur, aut a
precedente – si subsequens est – iuvetur. Et in quocumque homine
cuius[17] livor supra mensuram suam in superfluitate se extenderit, ceteri
humores in illo pacifici esse non possunt, nisi tantum in illis hominibus
sit, quos gratia dei infudit, aut in fortitudine ut Samsonem, aut in
sapientia ut Salomonem, aut in prophecia, ut Iheremiam aut in quibusdam paganis, ut Plato fuit, et sibi similes.

Et ubi alii predicti insaniunt, ibi erunt isti per gratiam dei in probitate
fortissimi, quia gratia dei permittit eos interdum esse in aliqua vicissitudine, ita quod interdum sunt in infirmitate, interdum in sanitate,
interdum in timore, interdum in robore, interdum in tristicia, interdum
in leticia; et hoc reparat in eis deus, ita ut cum sunt infirmi, facit eos
sanos, cum timidi, facit eos robustos, cum tristes, facit eos letos.

K: København, Ny kgl. saml. 90 b (references in the margins above are to page
and column in this manuscript)

1 corporis: *corr. from* corpus K   2 ne contrarium K   3 quatuore K   4 constat
K   5 suscitavit: *corr. from* sustentavit K   6 qui qui K   7 aeri *expunged before*
horrei K   8 eo K   9 est K   10 debebat K   11 deliciosa K   12 ipsas: *corr. from*
ipseis K   13 flecmaticis K   14 earum K   15 illos *repeated before* post K   16
excitant (n *expunged*) K   17 huius K

* While the 'quam' here relates to 'caritatis', at the close of the paragraph,
where the phrase 'recto amore caritatis' recurs, K gives 'quem', relating to
'amore'. The minor inconsistency may be purely scribal.

The passages edited above can be found in P. Kaiser's edition (Teubner, (Leipzig
1903)) on the following pages: (1) pp. 2–3; (2) pp. 8–11; (3) pp. 41–5; (4) pp. 65,
84; (5) pp. 104, 136–7, 33, 148–9; (6) pp. 35–6, 77–8, 235, 239; (7) p. 233; (8) pp.
87–9; (9) p. 51. I have not noted Kaiser's misreadings of K, of which numerous
samples were listed and corrected in the reviews of his edition by Alfred Ernout,
Revue de philologie XXVIII (1903) 159–62, and Paul von Winterfeld, *Anzeiger für
deutsches Altertum* XXIX (1904) 292–6.

The first letter to Guibert of Gembloux

147vb Guiberto monacho Hildegardis.[1]

Hec verba non a me nec ab alio homine dico, sed ea ut *in*[2] superna
visione accepi profero. O serve dei, per speculum fidei in quo[3] deum
cognoscendo attendis,[4] et o fili dei per formationem hominis, in quem
deus miracula sua constituit et signavit – quia, sicut speculum in quo
queque videntur vasi suo inponitur, ita racionalis anima corpori velut
fictili vasi inmittitur, quatinus per ipsam vivendo[5] regatur et[6] anima
per fidem celestia contempletur – audi quod indeficiens lumen dicit. –
250

Homo celestis et terrestris est: per bonam quidem scientiam racionalis anime, celestis, et per malam, fragilis et tenebrosus; et quanto se in
148ra bonis[7] cognoscit, tanto amplius deum diligit. Nam si / in speculo vultum suum[8] sordidatum et pulvere sparsum aspexerit, mundare et tergere illum[9] studet; ita etiam si se peccasse, et varietati vanitatum se inplicitum esse, intellexerit, gemat, quoniam in bona scientia se pollutum scit. Et cum psalmista plangat, dicens: 'Filia Babylonis misera . . .' [Psalm 136: 8f]. Quod est: Humana concupiscentia per spumam serpentis est confusa. Ipsa etiam pauper et eg⟨e⟩na[10] est, quoniam in speculativa scientia honorifica opinione caret, eo[11] quod gloriam eterne vite, quam per bonam scientiam gustat, a deo querendo non desiderat. Beatus autem est ille[12] qui tenebit hoc quod a deo vivit, et cuius scientia eum docet quod[13] deus eum creaverit et redemerit, et quod[14] propter liberationem hanc, qua deus ipsum liberavit, omnem malam consuetudinem peccatorum suorum conterit, omnemque[15] miseriam et paupertatem, quam in celestibus diviciis habet, supra petram illam – que firmamentum beatitudinis est – proicit.

Nam cum homo lutulentam putredinem se habere scit, et nequaquam a gustu peccatorum se continere valet, tunc[16] nigerrime aves eum totum sordidant, sed tunc etiam[17] ipse per racionalem animam, quam nec videt nec cognoscit, in deum credendo confidat. Et licet se[18] sic esse et[19] infinita vita vivere sciat, se tamen continere non potest quin frequenter peccet. Et ideo, o quam mirabilis – et lamentabilis – vox est, quod deus talia fictilia vasa quandoque miraculis suis stellata facit, cum tamen ipsa non valeant peccata deserere, nisi quantum per gratiam dei ab ipsis
148rb prohibe⟨n⟩tur.[20] Petrus namque secur⟨u⟩s[21] / non fuit, qui filium dei se numquam negatur⟨u⟩m[22] ardenter promisit, sic nec multi alii[23] sancti qui in peccatis ceciderunt, qui tamen postmodum[24] utiliores et perfectiores facti sunt, quam fuissent, si non cecidissent.[25]

O serve fidelis, ego paupercula feminea forma in vera visione hec verba iterum tibi dico. Si deo placeret quod[26] corpus meum sicut et animam in hac visione levaret, timor tamen ex mente et[27] corde meo non recederet, quia me hominem esse scio, quamvis ab infancia mea inclusa sim. Multi autem sapientes miraculis ita infusi sunt, quod[28] plurima secreta aperiebant,[29] sed propter vanam gloriam illa sibimet ipsis asscripserunt, et ideo ceciderunt. Sed qui in ascentione anime sapientiam a deo[30] hauserunt, et se pro nichilo computaverunt,[31] hii columpne celi facte[32] sunt – sicut et in Paulo contigit, qui ceteros discipulos predicando precessit, et tamen se quasi pro nichilo habebat. Iohannes quoque evangelista miti humilitate plenus erat, quapropter de divinitate multa hauriebat.

Et unde hoc esset, si ego paupercula me non cognoscerem? Deus ubi vult ad gloriam nominis sui, et non terreni hominis, operatur. Ego quidem semper trementem timorem habeo, quoniam nullam securitatem ullius possibilitatis in me scio; sed manus meas ad deum porrigo, quatinus velut penna, que omni gravedine virium caret, et per[33] ventum volat, ab[34] ipso sustinear, nec ea que video perfecte possum,[35] quamdiu in corporali officio sum et in anima invisibili,[36] quoniam in his duobus homini defectus est.

Ab infantia autem mea, ossibus et nervis et venis meis nundum
148va confortatis, visione*m* h*anc*[37] / in anima mea usque ad presens tempus semper *video*,[38] cum iam plusquam septuaginta annorum sim. Spiritus vero meus,[39] prout deus vult,[40] in hac visione sursum in altitudinem firmamenti et in vicissitudinem diversi aeris ascendit, atque inter diversos populos se dilatat, quamvis in longinquis regionibus et locis a me remoti sint; et quoniam hec tali modo video,[41] idcirco etiam secundum vicissitudinem nubium et aliarum creaturarum ea conspicio.[42] Ista[43] autem nec corporeis[44] auribus audio, nec cogitationibus cordis mei, nec ulla collatione sensuum meorum quinque[45] percipio, sed tantum in anima mea, apertis exterioribus oculis, ita ut numquam in eis defectum extasis paciar,[46] sed vigilanter die ac nocte illa video. Et assidue infirmitatibus constringor, et gravibus doloribus implicata sum, adeo ut mortem[47] inferre minentur, sed deus usque adhuc me sustentavit.[48]

Lumen igitur quod video locale non est, sed nube que solem portat multo ⟨et multo⟩ lucidius,[49] nec altitudinem, nec longitudinem nec latitudinem, in eo considerare valeo, illudque[50] umbra viventis luminis[51] michi nominatur; atque[52] ut sol, luna et stelle in aqua[53] apparent, ita scripture, sermones, virtutes, et quedam opera hominum formata in illo michi[54] resplendent.

Quidquid[55] autem in hac visione videro seu didicero, huius memoriam per longum tempus habeo, ita ut, quoniam illud aliquando[56] viderim et audierim, recorder;[57] et simul video et audio ac scio,[58] et quasi in momento hoc quod scio disco. Quod autem non video, illud nescio,
148vb quia indocta sum.[59] Et ea que scribo, illa invisione[60] vi-/deo et audio, nec alia verba pono quam illa que audio, latinisque[61] verbis non limatis ea profero, quemadmodum illa invisione[62] audio, quoniam sicut philosophi scribunt scribere in visione hac[63] non doceor. Atque verba que in visione ista video et audio[64] non sunt sicut verba que ab ore hominis sonant, sed sicut flamma choruscans, et ut nubes in aere puro mota.

Huius quoque luminis formam nullomodo cognoscere valeo, sicut nec speram solis perfecte intueri possum.

Et[65] in eodem lumine aliam lucem, que lux vivens michi nominata est, interdum et non frequenter aspicio,[66] *et quando et* quomodo *illam* videam proferre *non valeo*,[67] atque interim dum illam intueor,[68] omnis tristicia et omnis *angustia a me* aufertur,[69] ita ut tunc mores[70] simplicis puelle, et non vetule mulieris, habeam.

Sed et pre assidua infirmitate quam pacior, aliquando tedium habeo verba et visiones que michi ostenduntur ibi[71] proferre, sed tamen cum anima mea gustando illa videt, in alios mores ita convertor, quod (ut supra dixi) omnem dolorem et tribulationem oblivioni trado, et que tunc in eadem visione video et aud*i*o,[72] hec anima mea quasi ex fonte haurit, sed ille tamen semper plenus et inexhaustus manet.[73]

Anima autem mea nulla hora caret prefato lumine quod umbra viventis[74] luminis vocatur, et illud video velut in lucida nube firmamentum absque stellis inspiciam,[75] et in ipso video que frequenter loquor, et que interrogantibus de fulgore viventis[76] lucis respondeo.[77]

149ra In visione etiam vidi quod primus liber visionum mearum Scivias diceretur, quoniam per viam viventis lu-/minis prolatus est, non de alia doctrina. De coronis autem vidi, quod omnes ecclesiastici ordines clara signa secundum celestem claritatem habent, virginitas vero clarum signum – preter nigrum velamen et signum crucis – non habet. Unde et istud signum virginitatis esse vidi, scilicet ut albo velamine caput virginis tegeretur, propter candidam vestem quam in paradyso homo habebat et perdiderat, et supra caput ipsius rota tribus coloribus in unum coniunctis, quod sanctam trinitatem designat, cui quatuor rote adherent, quarum una in fronte agnum dei habens, in dextra parte cherubyn, et in sinistra angelum, retro autem hominem, et hec omnia ad trinitatem pendent.

Hoc datum signum deum benedicet, quia candore claritatis primum hominem vestierat. ⟨. . .⟩[78] Et hec in libro Scivias pleniter continentur. In vera itaque visione librum Scivias et alios scripsi, et in eodem opere adhuc laboro.

In duobus autem[79] modis, scilicet corporis et anime, me ipsam nescio, et me quasi pro nichilo computo, atque in deum vivum intendo, et omnia hec illi relinquo, quatinus ipse qui nec inicium nec finem[80] habet in omnibus istis a malo me conservet. Unde et tu, qui hec verba queris, cum omnibus illis qui ipsa fideliter audire desiderant, pro me ora, sic videlicet[81] ut in servitute dei feliciter[82] permaneam.

Sed et tu, o fili dei, qui illum in fide queris, et qui ab ipso petis ut te salvet, attende aquilam duabus alis suis ad nubem volantem, que tamen, si in una leditur, super terram residet, nec se levare potest, cum se libenter ad volandum elevaret. Sic etiam homo cum duabus racionali-

149rb tatis[83] – scilicet cum scien-/tia boni et mali – volat: dextra ala scientia bona est[84] et sinistra mala scientia est,[85] et mala bone ministrat, bonaque per malam acuitur et regitur, atque[86] in cunctis per illam sapiens efficitur.

Nunc autem,[87] o care fili dei, alas scientie tue deus[88] ad recta itinera elevet, ita ut, etsi[89] aliquando peccatum ex *gustu lambis*,[90] quoniam sic natus es ut[91] sine peccato esse non possis, *operando* tamen illud *non comedas*.[92] Bene[93] celestis armonia de homine sic faciente deo cantat, illum laudans, eo quod[94] cinerosus homo deum tantum diligat ut,[95] propter eum[96] se ipsum ex toto contempnens,[97] sibi non parcat, et a peccati opere se coerceat. Hoc modo, o probe miles, in certamine hoc esto, quatinus in celesti armonia esse possis, et ut tibi a deo[98] dicatur: Tu es ex filiis Israhel, quia per oculos *cancelli*[99] et per studium celestis desiderii in montem excelsum aspicis. Sed et omnes qui in litteris tuis michi transmissis notati sunt per spiritum sanctum regantur, et[100] in libro vite scribantur.[101]

Tu quoque, fidelis serve dei, dominum Sygerum compet⟨ent⟩er[102] ammone, ne a dextra *in*[103] sinistram declinet. Quod si voto ipsius aliquis resistit, ipse tamen, lorica fidei et galea celestis desiderii indutus, viriliter repugnet, et iter suum perficiet. Sed et consideret quia, cum primus homo voci uxoris sue plusquam voci dei obediret, presumptione sua periit, quoniam illi consensit. Si autem modus tribulationis istorum tantus est, ut vires ipsorum transcendere videatur, meminerint scriptum: 'Fidelis deus qui non pacietur vos temptari supra id quod potestis, sed faciet etiam cum temptatione proventum ut possitis sustinere' [I Corinthians 10: 13]. Cuius benigne promissionis ipse et uxor eius alacri expectatione roborati, unanimiter[104] in unum assensum conveniant, et consilium quod utilius est, sive vir sive femina illud dederit, teneatur, atque provideant ne prima deceptio in ipsis sit, videlicet ne vir feminam accuset, aut econtra femina virum, sed omnia hec secundum voluntatem dei perficiant. Igneus autem spiritus sanctus corda eorum ita accendat, ne umquam ab ipso recedant.

G: Bruxelles, Bibl. royale 5527–34, fols. 147vb–149rb (from Gembloux)
R: Wiesbaden, Hess. Landesbibl. 2 ('Riesenkodex'), fols. 380rb–381rb

1 *superscription om.* R H. de modo visionis sue R   2 ui G   3 qua R   4 attendis

R 5 p. i. corpus videndo R 6 et ut R 7 bono R 8 v. s. in speculo R
9 *om.* R 10 egna G 11 scilicet R 12 ille est R 13 quia R 14 qui R 15 et
omnem R 16 *om.* R 17 *om.* R 18 l. homo se R 19 et in i. v. R 20 ab
ipsis prohibetur G ipsis prohibetur (ab *om.*) R 21 securs G 22 negaturm G
23 a. m. R 24 postea R 25 *Cf.* Ordo Virtutum (*ed. Dronke*) *207–8*: qui nunc
in maiori luce fulgent / quam prius illorum causa fuisset 26 ut R 27 et ex R
28 ut R 29 aperirent R 30 adeo G 31 computabant R 32 facti R
33 et que per R 34 ad G 35 *sc.* videre   scire possum R 36 *corr. from* -is G
invisibilis R 37 visionis huius munere G 38 fruor G 39 et anima mea
(*recte?*) R 40 voluerit R 41 t. m. in anima mea v. R 42 conspicis G 43 Ita
G 44 exterioribus R 45 q. s. m. R 46 passa sim R 47 g. d. multociens ita
i. s. ut michi m. R 48 suscitavit R 49 et multo *om.* G sed multo et multo
nubi que solem portat lucidior est R 50 et illud R 51 *corr. from* -iis G
52 et R 53 aquis R 54 m. i. i. R 55 Quidquic G 56 ita quod aliquando
illud R 57 recordor R 58 video. audio. scio R 59 sed tantum litteras in
simplicitate legere instructa sum *add.* R 60 in visione (illa *om.* R) *I accept the
difficilior lectio of G (for* invisio, *'vision', cf. Lexicon s.v.), even though word-
divisions in G are often careless, because Hildegard would not normally have placed
demonstr. pron. before* in *with sb.* 61 et latinis R 62 illa in visione R 63 i. h. v. R
64 et verba in visione ista non sunt R (invisione ista G) 65 *om.* R 66 video R
67 quam nimirum quomodo videam multo minus quam priorem proferre
sufficio G 68 video R 69 o. michi t. omnisque dolor de memoria aufertur G
70 velut mores R 71 i. o. R 72 audeo G 73 sed illa (*sc. visio*) t. s. plena et
inexhausta m. (*recte?*) R 74 *corr. from* urentis G 75 aspiciam R 76 predicte
viventis R 77 *The next two paragraphs are missing in R* 78 *Probably a lacuna
here, since the* datum signum *and discussion* de coronis *are not found in* Scivias, *as
the next words would suggest* 79 itaque R 80 nec f. nec i. R 81 s. v. *om.* R
82 *om.* R 83 d. alis r. (*recte?*) R 84 volat. ita ut d. a. s. b. sit R 85 s. m. est R
86 et R 87 N. a. *om.* R 88 deus a. s. t. R 89 ita quod si (*recte?*) R 90 sensu
contingas G 91 quod (*recte?*) R 92 numquam t. i. ex assensu conmittas G et
tunc bene volas *add.* R 93 Nam R 94 quia (eo *om.*) R 95 diligit quod R 96
deum R 97 contempnit R sibi . . . coerceat *om.* G 98 adeo G 99 mentis G
100 per s. s. scientia ita r. ut R 101 *The letter ends here in R* 102 competier, *i
erased* G 103 ui G 104 unanimitur G

This is the first attempt to edit the complete surviving text of Hildegard's letter
to Guibert of Gembloux, using the longer version, in G, as base. (References in
the margins are to folio and column in this manuscript.) Even G, however,
contains at least one lacuna (see note 78 above). Pitra (pp. 331–4) published a text
based on R, and an anonymous Bollandist (*Acta Bollandiana* I (1882) 597–600)
printed a few of the G variants and the passages found only in G.

That these passages too are genuinely by Hildegard, I have no doubt: they
reply specifically to questions that Guibert had asked her, and the allusions to the
knight Sygerus (Siger of Wavra, on whom see esp. *Briefwechsel*, pp. 225, 229)
are corroborated by a letter of Guibert's to Hildegard (ed. Pitra, pp. 381–8). But
the evaluation of the numerous different readings in those parts of the letter that
G and R have in common remains delicate, and the text given above represents

a compromise. Both manuscripts show traces at different moments of attempts to 'improve' Hildegard's style, e.g. by changing her habitual 'ita quod' to 'ita ut'. In seven instances (see notes 37–8, 67, 69, 90, 92, 99) I have introduced readings from R into my text, because I believe they represent Hildegard's authentic phrasing, which has been made more conventional, or more 'latinate', by a redactor in G. It would be challenging to try to restore Hildegard's original wording throughout, but until there is a critical edition of all her major writings, the risks involved in such conjecturing would be too great.

Letters from the manuscript Berlin Lat. Qu. 674

I

26ra 'Ascendunt montes et descendunt campi in locum quem fundasti eis' [Psalm 103 : 8]. Hoc tale est: Ascensio montis potenciam dei significat, et descensio campi possibilitatem ipsius; in hisque duabus partibus omnia ponit ac dividit, quia celum in altitudinem posuit, et lumen suum – scilicet terram – sub ipsum, atque hoc in omni creatura fecit. Hoc superbia contradixit, et quandam equalitatis similitudinem cum deo se habere dixit, quod fieri non potest, quapropter etiam ab ipso ad nichilum computata est – quoniam si homo sine alis brachiorum ac manuum esset, humana forma que in ipso est ad nichilum computaretur. Divinitas celum et omnia occulta eius paravit, atque omnes creaturas in terris edificavit, et terra ipsas sustinet. Conatus autem structure superbie sine capite et sine alis est, ac ipsa uno pede vix stat, nec ambulare valet.

Quod illa sine capite et sine alis est, hoc est quod sine deo est, nec ullam possibilitatem standi habet, sed semper cadit, ac unumquodque opus suum sola voce[1] mendaciter constituit; et sine corpore veritatis

26rb super uno pede – qui mendacium significat – stare vult, sed / qui duos pedes habet uno pede ambulare non potest. Quapropter omnes fideles superbiam, que semper in mendatio persistit, fugiant, quia ipsa nec in ere nec in alia fictili re faber nominari potest, ideoque nec in celestibus nec in terrenis quicquam edificat, sed destructio et despoliatrix edificatorum est, quoniam celum perdidit et hominem decepit, velut scriptura habet.

II

36ra Deus mirabilis et invisibilis est, et occulta mysteria ipsius ⟨homo⟩[1] nulla possibilitate scire vel capere potest. Diabolus tamen, per primam[2] deceptionem suam, hoc quod celeste fuit in homine serpentino dolo suo destituit; sed deus novum quid salvare voluit. Ita etiam sepe fit cum aliqua inspiratio a vivente luce – que deus est – procedit, spiramen anime hominis tangens: si homo ille aliter quam debeat gloriatur, vel si alcius quam possit ascendit, hoc serpens mox in ipso deridet; unde que ex veritate procedunt audiantur, et que ex mendatio sunt misericorditer amoveantur, quia nemo in tanta perfectione est quin in aliquo mendax sit, quemadmodum David in spiritu sancto dicit: 'omnis homo mendax' [Psalm 115: 11].

III

41va Domine abbatisse H. Hildegardis. In vera visione hec verba vidi et audivi. O filia dei, que me pauperculam formam in amore dei matrem nominas, disce ut discretionem – que in celestibus et in terrestribus mater omnium existit – habeas, quoniam per ipsam anima regitur, et corpus in recta constrictione pascitur. Homo enim qui, in suspiriis penitencie, peccatorum suorum – que per suggestionem diaboli cogitando, loquendo, et operando commisit – meminerit, matrem Discretionem amplectatur et illi subdatur, ac in vera humilitate et obediencia secundum consilium magistrorum suorum peccata sua emendet. Sic⟨ut⟩[1] namque per incongruam pluviam tempestatis fructus terre leditur, et sicut inarata terra non rectum fructum sed inutiles herbas germinat, sic homo qui plus quam corpus suum sustinere possit laboraverit, per indiscretum laborem et per indiscretam abstinenciam anime sue inutilis efficitur.

Cum vero nigerrima avis (scilicet diabolus) senserit quod homo ab illicitis desideriis et a peccatis suis cessare voluerit, in ieiunia, in orationes, 41vb et in abstinenciam hominis illius velut coluber in cavernam suam / se involvit, eique in suggestione sua dicit: Peccata tua deleri non possunt, nisi corpus tuum per tristiciam et lacrimas, et per alios inmensos labores ita conculces, quod totum arescat. Unde idem homo, sine spe et sine gaudio vivens, sepe sensu deficit, et gravi infirmitate detinetur, et sic, per deceptionem diaboli merito sanctitatis despoliatus, ea que sine discretione incepit inperfecta relinquit, ac ita novissima eius peiora prioribus erunt.

Homo quoque qui secundum exemplum Iesu Christi in ligatura obediencie est, omni studio caveat ne secundum proprietatem suam sibi aliquid eligat plus in se ipsum quam in bonum consilium aliorum confidens, ita quod ne per superbiam que de celo ruit superetur, per hoc quod aliis bonis hominibus melior esse velit, cum illud bonum et sanctum computat quidquid a se ipso constituit. Homo enim a se ipso scire potest quod proprie voluntati sue acquiescere non debet, cum ipse in duabus naturis – corpus et anima – existit, et illa abinvicem dissenciunt, quia quod alteri placet hoc alteri displicet, et cum hoc quod in ipso ita sit, quomodo posset ipse cum salute anime proprie voluntati sue – que corporis est – consentire? Homo namque qui propter timorem et amorem dei propriam voluntatem suam contempserit, et se preceptis et

42ra doctrine et regule[2] / magistrorum suorum in vera humilitate bonorum operum, exempla aliis prebendo, subdiderit, ille se ipsum vivum tabernaculum in celesti Iherusalem facit, et super illum spiritus sanctus requiescit.

O carissima filia, non video tibi et illis duabus familiaribus tuis prodesse ut silvam aut clusam vel limina sanctorum petatis, cum vos signo Christi quo ad celestem Iherusalem tenditis signate sitis, quia si maiorem laborem quam sufferre possitis incipitis, per deceptionem diaboli, ut predictum est, cadetis.

In amore quoque Christi tibi dico quod de fine et de operibus hominum, ac etiam de illis que ipsis futura sint, loqui non soleo, sed illa que per spiritum sanctum in visione anime mee doceor, licet indocta sim, loquor et scribo; illos etiam quos michi conmendasti in orationibus meis gracie dei libenter conmendo. Ego etiam deum pro te libenter orabo, ut te ab omnibus que tibi inutilia sunt liberet, et a futuris malis te custodiat, et ut labores sanctorum operum cum sancta discretione ita perficias quod, splendore pure sanctitatis confortata et ardore vere caritatis dei accensa, ad summam beatitudinem pervenias, in qua in eternum vivas.

IV

46ra O filia Ade, adtende, quia in casibus tuis similia Ade facis – qui dominum suum contempsit, et inmundissimum vermem audivit, et ita honorem suum et angelicam vestem retrorsum proiecit, et pro paradyso gehennam in hereditatem suscepit! Sic et tu fecisti, quando celestem vestem quam indueras exuisti, et pompam huius mundi – cui renunciaveras – respexisti, licet te per hoc excusare velis, quod invita eandem vestem indueris. Sed cogita quod infans renitens in baptismo mergitur, /

46rb sed, licet ploret et eiulet, tamen Christianus fit.

O cara filia, ego lacrimosa intentione pro te et salute anime tue semper oro deum ut te resuscitare dignetur, quemadmodum quatriduanum Lazarum quem ad vitam revocavit – quatinus pater tuus celestis super te gaudeat, dicens: Ego inveni perditam ovem meam, que ex lupo rapta fuerat!

Memento etiam iunioris filii illius patrisfamilias, qui, accepta a patre

substancia, abiit in regionem longinquam, et ibi vivendo luxuriose consumpsit omnia, et ad tantam inopiam redactus ut porcos pasceret, et siliquas – cibum eorum – desideraret, et nemo illi daret. Sic et tu modo, desideriis carnis et incesto amore devicta, in hac die, tua – que ad pacem et habundanciam sunt – habes; sed pro certo venient tibi cito dies alieni et non tui, in quibus circumdabunt te inimici tui undique, et evulsam miseram animam tuam a corpore pertrahent secum, ad terram picis et sulphuris, ad terram mortis, opertam mortis caligine, ubi nullus ordo sed sempiternus horror inhabitat, ubi vermis qui non moritur et ignis qui non extinguitur carnes tuas – modo voluptati subditas – comedet et
46va occupet, nisi velocius prevenias / faciem domini in confessione, et cum amaris lacrimis penitencie et digna satisfactione corrigas delicta iuventutis tue.

Unde, o cara filia, obsecro te ut reinduas Christum, quem exueras, et flexis genibus fuge ad deum, ut te a morte resuscitet ad vitam, ante diem obitus tui. Nam dies tui breves sunt. Benignus dominus Iesus Christus, qui peccata nostra in cruce portavit, ipse tibi veram inspiret[1] peniten-ciam, ut te ad vitam revocet, quatinus in eternum vivas.

V

46va O fili dei, tu in vita tua similis es terre illi que utiles et inutiles herbas germinat, quia per naturam anime, que celestis est, aliqua bona facere delectaris, sed inutilia que ad te trahis illa prohibent, et impediunt te, ne bona perficere possis; et ita – creatoris tui preceptis ac celestis anime tue desideriis neglectis – ea que caro tua postulat sepissime facis.

Nunc autem ammonitio spiritus sancti te doceat ut fortissimus miles veri Salomonis, fortissimis armis gloriose indutus, in fortitudine et stabilitate contra gustum carnis et delectationis tue, et contra inimicos
46vb anime / tue – per quam vivis et ad deum tendis – viriliter et infatigabi-liter pugnes. Tu ergo varias cogitationes spiritalium viciorum a corde tuo, timore et amore illius qui te creavit et redemit, expelle.

Cum autem superbia vane glorie tibi accurrit, ut te sapientiorem et probiorem aliis existimes, et ita tibi displicent que agunt, tunc memento quia cinis es et in cinerem reverteris, et quod sine gracia dei nichil facere potes. Cum autem te incitat natura carnis tue, adtende passionem Christi, quam in cruce pacientissime tolleravit. Corpus etiam tuum tantum fatiga orationibus, vigiliis, ieiuniis et flagellis, quantum te peccatis consensisse cognoscis. Si ista feceris, inimicus tuus, per te superatus, in confusione sua rugiet, et deus super te gaudebit et electum et dilectum tabernaculum suum te faciet.

VI

44rb Oculi tui clare vident, quando per bonam intentionem ad deum aspicis
et sciencia tua vigilat, quando in turpitudine huius seculi te contines et
mens tua sursum volat, cum vicia fallentis diaboli et scurilitatem ac
vanitatem vicissitudin*u*m[1] morum hominum fugis. Tu tamen in
cogitationibus tuis diligenter fuge rusticos mores, qui in⟨s⟩cii[2] sunt
honoris rega*l*is[3] curie – scilicet iracundi*am*[4] et vindictam, que disci-
plinatos et honorificos mores comprimunt.

Ego enim in visione anime mee vidi te in altum montem ad pul-
cherrimam puellam aspicere, cuius facies elegantissima et cuius vestes /
44va candidissime apparuerunt, quarum ornatus pulchritudinem perfecte
perspicere, ut desiderabas, non potuisti. Et hec pulcherrima puella
floriditas caste mentis continencie est.

In cubiculo mentis tue hanc puellam pone, et ipsa smaragdinam
columpnam in fenestra celestis Iherusalem faciet, que inferius ex
nobilissimis lapidibus – topazio et saphiro – et superius purissimo auro,
omni genere nobilium lapidum intermixto, velut speculum fulgens et
lucida appareat, ita ut etiam plurimi, facies suas in illa considerantes,
feditatem vultus sui, scilicet pravitatem morum suorum, in contem-
platione illius ⟨cognoscant⟩.[5] Ignis spiritus sancti te dilectum amicum
filii virginis faciat, quatinus in summa beatitudine cum eo in eternum
gaudeas.

VII

42vb Secreta dei mysteria ab his comprehendi vel sciri non possunt que per
principium exorta sunt, sed tamen omnia iudicia eius iusta sunt, quia
nulla vacuita⟨s⟩[1] in ipso est, sed sicut fuit et est, ita est. Sicut autem
homo ex elementis constat, et elementa in unum coniuncta sunt nec
ullum eorum sine alio per se aliquid valet, sic etiam mores hominum
inequales sunt, licet ab uno spiramine exoriantur.

Mores hominum quatuor modis existunt: quidam duri, quidam
aerii, quidam quasi turbo, quidam ardentes. Qui duros mores habet,
ille in omnibus acer est et in nullis rebus suis in alium aspicit, sed omnia
sua solus secum computat, et hoc ei placet. Et qui aerios mores habet,
illius mens in vicissitudine semper est, et tamen deum timet et ideo se
ipsum in peccatis coercet, quia sibimet ipsi displicent illa que operatur.
43ra Qui au-/tem mores secundum turbinem habent, illi sapientes non sunt,
sed omnia sua cum stulticia miscent, et per verba sapiencie non edifi-
cantur, sed ea indignando exorrescunt. Et qui ardentes mores habent,

illi ad omnia que secularia sunt student et se a spiritalibus alienos faciunt, et pacem fugiunt, et ubicumque illam viderunt cum seculari studio eam offendunt.

Sed deus presumptionem illorum notat qui per obedienciam ad ipsum non respiciunt sed – quasi ipso adiutore et preceptore non indigentes – per se ipsos omnia sua constituunt, quod deus scopis angustiarum et iniuriarum contrarie adversitatis purgabit, quousque in penitencia rememorentur cum deo, quia diligendo et mandata eius observando solliciti non ambulaverunt.

De omnibus vero istis qui tales mores habent deus ad se colligit – cum in sciencia sua illa que contra salutem anime eorum sunt ad deum ⟨convertunt – eos qui tandem eum⟩² pertimescunt, ut in Saulo et aliis multis factum est.

O persona que secundum summum patrem pater nominaris, egritudo tua in aeriis moribus est, et ideo deum valde times, et illi qui duros mores et turbineos atque ardentes habent in ovili domini – quod tibi commissum est – sunt, et te comprimunt, nec ab eis consolationem 43rb ullius / unguenti habes. Tu autem gaude, quia deus te amat et per egritudinem qua gravaris animam tuam purgat, qua⟨m⟩³ in hereditatem suam constituet. Deus etiam locum tuum in oblivione non habet, sed vicissitudines morum qui sibi displicent purgabit. Tu vero nunquam in sciencia tua detrimentum loci tui quesisti; que faciebas, illi prodesse putabas. Nunc autem gaude de salvatione anime tue, quia vivus lapis in celesti Iherusalem eris.

VIII

51rb O serve dei, qui in officio Christi decoratus es, ne paveas gravedinem qua in sompnis exterreris, que ex¹ sanguineis humoribus tuis, ex melancolica complexione commotis, in te surgit. Unde somnus tuus gravis, et visiones somniorum tuorum sepissime vere non sunt, quoniam antiquus deceptor, licet sensus tuos non ledat, tamen deceptione sua in hoc eodem te conturbat. Ex dispensatione tamen dei tali compressione castigaris, ut per timorem istum carnalis concupiscencia in te constringatur. Singulis autem noctibus, manu cordi tuo superposita, ewangelium 'In principio erat verbum' devota intentione lege, et postea verba ista dic:

51va Dominus deus omnipotens, qui in plena / bonitate tua spiraculo me vite suscitasti, per sanctissimum indumentum mitissime humanitatis filii tui – quam propter me induit – obsecro, ne paciaris me ulterius huius inquietationis amaritudine torqueri, sed, propter amorem unigeniti filii tui, auxilio misericordie tue me ab ista fatigatione libera, et ab omnibus insidiis aeriorum spirituum defende.

Spiritus sanctus tabernaculum sanctificationis te faciat, quatinus in gaudiis summe beatitudinis semper cum deo vivas.

IX

49vb O filia creatoris, quoniam ipse te creavit, in caritate Christi tibi / dico
50ra quod in visione anime mee multa miracula dei video, et profunditates scripturarum per graciam dei intelligo, sed qui vel quales eventus hominibus venturi sunt in illa michi non revelantur.

In eadem autem visione cognovi animam mariti tui in magnis penis esse, sed non ad perditionem deputatam, quia, licet proprie voluntati sue plus quam deo serviret, tamen voluntatem ac desiderium quandoque bona operandi in corde suo habebat, que morte preventus operatus non est.

Cara domina, ea que homini futura sunt querere a deo[1] non presumo, cum ipsi ad salutem anime magis prosit ea nescire quam prescire, sed deum omnipotentem pro te libenter exorabo ut omnia tua ad salutem anime et corporis tui disponat.

Animam quoque mariti tui tribus annis – missis, elemosinis, et orationibus – omni die adiuvare quantum potes non desistas, quatinus a diris penarum afflictionibus per misericordiam passionis Christi liberetur. Tu etiam in deo confide et omnia tua illi committe, et ipse te non relinquet ac in eterna beatitudine te conservabit.

X

50ra O mitis pater, de variis eventibus hominum et que ipsis futura sint
50rb dicere non soleo, cum / ego paupercula et indocta feminea forma alia scire non possum quam ea que in vera visione doceor. Unde etiam pro illa matrona libenter orabo, ut gracia dei in corpore et anima regatur, et herede deo digne letificetur.

Ego autem in vera visione anime mee verba ista audivi: Tu, homo, cave ne alcius quam possibilitas tua sufferre possit ascendas, sed in omnibus causis tuis dulcissimam matrem virtutum, scilicet Discretionem, amplectere, ut ab ea per omnia ducaris ⟨et⟩[1] cadere non possis. Pastor enim qui virgam correctionis sine discretione tenet deo non placet, nec etiam ab ovibus suis diligitur, sed magis odio habetur. Bone pater, ovile tuum cum misericordia rege, imitans deum, qui magis vult misericordiam quam holocaustum, et stude etiam ut omnia opera tua in vera humilitate fiant, in qua verus sol, filius dei, ab arce patris in uterum virginis descendit, quatinus in eternum cum illo vivas.

262

XI

51rb O serve dei, anima ista de qua queris nondum purgatione penarum liberata est, unde diligenter pro ipsa deum exora, et gaude quia in numerum beatarum animarum a deo[1]·computata est. Spiritus sanctus te gracia sua accendat et in servitio suo te confirmet.

XII

30va Sol in mane oritur, et de loco in quo constitutus est omnes nubes lumine suo speculative perfundit, et omnes creaturas regit et illuminat ardore suo, usque ad vesperum procedendo: sicut etiam deus omnem creaturam – que homo est – creavit, eamque postea spiraculo vite vivificavit et illuminavit.

Sicut enim primum mane diei cum humido frigore et vicissitudine nubium surgit, sic et homo in puericia sua humidum frigus habet, quia caro sua crescit et ossa sua nondum medulla impleta sunt, nec sanguis illius in rubore suo plene rutilat. Ut autem tercia hora diei in cursu solis calescere incipit, ita quoque, per dentes cibos atterendo, gustum illorum capit, et per incessum pedum movetur.

Homo vero, puericia transacta, in iuventute audax, letus et serenus efficitur, secum disponendo quid incipere velit, quod si ad dextram 30vb partem se vertendo in luce solis bonum elegerit, fructu-/osus in bonis operibus efficietur; si autem ad sinistram partem, malum sequendo, declinaverit, pessimus in nequicia peccatorum nigrescet. Sed cum ipse usque ad nonam opus suum operando pervenerit, in carnibus et in medullis ac in ceteris v⟨i⟩ribus,[1] quibus prius crescendo proficiebat, tunc deficiendo arescit. Sic etiam summus fabricator etates mundi a prima usque ad vespertinum tempus ordinate constituit.

Tu autem, o pater, qui secundum patrem nominaris, considera qualiter incepisti, et quomodo vivendo processisti, quia in puericia tua stultus eras, et in iuventute tua cum temetipso letam securitatem habebas. Interim tamen quandam causam unicornis, tibi tunc ignotam, quesisti, que scilicet scriptura nostra fuit, que plurimum resonat de carnali indumento filii dei, qui, virginalem naturam diligendo, in ipsa velut unicornis in sinu virginis quiescens, dulcissimo sono pulcherrime fidei omnem ecclesiam ad se collegit.

Memor esto quoque, o fidelis pater, quid de paupercula mollis forme de eodem predicto indumento filii dei sepe audiebas, et quia per summum iudicem adiutor meus ablatus est, ideo scripturam nostram 31ra tibi modo commit-/to, suppliciter rogando quod eam caute serves ac diligenter corrigendo prospicias, ut etiam nomen tuum in libro vite

263

scribatur, in hoc imitando beatum Gregorium, qui propter onus Romani presulatus a cythareno sono infusionis spiritus sancti numquam dictando cessavit. Tu etiam ut probus miles celestia arma indue, opera stulticie iuventutis abluendo, ac in angelico vestimento monachilis habitus strennue labora in meridie, prius quam dies inclinetur, quatinus in celestibus tabernaculis in societatem angelorum cum gaudio suscipiaris.

The twelve letters are printed in the order in which they are discussed in chapter 6, pp. 183–95.

B: Berlin, Staatsbibl. Lat. Qu. 674 (references in the margins are to folio and column in this manuscript)

I Quomodo intelligatur ascendunt montes et descendunt campi. *superscript* B 1 *corr. from* vice B II De lapsu primi hominis et de salvatione per seculum. *superscript* B 1 ipsius nulla B 2 per primam *repeated and expunged* B III De discretione que mater est omnium virtutum *superscript* B 1 Sic B 2 regule / et B IV De apostasia. *superscript* B 1 inspirat B V Contra carnis gustum pugna. *superscript* B VI De continencie pulchritudine. *superscript* B 1 vicissitudinem B 2 incii B 3 regaris B 4 iracundie B 5 illius. Ignis B VII De hominum moribus quadripertitis *superscript* B 1 vacuita B 2 B *has lacuna between* deum *and* pertimescant; *my completion is purely conjectural* 3 qua B VIII Quomodo fantasie fugentur. *superscript* B 1 et B IX Quod hominum eventus non predixit. *superscript* B 1 adeo B X (*without superscript*) 1 ducaris cadere B XI De anime purgatione. *superscript* B 1 adeo B XII De etatibus hominis atque mundi. *superscript* B 1 uribus B

Women's Testimonies from the Register of Jacques Fournier

Grazida Lizier

^{56vb} Anno domini millesimo trecentesimo vicesimo, die undevicesimo mensis Augusti, Grazida, uxor Petri Licerii quondam de Monte Alionis, iurata ad sancta dei evangelia quod diceret veritatem, tam de se ut principalis quam de aliis ut testis, super crimine heresis de quo suspecta habebatur, et super incestu et strupro[1] commisso cum ipsa per Petrum Clerici, rectorem ecclesie de Monte Alionis, in iudicio constituta dixit et confessa fuit, quod septem anni sunt vel circa, in estate, dictus rector venit ad domum matris eius, que erat tunc in messibus, et sollicitavit ipsam quod permitteret se carnaliter cognosci ab eo; et ipsa, ut dixit, consensit sibi – que tunc, ut dixit, virgo erat, et poterat esse quattuordecim vel quindecim annorum vel circa, ut sibi videtur; et eam defloravit in borda in qua stant palee. Tamen, ut dixit, nullam violenciam sibi fecit, et postea frequenter eam carnaliter cognovit, usque ad mensem subsequentem[2] Ianuarii, et hoc semper in domo matris sue predicte, sciente et consenciente dicta matre sua. Et hoc, ut dixit, maxime de die fiebat. Postea, dicto mense Ianuarii, dictus rector dedit ipsam in uxorem Petro Licerii – quondam marito suo predicto – et postquam dederat eam in uxorem dicto marito suo, dictus sacerdos, sciente et consenciente dicto viro suo, frequenter, et per quattuor annos quibus dictus maritus eius vixit, eam carnaliter cognovit. Et quando maritus suus[3] interrogabat ipsam que loquitur si dictus sacerdos rem secum habuerat, ipsa respondebat quod sic, et maritus suus dicebat quod custodiret se ab aliis hominibus nisi a dicto sacerdote. Tamen, ut dixit, nunquam dictus sacerdos carnaliter eam cognovit quod maritus eius esset in domo, sed quando erat absens.

Interrogata si tunc sciebat, vel ex tunc scivit, quod dictus sacerdos esset, vel esse diceretur, cognatus germanus Fabrisse matris ipsius que loquitur, respondit quod non scivit hoc, nec audivit dici, nec eciam quod aliquo modo mater eius esset de consanguinitate dicti sacerdotis.

Interrogata si ipsa scivisset quod dicta mater eius fuisset consanguinea germana dicti rectoris, spuria tamen, ipsa se permisisset cognosci a dicto rectore, respondit quod non, et quia et[4] sibi placuit et dicto rectori quando se mutuo[5] carnaliter cognoscebant – propter quod peccare non credebat[6] cum eo.

Fuit interrogata per dictum dominum episcopum si, dum carnaliter cognoscebatur a dicto sacerdote – vel antequam maritum haberet vel dum erat in matrimonio – credebat peccare, respondit quod, quia illo tempore et sibi placebat et dicto rectori quod se mutuo carnaliter[7] cognoscerent, non credebat, nec ei videtur, quod peccaret; sed quia nunc non placet ei quod a dicto sacerdote cognoscatur, si nunc cognos-/ ceretur ab eo, peccare crederet.

Interrogata cum, tempore aliquo dum habebat maritum, inhoneste conversabatur cum dicto sacerdote, si credit vel credidit quod eque licite et sine peccato coniungeretur carnaliter cum marito sicut et cum sacerdote predicto, et e converso, respondit quod, licet magis videretur ei licitum quod coniungeretur carnaliter cum marito, tamen videbatur sibi, et eciam credebat, quod ita parum peccaret cum sacerdote sicut[8] et cum marito suo, quando ab eis carnaliter cognoscebatur.

Interrogata si habebat conscienciam de hoc quod se permittebat cognosci a dicto sacerdote, vel credidit[9] quod talis actus deo displiceret, respondit quod non habebat tunc conscienciam, nec credebat quod alicui rei deberet displicere concubitus eius cum dicto sacerdote – quia hoc sibi et dicto sacerdoti placebat.

Interrogata, si talis coniunctio eius cum dicto sacerdote fuisset ei prohibita per maritum suum, si credidisset peccare si postea se coniungeret cum dicto sacerdote, respondit quod, posito quod dictus maritus eius prohibuisset – quod tamen non fecit – adhuc ipsa non credidisset peccare si contra mariti sui prohibicionem se coniungeret carnaliter cum dicto sacerdote, cum hoc sibi et dicto sacerdoti placeret.

Interrogata si credit, quod si homo quicumque coniungat se carnaliter cum quacumque muliere non coniuncta sibi in consanguinitate, sive sit virgo sive corupta, sive in matrimonio sive extra matrimonium, solum quod viro et mulieri placeat talis concubitus, peccent, respondit quod, licet omnis carnalis coniunctio viri et mulieris deo displiceat, tamen ipsa non credit quod tales se coniungentes – ex quo placet eis mutuo – peccent.

Interrogata ex quo, ut dixit, credit quod omnis carnalis coniunctio viri et mulieris, eciam inter virum et uxorem, deo displiceat, si credit quod plus deo displiceat coniunctio mariti et uxoris, vel illorum qui non sunt coniuges, respondit quod magis displicet deo quando coniungunt se non coniuges quam quando coniuges se coniungunt.

Interrogata si credebat quod bene agentes et sancte viventes post

266

mortem irent ad paradisum, et peccatores intrarent infernum, et si credebat esse infernum vel paradisum, respondit quod nescit, sed audivit dici, quod paradisus est, et hoc credit ipsa; audivit eciam quod infernus est – sed hoc, ut dixit, nec credit nec discredit. Credit autem paradisum esse, quia est bona res, ut audivit dici, non credit autem nec ⟨dis⟩credit[10] infernum, quia mala res est, ut dicitur.[11] Et eodem modo interrogata de resurrexione, respondit quod nec credebat nec discredebat, licet audiverit frequenter dici quod resurgemus.

Interrogata si adhuc credit quod, quando viro[12] et mulieri placet carnalis eorum coniunctio, quod non sit peccatum, respondit quod non est peccatum, ut credit.

Interrogata[13] per quantum tempus stetit in illa credencia, respondit / quod ab[14] tempore illo quo fuit cognita a dicto sacerdote.

57rb

Interrogata quis docuit eam predicta,[15] dixit quod nullus, sed ipsamet.

Interrogata si docuit aliquam personam predicta, dixit quod non, quia super hoc non fuit interrogata.

Postque anno quo supra, die vicesimo primo mensis Augusti predicti, constituta in iudicio dicta Grazida in camera episcopali Appamiarum coram dicto domino episcopo, assistente sibi fratre Galhardo de Pomeriis, tenente locum domini inquisitoris Carcassone, quia suspecta videbatur de heresi Manichea, fuit interrogata per dictum dominum episcopum si credebat quod omnia corporalia que in hoc mundo videntur deus fecisset. Respondit quod res corporales bene ad usum humanum, et eciam utiles ad[16] res illas, deus fecit, sicut sunt[17] homines, bestie quibus homines vescuntur vel veuntur,[18] ut boves, oves, capre, equi, muli, et fructus terre et arborum, quibus homines vescuntur; sed, ut dixit, non credit quod deus fecerit lupos, muscas, cinsolas, et talia que hominibus sunt nosciva; nec credit eciam quod deus diabolum fecerit – quia res mala est, et nullam rem malam deus fecit, ut dixit.

Postque anno quo supra, die sexto decimo mensis Novembris, educta de carcere castri de Alamannis dicta Grazida, in quo carcere steterat per septem septimanas et aliquantulum plus, quia noluerat veritatem confiteri plene, ut videbatur, et constituta in iudicio in camera episcopali Appamiarum coram dicto domino episcopo, assistente sibi dicto fratre Galhardo, gratis et sponte, non metu vel vi tormentorum, ut dixit, confessa fuit et deposuit ut sequitur. –

Quod infra illud tempus quo dictus rector defloraverat eam et dedit ei maritum, quadam die de qua dixit se non recordari, ipsa stabat ad portam den Balle de Monte Alionis, cum Fabrissa matre sua, et dictus rector ascendebat versus castrum et remansit aliquantulum cum ipsis, et solaciando loquebantur de peccato luxurie. Et tunc dictus rector dixit quod habere rem cum muliere – solummodo quod ei placeat – peccatum non erat; dixit eciam quod tantum valebat una mulier sicut alia, et tantum peccatum erat cum una sicut[19] et cum alia, et hiis dictis in continenti[20] ascendit versus castrum de Monte Alionis.

Interrogata si alias consimilia verba dixit ei dictus rector, respondit quod non quod recordetur.

Interrogata si dictus sacerdos dixit ei quod infernus non esset, respondit quod non.

Interrogata si dictus rector dixit ei quod diabolus fecerit aliquas res huius mundi, dixit quod non.

Interrogata si ipsa credidit quod coniunctio carnalis viri et mulieris extra matrimonium peccatum non esset propter verba predicti rectoris, respondit quod sic – et propter hoc eciam ipsa non credebat peccare quando se carnaliter coniungebat cum dicto rectore.

Interrogata si ipsa credidit quod tantum peccatum sit habere rem cum una muliere sicut et cum alia propter verba predicti rectoris, respondit / quod non: immo, ut dixit, semper credidit quod gravius peccatum[21] esset habere rem cum consanguineis quam cum aliis mulieribus extraneis.

57va

Dixit eciam quod ipsa aliquando dixit dicto rectori quod intellexerat quod Fabrissa, mater ipsius, erat eius cognata germana, et dictus rector respondebat ei quod hoc nesciebatur, quia mater dicte Fabrisse fuerat filia Guillelmi Clerici, fratris Poncii Clerici, qui fuit pater dicti rectoris.

Interrogata quare a principio noluit confiteri quis docuerat eam predictas errores de peccato carnali, respondit quod, quando primo fuit citata, ipsa venit cum Alazaici Ademaria, que non poterat bene ire nec se cum aliis tenere, et in via, dicta Alazaicis dixit ei quod rector de Monte Alionis multa bona ei fecerat, et eam maritaverat, et quod non diceret aliquod malum de eo, eciam si iuraret dicere veritatem, quia[22] magnum quid est restaurare unam p⟨er⟩sonam,[23] et quod peccatum non erat, et quod staret bene firma et constans. Dixit eciam quod timebat, si veritatem predictam diceret de dicto rectore et fratribus eius, quod interficerent vel alias male tractarent ipsam.

Interrogata si volebat perseverare in confessionibus precedentibus factis per eam prius, respondit quod sic.

Interrogata si penitebat de predictis erroribus quos confessa fuit se credidisse, respondit quod sic, et fuit instructa per dictum dominum episcopum de contrario, qua instructione facta, dixit et confessa fuit se credere – et de cetero omnibus diebus vite sue crederet – quod omnis concubitus carnalis, excepto concubitu qui est inter virum et uxorem legittimam, est mortale peccatum. Item dixit se credere, et credituram in posterum, quod coniunctio carnalis mariti et uxoris legittime facta peccatum non est. Item dixit se credere, et semper de cetero, quod infernus est in quo omnes iniqui demones et homines perpetuo punientur et ⟨paradisus est in quo boni perpetuo⟩[24] glorificabuntur. Item dixit se credere nunc et in posterum quod omnes homines resurgent in eadem carne in qua nunc sunt,[25] in qua recipient unusquisque prout fecit, sive bonum fuerit[26] sive malum. Item dixit se credere quod deus omnes creaturas, tam corporales quam spirituales – eciam nocivas hominibus – et demones ipsos quantum ad naturam, deus bonus fecit; nec est aliqua creatura quam ipse non fecerit.

[Grazida's formal abjuration follows]

Mengarde Buscalh

103ra Item dixit quod sex anni sunt vel circa, tempore paschali, Petrus Clerici, rector de Monte Alionis, misit ad ipsam apud Pradas unum puerum; et[1] dixit ipsi loquenti quod dictus rector volebat quod ipsa iret apud Montem Alionem ad domum eius, quia procurator domini comitis vel iudex erat ibi; et ipsa cum dicto puero[2] ivit ad domum dicti rettoris, quem inveniens[3] in solario suo, et non inveniens aliquem alium[4] cum eo, peciit ab eo quare fecerat eam venire. Qui respondit ei quod per longum tempus adamaverat[5] eam, et volebat habere rem secum. Et cum ipsa, ut dixit, diceret ei quod non ⟨con⟩sentiret[6] sibi in hoc, quia magnum peccatum est, quia vidua erat, dictus rector respondit quod nullum peccatum erat nisi cum matre vel sorore. Et cum ipsa diceret ei quod, dicendo quod peccatum non erat[7] talis concubitus, diabolus eum faciebat loqui, dictus rector cominatus fuit ei, et eciam dixit: 'Et[8] quomodo tu audes michi contradicere in hoc, cum nulla mulier sit quam ego habere non possem, si tantum apud eam insisterem sicut institi apud te?' Et ipsa respondit ei quod, ex quo ita erat, placebat ei quod faceret voluntatem suam de ipsa. Et ibidem eam carnaliter cognovit; et postea iterum,[9] in eodem loco, alia vice carnaliter eam cognovit; processu temporis et in domo ipsius loquentis ter[10] eam carnaliter cognovit, ad quam dictus rector de nocte veniebat. Et perpetrato peccato suo recedebat ab ipsa.

105ra   Item dixit quod quando socrus eius predicta fuerat hereticata, ipsa loquens habebat unum filium duorum vel trium mensium infirmum, et dictus Guillelmus Buscalh dixit ei: 'Velles quod haberemus aliquem de illis bonis hominibus (loquens de hereticis) ut reciperet dictum filium tuum ad sectam eorum, si inciperet declinare ad mortem? – quia si reciperetur per eos et moreretur, esset angelus dei.' Et cum ipsa que-/

105rb reret ab eo, quid faceret ipsa de infante postquam fuisset receptus per hereticos, dictus Guillelmus dixit ei quod postea non daret lac dicto puero, nec aliquid aliud, sed quod eum permitteret sic mori. Quod ipsa audiens, dixit quod nullo modo dimitteret dare mamillam puero quamdiu viveret, quia ex quo Christianus erat, et non habebat[11] peccatum nisi de ipsa,[12] credebat quod si ipsa perderet dictum puerum, deus haberet eum.

106va   Et propter hoc dictus puer hereticatus non fuit, licet placuisset ipsi loquenti quod hereticatus fuisset, ⟨si⟩[13] postea eum lactare posset.

Guillemette Bathégan

114ra   [Arnaldus dixit] quod defuncti non faciebant aliam penitentiam nisi quod ibant sic vigilando de ecclesia ad ecclesiam. Et cum ipsa diceret ei quod bene patiebantur tunc ⟨si⟩[1] frigus vigeret, dictus homo respondit ei quod deffuncti querebant domum vel locum ubi erant multa ligna, et ibi se calefaciebant ad ignem, faciendo[2] ignem de predictis lignis.

    Dixit etiam ei quod dicta Fabrissa venerat ad ipsam que loquitur, et invenerat eam[3] in lecto. Et postea dixit ei dictus homo ex parte dicte filie sue quod faceret celebrare unam missam pro ea, et quod poneret mediam libram olei in aliqua lampade que arderet ante altare beate Marie. Et cum hiis dictis dictus homo vellet recedere, ipsa retinuit ipsum ad cenam. Et cenaverunt et[4] filius suus et dictus homo de pane, vino et carnibus, et post cenam dictus homo dixit ei quod dicta filia eius ibat cum quadam filia de Na Nespla defuncta et duabus aliis mulieribus, et quod ibat bene et ilariter sicut et alie. Et cum ipsa que loquitur diceret, 'Et quomodo[5] poterat dicta filia eius[6] ita velociter ire sicut et alie, cum ipsa pregnans et grossa mortua fuisset?' dictus[7] homo respondit quod dicta filia eius erat pulcra et fortis, et quod ita velociter ibat sicut et alie . . . in festo sequenti omnium sanctorum debebat intrare in requiem. Quia, ut dixit, nulla anima intrabat paradisum hominis vel mulieris magni usque ad diem iudicii, sed anime puerorum qui moriuntur infra septimum annum in continenti vadunt in gloriam dei.

Dixit etiam ei, ut videtur sibi, quod omnes anime hominum et mulierum, peracta penitentia quam faciunt eundo de ecclesia ad ecclesiam, ibant ad requiem, et postea in die iudicii omnes salvabuntur, ita quod nulla anima hominis vel mulieris peribit vel dampnabitur; cui ipsa respondit: 'Sic placeat deo quod nullus dampnetur!'[8]

Aude Fauré

133rb Interrogata si aliquis vel aliqua induxit eam ad errorem supradictum, dixit quod non, set supervenit sibi, ut credit, ex perseverancia supradicti peccati, quod non fuerat confessa illud.

Interrogata si unquam participavit vel conversa fuit cum hereticis, dixit quod non, nec unquam vidit hereticum, quod sciat.

Interrogata si fuit confessa vel revelavit dictum errorem alicui sacerdoti vel alii, dixit quod non – quousque nuper, in quadam gravi infirmitate quam passa fuit, in qua dixit se revelasse dictum[1] errorem dicto Guillelmo Fabri, marito suo, et Emengardi Garaude de Muro Veteri; et primo dicto viro suo per hec verba: 'Domine, quomodo potest esse hoc, quod non possum credere dominum nostrum?' Et tunc dictus maritus suus dixit sibi, reprehendendo – ut dixit – eam: 'Quo-
133va modo, maledicta? loqueris in bono sensu tuo?' Que respondit / quod sic. Et tunc idem maritus suus dixit sibi quod, si non fuerat confessa, quod* confiteretur, quia alias non staret cum eo, set quod dimitteret eam.

Interrogata si tunc, quando dixit predicta verba dicto marito suo, erat in bono sensu, dixit quod sic, et quod adhuc bene recordatur de predictis omnibus.

Item dixit quod in eadem infirmitate misit pro Emengardi Garauda dicti loci de Muro Veteri, cui Emengardi cum venisset ad eam dixit: 'Osta, cia,[2] quomodo potest esse quod non possum credere deum,[3] nec eciam possum credere quod hostia que elevatur in altari per Capellanum sit corpus Christi?' – et quod[4] tunc dicta Emengardis reprehendit eam valde, et dixit sibi multa verba inductiva ad credendum, et inter cetera[5] narravit sibi, ut dixit, quod⟨d⟩am[6] exemplum tale . . . Quo exemplo narrato dicta Auda dixit: 'O cia, tam bona verba habetis, et tam bene confortastis me!'

133vb 'Sancta Maria, domine, qualiter potest hoc esse? Nam quando sum in ecclesia et elevatur corpus Christi, non possum rogare[7] ipsum, nec possum ipsum respicere, set quando puto respicere ipsum, advenit[8] michi[9] "un essbegament"[10] ante occulos!'

134rb 'Cia, qualiter potest esse quod non possum credere deum, nec eciam cum[11] elevatur corpus Christi per Capellanum in altari possum rogare ipsum, nec credere quod sit corpus Christi?' Et tunc dicta Emengardis respondit: 'Co, Na Traytoressa, no sia! – nam iste locus et istud hospicium semper fuit mundus de tot mal, sec[12] de yregia!' et 'Caveatis vobis, ne vos asportetis ⟨illam⟩[13] nobis de alio loco, nec vituperetis locum istum!'[14] . . . Postque iterum dicta Auda interrogavit dictam Emengardim: 'Cia, qualiter rogatis deum, et que verba dicitis in elevacione corporis Christi, quando elevatur per Capellanum in altari?' Et dicta Emengardis respondit . . . 'Senher, trametestz me una lagrema de aquela vostra ayga que·m[15] lave le mieu cor de tota legesa et de tot peccat. In manus tuas, domine, comendo spiritum meum, redemisti me, domine deus veritatis.'

Item dicta Auda dixit eidem: 'Cia, que verba dicitis vos de mane, cum surgitis de lecto?' Et dicta Emengardis dixit quod dicebat talem[16] oracionem: 'Senher Dieus, tot poderos, a vos coma l'arma e 'l cors. Senher, vos me gardastz de peccar e de falhir[17] e de l'autra peccada e de la mieua meteysha, e[18] de fals testimoni, e m'amenastz a bona fi.' Post que verba predicta Auda dixit: 'Osta, cia, ta be m'avestz coffortada,[19] tam bona verba scitis et tam bene scitis rogare deum: si vos non fuissetis, perdita essem, et si contingeret me mori, putrefieret corpus meum in ecclesia Sancti Christofori et dyaboli portassent animam meam!' Et ibidem dicta Emengardis iterato dixit dicte Aude: 'Na Traytoressa, cavete bene vobis[20] quod credatis firmiter in deum, et credatis corpus Christi esse vere[21] in sacramento altaris, et audite quod exemplum dicam vobis'; et narravit sibi exemplum supra positum in confessione dicte Aude.

136rb Postque cum dicte due mulieres recessissent, ipsa Auda rediit ad cameram ubi iacebat dicta nutrix, et dixit sibi: 'Tu recepisti corpus Christi – credis quod illud quod recepisti sit corpus Christi?' Que nutrix respondit quod credebat firmiter. Cui dixit dicta Auda: 'Quomodo potest esse quod ego non possum[22] credere?' Et dicta nutrix[23] dixit ei: 'Domina, revertemini[24] ad deum', et 'Credatis firmiter illud esse corpus Christi.' Et dicta Auda dixit dicte nutrici quod rogaret deum, quod poneret in corde suo quod crederet; et dum dicta nutrix, ut melius poterat, rogaret deum, supervenit Guillelma, ancilla dicti hospicii dicte Aude, cui dixit dicta Auda: 'Guillelma, pone te in orationem, et roga beatam virginem Mariam de Monte Gaudio ut illuminet michi,[25] quod ego bene[26] possim credere deum' – quod et

272

fecit dicta Guillelma, flexis[27] genibus. Et cum orasset, statim dicta Auda fuit - ut dixit - illuminata, et credidit firmiter in deum, et credit adhuc, prout dixit.

Et cum predicta deposuisset, dicta Auda supplicavit humiliter dicto domino episcopo - cum magna contritione cordis, ut apparebat - ut sibi iniungeret penitenciam quam vellet, quia parata erat, ut dixit, eam recipere et complere, quantumcumque duram - supplicando tamen quod non inponeretur sibi penitencia publica, seu talis que deduceret eam ad verecundiam et vituperium seculi.

V: Vat. lat. 4030 (references in the margins are to folio and column in this manuscript)
Du: *Le registre d'Inquisition de Jacques Fournier*, ed. J. Duvernoy (3 vols., Toulouse 1965)

Grazida Lizier

1 strupro: *sic* V (stupro Du)   2 sequentem Du   3 ipsius Du   4 *om.* Du (C) [*quia* = '*that*']   5 *om.* Du (C)   6 non credebat peccare Du   7 mutualiter Du 8 *om.* Du   9 credebat Du (C)   10 credit V (*corr.* Du)   11 dixit Du   12 et *expunged before* viro V   13 Item V (*corr.* C)   14 a Du (C)   15 errorem predictam Du (*for* eam predicta V)   16 *Du's correction* - Adde: hominem - *should be rejected* (*see transl. above, p.* 205)   17 *om.* Du   18 *sc.* vehuntur utuntur Du (C)   19 *om.* Du   20 incontinenti (*one word*) Du   21 *om.* Du   22 1 *expunged after* quia V   23 psonam V   24 *The copyist has omitted a line* (*Du's text* - infernus est in quo . . . homines perpetuo punientur et glorificabuntur - *gives no sense*)   25 in qua nunc sunt *om.* Du (C)   26 *om.* Du (C, *but with unnecessary corr. to* fecerit)

Mengarde Buscalh

1 qui Du   2 petro V (*corr.* Du)   3 invenit Du   4 aliquem: *om.* Du   5 *sic* V ipse adamaverat Du   6 absentiret *with* ab *deleted* V assentiret Du   7 non erat peccatum Du   8 dixit ei: Quomodo Du   9 *om.* Du   10 *om.* Du   11 fecerat Du   12 ipsi Du   13 *suppl.* Du

Guillemette Bathégan

1 tunc frigus V   2 vel faciendo Du (C)   3 ipsam Du   4 *om.* Du   5 diceret in quo modo Du   6 sua Du   7 et dictus V   8 dampnaretur Du (C)

Aude Fauré

1 dictam Du (C)   2 cia: *sic* V, *here and in all other occurrences below; Du prints* tia *throughout*   3 Dominum Du (C)   4 *om.* Du (C)   5 inter eadem Du (C) 6 quodam V (*corr.* Du)   7 orare Du   8 supervenit Du   9 quoddam Du 10 anbegament Du (*Does the copyist's* essbegament *correspond to Prov.* esbayment

[*Levy*, '*Unruhe*', '*Sorge*'] *or* esbleugimen [*F. Mistral, Dict.*, '*éblouissement*']*?*)
11 cum eciam Du (*ignoring reversal-signs in V*)   12 tec V nec Du [*I owe the
emendation sec to Peter Ricketts*]   13 *I have supplied* illam (*sc.* '*heresiam*' – '*yregia*'
in the previous sentence)   14 istum nostrum Du   15 quē V que Du   16 *om.* Du
17 falhar Du (C)   18 e de lautra p. e de la m. m. e V et de l'autra p. et de la m.
m. et Du   19 cosfortada V coffortata Du (-ada C)   20 vos Du   21 *om.* Du
22 possim Du   23 mulier Du   24 revertamini Du (C)   25 me Du   26 *om.* Du
27 flexit V (C)

* For correctness of Latin this second 'quod' should be deleted; but it probably
reflects a colloquial vernacular looseness (cf. Grazida Lizier, above, p. 267: 'si
adhuc credit quod, quando . . . coniunctio, *quod* non sit peccatum').

The complete testimony of Grazida Lizier, and extracts from the testimonies of
Mengarde Buscalh, Guillemette Bathégan, and Aude Fauré, are edited afresh here
from the unique manuscript (V). It seemed advisable to mention explicitly in the
textual notes all my divergences of reading from Duvernoy's printed text, except
for very minor ones of spelling. (Punctuation is my own.) It was not till after this
editing had been done that I was able to see Duvernoy's fascicule, *Corrections*
(Edouard Privat, Toulouse 1972). In cases where a manuscript reading, as given
above, is also mentioned in *Corrections*, I have added '(C)' to my note.

The translations in chapter 7 are based on the texts as edited here. I have not
commented on passages in Duvernoy's French version (*Le registre d'Inquisition de
Jacques Fournier*, 3 vols. (Paris–La Haye 1978)), where his interpretation differs
from mine.

Marguerite Porete

Lyrical moments from _Le mirouer des simples ames_

I

116r   Amye, que voulez vous de moy?
      Je contiens tout ce qui fut et qui est et qui sera,
      je suis du tout remplie.
      Prenez de moy tout ce qu'il vous plaira –
      se vous me voulez toute, je ne contredis mie.
      Dictes, amye, que voulez vous de moy?
      Je suis Amour, qui du tout suis[1] remplie:
      ce que vous voulez,
      nous voulons, amye –
      dictes nous nuement vostre voulenté!

II

11r   Vertuz, a tousiours je prens   de vous congé:[2]
      Je en auray le cueur plus franc   et plus gay.
      Voustre service est troup constant –   bien le sçay.

      Je mis ung temps mon cueur en vous,   sans nulle dessevree,/
11v   Vous savez que je estoie a vous   trestoute habandonnee –
      Je estoie adonc serve de vous: or en suis delivree.

      J'avoie en vous tout mon cureur mis –   bien le sçay –
      Dont je vescu, ung tandis,   en grant esmay.

      Souffert en ay maint gref tourment,   mainte paine enduree:
      Merveilles est quant nullement   en suis vive eschappee.

      Mais puis que[3] ainsi est, ne me chault: je suis de vous sevree,
      Dont je mercie le dieu d'enhault[4] –   bonne m'est la journee!

      De voz dangers   partie sui,   ou en maint ennuy j'estoie[5] –
      Oncques mais   franche ne fui,   fors de vous dessevree;
      De voz dangers   partie suis,[6]   en paix suis demouree.★

III

6r   Vous qui en ce livre lirez,
      Se bien le voulez entendre,
      Pensez ad ce que vous direz,

Car il est fort a comprendre:
Humilité vous fault prendre,
Qui de science est tresoriere
Et des aultres vertuz la mere.

Theologiens ne aultres clers,
Point n'en aurez l'entendement
– Tant aiez les engins clers –
Se n'y procedez humblement,
Et que Amour et Foy ensement
Vous facent surmonter Raison,
Qui dames sont de sa maison.[7]

Raison mesmes nous tesmoigne
Ou xiiie de ce livre
Chappitre, et n'en a vergoigne,
Que Amour et Foy la font vivre;
Er d'elles point ne se delivre,
Car sur elle ont seigneurie,
Par quoy il fault qu'elle s'umilie.

Humiliez dont[8] voz sciences
Qui sont de Raison fondees,
Et mettez toutes voz fiances
En celles qui sont donnees
D'Amour, par Foy enluminees,
Et ainsy comprendrez ce livre,
Qui d'Amour fait l'ame vivre.

IV

102r Je vous prie, chere fille, lesser[9] ester:
il n'y a si grant clerc ou monde
qui vous en sceust parler …

Je vous prie, chere fille,
ma seur et la moye amye,
par Amour, se vous voulez,
que vous ne vueillez
plus dire les secrez
que vous savez –
les aultres s'en dampneroient
102v la ou vous / vous sauverez,
puisque Raison et Desir les gonvernent[10]

276

et Crainte[11] et Voulenté.
Sachez pourtant, mon eslite fille,
que paradis leur est donné.

Paradis? dit ceste eslite –
ne leur octroiez vous aultrement?
Aussi bien l'auront les murtrie⟨r⟩s,[12]
se ilz veulent mercy crier! –
mais nonpourtant[13]
je m'en vueil taire,
puisque vous le voulez,
et pource diray
vers de chançon au congé
de fine Amour.

V

103r   Penser plus ne m'y vault,
ne oeuvre, ne loquence:
Amour me trait si hault
– penser plus ne m'y vault –
de ses divins regars,
que je n'ay nulle entente.
Penser plus ne m'y vault,
ne oeuvre, ne loquence.

      . . .

103v   Amis, que diront beguines   et gens de religion
quant ilz orront l'excellence   de vostre divine chançon?
Beguines dient que je erre,   prestres clers et prescheurs,
Augustins et Carmes,   et les Freres Mineurs,
pource[14] que j'escri de l'estre   de l'affinee Amour.
Non fais, sauve leur raison   qui leur fait a moy ce dire:
Desir Vouloir et Crainte, certes,   leur toult la cognoissance,
                      et l'affluence
et l'union de la haultiesme   lumiere d'ardour
                    de divine Amour.

VI

104r   J'ay dit que je l'aymeray.
Je mens – ce ne suis je mie.
C'est il seul qui ayme moy –
il est, et je ne suis mie,

> et plus ne me fault
> que ce qu'il veult
> et qu'il vault.
> Il est plain
> et de ce suis plaine:
> c'est le divin noyaulx
> et amour loyaulx.

Ch: Chantilly Condé F xiv 26 (references in the margins are to folios in Ch)
Gu: 'Il "Miroir des simples ames" di Margherita Porete', ed. R. Guarnieri,
   Archivio italiano per la storia della pietà IV (1965) 501–635

1 suis de bonté remplie Gu   de bonte *in margin* Ch (*probably a gloss for 'du tout'*
in Ch's exemplar)   2 je p. c. d. v. a t. ChGu   3 puisque Gu   4 d'en hault Gu
5 ou je esté en m. e. ChGu   6 P. s. d. v. d. ChGu   7 *sic* Ch de la maison Gu
8 dont: *sic* Ch   donc (*orthogr.*) Gu   9 *corr. to* lessez Gu   10 gouvernent Gu
11 *two letters deleted after* crainte Ch   12 murtries Ch (*corr.* Gu)   13 non pour
tant (*three words*) Gu   14 Pour ce (*two words*) Gu

★ The addition of a further internal rhyme in the last lines here suggests that
Marguerite may have been familiar with some examples of Latin leonine verse,
where it is not uncommon to pass from one type (such as *leonini collaterales*) to
another (such as *tripertiti*) in the course of a single poem.

The six passages are printed in the order of discussion in chapter 7. There are few
substantial divergences of reading from Gu, either here or in the notes on prose
passages, pp. 318–19; but I have tried to suggest certain differences of emphasis
by choice of line-arrangement, punctuation, and capitals, and especially by
restoring the complete rhyme-scheme in II, and by suggesting the lyrical movement in the later part of IV (printed as prose in Gu).

Abbreviations

ACO	Acta Conciliorum Oecumenicorum (Berlin 1914ff)
Beiträge	Beiträge zur Geschichte der Philosophie und Theologie des Mittelalters
Bogin	M. Bogin (ed.), *The Women Troubadours* (New York 1976)
Boutière–Schutz	J. Boutière, A. H. Schutz (eds.), *Biographies des troubadours* (Paris ²1973)
Briefwechsel	Hildegard von Bingen, *Briefwechsel*, tr. A. Führkötter (Salzburg 1965)
Causae	*Hildegardis Causae et curae*, ed. P. Kaiser (Leipzig 1903)
CC (CM)	Corpus Christianorum (Continuatio Mediaevalis)
CCM	*Cahiers de civilisation médiévale*
CE	F. Buecheler (ed.), *Carmina Latina Epigraphica* (2 vols., Leipzig 1895–7); *Supplementum*, ed. E. Lommatzsch (1926)
CIL	*Corpus Inscriptionum Latinarum* (Berlin 1863ff)
Colloque	*Pierre Abélard, Pierre le Vénérable: Colloques internationaux du CNRS No. 546* (Paris 1975)
CSEL	Corpus Scriptorum Ecclesiasticorum Latinorum
DA	*Deutsches Archiv für Erforschung des Mittelalters*
Dessau	H. Dessau (ed.), *Inscriptiones Latinae Selectae* (3 vols. in 5, Berlin 1897–1916)
Diehl	E. Diehl (ed.), *Inscriptiones Latinae Christianae Veteres* (3 vols., Berlin ²1961)
Du Cange	C. Du Cange, L. Favre, *Glossarium Mediae et Infimae Latinitatis* (9 vols., Niort 1883–7)
Duvernoy (Du)	J. Duvernoy (ed.), *Le registre d'Inquisition de Jacques Fournier* (Bibl. Méridionale XLII, 3 vols., Toulouse 1965)
Echtheit	M. Schrader, A. Führkötter, *Die Echtheit des Schrifttums der heiligen Hildegard von Bingen* (Köln–Graz 1956)
Frank	I. Frank, *Répertoire métrique de la poésie des troubadours* (2 vols., Paris 1953–7)
GP	H. Geist, G. Pfohl, *Römische Grabinschriften* (München ²1976)
HC	Abélard, *Historia calamitatum* (see below, under 'Monfrin')
Hilbert	K. Hilbert (ed.). *Baldricus Burgulianus Carmina* (Heidelberg 1979)
JWCI	*Journal of the Warburg and Courtauld Institutes*
LDO	Hildegard of Bingen, *Liber divinorum operum* (P.L. 197, 741–1038)
Levy	E. Levy, *Provenzalisches Supplement-Wörterbuch* (8 vols., Leipzig 1894–1924)
Lexicon	A. Blaise, *Lexicon Latinitatis Medii Aevi* (CC, Turnhout 1975)
LVM	Hildegard of Bingen, *Liber vitae meritorum* (Pitra pp. 1–244)

ABBREVIATIONS

Manitius	M. Manitius, *Geschichte der lateinischen Literatur des Mittelalters* (3 vols., München 1911–31)
Manuel	Dhuoda, *Manuel pour mon fils* [*Liber manualis*], ed. P. Riché, tr. B. de Vregille, C. Mondésert (Sources Chrétiennes, Paris 1975)
Medieval Latin	P. Dronke, *Medieval Latin and the Rise of European Love-Lyric* (2 vols., Oxford ²1968)
Meyer (*Ges. Abh.*)	W. Meyer, *Gesammelte Abhandlungen zur mittellateinischen Rythmik* (3 vols., Berlin 1905–36)
MGH	Monumenta Germaniae Historica
Miroir	R. Guarnieri (ed.), 'Il "Miroir des simples ames" di Margherita Porete', *Archivio italiano per la storia della pietà* IV (1965) 501–635
Mlat. Jb.	*Mittellateinisches Jahrbuch*
Monfrin	J. Monfrin (ed.), Abélard, *Historia calamitatum* (Paris ³1967) [followed by two letters of Héloïse]
MS	*Mediaeval Studies*
NG	F. Blatt, *Novum Glossarium Mediae Latinitatis* (København 1957ff)
Opera	H. Homeyer (ed.), *Hrotsvithae Opera* (Paderborn 1970)
Passio	C. I. M. I. van Beek (ed.), *Passio Sanctarum Perpetuae et Felicitatis* (Nijmegen 1936); *Passio Sanctarum Perpetuae et Felicitatis, Latine et Graece* (Florilegium Patristicum XLIII, Bonn 1938)
PBB	[*Paul und Braunes*] *Beiträge zur Geschichte der deutschen Sprache und Literatur*
Pitra	*Analecta Sacra VIII: Sanctae Hildegardis Opera*, ed. J. B. Pitra (Monte Cassino 1882)
P.L.	Patrologia Latina
Poetae	*Poetae Latini Aevi Carolini* / *Poetae Latini Medii Aevi* (MGH, 1881ff)
'Problemata'	P. Dronke, 'Problemata Hildegardiana', *Mlat. Jb.* XVI (1981) 97–131
RAC	*Reallexikon für Antike und Christentum*
RB	*Revue Bénédictine*
RMAL	*Revue du moyen âge latin*
RP	*Romance Philology*
RTAM	*Recherches de théologie ancienne et médiévale*
Schultz	O. Schultz (ed.), *Die provenzalischen Dichterinnen* (Altenburg 1888)
Scivias	*Hildegardis Scivias*, ed. A. Führkötter, A. Carlevaris (CC CM XLIII–XLIII A, Turnhout 1978)
SM	*Studi medievali*
Tangl	M. Tangl (ed.). *Epistolae Selectae* I (MGH 1916)
TLL	*Thesaurus Linguae Latinae*
Trier 1980	*Petrus Abaelardus (1079–1142). Person, Werk und Wirkung*, ed. R. Thomas, J. Jolivet, D. E. Luscombe, L. M. de Rijk (Trierer Theologische Studien 38, Trier 1980)
Unterkircher	*Sancti Bonifacii Epistolae. Codex Vindobonensis 751 der Österreichischen Nationalbibliothek*, introd. F. Unterkircher (Codices Selecti XXIV, Graz 1971)
Winterfeld	P. von Winterfeld (ed.). *Hrotsvithae Opera* (MGH, 1902)
ZfdA	*Zeitschrift für deutsches Altertum*
ZfdP	*Zeitschrift für deutsche Philologie*
ZfrP	*Zeitschrift für romanische Philologie*

Notes

Preface

1 See especially pp. 24–6, 203ff below.
2 I have not attempted to cover Byzantine, Celtic or Norse texts. On the Byzantine side there are testimonies in diverse literary genres: see esp. H. Hunger, *Die hochsprachliche profane Literatur der Byzantiner* (2 vols., München 1978); some of the poetry of Eudokia and Kassia is printed, with German translation, by H. Homeyer, *Dichterinnen des Altertums und des frühen Mittelalters* (Paderborn 1979) pp. 113–71. On early testimonies of Norse women poets, see Guthrún P. Helgadóttir, *Skáldkonur fyrri alda* I (Akureyri 1961). The oldest Celtic poems attributed to women, as to Liadain in Irish (*Liadain and Curithir*, ed. and tr. Kuno Meyer (London 1902)) or to Heledd in Welsh (cf. most recently A. O. H. Jarman, in *A Guide to Welsh Literature* I (Swansea 1976) 93–7) raise delicate problems of how far the extant pieces reflect authentic originals.
3 Some remarks made by the eminent medieval historian Georges Duby, in an interview published not long after this book went to press (*Le Nouvel Observateur* (28 août au 3 septembre 1982) 14–17), are symptomatic of the unflagging vitality of such attitudes. Asked about the women 'qui ont pris la parole à cette époque', Professor Duby answered: 'Certes, il y a Marie de France. Je me demande ce qui se cache derrière ce nom . . . Quant à Héloïse, tout donne à penser que ses lettres ont été écrites ou récrites par un homme.'
4 *Poetic Individuality in the Middle Ages: New Departures in Poetry 1000–1150* (Oxford 1970) pp. 150–92, 209–31.
5 The series begun by Otto Müller Verlag, Salzburg, with *Wisse die Wege*, tr. M. Böckeler (1954), has recently been completed with *Das Buch von den Steinen*, tr. P. Riethe (1979). Most of the volumes in this series include abridgements. In Corpus Christianorum (CM XLIII–XLIII A) a new ed. of *Scivias* has appeared (1978), by A. Führkötter and A. Carlevaris. Professor Albert Derolez and I are engaged on an edition of the *Liber divinorum operum* for the same collection.

1. From Perpetua to the Eighth Century

1 *Passio* II 1. For fully expanded references, here and throughout, see the Bibliography below (pp. 320–32). I cite the *Passio* from van Beek's *editio maior* (1936), but have also consulted his *editio minor* (1938), with its valuable annotations, and the more recent bilingual texts of Ruiz Bueno and Musurillo. In addition, for Perpetua's own narrative (*Passio* III–X) I have collated van Beek's Codex 2 (Ambrosiana C 210 Inf., fols. 109vb–112rb). In translation below, when I have preferred a reading from this MS (A), this is signalled in a footnote, followed by van Beek's reading (ed.).
2 The author of the *Passio* specifies 'fratres duos (II 2); but in Perpetua's own account her father says 'si te praeposui omnibus fratribus tuis' (V 2). 'Omnibus' might be taken to include Dinocrates, the brother who had died young; or 'fratribus' might be

intended in the sense 'brothers and sisters' (cf. *TLL*, s.v. *frater*); or again, Perpetua might have had other brothers of whom the *Passio* author was not aware.

3 In the somewhat later *Acta minora*, which draw upon the *Passio* and upon Perpetua's account within it, her husband is said to be of noble birth like her, and he is mentioned as coming with the whole of her family to the hearing, to join them in persuading Perpetua to choose life, not death. In Perpetua's own testimony in the *Passio*, however, there is no suggestion that her husband was present along with her family either when they visited her in prison (v) or before the procurator (vi) – in fact she makes no reference to him at any point in her narrative. This enigma could admit several possible solutions, which it may be worth setting out here, even though, in our present state of knowledge, no one possibility seems to impose itself decisively.

(i) The author of the *Acta minora* may have known a slightly fuller version of the *Passio*, in which Perpetua did mention her husband's visit in a way such as the *Acta* suggest. An early reviser of the *Passio* might have had a motive for suppressing Perpetua's sentences about her husband – if, for instance, he had been an unheroic Christian, who was prepared to compromise with the authorities on the matter of the civic sacrifice, this would have been embarrassing to include in a work designed to demonstrate 'fidei . . . nova documenta' (1 1).

(ii) Sentences of Perpetua's that referred to her husband may have been excised at a later stage in the textual tradition, at any time between 203 and the earliest extant MSS (*ca*. 900). This could have been, e.g., because a later reviser had in mind an idealized ascetic stereotype of women saints whose only thoughts near death were of God (a stereotype fulfilled *par excellence* by the virgin martyrs), and hence preferred to eliminate details about Perpetua's relations with her husband. It is perhaps significant that, in the later part of the *Passio*, Felicitas' husband is similarly ignored. It is even possible that one of the three scenes between Perpetua and her father – which in many ways are surprisingly similar – was originally an encounter with her husband, and that this was transformed.

In the thirteenth century Jacobus de Voragine, even though he clearly had Perpetua's own text before him when he wrote the *Legenda aurea* (ed. Th. Graesse (Leipzig ²1850) ch. 173, pp. 798–9), wanted to present her in coarsened hagiographic clichés. So he makes Perpetua reject her family violently – not only her 'most wretched husband, who will not be able to live on after you', but even her infant son, whom allegedly Perpetua 'hurls down'! She curses her family in biblical tones: 'Depart from me, you enemies of God, for I know you not!', whereupon the Prefect orders her and the other Christians to be 'whipped for a very long time'. These fictions, needless to say, increase Perpetua's holiness in Jacobus' eyes.

(iii) Dölger's conjecture (1930, p. 27), that Perpetua's husband was no longer alive, seems to me implausible. If he had died just before or after the birth of his child, it is scarcely conceivable that the author of the *Passio* would have written simply 'matronaliter nupta', and not something like 'nuper viduata'; and one would have to assume massive ignorance on the part of the *Acta* author (who is generally held still to have written in the third century).

(iv) Perpetua does not refer to her husband because he was absent from Carthage during the last weeks of her life, and took no part in any of the events she narrates. That is, the author of the *Acta* was misinformed, or simply, having no information save that Perpetua had been married, added a few words about her husband on his own initiative, where he felt these would be appropriate. This would be the most 'rational' explanation.

(v) Finally one cannot rule out the possibility of an emotional element in Perpetua herself, which led her to exclude her husband wholly from her thoughts while she was writing, even though he was alive and in Carthage at the time. Here many biographic speculations would be possible – that she had a 'father-fixation', or that she had become estranged from her husband even before her imprisonment, perhaps because he had resented her flaunting of Christianity, are two examples. Yet no speculation of this kind, however intriguing, has any real support in the surviving evidence.

4 *Passio* II 3.

5 A number of scholars have wished to identify the author – or better, redactor – of the *Passio* with Tertullian; for the literature discussing his identity, and the question of his possible Montanism, see J. Quasten, *Patrología* I 182–4.

6 *Passio* II 3 ('sicut conscriptum manu sua et suo sensu reliquit').

7 The original language of the *Passio* has been much debated by earlier scholars, but the problem, as Å. Fridh (1968) showed, is more complex than had hitherto been surmised. After a detailed study, Fridh came to the conclusion – which is accepted here – that 'tandis qu'il est désormais hors de doute que les deux parties du rédacteur et de Perpétue ont été rédigées primitivement en latin et traduites ensuite en grec . . . il nous semble très probable que le cas du récit de Saturus est le contraire' (*Le problème*, p. 80). Cf. also R. Petraglio, *Lingua latina* (1976) p. 13, approving Fridh's arguments. E. R. Dodds, *Pagan and Christian* (1965), still argued for a Greek original. Even if Perpetua, 'liberaliter instituta', had also learnt to read some Greek (and presumably spoke a local North African tongue, e.g. with servants), it seems clear since Fridh's work that Latin was the principal language of her everyday life.

8 E. Auerbach, *Literatursprache* pp. 49–53; Dodds, pp. 47–53; M.-L. von Franz, *Aion* pp. 389–496; G. Misch, *Geschichte* I 2, 519–20.

9 Michi autem spiritus *A* (et mihi Spiritus *ed.*).

10 longitudinis *A* (magnitudinis *ed.*).

11 libere in seculo *A* (libere *ed.*).

12 I.e. confessed to being Christians.

13 The Gate of the Living (Porta Sanavivaria): the gate by which gladiators who won their combat, or whose lives were spared, left the arena.

14 See below p. 45.

15 Cf. for instance Fredegisus (Jolivet, 'Quelque cas de "platonisme grammatical"' p. 96 n 28): 'God established things and names according to measure, so that they are necessary to one another.'

16 Cf. also U. and P. Dronke, 'The Prologue of the Prose Edda', esp. pp. 162–5.

17 This is the more radical notion of naming implicit, for instance, in the 'grammatical platonism' of Thierry of Chartres: 'Idcirco enim est homo, quia appellatur homo. Idcirco est animal, quia appellatur animal' (Jolivet p. 98 n 40).

18 *Acta* (ed. van Beek 1936) V 9; VI 3.

19 Compare the (possibly authentic?) expression attributed to her at *Passio* XX 8: 'Quando producimur ad vaccam illam nescioquam?'

20 Cf. the 'Testimonia' in van Beek 1936, pp. 149*ff.

21 L. Kretzenbacher, *Bilder* pp. 16–42.

22 Dio Cassius LX 23 (cit. *ibid.* p. 37).

23 M. Eliade, *Le chamanisme* pp. 423ff.

24 H. Kees, *Bibliothek Warburg Vorträge 1928–9* (Leipzig–Berlin 1930) p. 10.

25 Eliade pp. 419ff.

26 Chrétien de Troyes, *Lancelot (Le chevalier de la charrette)*, ed. M. Roques (Paris 1958) 3002ff; cf. H. Zimmer, *The King and the Corpse* (New York 1948) pp. 166ff; A. K. Coomaraswamy, *Selected Papers* I (Princeton 1977) 471 (and n 39), 479 (and n 83); L. Coomaraswamy, 'The Perilous Bridge of Welfare', *Harvard Journal of Asiatic Studies* VIII (1944) 196–213.

27 Eliade p. 420; cf. also pp. 389, 400.

28 At the close of the *Passio* (XXI 8), the redactor refers the climbing of the ladder to the moment of death, echoing the words from Perpetua's first vision: 'Saturus, qui et *prior ascenderat*, prior reddidit spiritum; nam et Perpetua *sustinebat*.'

29 Cf. esp. F. Dölger, 'Der Kampf' (1932) pp. 177–88.

30 *Pagan and Christian*, p. 51.

31 Cf. van Beek 1938, p. 20.

32 A number of scholars (including Musurillo, *Acts*, and E. C. E. Owen, *Some Authentic Acts of the Early Martyrs* (Oxford 1927)) have actually falsified Perpetua's text at this point, translating *caseum* as 'milk'. Admittedly the milk (of paradise) would sound more religious – but it is not what Perpetua dreamt.

33 Cf. *De gen. an.* I 729 a, II 739 b; Soranus (ed. V. Rose) pp. 125f; S. Ott, 'Aristotle among the Basques: the "Cheese Analogy" of Conception', *Man* (N.S.) XIV (1980) 699–711; 'Problemata' pp. 114–16.

34 Cf. *Scivias* I 4; 'Problemata' pp. 114f.

35 There is a special problem concerning Perpetua's brother Dinocrates, who had died at the age of seven. It seems far-fetched to suppose that, if the head of the family was a pagan and Dinocrates' older brother and sister had only just become catechumens, the child should, long before this, have been baptized. Nonetheless, St Augustine suggested that this was so, while at the same time calling the authenticity of Perpetua's narrative in question (*De an. et eius origine* I 10), and in our day scholars such as Dölger have claimed that Augustine's interpretation is plausible. But Augustine was not reading this text impartially: he held the harsh opinion that all unbaptized children were necessarily damned; therefore he thought, if there were any truth in Perpetua's vision of Dinocrates being brought relief in the otherworld, this could only be because Dinocrates had been baptized. But this perverse reasoning and special pleading should not encourage readers today to make an unwarranted inference from Perpetua's text.

36 The situation admits of one other possible interpretation (though I do not think it a very likely one): namely that Perpetua's mother, aunt, and non-catechumen brother (or siblings) were indeed secret Christians, but that the redactor of the *Passio* did not know this. That is, they could have been Christians of an unheroic kind, who outwardly continued to observe the state religion, and who, while they might be happy at Perpetua's courage and defiance, were afraid to emulate it themselves.

37 Cf. E. Auerbach, *Mimesis* chs. I–IV; *Literatursprache* ch. I (and Excursus).

38 F. Dölger, 'Antike Parallelen' (1930) pp. 1–40.

39 M. Alexiou, *Ritual Lament*, pp. 202–5.

40 *Conf.* VI ii, 2.

41 Cf. Alexiou p. 46.

42 *Elegiae* IV 5, 2.

43 *Aen.* VI 426ff, 445ff.

44 *Elegiae* II 6, 29ff.

45 Cf. e.g. Ovid, *Metam.* IV 458–9.

46 Nonetheless, Dölger (1930) is right that there is no specific sense of a Christian purgatory about the vision. Jacques Le Goff's recent suggestion (*La naissance du Purgatoire* (Paris 1981) p. 74), that in Perpetua we have 'le plus ancien texte où se profile l'imaginaire du Purgatoire', is a little misleading here, in that it forces the visionary elements towards a later and more conventional Christian pattern; this of course is exactly what Augustine was to do, two centuries after Perpetua. If one wishes, for instance, to see in Perpetua's phrase 'video ... Dinocratem mundo corpore, bene vestitum, refrigerantem' a reference to the early Christian notions of an otherworld *locus refrigerii* (thus Le Goff, p. 76), it is important to realize that Perpetua also uses *refrigerare* twice with an unequivocally earthly significance ('ut ... emissi in meliorem locum carceris refrigeraremus', III; 'ut et nos et illi invicem refrigeraremus', IX).

47 Assuming that the reading *trahebat* at VIII 3 is correct; Lazzati (1956) suggested reconstructing the Latin text here on the basis of the Greek: 'et aqua de ea fluebat ...'

48 *Oneirocriticon* III 40 (cit. Dölger (1930) p. 31).

49 John 4: 14.

50 Von Franz pp. 445ff.

51 These parallels were well noted by von Franz. But I cannot accept her further parallel, between the serpent and Dinocrates: she sees both as obstacles that Perpetua in her dreams must overcome for the sake of her spiritual progress (p. 454). I would suggest that Perpetua crushes or rejects the serpent, but accepts Dinocrates. Or better, she transforms the Dinocrates element in herself from something anguished into something liberated.

52 *Passio* XII 7. The passage is mistranslated by Musurillo (*Acts* p. 121): 'Thanks be to God that I am happier here now than I was in the flesh.'

53 There are two other sayings attributed to Perpetua that have a ring of authenticity, in *Passio* XVI 3 and XVIII 5. See also n 19 above.

54 The redactor of the *Passio* tells us later (XVI 4) that this governor became a believer.

55 Perpetua's Latin reads (x 1–4): 'Pridie quam pugnaremus, video in horomate hoc: venisse Pomponium diaconum ad ostium carceris et pulsare vehementer. Et exivi ad eum et aperui ei; qui erat vestitus discincta candida, habens multiplices galliculas. Et dixit mihi: "Perpetua, te expectamus, veni ... Noli pavere: hic sum tecum et conlaboro tecum." Et abiit.'

56 For the Vetus Latina, see D. de Bruyne, 'Les anciennes versions' pp. 98–104.

57 Van Beek 1938, p. 34, citing Tertullian (*De pallio* 4), explains that while all wrestlers were anointed with oil, some also chose to be smeared with mud (πήλωσις), others – like the Egyptian here – to be covered in dust (κόνισις).

58 Certain details of language make me suspect that Perpetua, before her conversion, had read Apuleius' *Metamorphoses*, the most notable literary work produced in her region a generation or so before her birth. Thus especially in Apuleius' amphitheatre episode (x 29ff) I am struck by such expressions as 'dies ... muneri destinatus' (cf. *Passio* VII 9), on which the woman criminal had been 'condemned to the beasts' ('quam dixi propter multiforme scelus bestiis esse damnatam', x 34; cf. *Passio* x 5 'ad bestias damnatam esse'). In this context in Apuleius there also occur the relatively rare words 'flexuosus' (x 29, though used of dance-movements, not of paths, as in *Passio* x 3),

and 'adtonitus' (x 35), used, as in Perpetua (x 5) to evoke the rapt absorption of spectators. Such indications are naturally not conclusive, and I would suggest at most faint memories of a book that Perpetua had firmly left behind. Yet one must remember that the whole of her literary education had been non-Christian, and even her imagery in this dream shows that she had learnt at least a little of the nature of the Egyptian's world – that this was for her no merely abstract concept of the sinful.

59 *Scalam ad caelos subrectam* (ed. W. von den Steinen, *Notker* II 90). Notker's intuitive insight here comprehends not only the non-Christian aspects of the imagery but also the congruence of Perpetua's first and last visions, which he fuses in his poem, showing the Egyptian and the serpent as threatening forces that are confronted in a single *agôn*. In my discussion of this sequence (*The Medieval Lyric*, pp. 41–4), the influence of Notker – or sheer absentmindedness – led me to make a garbled reference to Perpetua's original ('as she reaches the top an angel rewards her with an apple-bough', p. 42), which should be deleted; and in the misleading phrase 'Perpetua's angel with the apple-branch' (p. 43), the word 'fencing-master' should be substituted for 'angel'.

60 Von Franz p. 490.

61 *Passio* xx 4–5.

62 Von Franz p. 491.

63 Dölger (1932) shows that in a whole range of early Christian writing martyrdom is presented as a fight against the devil; yet I cannot agree with the conclusion he draws from this, 'that Perpetua moves totally in the line of thought of the North African Christians' (p. 187). For in the texts Dölger adduces the fight against the devil is a dead metaphor. Nowhere, save in Perpetua, is a combat imagined that is filled with fantastic oneiric elements. What Perpetua shares with the common line of thought is minimal.

64 Ed. Ruiz Bueno, *Actas* pp. 803ff.

65 *Literatursprache* p. 42.

66 Cf. P. Dronke, 'Medieval Rhetoric' pp. 319–22.

67 The texts are conveniently assembled in van Beek 1936, pp. 149*–161*.

68 See esp. *Literatursprache* pp. 66–83.

69 I omit from the discussion here the *Cento Vergilianus* of Proba (ed. K. Schenkl, CSEL xvi 568ff), composed *ca.* 360, an ingenious and spirited attempt to re-tell biblical episodes – from the Creation to Christ's birth, miracles and resurrection – using as far as possible a poetic diction borrowed directly from Vergil. The piece (694 hexameters) is comparable in scale to a Book of the *Aeneid*. In the adaptation of Vergilian language the author is astonishingly successful: even the fifteen verses of dedication, to the two sons of Theodosius I, are too august to reveal anything concretely about Proba herself.

70 Thus for instance D. Ruiz Bueno (ed.), *Cartas di San Jerónimo* I 319, or E. S. Duckett, *Women and their Letters* p. 12. Similarly J. N. D. Kelly, *Jerome: His Life, Writings, and Controversies* (London 1975) p. 141, speaks of this letter as 'written in the name of Paula and her daughter but manifestly by Jerome himself'. Paradoxically, he adds: 'It is an idyllic piece . . . and stands in striking contrast with [Jerome's] querulous, often vituperative note . . . during these years' (*ibid.*). The possibility does not seem to have occurred to Canon Kelly that the reason for this striking contrast might be that the letter is not 'manifestly' by Jerome at all, but by the two women to whom it is ascribed in the MS tradition.

71 Compare the acute discussion of the 'empty' or 'newsless' letters of John Donne, in J. Carey's recent article, *Essays and Studies* N.S. xxxiv (1981) 45–65.

72 *Ep.* 46, 10.

73 Cf. especially J. Leclercq, 'L'amitié dans les lettres' pp. 391–410; *The Love of Learning* pp. 226–8; and the section 'Love, Praise, and Friendship' in my *Medieval Latin* I 192–220.

74 Cf. J. Daniélou, *Sacramentum futuri*; E. Auerbach, 'Figura'.

75 In the brief observations that follow, my indebtedness to Spitzer's study (*Literaturstudien* pp. 871–912) will be evident. The emphasis here, however, is somewhat different from his, and I have chosen to focus on moments that Spitzer has not specifically discussed.

76 *Itinerarium* (ed. O. Prinz) I 1–2, XV 1–3, XVI 2–3:

> Interea ambulantes pervenimus ad quendam locum, ubi se tamen montes illi, inter quos ibamus, aperiebant et faciebant vallem infinitam, ingens, planissima et valde pulchram, et trans vallem apparebat mons sanctus Dei Syna. Hic autem locus, ubi se montes aperiebant, iunctus est cum eo loco, quo sunt Memoriae concupiscentiae. In eo ergo loco cum venitur . . .
>
> Tunc ergo quia retinebam scriptum esse babtizasse sanctum Iohannem in Enon iuxta Salim, requisivi de eo, quam longe esset ipse locus. Tunc ait ille sanctus presbyter: 'Ecce hic est in ducentis passibus. Nam si vis, ecce modo pedibus duco vos ibi. Nam haec aqua tam grandis et tam pura, quam videtis in isto vico, de ipso fonte venit.' Tunc ergo gratias ei agere coepi et rogare, ut duceret nos ad locum, sicut et factum est. Statim ergo cepimus ire cum eo pedibus totum per vallem amenissimam, donec perveniremus usque ad hortum pomarium valde amenum, ubi ostendit nobis in medio fontem aquae optime satis et pure, qui a semel integrum fluvium dimittebat . . . Tunc dixit nobis ipse sanctus presbyter: 'In hodie hic hortus aliter non appellatur greco sermone nisi *cepos tu agiu Iohanni*, id est quod vos dicitis latine hortus sancti Iohannis.' . . .
>
> Ac sic ergo et ibi gratias Deo agentes iuxta consuetudinem perexivimus iter nostrum. Item euntes in eo itinere vidimus vallem de sinistro nobis venientem amenissimam, quae vallis erat ingens, mittens torrentem in Iordanem infinitum. Et ibi in ipsa valle vidimus monasterium cuiusdam fratris nunc, id est monachi. Tunc ego, ut sum satis curiosa, requirere cepi, quae esset haec vallis . . .

77 That is, where the Israelites lie buried who were struck dead by God for having eaten quails (Num. II: 34).

78 *Ep.* 54, 13 (cf. H. Pétré's discussion in the 'Sources chrétiennes' ed. of Egeria, pp. 15–16; *sed contra*, the 1982 'Sources chrétiennes' ed., p. 26).

79 Paulina's poem is (apart from Proba's – cf. n 69 above) the only one known to me between the time of Perpetua and the end of the fourth century where scholars have agreed both on the dating and on the ascription. For the satire attributed to Sulpicia (*Epigr. Bob.* 37), see most recently H. Fuchs, *Discordia Concors* I 32ff. Another renowned composition of disputed date, the *Pervigilium Veneris*, has also been ascribed – in my view very plausibly – to an anonymous woman poet: the idea was briefly mooted by P. Boyancé, and has been developed with sensitive detailed discussion in the new edition by L. Catlow (*Pervigilium Veneris* (Collection Latomus 172, Bruxelles 1980)).

80 P. Courcelle, *Les lettres grecques en occident de Macrobe à Cassiodore* (Paris 1948) esp. pp. 3–4, 16–18.

81 *CE* III (cf. also A. B. Purdie, *Latin Verse Inscriptions* pp. 29–31). The epitaph is followed on the tombstone by a verse fragment in praise of Paulina, composed as if her husband were answering from the grave, which an admirer must have added after her death.

82 *Conf.* IX x, 23–4.

83 *Ep.* 23, 3. Notwithstanding the personal depth of Paulina's epitaph, we must also reckon with the possibility that a political purpose was implicit: a vindication, in defiance of Christian opinion, of the beliefs by which Praetextatus had lived. This, together with the rôle Praetextatus had played in restoring the pagan Altar of Victory in Rome, may help to account for the violence of Jerome's outburst.

84 *CIL* II 3596; GP 25. On the celebration of conjugal love in epitaphs, see especially R. Lattimore, *Themes* pp. 275ff; Purdie pp. 66ff. On the wish to follow a loved person into death, see Lattimore pp. 203ff.

85 Dessau 8142; GP 26.

86 Dessau 8453; GP 27.

87 *CIL* XII 5193; GP 476.

88 *CE* 66; GP 122.

89 Dessau 8283; GP 108.

90 *CE* 1979; Diehl 3885 A. On doubts about the afterlife in Latin inscriptions, see Lattimore pp. 59ff; on denials of an afterlife, *ibid.* pp. 78ff. Lattimore, commenting on this epitaph, suggests – against Lommatzsch – that 'the sense is entirely pagan' (p. 61; but cf. also his examples of doubt in Christian epitaphs, p. 320).

91 *CE* 1138 (a second couplet, more traditionally formulaic in language, follows); GP 47.

92 *CE* 1263; GP 530.

93 *CE* 537; GP 329.

94 *CE* 369; GP 82.

95 *L'oeuvre poétique de Paulin d'Aquilée* (Stockholm 1979) p. 76 n 12.

96 Diehl 3484; GP 486:

> Helpis dicta fui, Siculae regionis alumna,
>   quam procul a patria coniugis egit amor,
> quo sine maesta dies, nox anxia, flebilis hora,
>   nec solum caro sed spiritus unus erat.
> Lux mea non clausa est tali remanente marito,
>   maiorique animae parte superstis ero . . .

97 Cf. P. Riché, *Education* pp. 267–8.

98 See Gregory of Tours, *Hist. Franc.* VI 40; VIII 21, 28; Paulus Diaconus, *Hist. Langob.* III 21–2 (tr. W. D. Foulkes and E. Peters (Philadelphia 1974), notes *ad loc.*, pp. 125–6).

99 *CC* CXVII 466–7:

> Et quia, augusta tranquillisima, casu faciente, parvuli nepotis mei didicit peregrinare infantia et ipsa innocentia annis teneris coepit esse captiva, rogo per redemptorem omnium gentium, sic vobis non videatis subtrahi piissimum Theodocium, nec ab amplexu matris dulcis filius separetur, sic vestra lumina semper exhilaret sua praesentia, simul et matris viscera augusto delectentur de partu: ut iubeatis agere, favente Christo, qualiter meum recipere merear parvulum, in amplexu refrigerentur viscere, quae de nepotis absentia gravissimo dolore suspirant, ut, quę amisi filiam, vel dulce pignus ex ipsa,

quod mihi remansit, non perdam, adusque de morte geniti crucior, relever per vos cito nepote redeunte captivo: quatinus, dum me dolentem atque illum innocentem respicitis, et de Deo, qui est universalis redemptio, mercedem gloriae recipiatis, absoluto captivo, et inter utramque gentem per hoc, propitiante Christo, caritas multiplicetur et pacis terminus extendatur.

100 E.g. 'refrigerentur viscere' (for 'viscera').
101 *Opera poetica* (ed. F. Leo, MGH), App. xxxi; cf. Riché, *Education* p. 339.
102 *Epist.* 1 (MGH) 450–3.
103 *Opera poetica* xi 6.
104 See esp. E. Dutoit, *Le thème de l'adynaton dans la poésie antique* (Paris 1936); E. O. Sveinsson, 'The Poet Kormakr and his Verses', *Saga-Book* xvii (1966) 18–60.
105 A further couplet, which occurs in only one of the five MSS of Eucheria's poem, is probably a later addition – cf. H. Homeyer, *Dichterinnen* p. 185, who prints the poem p. 186.
106 *Vita S. Desiderii* 8 (CC cxvii 352).
107 CC cxvii 355.
108 So, too, the previous letter (*ibid.* p. 354) has 'Dulcissimo et desiderantissimo (*sic*) filio Desiderio'.
109 The reference in the phrase (*ibid.* p. 355) 'viriliter istam causam prosequere facias' is obscure: is the 'cause' simply the Christian life?
110 Otloh, *Vita Bonifacii* 25 (ed. W. Levison, *Vitae S. Bonifacii*, MGH, p. 138).
111 Tangl no. 143 (line-arrangement P.D.):

> Quid est, frater mi,
> quod tam longum tempus intermisisti,
> quod venire tardasti?
> Quare non vis cogitare,
> quod ego sola in hac terra
> et nullus alius frater visitet
> me, neque propinquorum aliquis ad me veniet? . . .
> O frater, o frater mi,
> cur potes mentem parvitatis meae
> adsiduae merore,
> fletu atque tristitia
> die noctuque
> caritatis tuae absentia adfligere?
> Nonne pro certo scies, quia viventium omnium
> nullum alium propono tuae caritati?
> Ecce non possum omnia per litteras tibi indicare.
> Iam ego certum teneo, quod tibi cura non est de mea parvitate.

The rhymes and assonances here, while not completely regular, seem much too extensive to be fortuitous: they are Berthgyth's attempt at a particular kind of verbal artistry. For the spelling of the names of Berthgyth, Balthard and Hugeburc, and of the women in Boniface's circle, I follow Tangl (who retains the forms from the Vienna MS used in his edition), rather than alter to Anglo-Saxon forms (Berhtgyþ, Bealdheard, Hygeburg, etc.).
112 Cf. Dronke, *The Medieval Lyric* p. 91, where the lament 'Wulf and Eadwacer' is

translated in full. The Anglo-Saxon text is in *The Exeter Book*, ed. G. P. Krapp and E. V. K. Dobbie (New York 1936) pp. 179–80, 'The Wife's Complaint' *ibid.* pp. 210–11.

113 Job 10: 1; Ps. 26: 10; Gen. 1: 10; Cant. 8: 6 (all cited in Tangl no. 147, *ad loc.*).
114 *Ep.* 3, 2.
115 Cf. e.g. Tangl nos. 9, 140, and my *Medieval Latin* I 196ff.
116 Compare Heloise's expressions, cited below p. 128.
117 Ed. Tangl, no. 148.
118 Ed. Tangl, no. 67 (also in R. Rau, *Briefe des Bonifatius* pp. 206ff).
119 E. Gottschaller, *Hugeburc*, esp. pp. 80–1.
120 Cf. B. Bischoff, 'Wer ist die Nonne von Heidenheim?', pp. 387f.
121 MGH *Scriptores* XVI 86–7.
122 I accept Gottschaller's suggestion (p. 16) that the reading *nenia* ('trifling') from the fourth group of MSS is probably correct, rather than the *venia* of the oldest MS. On 'apocrypha', compare also Hrotsvitha's comments (see below pp. 65–8).
123 I Cor. 15: 9.

2. Dhuoda

1 See *Manuel* pp. 12-15, 24-7. On the genre up to and including the Carolingian period, see esp. the fine synthesis by P. Hadot, 'Fürstenspiegel' 555ff; the fullest discussion of Carolingian examples is in H. H. Anton, *Fürstenspiegel*. Other aspects are illuminated by K. Bosl, 'Il "santo nobile"', in S. Boesch Gajano (ed.), *Agiografia* pp. 161–90; C. Erdmann, *Entstehung*, esp. pp. 10–29, 78–80; P. Riché, *De l'éducation antique* pp. 40–6, 87–9; J. Wollasch, 'Eine adlige Familie'.
2 Meyer, *Ges. Abh.* III 72 ('Dhuoda zu lesen, ist freilich unerfreulich. Ihr Text erinnert an den des Gregor von Tours').
3 The phrase belongs to the Painter in Jacques Prévert's scenario for the film *Quai des brumes* (dir. Marcel Carné).
4 Section IX of the *Manuel* (pp. 326–37) is devoted to this pastime.
5 *Manuel*, p. 22.
6 There with the addition of a fairy-tale motif, that he pretends to have the children killed.
7 *Manuel* p. 27.
8 On the textual problems of this chapter-division, which diverges in the three MSS, cf. *Manuel* pp. 53–9.
9 *Manuel* p. 72, 3ff. For all passages cited in this chapter, I have collated the Barcelona MS (Biblioteca Central 569 (= Ba)), and note any variants other than purely orthographic ones that are not recorded in Riché's edition. Here Ba (fol. 57va) has 'in tua specie tenus formam legendi dirigo gaudens. Quod si absens . . .' ('tuam . . . gaudens quod' ed.). While *tua* is probably a scribal error, the punctuation in Ba would give the sense: 'I am gladly sending you this little work . . . So that, since I am not physically present . . .'
10 *Manuel* p. 80, 2ff.
11 in fragili sexu *Ba* (sensu *ed.*).
12 Ed. A. Wilmart, *Analecta Reginensia* (Città del Vaticano 1933) p. 264.
13 *Monarchia* III xvi. Of the many discussions of the passage, I would signal especially

E. Gilson, *Dante the Philosopher* (London 1948) pp. 191–224, and B. Nardi, *Dal 'Convivio' alla 'Commedia'* (Roma 1960) pp. 282–313.

14 *Manuel* pp. 74, 32 – 76, 65. I give a text of the first seven couplets (Ba 57v*b*):

Centrum qui poli   contines girum,
Pontum et arva   concludis palmo –

Tibi comendo   filium Wilelmum:
Prosperum largiri   iubeas in cunctis;

Oris atque semper   currat momentis,
Te super omnem   diligat factorem.

Filiis cum tuis   mereatur felici
Concito gradu   scandere culmen;

In te suus semper   vigilet sensus
Pandens: per secla   vivat feliciter;

Iesus, nunquam ille   incidat in iram,
Neque separatus   oberret a tuis:

Iubilet iocundus   cursu felici,
Pergat cum virtute   fulgens ad supra . . .

'Oris atque . . . momentis' probably echoes St Paul, 1 Thess. 5: 1: later in these verses (51) Dhuoda cites the Pauline 'pax et securitas' from the same chapter (5: 3).

15 contines Ba (continens *ed.*).

16 I would construe as follows: 'currat semper, omnibus momentis atque horis, te diligat . . .' (Cf. D. Norberg, *La poésie latine* p. 15, who, however, read 'curras' for 'currat', and interpreted this as 'succurras').

17 vigiles sensus Ba (vigilet s. *ed.* – necessary as correction).

18 per secla Ba (per saecula *ed.* – but metrically the form in Ba is preferable).

19 indignam (indignā) Ba – probably rightly, in apposition to 'similem' in the previous verse (indigna *ed.*).

20 On these Provençal concepts, see especially G. Cropp, *Le vocabulaire courtois des troubadours de l'époque classique* (Genève 1975).

21 'Ein Merowinger Rythmus über Fortunatus und altdeutsche Rythmik in lateinischen Versen' (*Ges. Abh.* III 42–87). The pages on Dhuoda (72–85) seem to me still the most careful and illuminating analysis of her practice of versification. Though I have taken account of the observations of Norberg (*Introduction* pp. 147–8) and Riché (*Manuel*, *passim*), the brief remarks here and below owe most to Meyer.

22 On medieval adonics see especially M. Lapidge, *SM* 3a serie, XVIII (1977) 249–314.

23 *Manuel* p. 114, 2ff.

24 *Ibid.* pp. 114, 15 – 116, 40.

25 intuere Ba (survival of a common Merovingian spelling; intueri *ed.*).

26 *Manuel* p. 146, 57–60. Cf. p. 154, 28–9 ('deo et hominibus acceptabilis'), and p. 156, 72ff, where Joseph is brought on again, among others, as an exemplar of the most serviceable counsellors of princes ('utilissimi illi ad consilium').

27 *Manuel* p. 176, 54–8 (the passage may be inspired partly by 1 Tim. 5: 1–3); the following paragraph, *ibid.* 66ff.

28 *Ars minor*, ed. H. Keil, *Grammatici Latini* IV 360, 2–6.

29 due nativitates Ba (82v*b*); duo n. *ed.*

30 The text should read: 'aliquis dicit: *Cum quibus et sine quibus vivere non possumus*' (apłs *Ba*; the confusion with *ałs* is readily understandable). Riché, printing 'Apostolus' and emending to '*Cum quibus ⟨vivimus⟩* . . .', sought the quotation – in vain – in the writings of St Paul (*Manuel* p. 299 n 3).

31 Ovid, *Amores*, ed. G. Lee (London 1968) III xi b, 1–7, in Lee's translation.

32 *Manuel* p. 344, 34ff.

33 *Ibid.* pp. 82, 28–32; 84, 1ff.

34 Concurrents: 'to each year was allotted by the computists a number (1 to 7) which represents the concurrents, or number of days between the last Sunday in the preceding year and the first of January' (C. R. Cheney, *Handbook of Dates* (London 1945) p. 9).

35 palacii *Ba* (palatio *ed.* – perhaps acceptable as a correction, though I do not think we can rule out Dhuoda's using gen. for abl.; on her use of cases, cf. *Manuel* pp. 41–2).

36 *Manuel* p. 84, 14ff.

37 Riché notes that both MSS of this passage have 'tuo . . . aspectum', and emends to 'aspectu'; but the confusion of abl. and acc., common in eighth- and ninth-century Latin, is found elsewhere in Dhuoda (cf. p. 41), so that emendation is not desirable.

38 meus valde marcessit animus *Ba* (valde *om. ed.*).

39 This is the text in *Ba*, fol. 58vb (utrorumque *ed.*). The MS reading is defensible: lit. 'out of longing for each of the two of you'.

40 *Manuel* p. 98, 2ff. In the last phrase cited, the Ba reading (noted *ed.*), 'ex tuo desiderio', should be retained (ex suo d. *ed.*). The sentence continues in Ba: 'psaltim ut sub mensa illius . . . possim procul conspicere catulos' (mensam *ed.*).

I would point out the extent to which Dhuoda here uses refrain-like phrases: e.g. 'Certe et ego' (cf. p. 96, 14); 'fragilis ad umbram' (cf. p. 104, 1); 'per omnia' (*passim*); 'indesinenter' (cf. p. 96, 16).

41 Particularly striking is the verbal analogy between Gregory (ed. H. Morf, *Auswahl aus den Werken des Gregor von Tours* (Heidelberg 1922) p. 4):

> *Potest enim*, ut credo, per meae linguae ista proferre, *qui ex arida cute in* heremo producens aquas, populi sitientis extinxit ardorem; aut certe constabit, eum rursus *os* asinae reserare, si labia mea *aperiens* per me indoctum ista dignetur expandere

and Dhuoda's

> *Potens est enim* ille *qui os* animalis muti loqui fecit, mihi secundum suam priscam clementiam *aperire* sensum . . .

42 *Manuel* p. 126, 18–23.

43 *Ibid.* pp. 310, 2ff; 318, 71ff; 320, 10ff.

44 *Ibid.* pp. 134, 17ff; 140, 2ff. The words italicized are from Ecclus. 3: 14–15.

45 *Ibid.* p. 346, 2.

46 *Ibid.* p. 348, 10–14.

47 Licet in me consistat *Ba* (86va) (L. i. m. ita consistat *ed.*).

48 See above, p. 31; the strophe cited is from the early eleventh-century song *Levis exsurgit Zephirus* (text with transl. and discussion in my book *The Medieval Lyric*, pp. 92–4).

49 *Manuel* p. 348, 2ff.

50 Precurrentium tempora *Ba* (Per recurrentium t. *ed.*, giving the Ba reading as 'per currentium t.'). I construe 'tempora precurrentium [annorum]' as an acc. of time how long, dependent on 'remansi'.

51 Riché takes this to refer to the hours of the divine office.

52 While Riché notes the verbal parallel in Gen. 7: 2, perhaps the references to recovery and forgiveness – Prov. 24: 16 and Mt. 18: 22 – are even more relevant to Dhuoda's thought here.

53 II Cor. 11: 26.

54 *Manuel* p. 350, 35–8.

55 For the expression, 'recuperatio', compare 'recuperetur' used in an eschatological sense at p. 332, 4.

56 This probably refers to the churchmen whom William can enlist to pray for Dhuoda too.

57 *Mis*, the archaic form of the gen. *mei*, known to Dhuoda from Donatus, is used here for added emphasis (see Riché *ad loc.*, who also notes the echo of this verse in the later passage).

3. Hrotsvitha

1 See especially B. Nagel, *Hrotsvit von Gandersheim*, and, for more recent work, the fine survey by D. Schaller, 'Hrotsvit' pp. 105–14. Since Schaller's essay, the most important work has been that of two Italian scholars: G. Vinay, *Alto medioevo latino* pp. 483–554, and F. Bertini, *Il 'teatro' di Rosvita*.

2 This claim is based on the closing lines of the legend *Theophilus*, which Homeyer (*Opera* p. 152), following Lehmann (*Erforschung des Mittelalters* III (Stuttgart 1960) 126), sees as a 'grace after meals (*Tischsegen*)'. While the legends could indeed have been read aloud at meals, both in the refectory at Gandersheim and elsewhere, I do not think this can be safely inferred from the *Theophilus* lines. In these, Hrotsvitha plays on the language of a *Tischsegen*, but even more on the much-cherished metaphorics of 'spiritual food' (see esp. K. Lange, 'Geistliche Speise', *ZfdA* XCV (1966) 81–122). That is, when Hrotsvitha bids Christ to 'benignly consecrate the dishes of the table I have proffered, making these banquets wholesome for those who taste them' (*Theophilus* 452–3), the primary meaning of the dishes and the banquets is the metaphorical one: they are Hrotsvitha's compositions.

3 Bertini p. 9.

4 That she should have the same name as Hrotsvitha I by pure coincidence, or by adoption, seems less probable. It may also be significant that she concludes her last poem, on the 'primordia Gandesheimensis . . . coenobii', with the reign of Hrotsvitha I's predecessor, Cristina (896–919), the youngest daughter of the founders, Liudolf and Oda: a certain reticence to go on to celebrate her own namesake would be understandable if she was also a kinswoman.

5 R. R. Bezzola, *Les origines* I 248.

6 On Hrotsvitha's rhymed prose, the discussion in K. Polheim, *Die lateinische Reimprosa* (1925), remains, in its wealth of detail, unsuperseded. There are many extensive, though unsystematic, uses of rhymed prose in earlier centuries – in Apuleius, in Augustine (especially the homilies), in Venantius Fortunatus' *Vita Radegundis*, in the sermons of Hrabanus Maurus, and in the brilliant homily of Scotus Eriugena on the Prologue of John (cf. *Jean Scot Erigène et l'histoire de la philosophie*, ed. R. Roques (Centre National de Recherche Scientifique, Paris 1977), pp. 243–52). Yet no one before Hrotsvitha employed rhymed prose so elaborately and consistently, and with such lavish use of 'rich' rhymes as well as assonances. It is in this last point that the link

with Rather is particularly interesting. Compare, for example, in his *Excerptum ex dialogo confessionali* (P.L. 136, 397 C – 398 C, line-arrangement P.D.):

> Confiteor etiam ipsi   Domino Deo omnipotenti,   quod his et plus his   omnibus voluptatum foedatus   flagitiis,   et contagionibus fuscatus   omnimodis,   semper sine ulla mentis sinceritate,   corporis et sanguinis sacramentum Domini,   fateor, percipi   indigne . . .
> Praeter haec peccavi iocando, equitando,   ambulando, stando,   se-dendo   sive iacendo,   et in his et in aliis   omnibus vitiis . . .

On rhymed prose in Rather's letters, see F. Weigle, 'Die Briefe Rathers von Verona, *DA* I (1937) 147–94; some letters – notably *Epp*. 1–6, 19, 20–3 – have consistent rhyme throughout ('völlig durchgereimt', p. 187). On Hrotsvitha's having received tuition from men (*magistri*) as well as women teachers, see n 46 below.

7 *Opera* p. 227. Cf. E. Cerulli, *Studia Islamica* XXXII (1970) 69–76.

8 In view of Hrotsvitha's precise wording, it is out of the question that she received the information 'through the mediation of her abbess' – as Homeyer (*Opera*, p. 124) thought possible; it is also highly unlikely that Hrotsvitha had, as Homeyer claims, 'not the oral report alone' but written information on the background of the events: this would make nonsense of Hrotsvitha's levelheaded and decisive contrast between oral and written sources.

9 Unfortunately Hrotsvitha's informant seems not to have explained to her the precise nature of Islamic religious observance, for when she touches on this in her poem she merely adopts Christian caricatures (e.g. making the Moslems into idol-worshippers), such as she would have found in polemic writings, or indeed could have picked up by hearsay in northern Europe, without the help of a Cordovan.

10 *Ruotgeri Vita S. Brunonis* 8, in *Lebensbeschreibungen einiger Bischöfe des 10.–12. Jahrhunderts*, ed. I. Ott, tr. H. Kallfelz (Darmstadt 1973) p. 190.

11 Despite the long customary tradition of naming several of Hrotsvitha's plays after men and not women characters (*Dulcitius*; *Calimachus*; *Abraham*; *Pafnutius*), I believe it is important, because of Hrotsvitha's emphasis on feminine protagonists, to return to her own nomenclature. Her second, third, fourth and fifth plays are entitled, respectively, *Passio sanctarum virginum Agapis Chioniae et Hirenae*; *Resuscitatio Drusianae et Calimachi*; *Lapsus et conversio Mariae neptis Habrahae heremicolae*; and *Conversio Thaidis meretricis*; the last play, commonly known as *Sapientia*, is entitled *Passio sanctarum virginum Fidei Spei et Karitatis*.

12 Ed. K. Strecker, MGH *Poetae* IV 1088–90; the text is also in Winterfeld pp. xx–xxiii.

13 '*Nunc Terentius exit foras audiens haec et ait.*'

14 Cit. W. Creizenach, *Geschichte des neueren Dramas* (3 vols., Halle ²1911–23), I 3. The passage occurs in the Prologue of a Life of St Mary of Cappadocia, written *ca*. 1180 by a monk Reinerus, at St Laurent in Liège (ed. B. Pez, *Thesaurus Anecdotorum Novissimus* (Augsburg 1721) IV iii, 83ff). Reiner (p. 85) claims that 'Frater etenim quidam pueris sive adolescentibus Terentium legebat. Sed scenica lectio plus obesse quam prodesse auditoribus infirmis solet.' In delirium (*extasis*), the master receives a warning threat from St Laurence, 'quod ludicris sordidaretur, dum comico uteretur'. This last phrase in particular suggests that the *scenica lectio* was no dispassionate textual study, but that the possibilities of *ludicra* were indeed exploited.

15 Bertini p. 108 (Homeyer, following Winterfeld, emends 'Expaveo' to 'Expavete').

16 See esp. the fine study by E.-R. Labande, 'Mirabilia mundi: Essai sur la personnalité d'Otton III', *CCM* VI (1963) 297–313, 455–76.

17 *Dichtung* pp. 91–104.

18 The two plays, however, are very different in characterization and tone. The holy man of the desert, shown as gently doting and fatherly in the first play, is a relentless, tormenting crusader in the second. Where Mary, the first heroine, is converted lovingly, Thais is humiliated and crushed. The second play is also distinguished by its didactic opening, Pafnutius teaching his disciples the theory of musical harmony; this at first sight irrelevant prelude serves to enrich the close with the theme of cosmic harmony ('caeli concentus', XII 6), extending to the Neoplatonic 'return' of souls ('felici reditu ad te reverti ... repetere principium sui originis', XIII 2-3 – cf. Boethius *Cons.* III m. 9, 20-1).

19 *Gong.* 570ff (*Opera* p. 122). In the Merovingian *Vita Gangulfi Martyris Varennensis* (ed. W. Levison, *Script. Rer. Merov.*, MGH, VII 142ff), Gongolf's wife speaks her mocking vow on a Friday, and thereafter every Friday must fart as many times as the words she speaks (p. 167).

20 'Dixerat' – Hrotsvitha here parodies epic style (cf. e.g. *Aen.* IV 331).

21 'Oh wanton boy, with impunity you make a boast of spurning . . .' (cf. e.g. *Anth. Graeca* XII 22).

22 *Dichtung* pp. 98f.

23 *Opera* p. 376.

24 See esp. O. B. Hardison Jr, *Christian Rite and Christian Drama in the Middle Ages* (Baltimore 1965) pp. 192ff; J. Drumbl, *Quem quaeritis* (Roma 1981) pp. 82ff.

25 See P. Aebischer, 'Le "Cant de la Sibil·la" . . .', in his *Neuf études sur le théâtre médiéval* (Genève 1972), esp. pp. 23f.

26 While we do not know the date of her death, there is no record of Hrotsvitha later than 973. It is ironic to recall that in 1007 Gandersheim, after sixty years of full independence under the rule of its abbesses, was made – despite fierce resistance – a dependency of the diocese of Hildesheim.

27 *In honorem Hludowici* (Ermold le Noir, ed. and tr. E. Faral (Paris ²1964)) 2062-3.

28 *Opera* pp. 37-9.

29 Cf. T. Janson, *Latin Prose Prefaces* p. 141.

30 1. *Dedicatio* 7-8 (*Opera* p. 40).

31 2. *Dedicatio* 5-6 (*Opera* p. 176).

32 *Basilius* 9-13 (*Opera* p. 177).

33 *Opera* p. 227.

34 Cf. E. Jeauneau, '"Pierre Abélard à Saint-Denis"', in *Abélard en son temps: Actes du colloque international . . .* (Paris 1981) pp. 161-73.

35 A detailed study of the presence of classical authors in the works of Rather and Liutprand would be rewarding. Whilst for Rather's letters there is a fine 'Verzeichnis der Zitate' in F. Weigle's edition (MGH, pp. 205-9), there is nothing comparable for Liutprand, though the recent edition of his works (in A. Bauer and R. Rau, *Quellen zur Geschichte der sächs. Kaiserzeit* (Darmstadt 1971)) has a number of valuable parallels in the notes, signalling, *inter alia*, the Terentian adaptations in the *Legatio*.

36 Cf. J. Grimm, A. Schmeller, *Lateinische Gedichte des X. und XI. Jh.* (Göttingen 1838), p. ix.

37 It is not likely that Hrotsvitha had read Plautus (though see also n 57 below); but her play on Terence's phrase, *Andria* 218 – *amentium, haud amantium* – is deliberate, and should be noted in the editions.

38 I have gathered a range of classical and medieval examples in *Medium Aevum* XXXIII (1964) 50.
39 Cf. *Opera* p. 496.
40 Cf. *Opera* pp. 494ff; some interesting new parallels between Hrotsvitha and earlier poets (including Lucan, Ovid, Venantius Fortunatus, and several Carolingians) are suggested in Schaller, 'Hrotsvit'.
41 This point was well observed by Vinay p. 511.
42 *Lapsus et conversio Mariae* (= *Abraham*) IX 5.
43 *Opera* pp. 235-7.
44 The word is 'humilitas' (glossed by Winterfeld, p. 346, as 'Herablassung'). It is the earliest recorded instance of this 'courtly' sense, which was to become widespread in vernacular love-poetry (see the excursus 'The Concept *umiltà*' in my *Medieval Latin* I 158-62).
45 'Dictatiuncula' appears to be attested before Hrotsvitha only in Jerome, *Contra Vig.* 3 (P.L. 23, 341-2), in a context of violent polemic about clerical chastity. Hrotsvitha will have known the passage, and sensed the mock-modesty of Jerome's diminutives, 'dictatiuncula' and 'lucubratiuncula' (*ibid.*).
46 This key-word, 'magistrorum', must on no account be emended to 'magistrarum' (K. Strecker *Hrotsvithae Opera* (Leipzig ²1930) *ad loc.*), or translated 'Lehrerinnen' (Homeyer *ad loc.*). Even if in this context we construe it as being of common rather than masc. gender, it is surely a testimony not to be rejected that Hrotsvitha had received tuition from men as well as women teachers. This point of text and translation is a small but revealing instance of how the 'cloistered nun' image could blind even distinguished specialists.
47 Jerome to Paulinus of Nola, *Ep.* 53, 2-3 (not only the occurrence of the two Greek words but also the context makes Hrotsvitha's knowledge of this passage likely).
48 *Parzival* 115, 21-34; 782, 5-12.
49 *Cons.* I pr. 1, 5 ('Eandem tamen vestem violentorum quorundam sciderant manus, et particulas quas quisque potuit abstulerant').
50 *Prologus* 26-9 (*Opera* pp. 387f).
51 I suggest there is no good reason for disbelieving Hrotsvitha's central statement in her letter to Gerberga, that she had no written sources for the *Gesta Ottonis*. Homeyer (*Opera* p. 390) argues that 'for the events in a time-span of over forty years she could not have relied on oral tradition alone; the correct chronological ordering of the events suggests that she used a chronicle', even if this was complemented by oral reports. In my view this, apart from doing violence to Hrotsvitha's explicit testimony, underestimates her powers of organizing material independently. It also takes no account of the possibility of her presence at court. Insofar, for instance, as some passages in the *Gesta* are paralleled in the works of Liutprand, the reason for this could be personal acquaintance rather than literary borrowing.
52 *Opera* pp. 385-6.
53 'Varietate': cf. Ps. 44: 10.
54 'Pigescat': the frequentative *pigescere* appears to be unrecorded elsewhere.
55 *Archicancellarie, vir discrete mentis* (*Die Gedichte des Archipoeta*, ed. H. Watenphul and H. Krefeld (Heidelberg 1958) IV). As E. H. Zeydel ('Knowledge of Hrotswitha's Works' p. 383) pointed out, a note in the Chronicle of the Bishops of Hildesheim states that Hrotsvitha wrote a poem about all the deeds of the three Ottonian emperors

(*Scriptorum Brunsvicensia . . . illustrantium*, ed. G. W. Leibniz (Hanover 1710) II 787: 'scripsit . . . trium Imperatorum Ottonum res gestas omnes'). Yet this chronicle is not from the eleventh century, as Zeydel claimed: its entries go as late as 1573 (*ibid.* II 806); thus there is no compelling reason to trust this detail and postulate a continuation of the *Gesta Ottonis* that has not survived. Again, the testimony might tempt one to speculate about Hrotsvitha's possible authorship of the lyrical sequence, 'Modus Ottinc' (*Carmina Cantabrigiensia*, ed. K. Strecker, MGH, no. 11), which in fact dwells on all three Ottos; on the other hand, it is far too brief a composition to be said to cover 'res gestas omnes'.

56 H. Delehaye, *Etude sur le légendier romain* (Bruxelles 1936), pp. 163, 168f.

57 *Passio . . . Agapis* (= *Dulcitius*) I 6; cf. also *Passio . . . Fidei* (= *Sapientia*) V 17. The word *conquiniscere* (to crouch, cower, or bow the head) occurs twice in Plautus, once in Priscian, citing verses from the oldest *fabula atellana*, and once in an epitome of Julius Valerius on Alexander; it does not seem to be attested elsewhere (see *TLL*, s.v.). In terms of transmission of texts, it is clearly likelier that Hrotsvitha had seen Priscian or the Alexander epitome than Plautus – but much that regards the sources of her diction still awaits detailed investigation.

58 *Passio . . . Agapis* XIV 3 (*Opera* p. 277).

59 *Praef.* 5 (*quia nec matura adhuc aetate vigens, / nec scientia fui proficiens*).

60 *Lapsus* (= *Abraham*) VII 15ff. Did Hrotsvitha get her unusual expression for 'dawn' (*matuta*) from Odo of Cluny's *Occupatio*, where it occurs twice (see *NG*, s.v.), rather than from Prudentius (*Symm.* II 562) or Ovid (*Fasti* VI 479)? The occurrence in Lucretius (V 656), cited by Homeyer along with Prudentius, should be discounted.

61 *Ecl.* X 49 (first noted by Vinay, p. 551); *Aen.* I 327.

62 *Primordia* 185–226 (*Opera* pp. 457–8).

63 Cf. Homeyer, *Opera* p. 457.

64 *Gesta Ottonis*, *Praef.* I (*Opera* p. 385).

65 D. H. Lawrence, 'Song of a man who has come through' (*Collected Poems*, 1932).

66 Cf. esp. M. Schapiro, *Late Antique, Early Christian and Medieval Art* (New York 1979) pp. 67–142.

67 H. Menhardt, 'Eine unbekannte Hrotsvitha-hs.' 233–6; B. Jarcho, *Speculum* II (1927) 343f; Zeydel pp. 382–5.

68 See below, pp. 85ff.

69 See below, pp. 91ff, and my discussion of the new edition of the *Carmina Ratisponensia*, ed. A. Paravicini (Heidelberg 1979), in *Sandalion* V (1982) 109–17.

4. Personal Poetry by Women: The Eleventh and Twelfth Centuries

1 Ed. Rosalie Green *et al.*; cf. also J. Autenrieth, 'Bemerkungen'.

2 *Die Dichtungen*, 'Das Jüngste Gericht' st. 35 (p. 68).

3 See Bibliography below, p. 329.

4 A few suggestions in Dronke, *Poetic Individuality* pp. 150ff.

5 Thus Manitius III 888 n 1 (though it also seems possible that in poem 142, ed. Hilbert, Baudri means he is Constance's spiritual father in a less specific sense).

6 O. Schumann, 'Baudri' pp. 162–3; F. J. E. Raby, *Secular Latin Poetry* I 344 n 1.

7 Hilbert 200, 51f.

8 Hilbert 137.

9 Ed. W. Bulst, 'Liebesbriefgedichte Marbods'; cf. my *Medieval Latin* I 213–16.

10 The poem is the short piece (thirteen leonine hexameters) entitled *Puella ad amicum munera promittentem* (ed. W. Bulst, *Carmina Leodensia* p. 16). Following Delbouille, I had formerly attributed this poem to Gautier, a friend of Marbod's. This attribution has now been disproved by Bulst (see esp. p. 26), and the lines must be seen as anonymous. That they were copied in the MS Liège 77 (s. XI/XII) which was presented *to* Marbod rules out the possibility of their being by Marbod himself (though they turn up among the love-verses in his *editio princeps* (Rennes 1524)).

11 III 888.

12 *De virginitate* (*Carmina*, ed. F. Leo, MGH, VIII 3) 227ff. Cf. W. Schmid, in *Fs. Günther Jachmann* (Köln–Opladen 1959) pp. 253–63.

13 Cf. esp. W. Bulst, 'Radegundis an Amalafred'. There are some recent observations in F. A. Consolino, '*Amor spiritualis . . .*' pp. 1351–68. Consolino discusses Fortunatus' verses, and also mentions Baudri's to Constance (pp. 1365–7), though she fails to see the humorous elements in the two poets.

14 To suggest that Fortunatus was merely writing in Radegunde's name (thus, e.g., J. Szövérffy, *Weltliche Dichtungen* I 281: 'Wir haben überhaupt keinen Grund anzunehmen, dass Radegunde je gedichtet hat') is inappropriate, since Fortunatus (*App.* XXXI) refers explicitly to poems of hers that Radegunde had sent him (see above p. 28).

15 *Appendix carminum* I and III.

16 See esp. P. Lehmann, *Pseudo-Antike Literatur des Mittelalters* (Leipzig 1927).

17 Cf. A. Hofmeister, 'Puer, Iuvenis, Senex', in *Fs. Paul Kehr* (München 1926), pp. 287–316.

18 Thus D. Schaller, 'Probleme', p. 31, announcing a forthcoming documentation by W. Bulst. Meanwhile Hilbert, p. 338, has distinguished between *Constantia domina*, to whom poem 200 is dedicated, and *Constantia virgo*, the recipient of poem 142. This, in the absence of specific evidence, seems far-fetched (as Hilbert himself appears to sense in his cautionary note on p. 333). Hilbert further suggests that there may have been a third Constantia in Baudri's life: the subject of the epitaph 213, according to him, is '*eadem aut alia*'. If *domna* Constantia (who was, presumably, *virgo*) was still alive in 1129, then this poem must have been composed in the last year of Baudri's life. It is much to be hoped that Bulst's promised discussion will resolve these questions. Provisionally, it seems safest to reckon with not more than one Constantia.

19 Hilbert 200, 12, 14; the passages cited in translation below are from this poem and from Constance's reply (*ibid.* 201).

20 E. R. Curtius, *Europ. Lit.* Excursus XIII.

21 Hilbert 137, 37.

22 Hilbert 99, 181ff.

23 *Her.* x 9ff; XIII 103ff (cf. my discussion in 'Learned Lyric', *SM* 3a serie XVII (1976) 5ff).

24 The passage is discussed below, p. 118

25 See Schaller, 'Probleme', p. 26 n 7.

26 *Cant.* 2: 5; 5: 8.

27 *Her.* I 2.

28 *Ibid.* VI 126.

29 *Carmina Ratisponensia*, ed. A. Paravicini (Heidelberg 1979); I have discussed the localization and dating of the verses, and a series of textual points, in *Sandalion* v (1982)

109–17. The Regensburg verses concerned with love are also edited and translated in my *Medieval Latin* II 422–47, and discussed *ibid.* I 221–9.

30 *Ruodlieb* XIV 52–80. (A new critical ed., by B. Vollmann, is in preparation; meanwhile the most accessible text is the Reclam one of F. P. Knapp (Stuttgart 1977).)

31 Paravicini 44, *Medieval Latin* xxxiii.

32 *Medieval Latin* xxxi (Paravicini 40, reading 'carnem' for 'carmen' in the fourth line cited).

33 Paravicini 22, *Medieval Latin* xvii.

34 'Nachtrag' pp. 282–9.

35 *Ibid.* p. 288.

36 *Epistolae* 49–50 (ed. Könsgen pp. 25–8; see in Bibliography, under Anonymous).

37 *Ibid.* p. 103 (emphasis Könsgen's).

38 *Her.* xx 80–90.

39 Cf. also *Epistolae* 87, 33ff.

40 Here the last words ('tu es ego et ego sum tu') are very close to some in a play of Plautus (*Stichus* 727–31), where the slave Stichus claims he is one with his rival, Sangarius, since both have a passion for the same girl. Yet the bawdy mirth of Stichus' song is far from the Troyes letter, and the verbal resemblance – noted by Könsgen *ad loc.* – may be a coincidence only. (On Plautine echoes in medieval Latin texts, see esp. M. Manitius, *Philologus* Suppl. VII (1900) 758ff.)

41 The Pauline allusions (noted by Könsgen) are, respectively, II Tim 4: 7; I Cor 9: 24; II Cor 12: 2.

42 At least another pentameter (and perhaps other elegiac couplets also) will have preceded the two valedictory verses, which are leonine hexameters, and the concluding words, which are in prose: 'Have pity on me, for I am truly fettered by my love for you. Farewell.'

43 See below p. 117.

44 Cf. Dronke, *The Medieval Lyric*, pp. 83f.

45 Neither the old collection, by O. Schultz (1888) – still indispensable for its critical apparatus – nor the welcome modern one of M. Bogin (1976) is quite complete: neither includes Azalaïs d'Altier or Germonda, or all the poems by anonymous *trobairitz* (see Bibliography pp. 321, 325).

46 Cf. G. Contini, *Poeti del Duecento* I 433: 'comunque, l'autenticità del personaggio non sembra facilmente revocabile in dubbio'; her texts, *ibid.* I 434–8.

47 Cf. the judicious discussion by Margit Frenk Alatorre, *Las jarchas mozárabes.*

48 Schultz 15 (p. 28). There are also some twelfth-century Latin love-letters between women, ed. in my *Medieval Latin* II 478–81.

49 I cite from the English translation: *Brigitte Bardot* (London 1960) pp. 17, 21.

50 Boutière–Schutz p. 498:

> Bels dous amics, ben vos puosc en ver dir
> Qe anc no fo q'eu estes ses desir,
> Pos vos conuc ⟨ni⟩·us ⟨pris⟩ per fin aman;
> Ni anc no fo q'eu non agues talan,
> Bels douz amics, q'eu soven no·us veses,
> Ni anc no fo sasons qe m'en pentis;
> Ni anc no fo, si vos n'anes iratz,
> Q'eu agues joi, tro qe fosetz tornatz;
> Ni anc . . .

51 I believe it was a strophe, rather than simply *distiques* (thus I. Frank, *Répertoire* II 213) –
for these would presuppose a rhyme 'veses' / 'pentis'.

52 *De vulg. eloq.* II vii.

53 Boutière–Schutz pp. 422–3:

> Dompna N'Almue⟨i⟩s, si·ous.plages,
> Be·us volgra prejar d'aitan:
> Qe l'ira e·l mal talan
> Vos fezes fenir merces
> De lui, qe sospir' e plaing
> E muor languen e·s complaing
> E qier perdon humilmen;
> Qe·us fatz per lui sagramen,
> Si tot li voletz fenir,
> Q'el si gart meils de faillir.
>
> Dompna N'Iseuz, s'ieu saubes
> Q'el se pentis de l'engan
> Q'el a fait vas mi tan gran,
> Ben fora dreichz q'eu n'agues
> Merces; mas a mi no·s taing,
> Pos qe del tort no s'afraing
> Ni·s pentis del faillimen,
> Qe n'aia mais chausimen;
> Mas si vos faitz lui pentir,
> Leu podes mi convertir.

54
> A⟨lais⟩
> Na Carenza, al bel cors avinen,
> Donatz conseil a nos doas serors,
> E, car sabetz meils triar lo meillors,
> Conseillatz mi segon vostr' escïen:
> 5 Penr*ai* marit, a *v*ostra conoissenza,
> O starai mi pulcela? – e si m'agenza,
> Que far filhos no cug qu*e* sia bos,
> *E* ses marit mi par trop angoissos.
>
> ⟨Yselda⟩
> Na Carenza, penre marit m'agenza,
> 10 Mas far enfantz cug qu'es grans penedenza,
> Que las tetinhas pendon aval jos,
> E·l ventrilhs es aruats *e* enojos.
>
> C⟨arenza⟩
> N'Alais i Na Yselda: ensenhamen,
> Pretz e beltat, joven, frescas colors
> 15 Conosc qu'avetz, cortezi' e valors,
> Sobre totas las autras conoissen;
> Per qu'ie·us conseil, per far bona semenza,
> Penre marit Coronat de Scienza,

En cui faretz fruit de filh glorïos:
20 Retengud' es pulcel' *a* qui l'espos.

N'Alaïs *i* Na Yselda, sovinenza
Ajatz de mi, i *l*'umbra de ghirenza;
Quan i seretz, prejatz lo glorïos
Qu'al departir mi retenga pres vos.

The MS, Q, has the letter *A* (= Alais) in margin before 1, *C* (= Carenza) before 13;
the *C* has not been noticed by any editor, nor has the significance of the *A* been seen.

3 saubez Q (saubes *Schultz*) la meilors Q (lo m. *Schultz*) 4 secundu uostra scienç Q
5 Penre Q (*em. Schultz*) nostra Q (*em. Levy*) 7 qui Q (que *Schultz*) 8 Essens Q
(*em. Levy*) 9–12 after 13–20 Q (*em. Bogin*) 11 tetinas si penden Q 12 El los
uentril aruat en noios Q 13 Nalaisina yselda Q (*em. Bogin*) 20 Retengutas pulsela
da quil spuse Q (*em. Schultz*) 21 Nalascina yselda Q 22 illumbra Q 23 los g. Q
(lo g. *Schultz*)

I have based my text on a photograph of the page in Q (Firenze, Bibl. Riccardiana
2909, s. XIV, fol. 42v*b*), most kindly lent me by Peter Ricketts. (The diplomatic text
of K. Bartsch, *ZfrP* IV (1880) 510f, is not wholly accurate.) In the main I follow the
normalizations of spelling in the edition of O. Schultz (p. 28); I list all departures from
Q other than purely orthographic ones. I also adopt several emendations from Schultz,
two from Levy (s.v. *filhon*), and two from Bogin (p. 144); I have further consulted
R. Nelli, *Ecrivains anticonformistes du moyen-âge occitan* (Paris 1977) pp. 255–9. At 12,
where the editions have corrected 'aruat' Q to 'cargatz', I have set 'aruats': the sense
demands a word that complements the drooping breasts and worn condition which,
as the previous line suggests, comes *after* childbearing, not during pregnancy.

Earlier editors conjured up an improbable lady 'Alaisina Iselda'. It is Bogin's merit
to have correctly distinguished 'N'Alais' from 'Na Iselda' (*sic* Bogin, though the Q
spelling 'Yselda', on both occasions, can be retained), and to have perceived what seems
poetically the right order of the verses (whereas in Q 9–12 follow 13–20). Her transposition (which unfortunately she does not discuss) elegantly resolves certain per-
plexities. With the MS order, followed by Schultz and retained by other editors, it is
hard to see how, after Carenza's exhortation to both girls to enter a divine marriage,
one (or both) could return to complaints about childbearing. If the Q order is retained,
I believe one would have to understand 'penre marit m'agenza' in 9 as meaning 'It
pleases me to take the divine husband you have just named' (which perhaps overstrains
the syntax). Then in 10 the adversative 'mas' would have to be emended to something
like 'car' – '*for* I think having children is a penance'. That is, if in these verses a *mystic*
marriage is being accepted, the speaker(s) could not possibly suppose it will bring
physical childbearing with it.

There is also a formal problem about Bogin's transposition, which she did not
consider. If her order is correct, it means that the poem is in effect a diptych: an eight-
line *cobla* and four-line *tornada* by Alais and Yselda are followed by a similar *cobla* and
tornada by Carenza. Pieces consisting of only one *cobla* plus *tornada* are relatively rare
in troubadour lyric – though see for instance Frank 553, 1; 577, 167 (here the genuineness of the *tornada* has been questioned); 577, 264; and especially 577, 36 (Peire d'Ussel's
'En Gui d'Uisel, be·m plai vostra canços'): not only has it the same versification and
rhyme-scheme as the three women's composition, but Peire's satiric challenge of his

clerical brother Gui's attempts to be a lover and love-poet (in the form of lines 1–12 above) will presumably have called forth a reply by Gui in the same form (that of Carenza's reply, lines 13–24 above). If Gui's riposte were extant, there would be complete formal similarity with the women's diptych.

At the same time, since such a diptych use of *cobla* plus *tornada* (8, 4; 8, 4) was evidently unusual, it is not hard to see how a copyist (perhaps in Q's exemplar) was tempted to place the two *tornadas* together at the close (giving 8, 8, 4, 4): such a form is relatively common (cf. e.g. Frank, 577, 21, or Bieiris de Romans's 'Na Maria, pretz e fina valors', Schultz p. 28, which Frank unaccountably omits), and could have been the one the copyist expected to find.

55 P. Dronke, 'Virgines' p. 101 and nn 18–21; Abelard, *HC* 467ff.
56 Cf. especially M. Bernards, *Speculum Virginum*.
57 'A chantar m'er de so q'ieu no volria', ed. M. de Riquer, *Los trovadores* III 800–2.
58 Cf. for instance *Cantigas d'amigo*, ed. J. J. Nunes (3 vols., Coimbra 1926–8) nos. 123, 236, 252, 490, 496. I am indebted to Professor Alan Deyermond for advice on this point.
59 While the love-story of Seguis and Valensa, to which the Countess alludes, is no longer recoverable, it is noteworthy that she sees herself in the man's rôle, not the woman's: she is the one who chooses actively, and who, by being more fervent, is also more vulnerable.
60 *Los trovadores* II 800.
61 *Biskupa Sögur* (København 1858) I 165f.
62 Since completing this chapter, I have seen two valuable recent essays concerned with *trobairitz*: a survey of the nature and poetic context of their songs by Pierre Bec, and some detailed observations by Antoine Tavera (see Bibliography pp. 322, 331). These do not conflict with the discussion above; while I wish to suggest a more radical originality in some of the *trobairitz* lyrics than does Professor Bec, I hope to have done so in a way that does not conflict with the caveats he has proposed. I have also, since this book went to press, attempted a more comprehensive interpretation of another *trobairitz*, Castelloza, to appear in an anthology, *Medieval Women Writers*, ed. Katharina M. Wilson (University of Georgia Press, forthcoming).

5. Heloise

1 See above, pp. 84–91.
2 This literary quality in letters is also evident in many less gifted letter-writers of the time: for insofar as anyone learnt to write letters at all in the early twelfth century, it was in an 'artificial' language, relying on many kinds of artifice. Besides, the infrequency of delivering letters itself implied that any letter dispatched was likely to be very carefully composed. Cf. the fine general discussion in G. Constable, *Letters* (1976).
3 This letter will not be discussed below. In *Trier 1980* I commented briefly on its verbal art, but did not treat the evidence of *cursus*. P. von Moos (*ibid.* p. 96 n 49) alludes to G. Constable as claiming that there is no *cursus* here: 'Heloise seems to have reserved her rhythmical prose for her letters to Abelard, since in her letter to Peter the Venerable there are any number of *clausulae* that would have been unacceptable to a papal scribe' (Constable, *Letters of Peter the Venerable* II 38). But this is a little misleading. The letter, in Constable's edition (I 400f), has fourteen sentences (if we include the *salutatio*, which

is a complete sentence). These fourteen display three strict *tardus* cadences ('Cluniacénsis persólveret', 'confirmarétis apícibus', 'nóbis exhíbeat'), three strict *velox* ('grátiae salutáris', 'descénderit gloriámur', 'dóminus impleátis'), and the *planus* 'nós commendástis'. It is possible that, if *g* before *i* was softened and fronted in current pronunciation, 'eulógio cibástis' and 'privilégium donástis' were likewise intended as *planus* cadences. While a statistically meaningful χ^2 test (cf. *Trier 1980*, pp. 54ff) cannot be set up for a sample of only fourteen *clausulae*, the distribution of cadences here is fully compatible with that in Heloise's letters to Abelard, and the rhymes that mark the rhythmic patterns here are, as I indicated (*Trier 1980*, pp. 70f), among Heloise's most highly developed ones.

4 'Chronologie' pp. 337–49.
5 There is a certain practical difficulty about referring to the letters. I speak of Heloise's first, second, and third letters to Abelard, and shall also at times designate these as *Epp.* II, IV, and VI respectively, since this indicates their place in the collected correspondence. That is their numbering in Migne, P.L. 178, where *Ep.* I is Abelard's *Historia calamitatum* (= *HC*), III and V are his two 'personal' replies to Heloise, and VII and VIII are the two long didactic letters *De origine sanctimonialium* and *Institutio seu regula sanctimonialium*. In the Muckle–McLaughlin ed. in *MS*, *HC* is not numbered, hence Heloise's epistles (II, IV, VI in Migne) become I, III, V in Muckle. As this numbering gives a less accurate impression of the collection, I shall not adopt it, but shall cite the appropriate volume and page of *Mediaeval Studies* (*MS*) where the letters are printed: thus

> XII (1950) 163–213 = Migne I
> XV (1953) 47–94 = Migne II–V
> XVII (1955) 240–81 = Migne VI–VII
> XVIII (1956) 241–92 = Migne VIII

As the Muckle–McLaughlin edition – much the best for the collection as a whole – unfortunately has no line-numbering, I add paragraph-references to make location easier. (Thus e.g. *MS* XVIII, 245, 1 refers to the first new paragraph on p. 245 of *Ep.* VIII.) For *HC* and Heloise's first and second letters, my primary reference is always to the ed. of J. Monfrin: as this has the advantage of lineation, line-references only are given. Since Monfrin gives only a very selective critical apparatus for the two Heloise letters, a reference to Muckle is always added in parenthesis. Where Jean de Meun's translation, which Muckle did not use, is of importance for establishing Heloise's text, I add a further reference to the recent ed. of this by F. Beggiato (*Le lettere*). The biblical, Patristic and classical citations in the letters are normally given below both Muckle's and Monfrin's texts, and are mostly not reproduced here. The *Problemata*, finally, do not yet exist in a reliable edition: I cite them from the unique manuscript (Paris, B.N. lat. 14511 (= P)), adding a reference in parenthesis to the corresponding column in P.L. 178.
6 On the formation of the *Problemata*, see below p. 135 and n 52.
7 Some detailed indications concerning this are given in my *Abelard and Heloise*. For a picture of older discussions, E. Gilson's masterly *Héloïse et Abélard*, esp. pp. 169–207, remains indispensable.
8 See below, pp. 133, 142–3.
9 See my *Abelard and Heloise*, pp. 28f, 52, 56–8.
10 *Trier 1980*, pp. 53–73.

11 This analysis of structure is offered as a way of illuminating the text, not as representing architectonics consciously imposed by Heloise.

12 This is how Jean's translation reads in the unique MS (Paris B.N. fr. 920):

> Tres chiers amis, *voz* homs m'a nouvelement monstré vostre epistre, que vous envoyastes a *nostre* ami pour confort.

The Latin editions of Monfrin and Muckle, by contrast, read:

> Missam ad amicum pro consolatione epistolam, dilectissime, vestram ad me forte quidam nuper attulit.

Neither Monfrin nor Muckle takes cognizance of the two vital readings in Jean – 'voz homs' and 'nostre ami' – and indeed Jean's editor, Beggiato, relegates these to the notes and emends Jean's text to make it accord with the Latin. In the Latin MSS, the only variants (noted by Muckle *ad loc.*) are that one MS (F) omits 'vestram', and that four (BDRY) read 'quidem' for 'quidam'. I suggest that the Latin MS which Jean – usually a faithful as well as skilled translator – had before him will probably have read:

> Missam ad amicum ⟨nostrum⟩ pro consolatione epistolam, dilectissime, vestrum ad me quidam nuper attulit.

13 'Abelard as Autobiographer', *Speculum* XLII (1967) 463–88.

14 Cf. D. De Robertis, *Maia* XVI (1964) 6–54.

15 '... de glorioso illo theologie tue opere' edd.; but *Theologia*, the name of Abelard's treatise, should be capitalized.

16 *Ep.* II 64–73 (*MS* XV, 69, 1); here and below, in citation from Heloise's writing, line-arrangement and punctuation are my own.

17 On the word-play (*annominatio*) in 'con-solari', see *Trier 1980*, p. 57.

18 Ed. and tr. P. Dronke, *Medieval Latin* II 483. On Boncompagno, see the new tr. and facs. ed. of his *Rota Veneris* by J. Purkart (New York 1975), and E. Ruhe, *De amasio ad amasiam* pp. 127ff (reviewed by D. Schaller, *Arcadia* XII (1977) 307–13).

19 Cf. Cicero, *De amic.* v–viii; Ambrose, *De officiis* III 22 (P.L. 16, 182); J. Leclercq, 'L'amitié'.

20 *Cons.* III pr. 3 – m. 5.

21 *De inv.* I xxxi.

22 *Remedia* 363.

23 See my 'Profane Elements', pp. 569–92. The motif, however, is also found in popular poetry, and while I know no popular examples datable before the twelfth century, this may simply be due to the gaps in what survives.

24 In the thirteenth century this loving descent to hell becomes a mystical paradox with Mechthild of Magdeburg, who exclaims (*Das Fliessende Licht* II 3) that she would gladly endure hell for the sake of divine Love.

25 *Ep.* II 71f (*MS* XV, 78, 2). Cf. Abelard's *Planctus Jacob* (ed. Meyer, *Ges. Abh.* I 367–8): 'reddebas sic me mihi'.

26 See especially Cicero, *De amic.* vii.

27 *MS* XV, 75, 4.

28 *MS* XVII, 253, 2.

29 Job 3: 5; Seneca, *Ep.* 24, 1. Heloise's expression 'dies illa' (IV 29), for the terrible day when Abelard dies, already carried liturgical and hymnic overtones of the last day, the day of doom: on the tradition of *Dies irae* chants prior to the famous thirteenth-century sequence, see esp. K. Strecker, 'Dies irae', *ZfdA* LI (1908) 227ff.

30 For the wish to be buried beside one's beloved husband, compare the remarkable letter of Queen Teresa of Portugal (†1130) to her son, Alfonso I:

> Finis meus prope est, fili amantissime, et iam mihi vilescunt omnia huius mundi, praeter te, quem cuperem videre. Sed videamus nos in meliori patria. Servos et ancillas meas tibi commendo, et fratres novae reformationis, sub cuius habitu et professione discedo. Sepultura mea, precor, sit iuxta patrem tuum, illustrem comitem Henricum, ut quos vita vidit consortes, mors videat inseparabiles (*Fasc. sanctorum ordinis Cisterciensis* I 314a).

31 *Phars.* II 4–15.

32 Cf. the poem *Quomodo primum amavit*, from Ripoll, s. XII², tr. and discussed in M. Thiébaux, *The Stag of Love* (Ithaca–London 1974) pp. 101–2.

33 See my discussion in *Poetic Individuality*, pp. 123–39.

34 Heloise's use of hyperbaton, esp. with such expressions as 'saltem', would repay closer investigation: it seems to be a distinctive trait in her style.

35 On the 'sacrilegious' aspect of sexuality, compare also Abelard's words, *MS* XV, 88, 1 and 89, 1; also, towards 1300, the testimony of Béatrice de Lagleize (Duvernoy I 226; 243).

36 Here Briseis uses plural forms ('nos humiles famulaeque tuae . . .'), as Heloise does so often.

37 *MS* XV, 83 (cf. also 87, 2).

38 *Ibid.* 86, 2.

39 Muckle, *MS* XVII, 242 *ad loc.* cites Cicero, *Tusc. Disp.* IV XXXV, 75, for this phrase; but even closer to Heloise's wording is Jerome, *Ep.* 125, 14: he has 'clavum clavo *expellere*' (cf. Heloise's 'expellit'), where Cicero has 'eiiciendum'. This letter of Jerome's is also cited by Heloise in her introduction to the *Problemata* (see below p. 136).

40 'Le silence d'Héloïse', *Colloque* pp. 425–68; 'Die Bekehrung Heloises' pp. 95–125.

41 *Trier 1980*, p. 92.

42 *MS* XVII, 242, 2.

43 James 2: 10; cf. *Probl.* 2, and discussion below.

44 *MS* XV, 252, 2.

45 *Ibid.* 252, 4.

46 Cf. *HC* 629ff (*MS* XII, 190f), and P. von Moos, 'Cornelia und Heloise'.

47 See the Excursus below, p. 142.

48 *Ep.* IV 265–8 (*MS* XV, 82, 1).

49 In the earlier passage, according to Muckle's apparatus, the MSS all read 'animi'; in the third letter, 'animae'. The theme is one that Abelard likewise reverts to in his *Regula* (*MS* XVIII, 265) and in answering one of the *Problemata* (15), as well as in other writings of his, such as the *Ethica*.

50 See the pioneering study by C. Waddell, *Trier 1980*, pp. 267–86.

51 Waddell (*ibid.* p. 43) has made the illuminating suggestion that this letter may have been the continuation of *Ep.* VIII (the *Regula*), which even in its most complete extant form ends very abruptly.

52 Thus for instance 7 is linked to 6 by 'etiam'; 10, 11 and 12 belong together (as the phrases 'in eodem evangelista' in 11 and 'quoque' in 12 make clear); the group 14–20 constitutes a series of 'quaestiones in Matthaeum', considering points in three consecutive chapters of Matthew (15 being explicitly related to 14 by 'postmodum'); 26 is attached to 25 (once more by 'etiam'), and *Problems* 30–6 again form a unified group: not only do they arise out of the same context in the first Book of Kings, but they also

have bridge-phrases such as 'postmodum' (31) and 'illud etiam' (34). So, too, 37–9, which arise out of the Gospels, are bridged by 'illud quoque' (38) and 'etiam' (39). Yet one other phrase reflects the later stage when the questions that had been sent ('dirigimus') were redacted so as to form a collected work: a reference in *Problem* 20, 'as we said a long way *above* (*sicut dudum superius diximus*)', relates to *Problem* 8.

53 P fol. 18ra (P.L. 178, 677 B).
54 I give the text (from P fol. 18rb–va) in *Trier 1980*, p. 70.
55 From this same letter of Jerome's (125, 4) Heloise adapts her expression 'Quorsum autem ista', in the first line cited above.
56 MS xv, 76, 3.
57 I have discussed some of the *Problemata* in more detail in *Trier 1980*, pp. 57–61.
58 Cf. e.g. 'Tibi nunc, domine, dum vivis incumbit' (*Ep.* vi, MS xvii, 253, 2).
59 In this it may not be anachronistic to see Heloise as resembling certain major letter-writers of our century (such as Rilke or Joyce), who, when writing intimate letters, were also aware that these would eventually be collected and seen by others than their first recipients, and hence lavished upon some initially private letters an enormous literary care.
60 *Ep.* ii 152ff (MS xv, 71).
61 *HC* 1333ff (MS xii, 206).
62 P.L. 178, 1771ff.
63 *Probl.* 5.
64 *Probl.* 25–7.

Excursus: Did Abelard Write Heloise's Third Letter?

1 J. F. Benton, 'A reconsideration of the authenticity of the correspondence of Abelard and Heloise', *Trier 1980*, p. 50.
2 See the crit. ed. by B. Boyer and R. McKeon (Chicago 1976–7) q. 130 *ad loc.*
3 *Le lettere* (ed. Beggiato) I 164 (cf. II 147, n 67).
4 *Trier 1980*, p. 43.
5 (1) MS xviii (*Ep.* viii), 269, lines 16–25 = MS xvii (*Ep.* vi), 245, lines 15–25
  (2) MS xviii, 270, lines 4–20 = MS xvii, 247, lines 14–31
  (3) MS xviii, 271, lines 10–21 = MS xvii, 247, lines 31–41
  (4) MS xviii, 271, lines 26–38 = MS xvii, 248, lines 5–16
  (5) MS xviii, 272, lines 14–25 = MS xvii, 245, line 29 to 246, line 10.
Some of these parallels are signalled by von Moos (*Trier 1980*, pp. 80f, with references to earlier scholarship), though he did not see their full extent.

6. Hildegard of Bingen

1 This is not to suggest that Hildegard knew any of the early Latin translations of Avicenna's writings: while some might have begun to circulate before the completion of her *Liber divinorum operum* (1173/4), we have absolutely no evidence that she had seen them.
2 *Goethes Werke* (Weimar 1887–1918) xxxiv.1, 'Kunst und Alterthum am Rhein und Main', p. 102: 'Ein altes Manuscript, die Visionen der heiligen Hildegard enthaltend, ist merkwürdig.' It seems less likely that Goethe was referring to the 'Riesenkodex'

(Wiesbaden 2), though this also contains the whole of Hildegard's visionary writings; it has no illuminations, however, and could be called 'merkwürdig' only by virtue of its size and the chain attached to it.

3 See especially H. Liebeschütz, *Das allegorische Weltbild*; B. Widmer, *Heilsordnung*.

4 This is Hildegard's title for it in her Prologue to *LVM* (Pitra p. 7).

5 L. Thorndike, *A History* II 124–54; C. Singer, *From Magic* pp. 199–239.

6 In this chapter, unless a footnote gives another reference, all texts are edited afresh below, pp. 231–64. The order of editing generally corresponds to that in the discussion. Surrounding passages of Latin, not translated here, are often also given.

The unusual aspects of Hildegard's style present a translator with many problems. The translations in this chapter are intended, among other things, to show how I construe the more problematic passages, and how I gauge the tone of the writing.

7 See esp. Prov. 8: 22ff; Wisd. 7–8; Ecclus. 1. I have given further documentation in *JWCI* XLIII (1980) 20ff and n 19.

8 *In Apoc.* 1 1 (P.L. 196, 686ff).

9 Pp. 230–4. Other visual abnormalities connected with migraine have recently been related to Hildegard's visions by F. Clifford Rose and M. Gawel, *Migraine: The Facts* (Oxford 1981) pp. 2–6: in particular, they mention the interruption of the visual field 'by shiny lines, arranged like constellations, a phenomenon known as fortification spectra, because of its resemblance to a castellated fort'; with this they compare Hildegard's 'ramparts of the heavenly city' (p. 6).

10 *Das Leben* p. 151 n 10.

11 Herwegen, 'Collaborateurs', *passim*. The Gent MS of *LDO*, however, contains both what was completed at the time of Volmar's death (1173), and copied either by his own hand or at his supervision, and at the same time a number of additions and corrections – substantial as well as stylistic – which are in another hand, and for which (as Hildegard's Epilogue (Herwegen pp. 308–9) tells) Abbot Ludwig of Trier and Hildegard's nephew Wescelinus were in some sense responsible. This was finely analysed by A. Derolez, *Essays . . . Lieftinck* II 23–33. In a subsequent essay, however, Derolez goes further:

> Hildegarde écrivait-elle elle-même et la tâche des collaborateurs se limitait-elle, comme on l'a cru, à 'employer la lime' et à corriger les fautes d'orthographe et de grammaire dues à sa connaissance défectueuse du latin? Les conclusions de notre étude précédente nous obligent à répondre négativement, et ceci à l'encontre des affirmations de l'auteur elle-même. ('Deux notes' p. 291).

This inference seems to go beyond the codicological evidence: it is possible to attribute stylistic changes to Ludwig and Wescelinus and still allow that all *substantial* changes and additions were inserted at Hildegard's dictation, or copied from notes she had made on wax tablets. Again, this does not rule out that the substantial changes and additions may also in their turn have been revised *stylistically* by the two clerics.

12 I have discussed this further in 'Problemata', sect. III ('Sources').

13 Ed. P. Dronke (Leiden 1978) p. 2.

14 Ed. *Echtheit* p. 107.

15 P.L. 197, 351f.

16 For the texts of the Barbarossa letters, and excellent historical discussion, see *Echtheit* pp. 124–31.

17 P.L. 197, 217f.

18 The rubrics of a number of these autobiographic passages in the Berlin MS read 'Visio secunda', 'Visio tercia', etc. Those in the *Riesenkodex* – in the form 'De secunda visione', 'De tercia visione . . .' – are mistranslated by Führkötter (*Das Leben* pp. 76ff): 'De secunda visione' does not mean 'Aus der zweiten Schau' but rather 'Über die zweite Schau'. That is, Hildegard is not giving extracts from visions, but giving an account of them.

19 *HC* 982ff (I am not, of course, suggesting that Hildegard knew Abelard's autobiographic letter).

20 *Ibid.* 1321ff.

21 P.L. 87, 415.

22 Text and melody in my *Poetic Individuality* pp. 209–19; discussion *ibid.* pp. 160–5.

23 P.L. 197, 1065ff.

24 The expression – 'Pater . . . salutis animarum mysticae plantationis filiarum mearum' – shows Hildegard's characteristic fondness for constructions with several genitives dependent on one another.

25 Cf. 1 Macc. 1.

26 Cf. Exod. 3: 14.

27 This letter, and Hildegard's letter to Richardis (translated and analysed below), are admirably edited and set in historical context in *Echtheit* pp. 131–41. Scriptural references are given there *ad loc.* Cf. also *Briefwechsel* pp. 94ff.

28 P.L. 197, 156f ('conviventi audacia', 156 D, should probably read 'conniventi').

29 Cf. F. Haug, 'Epistolae S. Hildegardis' pp. 60f.

30 Ed. *Echtheit* pp. 117f.

31 P.L. 197, 162. The wording, 'venisset', probably implies a visit rather than a permanent renunciation of her position, as Führkötter's translation – 'zurückgekehrt' (*Briefwechsel* p. 99) – might suggest.

32 *Ibid.* 163.

33 *V.N.* XXXI.

34 *Ibid.* XIX.

35 *Ibid.* VII.

36 Hildegard normally uses *oculi*, not *lumina*, for 'eyes'. The classical ring of her phrase here may be Boethian, or perhaps Ovidian: Philosophia addresses Boethius (*Cons.* I pr. 1) 'commota paulisper ac torvis inflammata luminibus'. In the *Metamorphoses*, Minerva is the 'torvi dea bellica luminis' (II 752), and Medusa has 'torva . . . lumina' (V 241); Hercules 'lumine torvo / spectat' (IX 27f); and Arachne looks with fierce eyes at the disguised goddess Pallas: 'aspicit hanc torvis' (VI 34). While it is certain that Hildegard knew the *Consolatio*, and it has not hitherto been suggested that she knew Ovid's *Metamorphoses*, the Ovidian expressions, which include 'spectat' and 'aspicit', are suggestive; a comparison of cosmological language in *Metam.* I and in Hildegard's *LDO* might be rewarding and might yield further results.

37 *Hist. Franc.* X 31.

38 R 201vb; Berlin Theol. Fol. 727 (= J) 116vab (cf. Pitra p. 244):
 . . . vivit et non vivit, cinerosa sentit et non sentit, ac [*et* J] miracula dei non per se, sed per illa tacta profert, quemadmodum chorda, per cytharedam tacta, sonum non per se, sed per tactum illius reddit. Et hec vera sunt, et qui verus est ea sic manifestari veraciter voluit. Quapropter si quis super eminentem mentem scripturarum, et

proprietatis sue, aliquid eis in contrarietate addiderit, penis hic descriptis subiacere dignus est; aut si quis aliquid ab eis per contrarietatem abstulerit, dignus est ut a gaudiis hic ostensis deleatur.

39 On Hildegard and Hermas, see esp. Liebeschütz pp. 51–6; P. Dronke, 'Arbor Caritatis' pp. 221–31.

40 Cf. *Echtheit* pp. 19f.

41 On the revisions of this passage, traceable in the Gent codex, see Derolez, *Essays* . . . *Lieftinck* II 23–33.

42 Cf. 'Problemata' p. 118 and n 64. The annotator of Hildegard's writings in Migne (P.L. 197, 123 n 50) takes pains to stress that Hildegard's view here is unorthodox, 'not congruent with the opinion of theologians'. Her attempt at a materialist interpretation of the demonic effect was too 'modern', we might say, for nineteenth-century theology.

43 I have published it for the first time in 'Problemata' pp. 127–9 (with discussion *ibid.* pp. 118–22).

44 The letter is preserved with Hildegard's correspondence, P.L. 197, 280–2.

45 'Te lucis ante terminum' st. 2 (ed. A. S. Walpole, *Early Latin Hymns* (Cambridge 1922) p. 299). On the question of the literal or allegorical perception of these phantoms in the Middle Ages, see the acute observations of J. Huizinga, *Über die Verknüpfung des Poetischen mit dem Theologischen bei Alanus de Insulis* (Koninklijke Akad., Amsterdam 1932) pp. 82–91 (with special reference to Hildegard, *ibid.* pp. 87ff).

46 P.L. 197, 336–7.

47 Compare Erwin Panofsky's perceptive comments on the modes in which Bernard of Clairvaux and Suger of Saint-Denis addressed each other (including *vestra Magnitudo* and *Sanctitas vestra*), and on the kinds of personal tension and disagreement that underlay the use of such extravagant formulae (Abbot Suger, *On the Abbey Church of St. Denis and its Art Treasures*, ed. and tr. E. Panofsky (Princeton ²1979) pp. 10f).

48 P.L. 197, 337–8.

49 The text is corrupt at this point in Migne (338 A): 'Deus etiam habet scrutinium, scrutationes in omni persona . . .' Corr. 'scrutinium scrutationis'?

50 *Les trois ordres.*

51 According to *Briefwechsel* p. 204, she is attested in a document of 1152. The date of her letter cannot be ascertained, but it may well be of the same period – late in Hildegard's life – as Guibert's first two letters (1175): when Hildegard describes to Guibert the way she received detailed instructions about costumes in a vision (see below, pp. 169, 253), it does not sound as though she means a vision experienced in the remote past. Thus the unusual modes of dress may have been introduced relatively late on the Rupertsberg – in the 1170s rather than the 1150s – at a time when the foundation, so poor at the start, had acquired enough wealth to afford queen-like diadems for a whole community. There is a particular aptness in these diadems: just as Hildegard herself had spiritual vision at the same time as natural vision, so her diadems are symbolic and at the same time real.

52 Guibert's two letters are printed in Pitra, pp. 328–31, 378–9. Hildegard's reply is printed, in a more complete version than Pitra's (pp. 331–4), below, pp. 250–6.

53 For earlier uses of this Pauline expression (cf. Eph. 3: 18) in medieval thought, see E. Jeauneau, *RTAM* 45 (1978) 118–28.

54 That is, Hildegard sees the answers in the *umbra*, but knows that their source is in the more rarely glimpsed blaze of light beyond the *umbra*.

NOTES TO PAGES 169-178

55 'Hoc datum signum deum benedicet': this use of acc. with *benedicere* has good biblical precedent – in the Vulgate, 'benedicere deum' is found particularly in the Book of Tobias.

56 See especially J. Bugge, *Virginitas*.

57 See Section x below.

58 P.L. 197, 269; cf. *Pastor Hermas* Vis. II 4; III 10–13; Boethius, *Cons.* I pr. I. Hildegard knew Boethius' text so well that she could recreate moments from it freely; the importance of the contents of the *Consolatio* for her cosmological thought would also repay detailed study.

59 P.L. 197, 192 D – 193 A. I have given a corrected text (based on R, fol. 343rb), with translation, in *Medieval Latin* 1 67f.

60 Cf. E. Jeauneau, 'La division des sexes chez Grégoire de Nysse et chez Jean Scot Erigène', in *Eriugena: Studien zu seinen Quellen*, ed. W. Beierwaltes (Heidelberg 1980) pp. 33–54.

61 Cf. Liebeschütz pp. 117f. The Manichaean texts I have in mind can be found in *Die Gnosis III: Der Manichäismus*, tr. J. P. Asmussen and A. Böhlig (Zürich–München 1980) pp. 103–88, 257–91; see also, more generally, G. Widengren (ed.), *Der Manichäismus* (Wege der Forschung, Darmstadt 1977). It should perhaps be underlined that there is no question of direct or conscious adoption by Hildegard of Manichaean ideas, and that she actively combated the Cathars, the 'neo-Manichaeans' of her own day (cf. esp. Pitra pp. 347–51, and A. Borst, *Die Katharer* pp. 91, 95). Nonetheless, the deep affinity between some of Hildegard's leitmotifs, such as Lucifer's challenge, and the *archaic* Manichaean mythologems, is undeniable.

62 'Per zelum dei': probably an objective genitive here, though Hildegard also (esp. in *Scivias* III 5) uses *zelus dei* with the force of a subjective genitive, to designate God's avenging zeal.

63 For ease of reference, the *Causae et curae* passages edited below (pp. 241–50) do not always follow the order in the manuscript, but are grouped thematically, in a way that corresponds to the discussion in this section.

64 Schipperges (*Heilkunde* p. 41) denied that any of the section-headings in the København MS could be by Hildegard. Yet here is a heading that seems essential for sense, and that presumably must be authorial: while it is possible in principle that the heading was inserted by a later hand, and that this entailed a modification of the sentence that follows, we have no evidence for such an assumption.

65 The comparison with the stag echoes Ps. 41: 2 ('Quemadmodum desiderat cervus ad fontes aquarum'). Hildegard's view, that woman's sexual delight is gentler than man's (cf. K56ab (*Causae* p. 76): 'De mulieris delectatione . . . levior in ea est quam in viro, quoniam huiusmodi ignis in ea tam fortiter non ardet ut in viro'), is the opposite of that in the Salernitan tradition – 'mulieres viris ferventiores sunt in libidine' (cf. *The Prose Salernitan Questions*, ed. B. Lawn (British Academy 1979) p. 4, and the parallels *ad loc.*).

66 *Heilkunde* p. 42. It is clear that Hildegard was familiar with the genre and form of *lunaria*, and in particular with the kind that predict the characteristics of children born under each of the lunar mansions. These belonged to the more popular medical tradition already in the early Middle Ages: e.g. there are two ninth-century copies (in the MS Sankt Gallen 751) of a *lunaris sancti Daniheli*, beginning 'Luna prima puer natus erit studiosus, vitalis' (A. Beccaria, *I codici di medicina* p. 378). What is unusual in Hilde-

gard's predictions is that she refers throughout to the date of *conception* of the child, not, like the *lunaria*, to the date of birth; the content of her predictions likewise appears to be her own (though this impression might have to be qualified after more comprehensive work on *lunaria*, many of which remain unpublished). Again, she does not venture (as do widespread works such as 'Alchandreus') to predict the child's exact life-span. The recent survey by C. Weisser, 'Das Krankheitslunar', gives a valuable guide to *lunaria* – not only those concerned with illness – and to their bibliography. For knowledge of this article, and helpful advice on Hildegard's relation to the *lunaria* tradition, I am indebted to Dr Charles Burnett.

67 The passage receives no mention in Jacques Le Goff's recent *La naissance du Purgatoire* (Paris 1981); but Le Goff (pp. 124–7) valuably signals the anecdotes in Gregory the Great's *Dialogi* (IV 42, 57) where the place of purgation is set in thermal baths on earth. It is probably these passages that lie behind Hildegard's attempt at scientific explanation.

68 Cf. P. Dronke, *Fabula* pp. 50–5; 'New Approaches' pp. 133–9.

69 Cf. R. Klibansky, E. Panofsky, F. Saxl, *Saturn and Melancholy*, esp. pp. 110f. The Latin physiognomic treatises, collected in *Scriptores Physiognomici Graeci et Latini*, ed. R. Förster (2 vols., Leipzig 1893), discuss the significance of physical features item by item, but do not assemble complete characterologies, and do not treat character in terms of the humoral temperaments. Compare also P. Diepgen, *Frau und Frauenheilkunde*, who, while claiming in a generalization that 'Die ganze Physiologie und Pathologie Hildegards wird von der antiken Tradition beherrscht' (p. 75), is forced to admit soon afterwards that Hildegard's characterization of feminine temperaments 'mir in dieser Form vorher nicht begegnet ist' (p. 76). Similarly with her physiology of menstruation: 'Wie weit Sankt Hildegard bei dieser Theorie eigene Wege geht, haben wir nicht feststellen können' (p. 157).

70 Lat. 'livosus': the formation, not recorded in the dictionaries, would appear to be Hildegard's own.

71 Cf. Klibansky *et al.*, Part I, *passim* (and especially the tables on pp. 62–3).

72 K 52 a (*Causae* p. 71): 'oculi eorum velud sagitte sunt ad amorem femine . . . et cogitationes eorum quasi procella tempestatum'.

73 It is a pity that this passage was not noticed by the authors of *Saturn and Melancholy*, since it would have prompted a modification of their central argument, that the Aristotelian conception of melancholy – condition of the diseased and of the brilliant mind – was largely forgotten in the Middle Ages and not rediscovered before the Quattrocento. For other medieval instances of this conception, see my review of the book, *Notes and Queries* CCX (1965) 354–6.

74 The passage in al-Mubashshir ibn Fātiq (1048/9) is translated by F. Rosenthal, *Das Fortleben der Antike in Islam* (Zürich–Stuttgart 1965) pp. 48f; cf. A. S. Riginos, *Platonica: The Anecdotes concerning the Life and Writings of Plato* (Leiden 1976) p. 152. The detail of Plato's weeping enters Western tradition with the thirteenth-century Spanish translation of al-Mubashshir, made under the aegis of Alfonso the Wise: *Los Bocados de Oro*, ed. H. Knust (Bibl. des litt. Vereins in Stuttgart 141, Tübingen 1879) p. 204. On the other hand, the equivalent passage in the Latin version, *Liber philosophorum*, that was made from the Spanish, omits the weeping, as the editor, E. Franceschini (*Atti del Reale Istituto Veneto* XC I (1931–2)) notes *ad loc.* (p. 463 n 1). F. Novotný, *The Posthumous Life of Plato* (Academia Prague 1977) p. 224 n 9, mentions that Firmicus Maternus, *Math.* VI 30, 24, suggests a horoscope for Plato that would account for his

being 'an interpreter of divine and celestial laws, and tempered with gentle speech and the power of divine genius'. The text of Firmicus was not widely diffused in the twelfth century, though it was known for instance to Bernardus Silvestris; whether there are traces of Firmicus' influence in Hildegard is a problem that would deserve detailed investigation.

75 Details are given in 'Problemata' pp. 117ff, together with text, translation and discussion of three of the unpublished letters. Below (p. 192), I revert briefly to the third letter published there (p. 131), because of its special importance for the question of Hildegard's self-understanding.

76 While a marginal entry shows that the MS belonged from an early period to S. Maria de Palatolis (Pfalzel bei Trier), which was a *Chorherrenstift*, it is not known whether any part of the MS was copied there. The hand that copied the *Vita*, the letters, and the 'Berlin fragment' in this MS (B), is of the beginning of the thirteenth century, and is identical with that of the illuminated Lucca MS of the *LDO* (*Echtheit* p. 80 and pl. xvi; the illuminations and some examples of the script of this MS, Lucca Bibl. Govern. 1942, are now available in a superb facsimile, *Sanctae Hildegardis Revelationes*, published by the Cassa di Risparmio di Lucca, 1973). Both the Lucca MS and B may have been copied in the Rupertsberg scriptorium (*Echtheit, loc. cit.*).

77 Cf. 'Problemata' p. 118 n 62, and the two new identifications of addressees proposed below.

78 Scotus Eriugena (*Periph.* III 35) had called 'the text of divine discourses [the Bible] and the sensible aspect of the visible world the two garments of Christ (*duo vestimenta Christi*)'. There is a remarkable archaic parallel to the notion of the earth as divine garment in the fragments of the pre-Socratic philosopher Pherecydes (H. Diels, W. Kranz, *Die Fragmente der Vorsokratiker*, 7. Pherekydes, B 1–3), but these were not accessible in Latin translation.

79 A similar juxtaposition is made by Notker, in his sequence *Sancti spiritus* (ed. W. von den Steinen, *Notker* II 54ff): 'Tu aspirando / das spiritales / esse homines' ('By your breathing you let human beings become spiritual'). On the sequences of Notker known to Hildegard, see 'Problemata' pp. 116f and n 57.

80 Cf. P.L. 197, 329f, and 338–41; also *Briefwechsel* pp. 207–10.

81 P.L. 197, 330 C, 340 D, 341 A.

82 So too an early Minnesinger, Meinhloh von Sevelingen, a contemporary of Hildegard's, composing perhaps in the 1170s, praises his lady as 'in rehter mâze gemeit' (*Minnesangs Frühling* 15, 12).

83 V. *Scivias*, Index verborum et elocutionum pp. 907–10, s.v. *voluntas*.

84 *Expositio Evang.* (ed. Pitra) p. 251. Cf. 'Problemata' pp. 114–16.

85 *LDO* I 4 (P.L. 197, 897 C).

86 Cf. K 53 b (*Causae* p. 73): 'sed in eis est temperata prudentia quam feminea ars habet'.

87 *Conf.* VIII xi, 27; on Hildegard's possible acquaintance with the *Confessions*, see also 'Problemata' p. 107.

88 A. Franz, *Die kirchlichen Benediktionen* II 52, 57f, 194, 229f.

89 *Carmina Burana* I 3, ed. O. Schumann, B. Bischoff (Heidelberg 1970) no. 7*.

90 Text in 'Problemata' p. 131; translation *ibid.* p. 126.

91 The correction was made by Schrader and Führkötter, *Echtheit* p. 81 n 25.

92 *Echtheit* p. 143.

93 Schrader and Führkötter alluded to this possibility but cast doubt on it (*Echtheit* p. 146

n 91). They suggested that another *scriptura* and another abbot might be in question. However, the extensive verbal parallels between the two letters make this, in my view, wholly unlikely. It would be necessary to discover a second abbot to whom Hildegard writes with such complete intimacy, and whom she also reminds that in his youth he was foolishly worldly, before one could plausibly suggest any recipient other than Ludwig for the second letter. The suggestion (*Echtheit, loc. cit.*) that it was unnecessary for Hildegard to *send* the copy of *LDO* to Ludwig because he himself came to her on the Rupertsberg, is not decisively supported by the words in the Epilogue of *LDO* (R 308r*b*):

> Tunc vero reverentissimus et sapientissimus vir coram deo et hominibus, Ludewicus abbas sancti Eucharii in Treveri, magna misericordia super dolore meo motus est, ita quod per se ipsum et per alios sapientes stabili instantia auxilium mihi fiducialiter prebuit, et quia ipse predictum felicem hominem [Volmarum] et me ac visiones *meas* [*quas* R] prius bene cognovit, in lacrimabili suspirio de illo, quasi eum a deo suscepissem, gaudebam.

Even if this could mean that Ludwig came to Hildegard, it does not necessarily do so: 'stabili instantia' can well mean 'with unfailing constancy' rather than 'by making a long stay'. And even if there was a visit of some length by Ludwig (or by Hildegard in Trier?), this in no way precludes his having been sent the manuscript in advance, which is the only plausible inference that can be made from the Berlin letter.

In Herwegen's ed. of the *LDO* Epilogue ('Collaborateurs' pp. 308f), the following readings especially need correction: 18 Quidam et: Quidam etiam *R* 19 gente: genere *R* 26 quum: quoniam *R*.

94 With the Latin text (edited below, pp. 263-4) compare the following lines in the *Schlüsselbrief* (*Echtheit* p. 143):

> ... teipsum coerce, ne per gratiam honorifici nominis vel per seculares mores a stabilitate bone intentionis tue amovearis... Deo etiam et tibi, mitis pater, gratias ago, quod infirmitati et dolori meo, que paupercula forma sum, condolere dignatus es, que modo velut orphana sola in opere dei laboro, quoniam adiutor meus, ut deo placuit, mihi ablatus est. Librum quoque per gratiam spiritus sancti in vera visione cum illo scripsi, et, qui nondum finitus est, mox tibi ad corrigendum representabo, cum perfectus et scriptus fuerit.

and the following in the *LDO* Epilogue (R 308r*b*, Herwegen p. 309):

> ... participes mercedis laborum illius faciam ... mercedem eterne claritatis in celesti Ierusalem dones.

95 W. Harms, *Homo Viator in Bivio* (München 1970); E. Panofsky, *Herkules am Scheide-wege* (Leipzig 1930).
96 *Le roman de Perceval*, ed. W. Roach (Genève 1956) 39-46.
97 *Cit. supra*, n 93.
98 P.L. 197, 107 B, 112 B-C.
99 *Echtheit* p. 13.
100 P.L. 197, 135 B.
101 The letter survives in B 54r*b*-56r*b*, and R 308v*a*-309v*a*. In the passages cited here, I basically follow the B text, and give variants (other than purely orthographic ones) from R. (Divergences from the text in P.L. 197, 218 C - 221 D, are not listed.) -

In visione que anime mee, antequam nata procederem, a deo opifice infixa est, coacta sum ad scribendum ista, pro ligatura qua a magistris nostris alligate sumus, propter quendam mortuum conductu sacerdotis sui apud nos sine calumpnia sepultum. Quem post paucos sepelitionis sue dies cum [om. B. *idem* add. BR] a magistris nostris *e* [*a* R] cimiterio eicere iusse *essemus* [*iussissent* BR], ex hoc non minimo terrore correpta, ad verum lumen ut soleo [*solito* R] aspexi, et vigilantibus oculis in anima mea vidi quod, si iuxta preceptum ipsorum corpus eiusdem mortui efferretur, eiectio illa in modum magne nigredinis ingens periculum loco nostro minaretur, et in similitudine atre nubis, que ante tempestates et tonitrua apparere solet, nos circumvallaret.

Unde et corpus eiusdem defuncti – utpote confessi, inuncti et communicati, et sine contradictione sepulti – nec efferre presumpsimus [*presumimus* R], nec [*ne* B] consilio seu precepto istud suadencium vel iubencium adquievimus: non consilium proborum hominum aut preceptum prelatorum nostrorum omnino parvipendentes, sed ne sacramentis Christi, quibus ille vivens adhuc munitus fuerat, iniuriam sevitate feminea facere videremur. Sed, ne ex toto inobedientes existeremus, a divinarum laudum canticis hactenus, secundum eorum interdictum, cessavimus, et a participatione dominici corporis – quam per singulos fere menses ex consuetudine frequentavimus – abstinuimus.

Super quo dum [om. B] magna amaritudine tam ego quam omnes sorores mee affligeremur, et ingenti tristicia detineremur, magno tandem pondere compressa verba ista in visione audivi . . . quoniam in hoc culpabilis essem, quod cum omni humilitate et devotione ad presenciam magistrorum meorum non venissem, ut ab eis licenciam communicandi quererem, maxime cum in susceptione illius mortui culpa non teneremur . . .

Aspexi etiam aliquid super hoc quod, vobis obediendo, hactenus a cantu divini officii cessantes, illud tantum [*-modo* R] legentes remisse celebramus, et audivi vocem a vivente luce procedentem, de diversis generibus laudum de quibus David in psalmo dicit: 'Laudate eum in sono tube, laudate eum in psalterio et cythara', et cetera, usque ad id: 'omnis spiritus laudet dominum' [Ps. 150: 3–6].

In quibus verbis per exteriora de interioribus instruimur, scilicet [om. R] quomodo, secundum materialem [*-ium* R] compositionem vel qualitatem instrumentorum, interioris hominis nostri officia ad creatoris maxime laudes convertere et informare debeamus. Quibus cum diligenter intendimus, recolimus qualiter homo vocem viventis spiritus requisivit, quam Adam per inobedienciam perdidit – qui ante transgressionem, adhuc innocens, non minimam societatem cum angelicarum laudum vocibus habeb*a*t, quas [*habebant quam* BR] ipsi ex spiritali natura sua possident, qui a spiritu – qui deus est – spiritus vocantur. Similitudinem ergo vocis angelice, quam in paradyso habebat, Adam perdidit . . .

Ut autem [*etiam* R] divine illius dulcedinis et laudationis, qua [*quam* BR] cum angelis [*c. a.* om. R] in deo priusquam caderet idem Adam iocundabatur, et non eius in hoc exilio recordarentur, et ad hec quoque ipsi provocarentur, idem sancti prophete, eodem spiritu quem acceperant edocti [*spiritu* om. B *eodemque s. a.* R], non solum psalmos et [om. B] cantica, que ad accendendam audiencium devotionem cantarentur, sed instrumenta musice artis diversa, quibus cum multiplicibus sonis proferrentur, hoc respectu composuerunt: ut tam ex formis vel qualitatibus eorumdem instrumentorum quam ex *sensu* [*verbis* B] verborum que in eis recitantur [*-rentur* R], audientes – ut predictum est – per exteriora ammoniti et exercitati, de interioribus erudirentur.

Quos videlicet sanctos prophetas studiosi[-*que* R] et sapientes imitati, humana et ipsi arte nonnulla organorum genera invenerunt, ut secundum delectationem anime cantare possent; et que cantabant in iuncturis digitorum, que flexionibus inclinantur, adaptav*erunt* [-*vit* BR], ut et recolentes Adam digito dei – qui *spiritus sanctus* est [*qui est formatus* B] – formatum, in cuius voce sonus omnis armonie et tocius musice artis, antequam delinqueret, suavitas erat [-*it* R]. Et si in statu quo formatus fuit permansisset, infirmitas [-*tem* B] mortalis hominis virtutem et sonoritatem vocis illius nullatenus ferre posset. Cum autem deceptor eius, diabolus, audisset quod homo ex inspiratione dei cantare cepisset, et per hoc ad recolendam suavitatem canticorum celestis patrie mutaretur, machinamentum calliditatis sue in [*ne* B] irritum ire videns, ita exterritus est, ut . . . confessionem et pulchritudinem atque dulcedinem divine laudis [*laudationis* R] et spiritalium ymnorum perturbare vel auferre non desistit. Quapropter summa vigilancia *vobis* [*nobis* B] et omnibus prelatis satagendum est, ut, antequam *os* [*omnes* B] alicuius ecclesie deo canencium per sentenciam claudatis . . . cavendum semper est [om. R], ne in iudiciis vestris circumveniamini a Sathana, qui hominem a celesti armonia et a deliciis paradysi extraxit . . .

Et quoniam interdum, in auditu alicuius canticionis [*cantionis* R], homo sepe suspirat et gemit, natura*m* celestis armonie recolens [*natura* B, *naturam anime* R], propheta, subtiliter profundam spiritus naturam considerans [*propheta spiritus n. c.* R], et sciens quia symphonialis est anima, hortatur in psalmo, ut confiteamur domino in cythara et [*in* add. R] psalterio decem cordarum psal*lamus* [*psalmus* B]: eius cytharam [-*ra* BR], que inferius sonat, ad disciplinam corporis, [*quod* add. B] psalterium, quod de superius [-*oribus* R] sonum reddit, ad intentionem spiritus, decem cordas ad completionem legis referri cupiens.

102 *De mus.* I 2:

Et primum ea [musica], quae est mundana, in his maxime perspicienda est, quae in ipso caelo vel compage elementorum vel temporum varietate visuntur. Qui enim fieri potest, ut tam velox caeli machina tacito silentique cursu moveatur? Etsi ad nostras aures sonus ille non pervenit, quod multis fieri de causis necesse est, non poterit tamen motus tam velocissimus ita magnorum corporum nullos omnino sonos ciere . . .

On the concept *musica mundana*, compare L. Spitzer, *Classical and Christian Ideas of World Harmony* (Baltimore 1963). There are some observations on Hildegard's conception of music in R. Hammerstein, *Die Musik der Engel* (Bonn–München 1962), esp. pp. 54–7, 108–9, and in M. I. Ritscher, *Colloquium Amicorum* pp. 309–26; cf. also J. Schmidt-Görg, *Fs. H. Lützeler* pp. 233f.

103 This alludes to the so-called 'Guidonian hand', a mnemonic teaching device attributed to Guido of Arezzo (*ca.* 990 – *ca.* 1050), assigning the degrees of the melodic gamut to the various joints of fingers and thumb of the left hand (cf. G. Reese, *Music in the Middle Ages* (New York 1940) p. 151, where the diagram of such a hand is reproduced).

104 Compare Hildegard's thoughts about Adam's original musical mastery in *Causae* (ed. below, p. 245).

105 On Joachim of Fiore's use of the *psalterium decem chordarum* in a range of allegorical images, see M. Reeves and B. Hirsch-Reich, *The Figurae of Joachim of Fiore* (Oxford 1972) ch. XII.

106 P.L. 197, 279 D.

7. From Hildegard to Marguerite Porete

1 See Bibliography below, pp. 325, 329f.

2 Cf. most recently K. Elm's essay 'Die Stellung der Frau in Ordenswesen . . .'. in *Sankt Elisabeth*, pp. 7–28.

3 There had been, admittedly, a vehemently subjective element in the visionary writings of Hildegard's younger contemporary, Elisabeth of Schönau (see Bibliography p. 324) – yet in her this went with a signal lack of imaginative and intellectual rigour. Compared with Elisabeth's outpourings, the literary control of a Hadewijch is at once evident.

4 In the case of the loss of Richardis, and in that of the Mainz interdict, opposition to Hildegard's stance admittedly continued (see above ch. 6. sects. III and X); yet significantly this opposition never took the form of an attempt to discredit Hildegard's *visio*.

5 Cf. A. Dondaine's discussion, *Revue de l'histoire des religions* CLXXVIII (1970) 49–56. Duvernoy in 1972 added a fascicule, *Corrections*, to his edition, though – at least in the testimonies I have read in MS – this catches only a proportion of the errors. Whilst much palaeographic and philological work on the *Registre* remains to be done, this must not lessen one's gratitude to Duvernoy for having made a complete text of the depositions available.

6 *Montaillou.*

7 For convenience, I use Gallicized name-forms in translations and discussion below (as does Le Roy Ladurie).

8 The translations here and below are in a sense 'free': in order to evoke as accurately as possible the Provençal words that the women themselves will have used in their testimonies, it is necessary not only to turn the Latin into direct speech but also to infer, from legalistic and condemnatory expressions in the official record, the 'unloaded' expressions that might lie behind these. Where no separate footnote indicates otherwise, the Latin texts corresponding to these testimonies are printed below, pp. 265–74, in the order in which they are here translated and discussed; at times surrounding passages of Latin, not translated in this chapter, are also given below.

9 Perhaps we should understand 'say (for certain that it was) so', since in the later interrogation Grazida admits to having heard rumours to that effect.

10 Lat. *solatiando*: see Du Cange, s.v. *solatiari* – 'animum relaxare, se divertir'. (Cf. Prov. *solatz*.)

11 For the theological view that sexual love in marriage 'cannot be entirely free from sin (*omnino peccato non careat*)', cf. Abelard, *Ep.* VIII, *MS* XVIII (1956) 278.

12 The best outline of Cathar beliefs is probably still that of Borst pp. 143ff.

13 See *Lexikon für Theologie und Kirche* I 708–12, s.v. 'Apokatastasis'. A number of the ways in which the theological concept left its mark in popular beliefs and legends are discussed in L. Kretzenbacher, *Versöhnung*.

14 The strict analogy with what Grazida had said of hell ('I don't believe in hell . . . for that is something evil') makes clear that she is here affirming, for the same reason, that she does not believe in Satan. She does not mean that there is a devil who has *aseitas* like God, or who can exist uncaused.

15 It is disappointing that Duvernoy, in his translation of *Le registre* (I 303), says in a footnote to Grazida's testimony: 'elle est consciemment insolente, bien que le procès-verbal ait l'apparence de la naïveté'. This judgement, by the scholar who through his

detailed work should have been in the best position to comprehend Grazida's thoughts, is inappropriately hostile and condescending.

16 Gaunilo, '*Quid ad haec respondeat . . .*' 6 (ed. M. J. Charlesworth, in *St Anselm's Proslogion* (Oxford 1965) pp. 162ff).

17 Both kinds of disbelief are exemplified by Béatrice de Lagleize (Duvernoy I 216ff).

18 See n 13 above. At the same time, some infiltration of learned influence, between Scotus Eriugena and the late thirteenth century, cannot be ruled out.

19 To cite only a few important studies, that complement one another: P. Rousselot, *Pour l'histoire du problème de l'amour*; F. Ohly, *Hohelied-Studien*; R. Herde, *Das Hohelied*; J. Leclercq, *Monks and Love*; *Monks on Marriage*.

20 However, Mengarde's statement that 'it's a great sin, since I was a widow' may reflect not only a Christian attitude to extramarital love but also an archaic taboo against widows' re-entering sexual bonds.

21 It is also possible that 'alia vice', coming in the wake of 'iterum', does not have temporal force but suggests another mode of intercourse.

22 The reference is to the child's inherited original sin, which had been washed away by his Christian baptism.

23 Duvernoy II 406–7, 411. In the textual notes that follow, Du = Duvernoy, V = the manuscript, Vat. lat. 4030.

24 Correcting to 'patri' (patre *V Du*).

25 Reading 'eam (persuasionem)': *sic V*; eum *Du*.

26 Translating 'aliquid' (*sic V*).

27 See below, pp. 217ff.

28 Duvernoy II 424.

29 V fol. 114rb (Du I 545):

> Item dixit ei quod filia ipsius que loquitur in brevi veniret ad eam et obscularetur (*sic V*) eam in lecto suo, et ex tunc melius dormiret . . . Item dixit ei . . . quod conaretur comedere et bibere quantum posset, et quod faceret quod viveret in presenti seculo quanto (*sic V*) plus posset, quia, ut dixit dictus Arnaldus ei, non est vita ita bona nec quod tantum valeat sicut vita presens.

30 Duvernoy I 151ff.

31 *Ibid.* I 261–2.

32 *Ibid.* I 215.

33 Neither Duvernoy nor Le Roy Ladurie distinguishes between Aude's disbelief in God and her disbelief in the 'real presence' in the host. Moreover, Le Roy Ladurie's interpretation of Aude as a masochist – 'on la verra supplier l'évêque de lui imposer pénitences publiques, pour que le monde la couvre d'opprobre' (p. 533) – is the exact opposite of what Aude says: she implores the bishop that her penance should *not* be public or humiliating (see her words, cited below p. 215).

34 See the fine analysis by G. Vinay, 'Otlone di Sant' Emmeram, ovvero l'autobiografia di un nevrotico', *Settimane di studio* XVII (Spoleto 1969) 1–23.

35 This sin (*peccatum*), which is distinct from Aude's failure of belief (*error*), is never disclosed.

36 I construe the vernacular exclamation 'osta' as a cry of distress (cf. Levy, s.v. *ostar* 7, who, however, gives the meanings 'hört auf! redet nicht so! nicht doch!', as if in answer to something said, whereas here it opens a dialogue).

37 Prov. 'Co, Na Traytoressa, no sia !' The phrase as recorded is difficult. I construe 'Co'
as interjection (mod. Fr. *'comment!'*), and 'no sia' as picking up the syntax of the
preceding lines: 'nec . . . sit', rather than as an imperative, like Duvernoy ('do not be
Mrs. Traitress'), for which one would expect *sias* or *siatz.*

38 Duvernoy II 89.

39 *Ibid.* II 94; cf. also above p. 124.

40 A place of pilgrimage in Foix (cf. Le Roy Ladurie pp. 491ff).

41 *Le livre* p. 9.

42 *Ibid.* p. 10.

43 This fantasy is based on a traditional theological conceit – cf. Alan of Lille, *Distinctiones*
(P.L. 210, 828 A):

> *Lambere*, proprie, *imitari*; unde Job: *Pulli aquilae lambunt sanguinem.* Aquila Christus,
> pulli martyres qui lambunt Christi sanguinem, id est imitantur eius passionem. Notat
> etiam *sumere*, unde praedicta auctoritas potest sic exponi: *Pulli aquilae*, id est fideles,
> *lambunt carnem et sanguinem*, id est sumunt carnem et sanguinem in Ecclesia Dei, et
> hoc Christi Jesu.

At the same time, the difference in tone between this and Angela's 'biberem sanguinem
eius fluentem ex latere suo' is evident.

44 *Le livre* pp. 12–15.

45 *Ibid.* p. 15.

46 *Corpus documentorum Inquisitionis haereticae pravitatis Neerlandicae* I, ed. P. Fredericq
(Gent 1889) 160 (no. 166).

47 Cf. Guarnieri, *Miroir* pp. 504–9 (on the question of an alleged medieval German
translation, and of other possible French MSS, *ibid.* pp. 501–2).

48 'Geistliche Prosa', in *Europäisches Spätmittelalter* p. 589. On the other hand, Ruh is too
categorical in saying there is no 'Zweifel, dass Marguerite der formalen Kunst der
zeitgenössischen Lyrik nie begegnet ist' (p. 592): even her use of canzone and rondeau
(the texts are cited below) should make one surmise that she had some acquaintance
with contemporary lyrical poetry. The whole question of Marguerite's literary and
theological formation remains to be solved in detail. Guarnieri (*Miroir* p. 510) rightly
underlines that 'la cultura così teologica come letteraria della Porete risulta a prima
vista', but unless new research brings further biographic details to light, the exact paths
of transmission, for instance, of the Dionysian mysticism that Marguerite knew may
not be ascertainable.

49 For this Guarnieri's study, 'Il movimento del Libero Spirito', which introduces her
edition of Marguerite, remains fundamental. By contrast, in N. Cohn's widely-read
The Pursuit of the Millennium (London 1957) p. 176, it is evident that the author has only
a hazy notion of Marguerite and does not know her work at firsthand.

50 Guarnieri, *Miroir* p. 521.

51 *Ibid.* p. 522.

52 *Ibid.* pp. 529, 534.

53 *Ibid.* p. 545.

54 *Ibid.* pp. 629–31 (the lyrical lines are printed below, p. 275).

55 *Ibid.* pp. 525, 527, 530f.

56 *De div. nom.* II.

57 Thus (e.g. *Miroir* p. 562) Raison addresses the soul as 'tres noble pierre en la largeur du

plain de verité'. At the first occurrence of the phrase (p. 527) the MS has the unexpected form 'la plane', but the context makes clear that the word for 'plain' (*le
plain, la plaine* – see Tobler–Lommatzsch s.vv.) is intended: 'Ceste ame . . . si siet en
la vallee d'Umilité, et en la plane de Verité, et se respouse en la montaigne d'Amour'.
For Plato's metaphor, see *Phaedrus* 248 b.

58 *Symposium* 203 c.
59 Guarnieri, *Miroir* pp. 608–9.
60 Printed by Guarnieri, *Miroir* pp. 649–60.
61 *Ibid.* pp. 524–5; the verses are printed above, p. 275.
62 On Cathar analogues to this conception of an invisible Church of the Spirit, still
tenacious in Marguerite's time, see Duvernoy II 53 and Le Roy Ladurie p. 559.
63 I have amplified this, with documentation, in a discussion of Joachim and Dante, *RP*
XXIX (1975) 1–19.
64 Here the MS (fol. 25v) has 'saincte eglise le petite', but Guarnieri (*Miroir*) corrects
silently to 'la'.
65 Guarnieri, *Miroir* pp. 538–9.
66 Gottfried of Strassburg, *Tristan* 45ff; Guido Guinizelli, 'Al cor gentil rimpaira sempre
amore' (ed. Contini II 460–4).
67 Guarnieri, *Miroir* p. 555. There is a striking parallel to this ideal of the acceptance by
the visible Church of the higher Church of the Spirit in Joachim, *Tractatus super quatuor
evangelia*, ed. E. Buonaiuti (Roma 1930) pp. 87f.
68 Guarnieri, *Miroir* p. 586.
69 Printed above, pp. 275f.
70 Guarnieri, *Miroir* p. 588.
71 *Ibid.* pp. 537–8.
72 The MS has 'choses passees' (not 'passes', Gu, *Miroir*).
73 The lyrical passages that follow are printed above, pp. 276–7.
74 Cf. Cant. 4: 7–10 ('amica mea . . . soror mea'), etc.
75 Marguerite's use of several genitives dependent on one another is strikingly reminiscent
of one of Hildegard's stylistic mannerisms (see above, p. 308 n 24).
76 Cf. G. Koch, *Frauenfrage*, esp. pp. 62–72, and 170–3 (referring also to the Waldensians).

Bibliography

My principal aim in this Bibliography is to chart the primary sources – the writings and testimonies of all the women, from *ca.* 200 to *ca.* 1300 A.D., that I read while preparing this book. These primary entries are distinguished by capitals. To make each entry as succinct as possible, only one edition – the standard text, or the most recent one – is generally adduced; often this is followed by some indications of secondary literature, concerned with that particular writer or text, which I found of special interest. (Other works, and studies that extend to more than one writer, are listed under the names – uncapitalized – of their authors, in the general alphabetical order.)

No attempt is made here to provide a comprehensive picture of the secondary literature on any writer or text, since a bibliography planned on that basis would alone take up a substantial volume. Instead, where possible, I have signalled certain works with '[B]', to indicate that they contain extensive further bibliography for their subject.

This Bibliography does not include: (i) works that are cited in the footnotes of the book in order to document specific points, but that have no direct bearing on writings by medieval women; (ii) works of classical authors (though these are frequently cited in the course of the book, according to standard editions); (iii) *lost* writings by medieval women, such as letters that can be inferred from surviving answers by men correspondents; (iv) the majority of historical studies about medieval women, where these do not specifically treat testimonies by women themselves.

Abels, R., E. Harrison, 'The Participation of Women in Languedocian Catharism', *MS* XLI (1979) 215–51

AELFFLED (†713): Letter to Adola, ed. Tangl no. 8; cf. Unterkircher fol. 32r–v

ALAIS, CARENZA, YSELDA (s. XII–XIII): 'Na Carenza, al bel cors avinen', ed. above pp. 300–2

ALAMANDA (s. XII²): 'Si·us quer conselh', ed. A. Kolsen, *Giraut de Bornelh* (2 vols., Halle a. S. 1910) no. 57

Alexiou, M., *The Ritual Lament in Greek Tradition* (Cambridge 1974)

ALMUCS DE CASTELNAU, ISEUT DE CAPIO (s. XII²): 'Dompna N'Almucs', ed. Boutière–Schutz pp. 422–4, Bogin p. 92

AMALASWINTHA (534): Four letters, in Cassiodorus, *Variae* X 1, 3, 8, 10, ed. MGH, *Auct. Ant.* XII 297ff

ANASTASIA (s. VI in.): Letter to Pope Hormisdas, ed. O. Günther, CSEL XXXV 2, Ep. 165

ANGELA OF FOLIGNO (1248–1309): *Le livre*, ed. P. Doncoeur, F. Pulignani (Paris–Toulouse 1925); ed. and tr. M.-J. Ferré, L. Baudry (Paris 1927)
   Cf. also A. Blasucci, *La Beata Angela da Foligno* (Foligno 1978); 'Angela da Foligno', in *Bibliotheca Sanctorum* I (Roma 1961) 1185–90.

ANONYMOUS
   Latin texts:

(1) 'Nisi, tanti seminis, silentium meum' (s. VI, from Radegunde's convent at Poitiers?), ed. C. P. Caspari, *Briefe, Abhandlungen und Predigten* (Christiania 1890) pp. 178–82, commentary *ibid.* pp. 398–404; MGH, *Epist.* III 716–18

(2) *Visio cuiusdam pauperculae mulieris* (s. IX in.), ed. H. Houben, *Zeitschrift für die Geschichte des Oberrheins* CXXIV (1976) 31–42

(3) *Carmina Ratisponensia* (s. XI²), ed. A. Paravicini (Heidelberg 1979); cf. P. Dronke, *Sandalion* V (1982) 109–17; *Medieval Latin* I 221–9, II 422–47

(4) *Puella ad amicum munera promittentem* ['Gaudia Nimpharum . . .'] (s. XI²), ed. W. Bulst, *Carmina Leodensia* VI

(5) *Epistolae duorum amantium* (s. XII¹), ed. E. Könsgen (Leiden–Köln 1974)

(6) Tegernsee love-letters (s. XII): Letters I–III ('S. suo dilecto', 'H. quondam carissimo', 'Accipe scriptorum'), VI–VII ('C. super mel', 'G. unice sue rose'), and possibly V ('C. Cara Karissime'), are written by women (ed. *Medieval Latin* II 472–82); also by a woman are 'H. flori florum' and 'Suo sua sibi se' (ed. K. Lachmann, M. Haupt, *Minnesangs Frühling* (Leipzig 1857) pp. 221–4). On the ed. by J. Kühnel (Göppingen 1977), see D. Schaller, 'Zur Textkritik und Beurteilung der sog. Tegernseer Liebesbriefe', *ZfdP* CI (1982) 104–21

Provençal texts (s. XII–XIII):

(1) 'Amics, en gran cossirier', ed. W. T. Pattison, *The Life and Works of the Troubadour Raimbaut d'Orange* (Minneapolis 1952), xxv, where the whole *tenso* is ascribed to Raimbaut; similarly in M. de Riquer, *Los trovadores* I 452-4

(2) 'Bona domna', ed. Schultz, II

(3) 'No·m posc mudar', ed. M. de Riquer, *Los trovadores* I 576f

(4) 'Quan Proensa ac perduda proeza', ed. Schultz, IV

(5) 'Quan vei los praz verdezir', ed. K. Bartsch, *Chrestomathie Provençale* (Marburg ⁶1904), cols. 249–52

(6) 'Si·m fos grazitz', ed. Schultz, III

Catalan text (s. XIII):

'Lassa, mays m'agra valgut', ed. J. Massó i Torrents, *Estudis Universitaris Catalans* XXI (1936) 405f

Anton, H. H., *Fürstenspiegel und Herrscherethos in der Karolingerzeit* (Bonn 1968)

AUDE FAURÉ (s. XIV in.): Testimony, see above pp. 271–4, and Duvernoy II 82–105; see also Index of Manuscripts

Auerbach, E., 'Figura', *Gesammelte Aufsätze zur romanischen Philologie* (Bern–München 1967), pp. 55–92

Literatursprache und Publikum in der lateinischen Spätantike und im Mittelalter (Bern 1958)

Mimesis (Bern ²1959)

AVA (†1127): *Die Dichtungen der Frau Ava*, ed. F. Maurer (Tübingen 1966); cf. R. Kienast, 'Ava-Studien I–III', *ZfdA* LXXIV (1937) 1–36, 277–308, LXXVII (1940) 85–104; M. Wehrli, *Formen mittelalterlicher Erzählung* (Zürich 1969) pp. 51–71

AZALAIS D'ALTIER (s. XIII¹): 'Tanz salutz e tantas amors', ed. V. Crescini, *ZfrP* XIV (1890) 128–32

AZALAIS DE PORCAIRAGUES (*fl.* 1173): 'Ar em el freg temps vengut', ed. M. de Riquer, *Los trovadores* I 459-62

Baker, D. (ed.), *Medieval Women* (Studies in Church History, Oxford 1978)

Barber, M. C., 'Women and Catharism', *Reading Medieval Studies* III (1977) 45-62

BAUDONIVIA (s. VII in.): *De vita S. Radegundis*, ed. MGH, *Script. Rer. Merov.* II 364–95

BIBLIOGRAPHY

BEATRIJS VAN TIENEN [Beatrice of Nazareth] (1200–68): *De autobiografie van de Z. Beatrijs van Tienen*, ed. L. Reypens (Antwerpen 1964)
Seven manieren van Minne, ed. L. Reypens, J. van Mierlo (Leuven 1926)

Bec, P., '"Trobairitz" et chansons de femme', *CCM* XXII (1979) 235–62

Beccaria, A., *I codici di medicina del periodo presalernitano* (Roma 1956)

Bernards, M., *Speculum Virginum* (Köln–Graz 1955)

BERTHA OF TUSCANY (906): Letters to Caliph Muktafi [extant in Arabic], tr. G. Levi della Vida, 'La corrispondenza di Berta di Toscana col Califfo Muktafi', *Rivista storica italiana* LXVI (1954) 21–38

BERTHA OF VILICH (1056/7): *Vita Adelheidis Abbatissae Vilicensis*, ed. MGH, *Scriptores* XV 2, 755–63 (*Prologus alter ad Vitam, Analecta Bollandiana* II 211f); cf. J. Schlafke, 'Leben und Verehrung der hl. Adelheid von Vilich', in D. Höroldt (ed.), *Tausend Jahre Stift Vilich 978–1978* (Bonn 1978)

BERTHGYTH (*fl. ca.* 770): Letters to Balthard, ed. Tangl nos. 143, 147, 148; cf. Unterkircher fols. 33v, 34v–35v

Bezold, F. von, *Über die Anfänge der Selbstbiographie und ihre Entwicklung im Mittelalter* (Erlangen 1893)

Bezzola, R. R., *Les origines et la formation de la littérature courtoise en Occident (500–1200)* (3 vols. in 5, Paris 1958–63)

BIEIRIS DE ROMANS (s. XIII¹?): 'Na Maria, pretz e fina valors', ed. Schultz, 15

Bischoff, B., 'Die Kölner Nonnenhandschriften und das Skriptorium von Chelles', in his *Mittelalterliche Studien* I (Stuttgart 1966) 16–34
see also under HUGEBURC

Borst, A., *Die Katharer* (MGH, Stuttgart 1953)

Bosl, K., 'Il "santo nobile"', in S. Boesch Gajano (ed.), *Agiografia altomedioevale* (Bologna 1976), pp. 161–90

BRUNHILDA [Brunichildis] (s. VI²): Letters, ed. W. Gundlach, *Epistulae Austrasicae* (CC CXVII 403ff) nos. 26, 27, 29, 30, 44

Brunhölzl, F., *Geschichte der lateinischen Literatur des Mittelalters* I (München 1975)

de Bruyne, D., 'Les anciennes versions latines du Cantique des Cantiques', *RB* XXXVIII (1926) 97–122

BUGGA [Heaburg] (*ca.* 720): Letter to Boniface, ed. Tangl no. 15; cf. Unterkircher fol. 20v–21r

Bugge, J., *Virginitas* ('s Gravenhage 1975)

Bulst, W., *Carmina Leodiensia* (Sitzb. d. Heidelberger Akad. d. Wiss., 1975, Abh. 1, Heidelberg 1975)
'Liebesbriefgedichte Marbods', in *Liber Floridus: Fs. Paul Lehmann* (St Ottilien 1950) pp. 287–301
see also under RADEGUNDIS

BURGINDA (s. VII/VIII): Letter to a young man, ed. P. Sims-Williams, *Medium Aevum* XLVIII (1979) 1–22 [The letter would seem to be an autograph, hence the diplomatic text, *ibid.* p. 6, should probably be accepted without emendation, assuming only the word-division 'fle tu' in line 12]

CAESARIA [Abbess at Arles] (s. VI²): Letter (before 587) to Richilda and Radegund, ed. MGH, *Epist.* III 450–3

Carrol, B. A. (ed.), *Liberating Women's History* (Urbana 1976)

CASTELLOZA (s. XIII¹): Four songs, ed. W. D. Paden *et al.*, *RP* XXXV (1981) 158–82

CHIARA D'ASSISI [St Clare] (1194–1253): *Scripta*, ed. I. M. Boccali, *Concordantiae verbales opusculorum S. Francisci et S. Clarae* (Assisi 1976) pp. 167–218

CHRISTINA OF MARKYATE (*ca.* 1096/8 – *ca.* 1155/66): *The Life of Christina of Markyate*, ed. C. H. Talbot (Oxford 1959)

Chydenius, J., *Love and the Medieval Tradition* (Soc. Scient. Fennica, Helsingfors 1977)
   The Symbolism of Love in Medieval Thought (Soc. Scient. Fennica, Helsingfors 1970)

CLARA D'ANDUZA (s. XIII¹): 'En greu esmai', ed. Schultz, 13

CLEMENCE OF BARKING (*fl.* 1163–9): *The Life of St Catherine*, ed. W. McBain (Anglo-Norman Text Society, Oxford 1964)
   La vie d'Edouard le Confesseur, ed. Ö. Södergård (Uppsala 1948) [often attributed to an anonymous nun at Barking]

COMPIUTA DONZELLA (s. XIII²): Three sonnets, ed. G. Contini, *Poeti* I 433–8

COMTESSA DE DIA (s. XII²?): Five songs, ed. G. Kussler-Ratyé, *Archivum Romanicum* I (1917) 161–82; four also ed. M. de Riquer, *Los trovadores* II 791–802; the fifth – the woman's strophes in 'Amics, en gran cossirier', *ibid.* I 452–4 – may well not be by the Comtessa (see above, p. 321)

Consolino, F. A., 'Amor spiritualis . . .', *Annali della Scuola Normale di Pisa* VII (1977) 1351–68

Constable, G., *Letters and Letter-Collections* (Typologie des sources du Moyen Age occidental, Fasc. 17, Turnhout 1976)
   (ed.), *The Letters of Peter the Venerable* (2 vols., Cambridge, Mass. 1967)

CONSTANTIA (*ca.* 1065–after 1129): Verse epistle to Baudri of Bourgueil, ed. Hilbert; cf. O. Schumann, 'Baudri von Bourgueil als Dichter', in *Ehrengabe für Karl Strecker* (Dresden 1931) pp. 158–70

Contini, G. (ed.), *Poeti del Duecento* (2 vols., Milano–Napoli 1960)

Curtius, E. R., *Europäische Literatur und Lateinisches Mittelalter* (Bern ²1954)

Daniélou, J., *Sacramentum Futuri* (Paris 1950)

DHUODA (*ca.* 803–after 843): *Manuel [Liber Manualis]* – see List of Abbreviations, and Index of Manuscripts
   Poems, ed. K. Strecker, MGH, *Poetae* IV 2, 701–17
   Cf. also Ph. A. Becker, 'Dhuodas Handbuch', *ZfrP* XXI (1897) 73–101; G. Mathon, 'Les fondements de la morale chrétienne selon le "Manuel" de Dhuoda', in *Sapientiae Doctrina. Mélanges . . . Dom Hildebrand Bascour O.S.B.* (Leuven 1980); W. Meyer, *Ges. Abh.* III 72–85; P. Riché, 'Les bibliothèques . . .', *Le Moyen Age* LXIX (1963) 87–103; J. Wollasch, 'Eine adlige Familie . . .', *Archiv für Kulturgeschichte* XXXIX (1957) 150–88

Diepgen, P., *Frauen und Frauenheilkunde in der Kultur des Mittelalters* (Stuttgart 1963)

Dodds, E. R., *Pagan and Christian in an Age of Anxiety* (Cambridge 1965)

Dondaine, A., 'A propos d'un livre récent' [Review of J. Duvernoy, *Le registre d'Inquisition de Jacques Fournier*], *Revue de l'histoire des religions* CLXXVIII (1970) 49–56

Dronke, P., *Medieval Latin*, and 'Problemata' – see List of Abbreviations
   'Arbor Caritatis', in *Medieval Studies for J. A. W. Bennett* (Oxford 1981) pp. 207–53
   Fabula: Explorations into the Uses of Myth in Medieval Platonism (Leiden–Köln 1974)
   The Medieval Lyric (London–New York ²1977)
   'Medieval Rhetoric', in *Literature and Western Civilization*, ed. D. Daiches, A. Thorlby (London 1973) II 315–45
   'New Approaches to the School of Chartres', *Anuario de Estudios Medievales* VI (1969 [1971]) 117–40

Poetic Individuality in the Middle Ages: New Departures in Poetry 1000–1150 (Oxford 1970)

'Profane Elements in Literature', in *Renaissance and Renewal in the Twelfth Century*, ed. R. L. Benson, G. Constable (Cambridge, Mass. 1982) pp. 569–92

'The Prologue of the Prose Edda' (with Ursula Dronke), in *Sjötíu Ritgerthir helgathar Jakobi Benediktssyni* (2 vols., Reykjavík 1977) I 153–76

'Virgines caste', in *Lateinische Dichtungen des X. und XI. Jhdts.: Festgabe Walther Bulst* (Heidelberg 1981) pp. 93–117

Duby, G., *Medieval Marriage* (Baltimore 1978)

Les trois ordres ou l'imaginaire du féodalisme (Paris 1978)

Duckett, E. S., *Women and their Letters in the Early Middle Ages* (Baltimore 1965)

Duvernoy, J. (ed.), *Le registre* – see List of Abbreviations

Corrections [to *Le registre*] (Toulouse 1972)

(tr.), *Le registre d'Inquisition de Jacques Fournier* (3 vols., Paris–La Haye 1978)

EANGYTH, BUGGA (719–22): Letter to Boniface, ed. Tangl no. 14; cf. Unterkircher fols. 21v–23v

Eckenstein, L., *Woman under Monasticism* (Cambridge 1896)

The Women of Early Christianity [revised by C. Roscoe] (London 1935)

EGBURG (716–18): Letter to Boniface, ed. Tangl no. 13; cf. Unterkircher fols. 64r–65r

EGERIA (381–4): *Itinerarium* [*Peregrinatio Aetheriae*], ed. O. Prinz (Heidelberg ⁵1960); *Journal de voyage*, ed. H. Pétré (Sources Chrétiennes, Paris 1948); ed. P. Maraval, M. C. Díaz y Díaz (Sources Chrétiennes, Paris 1982)

Cf. also A. A. R. Bastiaensen, *Observations sur le vocabulaire liturgique dans l'Itinéraire d'Égérie* (Nijmegen–Utrecht 1962); E. Löfstedt, *Philologischer Kommentar zur Peregrinatio Aetheriae* (Uppsala 1911); L. Spitzer, 'The Epic Style of the Pilgrim Aetheria', in his *Romanische Literaturstudien 1936–1956* (Tübingen 1959) pp. 871–912; G. F. M. Vermeer, *Observations sur le vocabulaire du pèlerinage chez Egérie et chez Antonin de Plaisance* (Nijmegen–Utrecht 1965)

Eliade, M., *Le chamanisme et les techniques archaïques de l'extase* (Paris 1951)

ELISABETH OF SCHÖNAU (*ca.* 1129–64): *Die Visionen und Briefe der heiligen Elisabeth*, ed. F. W. E. Roth (Brünn [Brno] ²1886)

Cf. also K. Köster, 'Elisabeth von Schönau. Werk und Wirkung . . .', *Archiv für mittelrheinische Kirchengeschichte* III (1951) 243–315; 'Das visionäre Werk Elisabeths von Schönau', *ibid.* IV (1952) 79–119; *Dictionnaire de Spiritualité* IV (1960) 585–8; L. Oliger, 'Revelationes B. Elisabeth', *Antonianum* I (1926) 24–83

Sankt Elisabeth. Fürstin, Dienerin, Heilige: Aufsätze, Dokumentation, Katalog, ed. Philipps-Universität Marburg . . . (Sigmaringen 1981)

Elm, K., 'Die Stellung der Frau in Ordenswesen, Semireligiosentum und Häresie zur Zeit der hl. Elisabeth' [B], in *Sankt Elisabeth* pp. 7–28

EPITAPHS [by women] (s. II–VI): see above pp. 24–6, and references to sources in the notes *ad loc.*

Erdmann, C., *Die Entstehung des Kreuzzugsgedankens* (Stuttgart 1935)

Erickson, C., K. Casey, 'Women in the Middle Ages: A Working Bibliography' [B], *MS* XXXVII (1975) 340–59

EUCHERIA (s. VI²): 'Aurea concordi quae fulgent fila metallo', ed. and tr. H. Homeyer, *Dichterinnen* pp. 185–7

EUDOXIA (s. V): Letter to Theodosius II, ed. E. Schwartz, ACO II 3 (*Epistularum ante Gesta Coll.* III 1, 21); P.L. 54, 861–4

EUPHEMIA (s. VI in.): Letter to Pope Hormisdas, ed. O. Günther, CSEL XXXV 2, *Ep.* 194

La femme dans les civilisations des Xe–XIIIe siècles: Colloque, CCM XX (1977) 93–263; also publ. separately (Poitiers 1977)

de Fontette, M., *Les religieuses à l'âge classique du droit canon* (Paris 1967)

Franz, A., *Die kirchlichen Benediktionen im Mittelalter* (2 vols., Freiburg i. Br. 1909)

Frenk Alatorre, M., *Las jarchas mozárabes y los comienzos de la lírica románica* (México 1975)

Frings, Th., E. Lea, 'Nachtrag und Bestätigung', *PBB* (Halle) LXXIX (1967) 282–9

GALLA PLACIDIA (s. V): Letters to Theodosius II and Pulcheria, ed. E. Schwartz, ACO II 3, *Epistularum ante Gesta Coll.* III 1, 18, 20; P.L. 54, 859–62, 863–7

Gardiner, D., *English Girlhood at School. A Study of Women's Education through Twelve Centuries* (Oxford 1929)

GARSENDA (*fl. ca.* 1200): 'Vos que·m semblatz dels corals amadors', ed. Schultz, 4

Gellinek, C., 'Marriage by Consent in Literary Sources of Medieval Germany', *Studia Gratiana* XII (1957) 557–79

GERMONDA (*fl.* 1227–9): 'Greu m'es a durar', ed. J. Véran, *Les poétesses provençales* (Paris 1946) pp. 194–219

GERTRUDE [Nun on the Rupertsberg] (s. XII/XIII): Letter to Guibert of Gembloux, ed. *Catal. Codicum Hagiog. Brux*, I i (Bruxelles 1886) 556

GERTRUDE OF HELFTA (1256–1301/2): *Les exercices* [*Exercitia*], ed. J. Hourlier, A. Schmitt, *Oeuvres spirituelles* I (Sources Chrétiennes, Paris 1967)

Le héraut [*Legatus*], ed. P. Doyère, *Oeuvres spirituelles* II–IV (Paris 1968ff) [In the *Legatus*, only Bk II – *Oeuvres* II 225–353 – is by Gertrude herself]

GISLA [Abbess of Chelles], ROTRUDA [Daughter of Charlemagne] (800): Letter to Alcuin, ed. MGH, *Epist.* IV 323–4

Gössmann, E., 'Anthropologie und soziale Stellung der Frau nach Summen und Sentenzenkommentaren des 13. Jhdts.', *Miscellanea Mediaevalia* XII (1979) 281–97

GRAZIDA LIZIER (s. XIV in.): Testimony, ed. above pp. 265–9 (cf. Duvernoy I 302–6); see also Index of Manuscripts

Greenhill, E. S., *Die geistigen Voraussetzungen der Bilderreihe des Speculum Virginum* (Beiträge, Münster 1962)

Grimal, P. (ed.), *Histoire mondiale de la femme* (3 vols., Paris 1967)

GUDELINA (535): Two letters in Cassiodorus, *Variae* X 21, 24, ed. MGH, *Auct. Ant.* XII 311, 313

GUILLELMA DE ROSERS (*fl. ca.* 1250): 'Na Guillelma, man cavalier arratge', ed. F. Branciforti, *Il canzoniere di Lanfranco Cigala* (Firenze 1954) pp. 172–80

GUILLEMETTE BATHÉGAN (s. XIV in.): Testimony – see above p. 270, and Duvernoy I 537–9; see also Index of Manuscripts

H., [DOMNA] (*fl.* 1220–40): 'Rofin, digatz m'ades de cors', ed. Schultz, 12

HADEWIJCH (*fl.* 1230–50): *Brieven*, ed. J. van Mierlo (Antwerpen 1947)

Mengeldichten, ed. J. van Mierlo (Antwerpen 1952)

Strofische Gedichten, ed. E. Rombauts, N. De Paepe (Zwolle 1961)

Vizioenen, ed. J. van Mierlo (Leuven 1924)

The Complete Works, tr. Mother Columba Hart, O.S.B. (London 1980)

Cf. also N. De Paepe, *Hadewijch. Strofische Gedichten: Een studie van de minne* . . . (Gent 1967); *Hadewijch, Strofische Gedichten, een Keuze; Grondige studie* . . . (2 vols., Gent–Leuven 1972); T. M. Guest, *Some Aspects of Hadewijch's Poetic Form in the 'Strofische Gedichten'* ('s Gravenhage 1975)

Hadot, P., 'Fürstenspiegel', *RAC* VIII (1972) 555ff

Helgadóttir, G. P., *Skáldkonur fyrri alda* I (Akureyri 1961)

HELOISE (*ca.* 1100–63): Letters to Abelard – 'Domino suo, immo patri', ed. Monfrin pp. 111–17; ed. J. T. Muckle *MS* xv (1953) 68–73; 'Unico suo post Christum', ed. Monfrin pp. 117–24, ed. J. T. Muckle *MS* xv 77–82; 'Suo specialiter, sua singulariter', ed. J. T. Muckle *MS* XVII (1955) 241–53

Letter to Peter the Venerable, ed. G. Constable, *The Letters* I 400f

Problemata, ed. P.L. 178, 677–730; see also the Index of Manuscripts

Le lettere di Abelardo ed Eloisa nella traduzione di Jean de Meun, ed. F. Beggiato (2 vols., Modena 1977)

Cf. also *Colloque*, and *Trier 1980* (see List of Abbreviations); P. Bourgain, 'Héloïse', in *Abélard en son temps. Actes du colloque international . . . (14–19 mai 1979)* (Paris 1981) pp. 211–37; P. Dronke, *Abelard and Heloise in Medieval Testimonies* (Glasgow 1976) [B]; E. Gilson, *Héloïse et Abélard* (Paris ³1964); C. S. Jaeger, 'The Prologue to the "Historia Calamitatum" and the Authenticity Question', *Euphorion* LXXIV (1980) 1–15; J. Leclercq, '"Ad ipsam sophiam Christum": Le témoignage monastique d'Abélard', *Revue d'ascétique et de mystique* XLVI (1970) 161–82; D. E. Luscombe, *Peter Abelard* (Historical Association, London 1979) [B]; R. Mohr, 'Der Gedankenaustausch zwischen Heloise und Abelard . . .', *Regula Benedicti Studia, Annuarium Internationale* V (1977) 307–33; J. Monfrin, 'Les lettres d'amour d'Héloïse et d'Abélard', *Le Monde* XV (1979) suppl. to no. 10795; P. von Moos, 'Cornelia und Heloise', *Latomus* XXXIV (1975) 1024–59; 'Die Bekehrung Heloises', *Mlat. Jb.* XI (1976) 95–125; 'Palatini quaestio . . .', *ibid.* IX (1973) 124–58; *Mittelalterforschung und Ideologiekritik* (München 1974) [B]; H. Silvestre, 'Pourquoi Roscelin n'est-il pas mentionné dans l'*Historia calamitatum*?', *RTAM* XLVIII (1981) 218–24; D. Van den Eynde, 'Chronologie des écrits d'Abélard pour Héloïse', *Antonianum* XXXVII (1962) 337–49; P. Zerbi, 'Abelardo ed Eloisa: il problema di un amore e di una corrispondenza', in W. Van den Hoecke, A. Welkenhuysen (eds.), *Love and Marriage*, pp. 130–61; P. Zumthor, 'Préface', in *Abélard et Héloïse, Correspondance* (Paris 1979) pp. 7–40. Peggy Kamuf, *Fictions of Feminine Desire. Disclosures of Heloise* (Lincoln–London 1982), which appeared when the present book was in press, is rich in stimulating and original perceptions (for Heloise's letters see esp. pp. 1–43).

HELPIS (s. VI?): Epitaph – 'Helpis dicta fui, Siculae regionis alumna', ed. and tr. GP 486

HERCHENAFREDA (s. VII¹): Letters to her son, Desiderius, ed. B. Krusch, *Vita S. Desiderii*, CC CXVII 353–6

Herde, R., *Das Hohelied in der lateinischen Literatur des Mittelalters bis zum 12. Jahrhundert* (Münchener Beiträge 3 (1968) and *Studi medievali* 3a serie, VIII (1967) 957–1073)

HERRAD OF HOHENBOURG (1125/30–95): *Hortus deliciarum*, ed. Rosalie Green *et al.* (2 vols., London–Leiden 1979); cf. J. Autenrieth, 'Einige Bemerkungen zu den Gedichten im *Hortus deliciarum*', *Fs. Bernhard Bischoff* (Stuttgart 1971) pp. 307–21

HILDEGARD OF BINGEN (1098–1179): Works: P.L. 197, and the following entries in the List of Abbreviations: *Causae*; *Echtheit* [B]; Pitra; 'Problemata'; *Scivias*; see also the Index of Manuscripts

'Ein unveröffentlichtes Hildegard-Fragment', ed. H. Schipperges, *Sudhoffs Archiv* XL (1956) 41–77

The German translations (often abridged) comprise (Otto Müller Verlag, Salzburg): *Wisse die Wege*, tr. M. Böckeler (1954); *Heilkunde*, tr. H. Schipperges (1957); *Natur-*

BIBLIOGRAPHY

kunde, tr. P. Riethe (1959); *Welt und Mensch*, tr. H. Schipperges (1965); *Briefwechsel*, tr. A. Führkötter (1965); *Lieder*, ed. and tr. P. Barth, M. I. Ritscher, J. Schmidt-Görg (1969); *Der Mensch in der Verantwortung*, tr. H. Schipperges (1972); *Das Buch von den Steinen*, tr. P. Riethe (1979)

W. Lauter, *Hildegard-Bibliographie* (Alzey 1970) [B: for most texts and literature up to 1969]

Das Leben der hl. Hildegard von Bingen [the twelfth-century *Vita*], tr. A. Führkötter (Salzburg ²1980); M. Schrader, A. Führkötter, *Die Herkunft der hl. Hildegard* (Mainz 1981)

Cf. also M. L. Arduini, 'Alla ricerca di un Ireneo medievale', *SM* 3a serie XXI (1980) 269–99; G. Baader, 'Naturwissenschaft und Medizin im 12. Jhdt. und Hildegard von Bingen', *Archiv für mittelrheinische Kirchengeschichte* XXXI (1979) 33–54; A. Ph. Brück (ed.), *Hildegard von Bingen 1179–1979. Fs. zum 800. Todestag* (Mainz 1979); A. R. Calderoni Masetti, G. Dalla Regoli, *Sanctae Hildegardis Revelationes* [Lucca MS 1942] (Lucca 1973); A. Derolez, 'The Genesis of Hildegard of Bingen's *LDO*', *Litterae Textuales. Essays presented to G. I. Lieftinck* (2 vols., Amsterdam 1972) II 23–33; 'Deux notes concernant Hildegarde de Bingen', *Scriptorium* XXVII (1973) 291–5; F. Haug, 'Epistolae S. Hildegardis secundum codicem Stuttgartensem', *RB* XLIII (1931) 59–71; I. Herwegen, 'Les collaborateurs de Sainte Hildegarde', *RB* XXI (1904) 192–203, 302–15, 381–403; J. Leclercq, 'Nouveaux témoins de la survie de St Bernard', *Homenaje a Fray Justo Pérez de Urbel* (2 vols., Silos 1976–7), II 93–109; H. Lehrbach, *Katalog zur internat. Ausstellung 'Heilige Hildegard von Bingen 1179–1979'* (Mainz 1979); H. Liebeschütz, *Das allegorische Weltbild der heiligen Hildegard von Bingen* (Darmstadt ²1966); M. Pereira, 'Maternità e sessualità femminile in Ildegarda di Bingen', *Quaderni storici* XLIV (1980) 564–79; M. I. Ritscher, 'Zur Musik der hl. Hildegard', *Colloquium Amicorum: Joseph Schmidt-Görg zum 70. Geburtstag* (Bonn 1967) pp. 309–26; M. Schmidt, 'Maria – "materia aurea" in der Kirche nach H. von B.', *Münchener Theologische Zeitschrift* XXXII (1981) 16–32; J. Schmidt-Görg, 'Zur Musikanschauung in den Schriften der hl. Hildegard', *Der Mensch und die Künste. Festschrift H. Lützeler* (Düsseldorf 1962) pp. 230–7; B. Widmer, *Heilsordnung und Zeitgeschehen in der Mystik Hildegards von Bingen* (Basel–Stuttgart 1955)

Homeyer, H., *Dichterinnen des Altertums und des frühen Mittelalters* (Paderborn 1979)

HROTSVITHA OF GANDERSHEIM (*ca.* 935 – *ca.* 1000): Works: see List of Abbreviations, under *Opera* and Winterfeld

Cf. also F. Bertini, *Il 'teatro' di Rosvita* (Genova 1979); E. Cerulli, 'Le Calife Abd ar-Rahmān III . . .', *Studia Islamica* XXXII (1970) 69–76; K. De Luca, 'Hrotsvit's "Imitation" of Terence', *Classical Folia* XXVIII (1974) 89–102; E. Franceschini, 'I "tibicines" nella poesia di Hrotsvitha', *Archivum Latinitatis Medii Aevi* XIV (1939) 40–65; A. D. Frankforter, 'Hroswitha of Gandersheim and the Destiny of Women', *The Historian* XLI (1979) 295–314; A. L. Haight (ed.), *Hroswitha of Gandersheim* (New York 1965) [B]; B. I. Jarcho, 'Stilquellen der Hrotsvitha', *ZfdA* LXII (1925) 236–40; H. Menhardt, 'Eine unbekannte Hrotsvitha-hs.', *ZfdA* LXII (1925) 232–6; B. Nagel, *Hrotsvit von Gandersheim* (Sammlung Metzler, Stuttgart 1965) [B]; D. Schaller, 'Hrotsvit von Gandersheim nach Tausend Jahren', *ZfdP* XCVI (1977) 105–14 [B]; M. Schütze-Pflugk, *Herrscher- und Märtyrerauffassung bei Hr. von Gandersheim* (Wiesbaden 1972); E. H. Zeydel, 'Knowledge of Hrotsvitha's Works Prior to 1500', *Modern Language Notes* LIX (1944) 382–5

327

BIBLIOGRAPHY

HUGEBURC OF HEIDENHEIM (s. VIII²): *Vita Willibaldi Episcopi Eichstetensis*, ed. MGH, *Scriptores* XV i, 86–106

Vita Wynnebaldi Abbatis Heidenheimensis, ed. *ibid.* 106–17

Cf. B. Bischoff, 'Wer ist die Nonne von Heidenheim?', *Studien und Mitteilungen zur Gesch. des Benediktinerordens* XLIX (1931) 387f; E. Gottschaller, *Hugeburc von Heidenheim* (Münchener Beiträge 12, 1973)

Hunger, H., *Die hochsprachliche profane Literatur der Byzantiner* (2 vols., München 1978)

IDA [Abbess of Bingen] (s. XII/XIII): Letter to Guibert of Gembloux, ed. *Catalogus Codicum Hagiog. Brux.* I i (Bruxelles 1886) 555f

IMMA [Wife of Einhard] (s. IX¹): Letters (828–36), ed. MGH, *Epist.* V 128–9

ISABELLA (s. XIII¹): 'N'Elias Cairel, de l'amor', ed. Schultz, 7

JACQUES FOURNIER (†1342): Record (1318–25) of testimonies, incl. those of thirty-six women – see List of Abbreviations under 'Duvernoy', and Index of Manuscripts; four of the women are given separate entries in this Bibliography – see under AUDE FAURÉ; GRAZIDA LIZIER; GUILLEMETTE BATHÉGAN; MENGARDE BUSCALH

Janson, T., *Latin Prose Prefaces. Studies in Literary Conventions* (Stockholm 1964)

Prose Rhythm in Medieval Latin from the 9th to the 13th Century (Stockholm 1975)

Jolivet, J., 'Quelques cas de "platonisme grammatical" du VIIe au XIIe siècle', *Mélanges René Crozet* (2 vols., Poitiers 1966) I 93–9

Jourdain, Ch., 'Mémoire sur l'éducation des femmes au Moyen Age', *Mémoires de l'Académie des Inscriptions et des Belles-Lettres* XXVIII (1874) 77–133

JULIANA ANICIA (s. VI in.): Letters to Pope Hormisdas, ed. O. Günther, CSEL XXXV 2, *Epp.* 164, 198

'SCHWESTER KATREI' (s. XIV¹): text ed. F. Pfeiffer, *Deutsche Mystiker des 14. Jahrhunderts* II (Leipzig 1857) 448–75

Klibansky, R., E. Panofsky, F. Saxl, *Saturn and Melancholy* (London 1964)

Kliman, B. W., 'Women in Early English Literature', *Nottingham Medieval Studies* XXI (1977) 32–49

Koch, G., *Frauenfrage und Ketzertum im Mittelalter* (Berlin 1962)

Kretzenbacher, L., 'Der Schwierige Weg nach oben', in his *Bilder und Legenden* (Klagenfurt 1971) pp. 16–42

Versöhnung im Jenseits (Bayerische Akad. d. Wiss., Sitzb. 1971, Part 7)

Kuhn, H., *Dichtung und Welt im Mittelalter* (Stuttgart 1959)

Labalme, P. H. (ed.), *Beyond their Sex: Learned Women of the European Past* (New York 1980)

Lattimore, R., *Themes in Greek and Latin Epitaphs* (Urbana 1942)

Leclercq, J., 'L'amitié dans les lettres du moyen âge', *RMAL* I (1945) 391–410

'Le genre épistolaire au moyen âge', *ibid.* II (1946) 63–70

The Love of Learning and the Desire for God (New York ²1974)

Monks and Love in Twelfth-Century France (Oxford 1979)

Monks on Marriage. A Twelfth-Century View (New York 1982)

Lehmann, A., *Le rôle de la femme dans l'histoire de France au moyen âge* (Paris 1952)

Le rôle de la femme dans l'histoire de la Gaule (Paris 1944)

LEOBGYDA (soon after 732): Letter to Boniface, ed. Tangl no. 29; cf. Unterkircher, fol. 21r–v

Le Roy Ladurie, E., *Montaillou* (Paris 1975)

LIADAIN (s. VII?): Poems and strophes attributed to her in *Liadain and Curithir* (s. IX), ed. and tr. Kuno Meyer (London 1902)

LOMBARDA (s. XIII in.): 'Nom volgr' aver per Bernard Na Bernarda', ed. Boutière–Schutz pp. 417ff

McDonnell, E. W., *The Beguines and Beghards in Mediaeval Culture* (Brunswick N.J. 1954)

Manselli, R., 'Amicizia spirituale . . .', *Studi e materiali di storia delle religioni* XXXVIII (1967) 302–13

   La religion populaire au moyen âge (Montréal 1975)
   Spirituali e Beghini in Provenza (Roma 1959)
   Studi sulle eresie del secolo XII (Roma 1953)

MARGUERITE D'OINGT (†1310): *Les oeuvres*, ed. A. Duraffour, P. Gardette, P. Durdilly (Paris 1965)

MARGUERITE PORETE (†1310): Works – see List of Abbreviations, under *Miroir*, and Index of Manuscripts

   Cf. also M. Doiron, 'Margaret Porete: *The Mirror of Simple Souls*, A Middle English Translation', *Archivio italiano per la storia della pietà* v (1968) 241–355 ['The Glosses by "M.N." . . .', ed. E. Colledge, R. Guarnieri, *ibid.* 357–82]; 'The Middle English Translation of *Le Mirouer des Simples Ames*', *Dr L. Reypens-Album* (Antwerpen 1964) pp. 131–52

MARIA DE VENTADORN (s. XII ex.): 'Gui d'Uissel, be·m pesa de vos', ed. J. Audiau, *Troubadours d'Ussel* (Paris 1922), xv

MARIE [of Chatteris?] (before 1285): *La Vie Sainte Audrée*, ed. O. Södergård (Uppsala 1955)

MARIE DE FRANCE (s. XII²): *Espurgatoire S. Patrice*, ed. K. Warnke (Halle 1938)
   Les fables: Die Fabeln, ed. K. Warnke (Halle 1898)
   Les lais, ed. J. Rychner (Paris 1969); ed. and tr. D. Rieger (München 1980)
   Cf. also G. S. Burgess, *Marie de France: an analytical bibliography* (London 1977) [B]; P. Ménard, *Les lais de Marie de France* (Paris 1978); E. Sienaert, *Les lais de Marie de France. Du conte merveilleux à la nouvelle psychologique* (Paris 1978); L. Spitzer, 'Marie de France – Dichterin von Problem-Märchen', *ZfrP* L (1930) 29–67; 'The Prologue to the Lais of Marie de France', in his *Romanische Literaturstudien 1936–1956* (Tübingen 1959) pp. 3–14

Marriage in the Middle Ages: Five papers, ed. J. Leyerle, in *Viator* IV (1973) 413–501

MARSILIA [Abbess of St Amand, Rouen] (*ca.* 1108): *Miraculum S. Amandi*, ed. *Acta Sanctorum* Febr. I, 902–3

Massó i Torrents, J., 'Poetesses i dames intel·lectuals', *Estudis Universitaris Catalans* XXI (*Homenatge a A. Rubió i Lluch*, 1936) 405–17

MATHILDE COUNTESS OF MORIT (s. XII): Letter to Abbot Rupert of Tegernsee (1166), ed. G. Sandberger, *Der Schlern* LII (1978) 503–7

MECHTHILD OF HACKEBORN (1241–*ca.* 1298): *Liber specialis gratiae*, ed. by Solesmes monks, in *Revelationes Gertrudianae ac Mechtildianae* II (Paris 1877) 1–436; cf. also Mechtild [*sic*] of Hackeborn, *The Booke of Gostlye Grace*, ed. T. A. Halligan (Studies and Texts 46, Toronto 1979)

MECHTHILD OF MAGDEBURG (*ca.* 1212–*ca.* 1294): *Offenbarungen, oder Das Fliessende Licht der Gottheit*, ed. P. Gall Morel (Regensburg 1869); *Lux divinitatis*, ed. by Solesmes monks, in *Revelationes* II 437–707; *Das Fliessende Licht der Gottheit*, introd. and tr. M. Schmidt [with an essay by H. Urs von Balthasar] (Einsiedeln–Zürich–Köln 1955)

Cf. also W. Mohr, 'Darbietungsform der Mystik bei Mechthild von M.', *Fs. F. von der Leyen* (München 1963) pp. 375–99; H. Neumann, 'Problemata Mechtildiana', *ZfdA* LXXXII (1948/50) 143–72; 'Fragmenta Mechtildiana inedita', *Annales Acad. Sc. Fennicae* (1954) pp. 161–77; 'Ein ungedrucktes Mechthild-Fragment', *Festgabe Ulrich Pretzel* (Berlin 1963) pp. 316–26; see also the entries under K. Ruh below

MENGARDE BUSCALH (s. XIV in.): see above pp. 269–70, and Duvernoy I 488–507; see also Index of Manuscripts

Metral, M.-O., *Le mariage: les hésitations de l'Occident* (Paris 1977)

Metz, R., 'Recherches sur la condition de la femme selon Gratien', *Studia Gratiana* XII (1957) 379–97

van Mierlo, J., 'Béguinages', *Dictionnaire d'histoire et de géographie ecclésiastiques* VII (1933) 457–73

Minnesangs Frühling see under ANONYMOUS

Misch, G., *Geschichte der Autobiographie* (4 vols. in 8, Bern–Frankfurt 1949–69)

Morewedge, R. T. (ed.), *The Role of Women in the Middle Ages* (Albany 1975)

Noonan, J. T., Jr, 'Marital Affection in the Canonists', *Studia Gratiana* XII (1957) 481–509

Norberg, D., *Introduction à l'étude de la versification latine médiévale* (Stockholm 1958)
   La poésie latine rythmique du haut moyen âge (Stockholm 1954)

Notker Balbulus (*ca.* 840–912): *Liber Hymnorum*, ed. W. von den Steinen, *Notker der Dichter und seine geistige Welt* (2 vols., Bern 1948)

Ohly, F., *Hohelied-Studien* (Wiesbaden 1958)

Parisse, M., 'Les Chanoinesses dans l'Empire germanique', *Francia* VI (1978) 107–26

PAULA, EUSTOCHIUM (s. IV ex.): Letter to Marcella, ed. D. Ruiz Bueno, in *Cartas de San Jerónimo* (2 vols., Madrid 1962) I 318–34 (*Ep.* 46)

PAULINA (s. IV ex.): 'Splendor parentum nil mihi maius dedit', ed. F. Buecheler, *CE* III

PERPETUA (*ca.* 181–203): see List of Abbreviations, under *Passio*, and Index of Manuscripts
   Cf. also F. Dölger, 'Antike Parallelen zum leidenden Deinokrates', *Antike und Christentum* II (1930) 1–40; 'Der Kampf mit dem Ägypter', *ibid.* III (1932) 177–88; M.-L. von Franz, in C. G. Jung, *Aion* (Zürich 1951) pp. 389–496; Å. Fridh, *Le problème de la Passion des saintes Perpétue et Félicité* (Stockholm 1968); G. Lazzati, 'Note critiche al testo', *Aevum* XXX (1956) 30–5; H. J. Musurillo, *The Acts of the Christian Martyrs* (Oxford 1972); E. C. E. Owen, *Some Authentic Acts of the Early Martyrs* (Oxford 1927); R. Petraglio, *Lingua latina e mentalità biblica nella Passio Sanctae Perpetuae* (Brescia 1976) [B]; D. Ruiz Bueno, *Actas de los mártires* (Madrid ²1962)

PERVIGILIUM VENERIS (s. IV²?): ed. L. Catlow (Collection Latomus 172, Bruxelles 1980)

Phipps, W. E., 'The Plight of the Song of Songs', *Journal of the American Academy of Religion* XLII (1974) 82–100

Plummer, J. F. (ed.), *Vox Feminae: Studies in Medieval Woman's Songs* (Studies in Medieval Culture 15, Kalamazoo, Michigan 1981)

Polheim, K., *Die lateinische Reimprosa* (Berlin 1925)

Power, E., *Medieval Women* (Cambridge 1975)

PROBA (*fl. ca.* 360): 'Romulidum ductor, clari lux altera solis' (*Cento* ed. CSEL XVI i, 568–609); cf. R. Herzog, *Die Bibelepik der lateinischen Spätantike* (München 1975) pp. 3–51

PULCHERIA (s. V): Letter to Pope Leo I, ed. E. Schwartz, ACO II 3, *Epist. ante Gesta Coll.* III I, 29; P.L. 54, 905–8

Purdie, A. B., *Latin Verse Inscriptions* (Fribourg–London 1935)

Quasten, J., *Patrología* [Spanish tr., with additions] (3 vols., Madrid 1968–81)

Raby, F. J. E., *A History of Secular Latin Poetry in the Middle Ages* (2 vols., Oxford ²1957)

RADEGUNDIS [St Radegund] (†587): Carmina – see *Venanti Fortunanti Opera Poetica* (ed. F. Leo, MGH, *Auct. Ant.* IV 1), App. 1 and III; cf. also W. Bulst, 'Radegundis an Amalafred', *Bibliotheca docet: Fs. Carl Wehmer* (Amsterdam 1963) pp. 369–80

Testamentum, ed. MGH, *Diplomata* I 8–11

Rau, R. (ed. and tr.), *Briefe des Bonifatius. Willibalds Leben des Bonifatius* (Darmstadt 1968)

Rauh, H. D., *Das Bild des Antichrist im Mittelalter* (Beiträge, Münster 1973)

Riché, P., *Education et culture dans l'Occident barbare* (Paris ³1972)

De l'éducation antique à l'éducation chevaleresque (Paris 1968)

Rieger, D., 'Die trobairitz in Italien', *Cultura Neolatina* XXXI (1971) 205–23

Ringler, S., *Viten- und Offenbarungsliteratur in Frauenklöstern des Mittelalters* (Münchener Texte und Untersuchungen 72, 1980)

Riquer, M. de (ed.), *Los trovadores* (3 vols., Barcelona 1975)

Rousselot, P., *Pour l'histoire du problème de l'amour au moyen âge* (Beiträge, Münster 1908)

Ruh, K., 'Geistliche Prosa', in *Europäisches Spätmittelalter* [*Neues Handbuch der Literaturwissenschaft VIII*], ed. W. Erzgräber (Wiesbaden 1978) pp. 565–606

(ed.), *Altdeutsche und altniederländische Mystik* (Wege der Forschung, Darmstadt 1964)

Ruhe, E., *De amasio ad amasiam* (München 1975) [reviewed by D. Schaller, *Arcadia* XII (1977) 307–13]

Sanders, G. M., 'Sur l'authenticité des Carmina Latina Epigraphica funéraires', *Akten des VI. Internat. Kongresses für Gr. u. Lat. Epigraphik* (München 1973) pp. 410–12

Schaller, D., 'Probleme der Überlieferung und Verfasserschaft lateinischer Liebesbriefe des hohen Mittelalters', *Mlat. Jb.* III (1966) 25–36

Schmid, J., 'Heilige Brautschaft', *RAC* II 528–64

Shahar, S., 'De quelques aspects de la femme dans la pensée et la communauté religieuses aux XIIe et XIIIe siècles', *Revue de l'histoire des religions* CLXXXV (1974) 29–77

Shapiro, M., 'The Provençal *Trobairitz* and the Limits of Courtly Love', *Signs* III (1977/8) 560–71

Singer, C., *From Magic to Science* (New York ²1958)

SULPICIA [attribution doubtful] (s. v): 'Musa, quibus numeris heroas et arma frequentas', *Epigrammata Bobiensia* 37, ed. F. Munari (Roma 1955), W. Speyer (Leipzig 1963); cf. also H. Fuchs, 'Das Klagelied der Sulpicia', in *Discordia Concors, Festgabe für E. Bonjour* I (Bern 1968) 32ff

Szövérffy, J., *Weltliche Dichtungen des lateinischen Mittelalters* I (Berlin 1970)

Tavera, A., 'A la recherche des troubadours maudits', in *Exclus et systèmes d'exclusion dans la littérature et la civilisation médiévales* (Senefiance, no. 5, Aix-en-Provence–Paris 1978) pp. 137–61

Taviani, H., 'Le mariage dans l'hérésie de l'an Mil', *Annales: Economies, Sociétés, Civilisations* XXXII (1977) 1074–89

TERESA [Queen of Portugal] (1075/80–1130): Letter to her son Alfonso, ed. Chr. Henriquez, *Fasciculus sanctorum ordinis Cisterciensis* I (Köln 1631) 314

Thorndike, L., *A History of Magic and Experimental Science* I–II (New York–London 1923)

Thouzellier, C., *Catharisme et Valdéisme en Languedoc à la fin du XIIe et au début du XIIIe siècle* (Paris 1966)

Hérésies et hérétiques (Roma 1969)

Thraede, K., *Grundzüge der griechisch-römischen Brieftopik* (München 1970)

331

'Frau', *RAC* VIII (1972) 197–269

TIBORS (*ca.* 1130–82): 'Bels dous amics', ed. Boutière–Schutz pp. 498f

TROTULA (s. XI): *De mulierum passionibus*, ed. in *Medici antiqui omnes* (Venezia 1547) pp. 70–81; on this text, whose authorship has been long disputed, see most recently *Trotula de Ruggiero, Sulle malattie delle donne*, introd. P. Cavallo Boggi, tr. M. Nubié, A. Tocco (Torino 1979) [B]; cf. also H. P. Bayon, 'Trotula and the Ladies of Salerno', *Proc. of the Royal Soc. of Medicine* XXXIII (1939/40) 471–5; P. O. Kristeller, 'The School of Salerno', *Bul. of the History of Medicine* XVII (1945) 138–94; E. F. Tuttle, *ibid.* L (1976) 61–72

Van den Hoecke, W., A. Welkenhuysen (eds.), *Love and Marriage in the Twelfth Century* (Mediaevalia Lovaniensia VIII, Leuven 1981)

Véran, J., *Les poétesses provençales* (Paris 1946)

Vinay, G., *Alto medioevo latino: conversazioni e no* (Napoli 1978)

Weigand, R., 'Die Lehre der Kanonisten ... von den Ehezwecken', *Studia Gratiana* XII (1957) 445–78

Weisser, C., 'Das Krankheitslunar aus medizinhistorischer Sicht', *Sudhoffs Archiv* LXV (1981) 390–400

Index of Manuscripts

General Index

GENERAL INDEX

Ovid (cont.)
  passim, 107, 109, 119, 126f, 298f, 305;
  Metamorphoses, 26, 95, 308; Remedia, 118

Passio S. Anastasiae, 77
Passio SS. Montani et Lucii, 15f
Pastor Hermas, 161, 169f
Paula, 17–19
Paulina, 21–3, 25f, 287f
Paulinus of Aquileia, 25
Perpetua, x–xi, 1–17, 22f, 36, 281–6; Acta
  minora, 5, 16, 282ff; Passio SS. Perpetuae et
  Felicitatis, 1, 10, 15f, 281ff
Persius, 112, 134
Pervigilium Veneris, 287
Petrarch, 38, 110
Pherecydes, 312
Philosophia, 74f
Plato, 182f, 195, 221, 250, 311, 319
Plautus, 295, 297, 299
Praetextatus, Vettius Agorius, 21–3
prayer, 11, 22, 32, 50f, 53f, 191f
Proba, Cento Vergilianus, 286f
Propertius, 11
purgatorial fires, 179, 247

Quem quaeritis, 63
Quodvultdeus, 16

Radegunde, 27ff, 56, 86, 298
Ramón Lull, 218
Rather of Verona, 56f, 69, 294f
Regensburg love-verses, 83, 91f, 98f, 298f
Reinerus of Liège, 294
Richard of St Victor, 146
Richardis of Stade, 150–9, 199, 201
Riché, P., 36, 38, 45, 290–3
Riquer, M. de, 104
rota, 172f, 175, 241f
Ruh, K., 217, 318
Ruodlieb, 83, 91f
Ruotger, 57

Sainte Eglise la Grande, Sainte Eglise la
  Petite: see 'Ecclesia'
Salernitan Questions, 310
Samson, 124, 182f, 250
Sapphic strophes, 46f, 51
Satan: see 'Lucifer'
Saturus, 2, 12f, 16, 284
scenica lectio, 58
Schipperges, H., 178f, 310
Schrader, M., 193, 312f
sea (literary motif), 31f, 219; see also 'water'
Sedulius, 33

Seneca, 114, 141, 304
serpent, 2, 6, 8f, 15, 185
sexuality, 170, 173–83, 204ff, 244–9
shepherd, 5f, 9, 81f, 153
Sibyl (Signs of Judgment), 63
Singer, C., 144, 147
Solomon, 182f, 189, 250; see also 'Bible'
Soranus, 9
Spitzer, L., 19f, 287
Suger of Saint-Denis, 309
Sulpicia, 287
Sybille Peire, 211f

temperaments: see 'humours'
Tengswindis, 165–7, 169, 171, 200
tenso, 98
Terence, 55, 57ff, 68ff, 78ff, 95; Adelphoi, 72;
  Andria, 72, 295; Eunuchus, 72; Hautonti-
  morumenos, 96
Terentius et Delusor: see 'Altercation'
Teresa (Queen of Portugal), 305
Theodoric (Hildegard's biographer), 163f
Theodulf, 36
Thierry of Chartres, 179, 283
Thietmar of Merseburg, 57
thirst of the dead, 3, 11f
Thorndike, L., 144
Tibors, 99f, 299
Tibullus, 11
trobairitz, viii, x, 97–106, 299–302

Valerius, 152
Venantius Fortunatus, 26, 28f, 85f
Vergil, 7–9, 70; Aeneid, 8, 11, 15, 79f, 295;
  Eclogue x, 79f
vision, 1–17 passim, 145ff, 168f, 200, 231ff, 252f,
  261; see also 'dream'
Vitae Patrum: see 'Lives of the Fathers'

Walahfrid Strabo, 36
Wallāda, 98
water (literary motif), 2–4, 11f, 15; see also
  'sea'
Wife's Complaint, The, 31, 290
will, Hildegard's theory of, 187ff, 257–9
William (son of Dhuoda), 37–54
William of Conches, 41, 148, 179, 195
winileodas, 31, 52
Wolfram von Eschenbach, 74
Wulf and Eadwacer, 31, 289f

youth (iuventus, jovens) (courtly value), 86,
  194f, 263f
Yselda, 101–3, 300–2